Strengthen for Service

Percy Dearmer (1867–1936)
The driving force behind *The English Hymnal,* while serving
as Vicar of St Mary-the-Virgin, Primrose Hill, London.

Strengthen for Service
100 Years of the English Hymnal
1906–2006

Edited by
Alan Luff

CANTERBURY
PRESS
Norwich

© English Hymnal Company Ltd 2005

© for his chapter, 'The Musical Typography of *The English Hymnal*', Andrew Parker 2005

First published in 2005 by the Canterbury Press Norwich (a publishing imprint of Hymns Ancient & Modern Limited, a registered charity) St Mary's Works, St Mary's Plain, Norwich, Norfolk, NR3 3BH

www.scm-canterburypress.co.uk

British Library Cataloguing in Publication data

A catalogue record for this book is available from the British Library

ISBN 1-85311-662-9/9781-85311-662-9

Typeset by Fakenham Photosetting Limited
Printed and bound by Cambridge Printing

CONTENTS

CONTENTS

FOREWORD

Rowan Williams

I first handled the unmistakeable squat green book on my first visit to an Anglican church at the age of eleven. When – a matter of weeks later – I joined the choir, it became more and more familiar: and when, fourteen years later, I landed up in the college at Mirfield, I was delighted to find the same solid little volume, complete and unexpurgated, in front of me, and I knew I was going to be at home musically and liturgically.

It was a fascinating book for a musical small boy. These were not just the hymn tunes I was used to from my Presbyterian background; some of them were haunting folk-songs of a sort I had never heard in church; some were part of the massive heritage of continental Lutheranism; and then there were those baffling and tantalizing pages with the squiggles on them, my first acquaintance with plainsong. Add to this an imaginative choirmaster prepared to let us loose on the not so well-known bits, and it was a recipe for a lively few years of singing.

Perhaps not everyone would think of the *The English Hymnal* (*EH*) as a lively book. The late Dom Anselm Hughes complained about it as a monument to a particular sort of North London suburban tastefulness – the Edwardian ecclesiastical equivalent of sun-dried tomatoes in Islington. But this has more to do with the internal civil wars of Anglo-Catholicism than with any reasoned judgement. You can of course see a bit of what Hughes meant; and Percy Dearmer's later development would no doubt have made that robust Anglo-Papalist feel quite vindicated. But the faint aroma of whimsical refinement is very faint indeed (compared with the overwhelming gusts of it in Dearmer's later labours). More obvious is the sheer musical energy, the international (or rather, I suppose, European) horizon, and the bold sense that the Christian year was a colourful, wholly engaging backcloth to the life of discipleship, appropriately celebrated with the best that could be found.

That's not to say that there are no uninspired patches. The hilariously dreary office hymns 'from the Epiphany until Lent' were a source of unregenerate merriment to Mirfield students, as they have been, no doubt, to lots of others. And the propers at the end – well, as the late Father James Owen of Little St Mary's in Cambridge used to say, no doubt there are many beautiful reasons for them ... The goal of comprehensively wallpapering the Calendar is a worthy one, but it has its pitfalls.

Yet overall, the *EH* remains a triumph. After all, it is given to few hymn books to be overseen by a composer of the stature of Vaughan Williams, whose original work for the *EH* has been wonderfully enduring. And in his arrangements and harmonizations, he never puts a foot wrong, and sets a uniformly superb standard for the other collaborators; compared with the banalities of the harmonies in some contemporary hymn books, his versions are gems (take 'Lo, he comes, with clouds descending', for example). If I wanted to identify a large part of what the *EH* gave me as a young singer and a young Anglican, it was a conviction that excellence in worship was not an elitist or dilettante thing, but a matter of taking seriously what God's people deserved. Dearmer had his quirks, but he believed that every church deserved excellence because God's people were worth it. We may dispute quite how far the taste of the *EH* escaped from a particular middle-class climate – but Dearmer would, I think, have replied firmly that if you have defensible convictions about what is good, living and creative, you have a duty to share it. And in this regard, the Christian past is not a museum but a treasury of things that can enhance life.

Too often, the arts in church, music in particular, refuse to aim too high, on the no doubt laudable principles that there is less distance to fall if you get it wrong and less risk of confusing faith with taste. It is the time-honoured defence of terrible plaster statues and inane choruses, and it is very far from being completely wrong. Quite often, taste has to be put on hold because the responses that faith draws out are raw and difficult, with the rawness and difficulty of St Mark's Greek, to take the obvious example. But: there is an opposite risk, of confusing faith with the easiest emotions, pressing the buttons of facile mass response. To be wary of identifying genuinely religious art with what we regard as aesthetically right is a proper caution against excluding the 'extremism' that arises from encounter with a strange and disturbing God. Yet it is just this which ought to make us equally cautious about deliberately lowering our sights and settling for stock responses. Any religious art which sets out, consciously or unconsciously, to reduce what human beings can experience in God's presence is dangerous – dangerous to the soul and dangerous for mission.

It seems a long way from the *EH* to 'Mission-Shaped Church' and our current concerns to develop new flexibility in the style of worship and common life. But properly understood, they do not occupy different universes. Both are about taking God's people seriously. The *EH* came from a milieu that was in revolt against both trivialized and dull piety and social complacency and injustice. It represented that vital strand of Catholic tradition in the Anglican Church which saw the faith and the liturgy as transforming and critical elements in an otherwise static society. It assumed that the rhythm of the Christian year was not just a matter of ecclesiastical convenience but a map of the soul's seasons; to grow up as a Christian involved the passage through darkness and light, hope and fulfilment, over and over again, letting the one story of God's action in Jesus become your own.

So what the *EH* stands for is not an archaic churchiness, but the commitment to a faith that is culturally adventurous, that expects God's people to be heirs of a humanly rich environment, but that most basically of all assumes that exploring God's revealed work is a challenge and a joy, in which our heritage is not an embarrassment but a vast resource of wisdom, delight and enlargement. All that was part of what the *EH* began to give me as a young Christian, and it is very good to be able to pay my debts to it. I hope that the vision that motivated it – a vision that felt pretty risky and unconventional at the time to many people – will go on stirring Anglican Christians for a good few centuries more.

✠ Rowan Cantuar:

INTRODUCTION AND ACKNOWLEDGEMENTS

This commemorative volume seeks to celebrate the centenary of what is widely acknowledged to be one of the landmarks in hymn-book publication. It is sponsored by the English Hymnal Company, which has, since the appearance of *The English Hymnal* in 1906, dealt with the administration of the book and its development.

The English Hymnal Company has been, over the years, a group of clergy and musicians who love the book and who wish to see its best interests furthered. Thus, in looking back over past minutes of the company, much of the business has certainly been concerned with relationships with Oxford University Press, with copyright and with the publication of the book's various editions. But the company has another, charitable, side. As the original directors died, many of them left shares to a charitable trust, which became, in 1950, the Ecclesiastical Music Trust. Trustees of this hold up to half of the company shares and, through it, are enabled to make modest grants to choristers and others involved in musical endeavour.

The directors of the company felt it their duty, as the fiftieth anniversary of the book approached, to make plans for celebration. Thus, in 1949, the minutes speak about the production of a brief history in time for 1956 and of a dinner at the Athenaeum, to which the Archbishop of Canterbury, the Editor of *The Times* and, for some reason, Sir Walter Monckton, were to be invited! An account of these plans – fulfilled and unfulfilled – are found in the present volume.

Fifty years later, as the millennium dawned, the present directors of the company began to turn their attention to how the centenary in 2006 might be celebrated.

One project is to provide a supplement of hymns and liturgical material which can be used alongside *The New English Hymnal* and plans are afoot for Canterbury Press to publish this during 2006.

It was also felt that there was a need for a scholarly reflection on the hundred years of *The English Hymnal* and how it had influenced the worshipping life of the Church of England.

And so it was, in January 2003, that a group of musicians and clergy met for a two-day reflection at the Deanery in Hereford and the plan of the book began to take shape. One of those present, Canon Alan Luff, soon emerged as ideally suited to edit the proposed book and I speak on behalf of all the directors when I thank Alan most warmly for his vision and his skill in working so well with the contributors and in enabling the book to come into being. One of those present at that first meeting was Canon Alan Dunstan, whose experience and skill we very much wanted to see reflected in the book. Sadly,

Alan died during 2004 and the book is poorer for the loss of a contribution from such a great champion of good hymnody.

The publication of the book by Canterbury Press is gratefully acknowledged as is the tremendous help and support received by us from Gordon Knights, Christine Smith, Mary Matthews and Clive Edwards.

In the biographical note, readers will see the breadth of experience represented by the contributors – a poet, a historian, hymnologists, academic musicians, a publisher, clergy – reflecting, we hope, the many areas in which *The English Hymnal* broke new ground a century ago.

Thanks, too, are due to the Revd Charles Whitney for his undertaking the task of providing indices for the book in a very short space of time.

May I add a special word of thanks to His Grace the Archbishop of Canterbury for his very kind acceptance of our invitation to write a Foreword. Archbishop Rowan has known and loved the book from an early age and has often acknowledged its influence on his life and spirituality – we are delighted to have his support in this project.

The title of this book perhaps deserves a mention. We considered the first line of several hymns as having a particular significance in *The English Hymnal*. At first *From Glory to Glory* emerged as 'front-runner' – words which may reflect the honour in which *The English Hymnal* has been held by successive generations and its wide influence in the church. It dawned on us, however, that this title might have rather triumphalist overtones and none of us wishes to predict that the hymnal which has nourished us should necessarily be the one which appeals to future generations – not least in an age when the whole notion of a 'hymn book' is under review.

A better title, we feel, is the one chosen – *Strengthen for Service* – its translated Syriac words providing one of the finest hymns in the Eucharistic section of *The English Hymnal* and one which so powerfully makes the link between worship and daily life. It is a title which we hope not only characterizes the way in which *The English Hymnal* has sought to serve church and liturgy during the past century, but also expresses the hope that its contents will continue to serve, nourish and enrich the church of the future.

Michael Tavinor
The Deanery, Hereford
September 2005

CONTRIBUTORS' BIOGRAPHIES

Robert Atwell is an Anglican priest. After six years as Chaplain of Trinity College, Cambridge, he became a Benedictine monk, spending the next ten years in a monastery in the Cotswolds. He is the compiler of two volumes of daily readings for the liturgical year, *Celebrating the Saints* (2004) and *Celebrating the Seasons* (1999), and of three poetry anthologies, *Love*, *Gift* and *Remember* (2005), all published by Canterbury Press. He is currently vicar of the parish of St Mary-the-Virgin in Primrose Hill, London, where Percy Dearmer was himself incumbent, and where in large measure *The English Hymnal* came to birth.

John Bawden was a lay-clerk at Guildford Cathedral in the late 1970s, and until recently continued to sing as a freelance deputy tenor with a number of professional church and concert choirs, including those of Winchester Cathedral and Westminster Abbey. He now devotes most of his time to conducting, leading choral workshops, arranging, and researching and writing programme notes for record companies and choral societies in the UK and North America. He is the author of the sleeve-notes for Priory Records' *Complete New English Hymnal* series, the final volume of which is due to be released in 2006. John is currently Musical Director of Fareham Philharmonic Choir and Associate Conductor of Godalming Choral Society.

Ian Bradley grew up with *The English Hymnal*, and when asked by *The Tablet* in 2000 to nominate his book of the century had no hesitation in describing it as 'the greatest influence on my life … It has influenced my faith and coloured my Christian pilgrimage by filling it with companions, images and phrases from the great treasury of English language hymnody'. The author of *The Penguin Book of Hymns*, *The Penguin Book of Carols* and *Abide With Me: The World of Victorian Hymns* (SCM Press, 1997), he has fought a one-man crusade to promote the hymn tunes of Arthur Sullivan, and was responsible for the CD in the 'Hymnmakers' collection devoted to Sullivan's tunes, *Nearer My God to Thee*. A minister in the Church of Scotland, he is Reader in Practical Theology and Church History in the University of St Andrews. His latest books are *Oh Joy! Oh Rapture! The Enduring Phenomenon of Gilbert and Sullivan* (2005) and *The Daily Telegraph Book of Hymns* (2005).

Elizabeth Cosnett has lived most of her life in Liverpool. In 1996 she retired from a career as a teacher and lecturer in English. Her interest in hymnody is closely linked with a love of poetry, which was developed in her MA thesis, 'The Poet as Hymn Writer'. She joined the Hymn Society of Great Britain and Ireland, and has served as its Executive President, and has participated in hymnic activities in various countries. Her book *Hymns for Everyday Saints* was published in 2001.

Martin Draper is Chairman of the English Hymnal Company, and has been a lover of *The English Hymnal* from his teenage years onwards. His first post after ordination was assistant curate in the parish of St Mary-the-Virgin in Primrose Hill, the birthplace of the original edition. He later served at St Matthew's Westminster, as Chaplain of St George's Paris and as Archdeacon of France. He has been a director of the English Hymnal Company since 1979.

Donald Gray was Canon of Westminster and Chaplain to the Speaker of the House of Commons, 1987–98. Previously Rector of Liverpool, he served on the Liturgical Commission as a member and consultant for over twenty-five years, and as a member of the Joint Liturgical Group, 1969–96 (Chairman, 1989–94). A former President of *Societas Liturgia*, he is currently Chairman of the Alcuin Club and President of the Society for Liturgical Study. Dr Gray was involved in the establishment of the International Anglican Liturgical Consultation and was its first Chairman. He was a member of the English Language Liturgical Consultation, through which he worked on the *Revised Common Lectionary* and other ecumenical liturgical texts.

Rhidian Griffiths was educated at Oxford and Aberystwyth. He joined the staff of The National Library of Wales in Aberystwyth in 1980, and is currently its Director of Public Services. Among his published works are articles on Welsh music history and bibliography, including contributions to the Glamorgan and Cardiganshire County Histories and to several books and journals. An officer of the Welsh Folk-Song Society, he has written on the relationship between folk music and hymn tunes in Wales, in articles published in the Society's journal, *Canu Gwerin* (Folk Song), and in the Amy Parry-Williams memorial lecture for 1991, *Ffiniau* (Boundaries). He was a member of the editorial board of the Welsh interdenominational hymnal *Caneuon Ffydd* (Songs of Faith), published in 2001.

John Harper is Director General of The Royal School of Church Music. He is also Research Professor at the University of Wales, Bangor. His *Guide to Western Liturgy* (1991) is used worldwide, and has been translated into Polish and Japanese. He is editor of the series, *Music for Common Worship*, the monastic hymnal, *Hymns for Prayer and Praise*, and of the *Musica Britannica* edition of Orlando Gibbons's consort music. He is Chairman of The Plainsong and Medieval Music Society, and has been closely involved in the reconstruction of two Tudor organs as part of the Early English Organ Project. He has taught at the universities of Birmingham, Oxford and Bangor (where he was Chair of Music), founded the Centre for Advanced Welsh Music Studies and established the bilingual journal, *Hanes Cerddoriaeth Cymru/Welsh Music History*. He directed the music of St Chad's Cathedral in Birmingham, the Edington Music Festival and Magdalen College Chapel, Oxford, and continues to compose music for the Church.

CONTRIBUTORS' BIOGRAPHIES

Anthony Harvey taught theology at Oxford, and then for seventeen years was Canon and Sub-Dean of Westminster, where he was involved in various forms of inter-faith work and social action. He was a member of the Church of England Doctrine Commission and of the Archbishop's Commission on Urban Priority Areas, and is the author of a number of books on the New Testament and Christian ethics.

Paul Iles was Canon Residentiary and Precentor of Hereford Cathedral for twenty years, having been a parish priest in Bristol and Oxford. He has written a number of books about prayer and devotion and has contributed a study of the cathedral's liturgy and music to the millennium history of Hereford Cathedral.

Alan Luff read classics and theology at Oxford. He prepared for the ministry at Westcott House in Cambridge and was ordained in Manchester in 1956. He was Precentor of Manchester Cathedral, 1962–69, vicar of Penmaenmawr in the Diocese of Bangor, 1969–79, Precentor of Westminster Abbey, 1979–92, and Canon of Birmingham, 1992–94. His interest in hymns deepened with membership of Dunblane Music Consultation, and he lectured on Welsh hymns to the Hymn Society, leading to writing *Welsh Hymns and Their Tunes* (1990). He has served as Secretary, Chairman and Vice Executive President of the Hymn Society, and as Vice President of the International Fellowship for Hymnology. He has written hymns, texts and tunes.

Bernard Massey was educated at Queen Mary College, London. He taught in the Mechanical Engineering Department of University College London, 1952–85, and wrote three science and engineering text-books. He was organist and choirmaster of the Congregational (later United Reformed) Church in Redhill, Surrey, 1964–88, editor of the *Bulletin* of the Hymn Society, 1975–2001 and 2003–04, and a member of the music sub-committees for *Hymns and Psalms*, 1983, and *Rejoice and Sing*, 1991.

Julian Onderdonk is a cultural historian specializing in twentieth-century British music and society. His essays have appeared in *Folk Music Journal*, *Vaughan Williams Studies* (1996), *English Dance and Song*, and *Vaughan Williams Essays* (2003), and he is currently working on a book that examines the social and political underpinnings of Vaughan Williams' nationalist activities. He has taught at New York and Pennsylvania State universities, Williams College, and is now Assistant Professor of Music History at West Chester University of Pennsylvania.

Andrew Parker studied at King's College Cambridge under David Willcocks and Margaret Bent. He is historian of the King's College Choir. As a musicologist, editor and engraver he has particular interest in paper bibliography in mid-sixteenth-century Venice, as well as hymnology. He has designed and originated *Common Praise* (2000), *The Irish Presbyterian Hymnbook* (2004) and *Church Hymnary* (2005) for SCM-Canterbury Press. He is currently involved in creating *Hymnview*, interactive software for browsing and accessing copyright-controlled materials in CD-ROM editions of hymn books.

Paul A Richardson is Professor of Music and Assistant Dean for Graduate Studies in Music in the School of Performing Arts at Samford University in Birmingham, Alabama, where he teaches voice and church music. A past President of The Hymn Society in the United States and Canada, he served on the editorial committee for *The Worshiping Church* (1990) and contributed to its *Worship Leaders Edition* (1991). He also contributed to the *Handbook to The Baptist Hymnal* (1992) and *The New Century Hymnal Companion* (1998). Together with Harry Eskew and David Music, he co-wrote *Singing Baptists: Studies in Baptist Hymnody in America* (1994). He recently completed a revised and expanded edition of Erik Routley's *A Panorama of Christian Hymnody* (2005). His articles and reviews appear in a variety of periodicals related to hymnology, church music and worship.

Ian Sharp is Emeritus Senior Fellow in Church Music at Liverpool Hope University, where he lectured in music, music education and education studies from 1969, retiring in 2003 as Foundation Dean. He was educated at Lincoln College, Oxford (Organ Exhibitioner), and at the universities of Birmingham, York and Liverpool. He is a Fellow and Choirmaster of the Royal College of Organists and the composer of a number of hymn tunes, many of them to texts by Elizabeth Cosnett. His publications reflect his practical interests in church music, music education and children's hymnody. He is currently a member of the Executive Committee of the Hymn Society of Great Britain and Ireland and an Associate Editor of its Bulletin.

Michael Thompson was educated at the universities of St Andrews and Durham. He was ordained for the diocese of Llandaff. A former Sacrist of Westminster Abbey, he has also served parishes in the dioceses of London, Peterborough, Southwell and Lincoln. He is incumbent of St Bartholomew's in Dublin, and a Minor Canon of St Patrick's.

Kenneth Trickett is a retired chartered accountant, a lifelong Methodist, and a collector and reviewer of hymn books. He was a member of the Main Committee for *Hymns and Psalms* (1983) and, with J Richard Watson, edited the *Companion* (1988) to that book. For fifty years he has been a member of The Hymn Society of Great Britain and Ireland and of The Methodist Church Music Society.

CONTRIBUTORS' BIOGRAPHIES

J Richard Watson is Emeritus Professor of English at the University of Durham. He is the author of *The English Hymn* (1997, 1999), *An Annotated Anthology of Hymns* (2002, 2003), and *Awake My Soul* (2005). He was Vice-President of the Charles Wesley Society, 1994–2003, and served on the committee for the Methodist book, *Hymns and Psalms* (1983). He co-wrote with Kenneth Trickett and others *Companion to Hymns and Psalms* (1988). He was the Free Churches' representative on the Archbishops' Commission on Church Music, 1988–92, and served on the committee for *Common Praise* (2000), the new edition of *Hymns Ancient & Modern*. He is currently General Editor of a project to replace John Julian's *A Dictionary of Hymnology* (1892, 1907) to be published by SCM-Canterbury Press in 2007.

Simon Wright is Rights Publishing Manager in the Music Department of Oxford University Press, where his responsibilities include the worldwide administration of *The English Hymnal* copyrights. He has written extensively on the history of OUP's music publishing, and is the author of a book on the Brazilian composer Heitor Villa-Lobos.

ACKNOWLEDGEMENTS

Photographs
All photographs are copyright.

Frontispiece
Percy Dearmer — © Lambeth Palace Library, London SE1 7JU.

Plate section
Ralph Vaughan Williams — © The RVW Archive.
Athelstan Riley — © Noël Riley. From the Riley family archive.
Alfred F A Hanbury-Tracey — © Revd Colin Alsbury. Anglo-Catholic History Society.
Thomas Alexander Lacey — © Christopher Guy and The Chapter of Worcester Cathedral.
Gilbert Keith Chesterton — © The National Portrait Gallery, London.
St Mary-the-Virgin, Primrose Hill — © The Vicar and PCC of St Mary-the-Virgin.
All Saints Church, Down Ampney — © Phil Draper. www.churchcrawler.co.uk

Music extracts
The sources of music extracts is indicated, together with copyright acknowledgements where applicable.

Musical Typography of The English Hymnal *(Parker)*
Example 1   *Caslon's Sampler* c1785
        2   *The Harmonicon* 1823
        3   *The English Hymnal Second Edition No. 383*
            REPTON Charles Hubert Hastings Parry (1848–1918) *The English Hymnal Second Edition No. 383*
        4   EASTER HYMN *Lyra Davidica* 1708. *The English Hymnal No. 133*
        5   THIRD MODE MELODY Thomas Tallis (*c*1515–85) *The English Hymnal No. 92ii*
        6   DER TAG BRICHT AN Melchior Vulpius (*c*1560–1616) *The English Hymnal No. 101*
        7   Good Friday Reproaches *The English Hymnal No. 737 (First and Second Editions)*

ACKNOWLEDGEMENTS

The Music of The English Hymnal *(Bawden)*
Example 1   ORIENTIS PARTIBUS Harmony by Ralph Vaughan Williams
(1872–1958) © Oxford University Press, Oxford. *The English
Hymnal No. 129*
         2   SALVE FESTA DIES Ralph Vaughan Williams (1872–1958) ©
Oxford University Press, Oxford. *The New English Hymnal
No. 109ii*
         3   ST JOSEPH OF THE STUDIUM Sir Joseph Barnby (1838–96)
Hymns Ancient & Modern Standard Edition No. 441
         4   WEIMAR Melchior Vulpius (c1560–1616) *The English Hymnal
No. 187*
         5   MARCHING Martin Shaw (1875–1958) © Curwen &
Sons/Music Sales Ltd, London. *The English Hymnal No. 503*
         6   PALACE GREEN Michael Fleming (b.1928) © The Royal
School of Church Music, Dorking. *The New English Hymnal
No. 447*

A Moral Issue? (Harvey)
Example 1   ST PHILLIP William Henry Monk (1823–89) *The New English
Hymnal No. 69*
         2   HEILIGER GEIST (BERLIN) Johann Crüger (1598–1662) *The
English Hymnal No. 76*

Folk-Songs in The English Hymnal *(Onderdonk)*
Example 1   KING'S LYNN traditional melody. *The English Hymnal No. 562*
         2   DANBY traditional melody. *The English Hymnal No. 295*
         3a THE MERCHANT'S DAUGHTER traditional melody in the
Lucy Broadwood Collection, re-set from *The Journal of the Folk
Song Society No. 4*
         3b RUSPER traditional melody. *The English Hymnal No. 379*
         4a LORD RENDAL traditional melody in the Cecil Sharp
Collection, re-set from an unknown source
         4b LANGPORT traditional melody. *The English Hymnal No. 656*

Ralph Vaughan Williams (1872–1958)
Arguably the greatest British composer and arranger of the twentieth century. He was appointed Music Editor of *The English Hymnal* at only 32 years of age. He declined all honours during his lifetime, with the exception of the Order of Merit conferred upon him in 1938.

Athelstan Riley
(1858–1945)

An uncompromising High Church layman. The group established by Dearmer regularly met at his house.

Reverend, the Honourable
Alfred F. A. Hanbury-Tracy
(1846–1929)

Leader of Dearmer's group, he came from an aristocratic background and was Vicar of St Barnabas, Pimlico, London.

Thomas Alexander Lacey
(1853–1931)

An extremely gifted liturgist, and unrivalled expert in medieval Latin, he translated ancient Office Hymns into magnificent English.

Gilbert Keith Chesterton
(1874–1936)

One of Dearmer's religious protégés, who converted from Anglicanism to Roman Catholicism in 1922.

St Mary-the-Virgin, Primrose Hill, London.

The great Lenten veil designed by Percy Dearmer. As the Palm Procession enters
the church, the Prophetic Anthem is sung and the veil lowered, exposing the Rood.

All Saints' Church, Down Ampney, Gloucestershire

Vaughan Williams was born at the Rectory, and named the tune he wrote
to accompany '*Come down, O love divine*' after his beloved home village.

THE BIRTH AND BACKGROUND OF
THE ENGLISH HYMNAL

Donald Gray

It is an evident truism that any work of art emerges from the cultural milieu in which it has been conceived. It will be decisively shaped, moulded and influenced by the prevailing fashions and philosophies. It might seem, at first sight, somewhat extravagant to claim 'work of art' status for a hymn book. But now we have no hesitation in accepting the important category of 'popular culture', it surely must be accepted that, during the majority of the twentieth century, hymns and hymn singing was a significant ingredient in the musical repertoire of most people – part of their culture.

It is a fact that those principally involved in the conception of *The English Hymnal* were highly sensitive to the direction in which various art forms were leading, both at the *fin de siècle* and on into the new century. They did not hesitate to advocate bringing these new insights into the service of the church and its worship; they were seized of a vision of instilling new life into its music and dispensing with what they considered the often unworthy accretions of the immediate past both in the words and music. It was an exciting period artistically and culturally, why should not Divine Worship reflect the glories of the age, they believed?

The original vision

The two principal animators involved in the production of this new hymn book were both cognizant of the prevailing currents in the cultural scene. Both Percy Dearmer and Ralph Vaughan Williams were alive to, and actively interested in, the aesthetic world of the day.

Dearmer had long been influenced artistically, as well as politically, by the work of William Morris and the other pioneers of the Arts and Crafts Movement. He was the son of an artist, who also had not inconsiderable musical talent. Thomas Dearmer had met Percy's mother as the visiting drawing master at the school for young ladies which she ran in Maida Vale. Not surprisingly Percy had an in-born feel for things artistic and later he was to marry, as his first wife, an artist who was totally taken up by Arts and Crafts design and contributed to some of the early twentieth-century leading cultural journals.[1]

Going up to Oxford in 1886 Percy Dearmer was to discover a place buzzing with new and original ideas. He himself contributed to the general gaiety and colourfulness of the times with his bright blue shirts worn with loud checks and the accompanying flowing Liberty ties. He decorated his rather dark rooms in Peckwater Quad in Christ Church with Morris tapestries even before he was influenced by the political writings of his hero. When he started to read Morris, the artist's son became convinced of the social, political and indeed religious implications behind his instinctive need to celebrate and honour beauty. Dearmer was later to write that he learnt from Ruskin through Morris that 'what we call by the light name of ugliness is a moral as well as an aesthetic evil – corrupt, sinister and polluting'.[2]

In all this he was to be supported and encouraged by his wife, Mabel, 'an artist in all her being'. On ordination in 1891 Dearmer went to work as a curate at St Anne's South Lambeth, a grim parish dominated by the gas works. After their marriage in May 1892 Percy and Mabel attempted to brighten up their tiny house with contemporary and fashionable *objets d'art* from artists of the Arts and Crafts Movement. This was not just an aesthetic decision: it reflected their social and political concerns.[3]

The Movement was founded in the late nineteenth century by a group of British artists and social reformers inspired by John Ruskin and William Morris. They sought to stem the tide of Victorian mass production, which they believed degraded the worker and resulted in 'shoddy wares'. The Movement was an attempt to redefine the role of art and craftsmanship. As a consequence it sought to restore dignity to labour, create opportunities for women and underpin many of the needed social reforms.[4]

So the Dearmers' modest home was decorated with Morris wallpapers and chintzes with Morris tapestries on the doors. On the walls were engravings by Edward Burne-Jones who had studied theology along with Morris and had at one time seemed destined for ordination. As wedding presents Mabel and Percy's friends gave them lamps and crockery by William Arthur Smith Benson, the architect, metal worker and furniture designer who was a founder member of the Art Workers Guild and succeeded Morris as chairman of Morris & Co. on his death in 1896. Around the house were de Morgan vases and jars. William Frend de Morgan was a influential potter and designer who designed stained glass and tiles for Morris & Co. A friend, Percy Widdrington, recorded, 'He and Mabel spent a prodigal sum on decoration, but there was a striking lack of furniture.'[5]

All this witnesses to the primary concerns, artistic, sociological and theological, of Dearmer. Add to this his growing intimacy with the artistic colleagues and associates of his wife.

Mabel White trained at Herbert Herkomer's art school in Bushey and for many years supplemented their income with her artistic work. Her art was said to be influenced by Aubrey Beardsley, an *enfant terrible* of the contemporary artistic world. Beardsley was the first art editor of the influential *Yellow Book* which was startling in its time and gained an immediate notoriety. It was said that he and his fellows 'incorporated the sinuous lines of *Art Nouveau* ... producing a distinctive decadent style'. The fact that Mabel contributed to such a racy publication must have raised many a clerical eyebrow!

She also specialized in children's books illustration. The Arts and Crafts period encompassed a golden age in children's book illustrations. With many friendships in both the artistic and literary scene and their commitment to political causes, not least feminism, the Dearmers were at the cutting edge of cultural life and far from being imprisoned in any ecclesiastical ghetto.[6]

Choice of Musical Editor

Consequently, when Dearmer started to look for a Musical Editor for the new hymn book he did not seek advice from the narrow confines of either the church musical establishments or a safe and prudent ecclesiastic. He was influenced in his decision by two people, Henry Scott Holland and Cecil Sharp. Dearmer had been closely associated with Holland since Oxford days. During the year after his graduation and before ordination Dearmer had worked for both Charles Gore and Holland, based at Pusey House in Oxford. He was secretary of the Oxford branch of The Christian Social Union of which Holland was Chairman. The purpose of the CSU was, as Gore put it in a tribute to Holland, 'stirring up the church to its realization of what the teaching of its Master about human brotherhood, and the equal spiritual value of every human soul, really means'. They were Christian Socialists for whom the doctrine of the incarnation, the doctrine of the Holy Trinity, the doctrine of redemption through sacrifice, the doctrine of the Church and the Sacraments all alike spoke to them of social duty and supplied them with the motives and forces for social redemption. 'Social enthusiasm', Gore said, 'flowed inevitably from that fountain and that fountain alone.'[7]

Dearmer's other advisor was a layman and a musician. Cecil Sharp had thought that his musical career lay in composing, but on his return from nine years in Australia in 1892 he was gradually beguiled by the discovery of folk-song, the collection and recording of which became his life's work. It is reckoned that it was probably just in time to save a great mass of beautiful material.[8] Sharp was also 'left of centre' in his politics with Father Charles Manson, a fiery Christian Socialist, as a mentor. His sister, Evelyn, was a writer on the staff of the *Yellow Book* who also wrote children's books. Mabel Dearmer became a friend and illustrated her books. Later Evelyn, like Mabel, became a campaigning journalist for women's suffrage and spent two spells in Holloway Prison. It is very likely that Evelyn introduced Percy to her brother.[9]

Who was it that this combination of a Christian Socialist priest and a Fabian Society pioneer collector and arranger of English folk-songs and dancing recommended as Musical Editor of the proposed hymn book? It was not one of the musical knights of the time, nor someone distinguished from the Cathedral musical establishment. He had what might be described as an 'ecclesiastical connection'; the fact that he had been born in his father's parsonage at Down Ampney in Gloucestershire. Sadly his father died when he was only two years old. He was Ralph Vaughan Williams. He, like Sharp, had become intrigued by folk-song. Vaughan Williams had written to Sharp in 1903 following a lecture on the subject which he had given at the Hampstead Conservatoire. It was the beginning of a long partnership.[10] Sharp's biographer writes,

> Always in the background, ready to take an active part when called upon when the need arose, was Ralph Vaughan Williams, a lifelong friend of Cecil Sharp. The encouragement and sound advice that he gave cannot be over-estimated.[11]

Vaughan Williams always maintained that, although he had been confirmed at Charterhouse, his religious views on leaving school were basically atheistic. His second wife, Ursula, said that although he later 'drifted into a cheerful agnosticism', he was never a professing Christian.[12] However, this had not prevented him from becoming a church musician at the outset of his musical career.

From 1895 until 1899 he was organist at St Barnabas Pimlico. The Vicar was the Revd the Hon. A F A Hanbury-Tracy, who was later to be a colleague on the *English Hymnal* Committee. St Barnabas was the church for which J M Neale produced his *Hymnal Noted* and which had a long tradition of experimenting with hymnody. G R Woodward, a pioneer in the revival of plainsong in the Church of England, had been a curate at St Barnabas, and its first Priest-Precentor was the distinguished nineteenth-century musician, the Revd Sir Frederick Gore-Ouseley, who eventually took the choir boys from Pimlico to his own foundation at Tenbury Wells.

So Vaughan Williams had a background in church music and some experience in the Anglo-Catholic tradition. In fact he must have first met Henry Scott Holland at St Barnabas. Holland's favourite aunt (Miss Jane Gifford) was a pillar of the church and he enjoyed joining her at worship there whenever possible. Nevertheless, when recalling the circumstances of Dearmer's invitation to become Musical Editor of the hymn book Vaughan Williams was able to adopt a certain mock surprise.

> It must have been in 1904 that I was sitting in my study in Barton Street, Westminster, when a cab drove up to the door and 'Mr Dearmer' was announced. I just knew his name vaguely as a parson who invited tramps to sleep in his drawing room; but he had not come to me about tramps. He went straight to the point and asked me to edit the music of a hymn book. I protested that I knew very little about hymns but he explained to me that Cecil Sharp had suggested my name, and I found out afterwards that Canon Scott Holland had also suggested me as a possible editor, and the final clinch was given when I understood that if I did not do the job it would be offered to a well-known church musician with whose musical ideas I was much out of sympathy. I thought it over for twenty four hours

and then decided to accept but I found the work occupied me two years and that my bill for clerical expenses alone came to two hundred and fifty pounds. The truth is I determined to do the work thoroughly, and that, besides being a compendium of all the tunes of worth that were already in use, the book should, in addition, be a thesaurus of all the finest hymn tunes in the world – at all events all such as were compatible with the metres of the words for which I had to find tunes. Sometimes I went further, and when I found a tune for which no English words were available I took it to Dearmer, as literary editor, and told him he must write or get somebody else to write suitable words.[13]

In addition to all this, Holland, Sharp and Dearmer, being each in their different ways in tune with the artistic, cultural and political atmosphere of those early days of the twentieth century, knew instinctively that they were recruiting for the task a rising star in the English musical firmament. The emphasis here must be on 'the English musical firmament'. Vaughan Williams believed that music could and should be national. He thought the often-quoted description of music as 'the universal language' was unfortunate. He wrote:

Some music may appeal only in its immediate surroundings; some may be national in its influence and some may transcend these bounds and be world-wide in its acceptance. But we may be quite sure that the composer who tries to be cosmopolitan from the outset will fail, not only with the world at large, but with his own people as well.[14]

In this he was underlining Sharp's dismal contention that 'from the age of Purcell down to recent days music in England has been in the hands of the foreigner'. Neither Sharp nor Vaughan Williams was advocating the abandonment of non-English music, that would be unthinkable, rather they were anxious to secure the place of English music, in particular that deriving from the rich soil of folk-song.[15]

The need for a new hymnal
Now the scene was set for the work of producing this new book. The idea of a new hymn book had been in the mind of Dearmer and others for some while, but he was the moving force. For him it was part of a life-time campaign.

I will only say with all the solemnity of which I am capable that you will not with the hymn books at present in general use either hold the present generation or secure any influence with the next. While our hymns are what they are, the best and most intelligent people must increasingly go away from us. We could not respect them were it otherwise.[16]

Hymns, he believed, 'made it possible to keep our worship in touch with the age'. This was a considerably radical thought in those days. Worship was very much privatized and only interested in personal salvation. Condemning *Hymns Ancient & Modern* Dearmer said it had all the defects of its age.

> It was an age with which we have very little in common; the religious world was interested in its own salvation, but was much less interested in God, and not at all in its neighbour – except when he lived a very long way off; and therefore great as were the additions made to the narrow and jejune popular theology of the day, there were still serious defects. There are many hymns about the life of Christ, but even at Christmas none of them dwell upon the fact that Christianity involves peace and goodwill upon earth; there are a few hymns about the Holy Spirit, and one or two rather mechanical or mathematical ones about the Trinity, but almost none about the eternal Father.[17]

Hymns Ancient & Modern was the most widely used book in the Church of England. It was the result of what was at first a grudging acceptance of the hymn in Anglican worship. Hymns had begun to appear in the late eighteenth and early nineteenth centuries. Hymnody arrived in the first place with metrical Psalms, which were acceptable because they were the words of Scripture. Horton Davies, in his four-volume magisterial survey *Worship and Theology in England*, says that while they did not break the laws of God, they played ducks and drakes with the laws of metre. 'The awkward inversions and plodding progressions of their sad doggerel were calculated to dampen the ardour of the most enthusiastic singers!'[18]

At first Tractarians regarded hymns with the greatest suspicion, being reminiscent of Protestant Nonconformity. Through the work of such people as the Wesleys, hymns had become a staple of Nonconformist worship. Under the leadership of J M Neale that view changed with the appearance in 1851 of *Hymnal Noted*. This was a collection of translations of Latin hymns, together with their plainsong. About the same time less 'advanced' churchmen adopted other collections. These trends came together with the appearance in 1861 of *Hymns Ancient & Modern*. This book, it has been said, was remarkable for its eclecticism, bringing together examples of plainsong, metrical psalmody, chorale and old church-tune. To this mixture were added new tunes of a distinguished type by such 'modern' composers as J B Dykes, F A Gore Ouseley and W H Monk.[19]

Hymns Ancient & Modern was first published in 1861, and it soon became something of a national institution. Even so the Proprietors, a group of Church of England clergymen, were engaged in the continual process of change and revision. First of all an appendix was added to the book in 1868, and then a completely revised edition appeared in 1875, to which a supplement was added fourteen years later. It was this 1889 edition that Dearmer and a group of friends found sufficiently unsatisfactory that they decided to get together to consider the possibility of producing their own supplement for that hymn book.[20] The group was an intriguing one. It was led by the Hon. A F A Hanbury-Tracy, the Vicar of St Barnabas Pimlico. Other members were George Ratcliffe Woodward, Hanbury-Tracy's former curate and an early advocate of both plainsong and the English carol, Athelstan Riley, an uncompromising conservative High Church layman, and D C Lathbury, a historian and a biographer of Dean Church.

It was to this multi-talented group that Vaughan Williams was added. They met chiefly at the home of Athelstan Riley in Kensington Court, occasionally at Dearmer's St Mary's Vicarage in Primrose Hill or at St Barnabas Vicarage in Pimlico. At first there were frequent meetings, but hearing that a completely new edition of *Hymns Ancient & Modern* was in the offing, they decided to pause for a while and wait to make a judgement on the new hymnal. It was published in 1904 to a chorus of disapproval and disappointment, some of which was hasty and ill-judged. A later critic analysed the reaction.

> Controversies broke out upon the appearance of *A & M 1904*, and spread to the daily press. Very typical was the storm which raged around the herald angels at Christmas, who had to disappear in favour of the original line, 'Hark, how all the welkin rings!'. Why did the 1904 book fail eventually? Those responsible for the choice and purchase of hymn books had certainly received a number of minor shocks when they looked into their advance copies. Some of the old favourites had either appeared in reformed and corrected dress or had vanished altogether. Yet it could not have been long before the improvements and advantages of the new book would have been realized, as the dust of controversy died down. But two years was too short a time for the echoes to cease, and in 1906 there appeared *The English Hymnal*, accompanied by a flourish of trumpets from the *Church Times*, which was then in the zenith of its influence, and never ceased to promote this new book.[21]

Effectively the 1904 edition of *Ancient & Modern* never took off. Those who had used the old book much preferred what they had, with the result that the 1889 edition was republished in 1916 with a second supplement, Erik Routley in an article 'That Dreadful Red Book' tells how it was the victim of 'a press campaign of unprecedented violence'.

> The astute Proprietors had taught people to think of *A & M*, as the hymnal around which all the others revolved. Others were left or right of it north, south, east or west of it. It was there in the middle. Take it away from that position and nobody will know where he is. It became an institution like the monarchy – beyond serious criticism, subject to affectionate loyalty, subject

occasionally to affectionate ridicule, but a landmark which to remove was to come under the curse. At any rate, that's how the papers seem to have seen it.[22]

The coast was clear for High Church critics of *Ancient & Modern* to do their own work. There was now no excuse not to set to and produce a book containing the material they believed was needed for their style of worship. This would also be a collection able to uphold the artistic standards essential, in their opinion, in such a project. In order to accomplish the task the committee was enlarged by the inclusion of W J Birkbeck, an expert on the Orthodox Church, and Canon T A Lacey, an extremely gifted liturgist, the author of the Alcuin Club's best-selling *Liturgical Interpolations*. Woodward, however, soon left the committee. It is said he resigned due to the fact that he could not accept the inclusion of a hymn written by someone who was not a confessing Christian. The words were 'To Mercy, Pity, Peace and Love' by William Blake.[23]

The Hymnal Committee
The new volume was originally to be called *English Hymns* and was to contain words only, but within weeks of commencing the work it became obvious that they must abandon the idea of merely producing some kind of supplement and must undertake the much more demanding task of compiling a completely new hymn book.

The Committee recommenced its work with Vaughan Williams and Dearmer shouldering the major part of the task. In 1956 Vaughan Williams was asked to contribute 'some reminiscences of *The English Hymnal*' to a booklet called *The First Fifty Years* published by the Oxford University Press. A comparison of Vaughan Williams' original manuscript with the printed version reveals an interesting omission. In his draft the composer admitted to feeling 'rather at sea' during his first Committee Meeting. It was, he said, a new experience for him to be faced by an eager group of High Church parsons.[24]

When in 1904 Percy Dearmer asked Vaughan Williams to be Musical Editor, he told him that the work would probably take two months, and that each of the founders would put down five pounds for out-of-pocket expenses. In fact the work took two years. In a 1956 broadcast, to celebrate its fiftieth year, Vaughan Williams said:

> I decided, if I was to do the book at all I must be thoroughly adventurous, and honest... As regards honesty: the actual origin of the tune must be stated, and any alteration duly noted. But this does not mean that the original version must necessarily be adhered to. I always tried to find what I believed to be the best version... Cecil Sharp had just made his epoch-making discovery of the beautiful melody hidden in the countryside: why should we not enter into our inheritance in the church as well as the concert room? So you will find a lot of folk-songs in *The English Hymnal*. Our first territory to explore was of course the English and Scottish six-

teenth and seventeenth century psalters, many fine tunes out of which had been neglected in modern hymnals. In these tunes I restored what the Scots call the gathering note and in England we designate more pompously, the long initial. I explored particularly Wither's *Hymns and Songs of the Church* because they contained beautiful tunes by Gibbons... Also Archbishop Parker's *Psalter* containing fine tunes by Tallis. The eighteenth-century psalm books contain many fine tunes which had been allowed to drop out. Then there are the strong Methodist tunes of the eighteenth century. Another fruitful source of good melodies was the Welsh hymnbooks. The German choral was, up to a point, represented in the nineteenth century C of E hymn books, but often in a distorted form: so far as possible *The English Hymnal* has restored the originals. I intended the music to be congregational, both in matter and manner: the choir and organist acting as leaders. They have their opportunity to show off in other parts of the service but in hymns they must be the servants of the congregation.[25]

When the *English Hymnal* compilers began their work there was available as a bench mark another piece of work in the area of hymnody to set alongside *Hymns Ancient & Modern*, but of an entirely different calibre. We have already alluded to the cultural ferment of the times and J R Watson in his *The English Hymn* (1997) picks up the same point. The challenge to *Hymns Ancient & Modern*, he points out, came from within the church itself and was connected with the aesthetic movements of the last quarter of the nineteenth century. Watson mentions Ruskin and Pater, but we would add other luminaries of the Arts and Crafts and *Art Nouveau* Movements. However there is no disagreement in acknowledging the importance of the work of Robert Bridges.[26]

In a letter of October 1893 Robert Bridges said that he was 'beginning to print the hymns we have collected or set for the choir here'. Having abandoned his medical career Bridges moved in 1882 to Yattendon, Berkshire. For nine years he was Precentor at the church there and trained the choir. Although a poet he was concerned with the music as well as with the words. He had little time for the mid-Victorian music of Dykes and Monk and introduced plainsong and taught his choir other music which he believed was worthy to be used in Divine Worship.

Music being the universal expression of the mysterious and supernatural, the best that man has ever attained to, is capable of uniting in common devotion minds that are only separated by creeds, and it comforts our hope with a brighter promise of unity than any logic offers. And if we consider and ask ourselves what sort of music we should wish to hear on entering a church, we should surely, in describing our ideal, say first of all that it must be something different from what is heard elsewhere; that it should be a sacred music, devoted to its purpose, a music whose peace should still passion, whose dignity should strengthen our faith, whose unquestion'd beauty should find a home in our hearts, to cheer us in life and death.[27]

Convinced that too frequently those who could not afford expensive things were forced to accept the 'cheap and nasty', Bridges arranged for the publishing of a cheap but aesthetically pleasing edition of his hymnal in addition to the luxury edition produced by Oxford University Press. He hoped that the latter would be 'one of the handsomest music books ever printed'. The book is indeed worthy of such a claim. Its typography, its paper and its printing are a joy. It has been said it was an aesthetic experience to look at and handle, a book which was clearly making a statement over and against the simple and serviceable presentation of *Hymns Ancient & Modern*. It was published between 1895 and 1898.

The Yattendon Hymnal was widely admired and the *English Hymnal* Committee tried, in vain, to persuade Robert Bridges to join them. Finding it was likely to spend much of its time on hymns he thought insipid and sentimental he declined the invitation.[28] However, *The English Hymnal* included thirteen hymns from *The Yattendon Hymnal*, notably the translations of 'O Sacred Head, sore wounded' and 'The duteous day now closes', for which the Editors expressed themselves as being 'under a very great obligation to Mr Robert Bridges'.

There is no doubt that Bridges' work at Yattendon influenced *The English Hymnal* even if Dearmer, Vaughan Williams and company were unable to persuade the future Poet Laureate to share in their task. Routley said *The Yattendon Hymnal* did so much to give *The English Hymnal* its character. Bridges' greatest contribution to hymnody lies in his passionate concern for standards. These were set out in *The Yattendon Hymnal* and proved a major inspiration for the makers of *The English Hymnal*.

As the work progressed a number of authors helped with the words of the book. Dearmer was particularly grateful to his friend Laurence Housman (brother of A E) who was at the time Art Critic of the *Manchester Guardian* and later a playwright and a pioneer feminist, pacifist and socialist. Erik Routley thought that although the editors of the *Ancient & Modern* revision of 1904 were trying sensitively to reflect the needs of the day they failed at the very point that *The English Hymnal* succeeded. It is a sad fact that the *Ancient & Modern* committee contained no wordsmiths, they were all musicians, with not a poet among them. They failed to 'scoop' the Yatttendon book which had a poet as its principal author.

What is so successful in *The English Hymnal*, Routley reckons, is 'its youthful zest and sparkle'. Whereas the *Ancient & Modern* editors of 1904 didn't ask the right questions, Dearmer and Vaughan Williams did. In the 1904 book there is not a single folk-song and not a single French Diocesan tune. While 1904 was pedagogic and conservative he judged 'Dearmer and VW were adventurers'.[29] However, some members of the Episcopal bench were to be of the opinion that the *English Hymnal* compilers had ventured too far! But that is to anticipate.

It is said that the 1904 revision of *Ancient & Modern* took ten years. The remarkable fact, as we have seen, is that the work of compiling *The English Hymnal*, without any sign of haste or hurry, of cutting corners or carelessness, took no more than two years. All through 1905 the committee met twice a week. The brunt of the work, as has been said, was borne by Dearmer and Vaughan Williams. Evelyn Morrison, who did all the typing of the *Hymnal*, recalled how Dearmer would stand at the door of St Mary's Primrose Hill after service in order to catch her as she went out, the belt of his cassock stuck all round with scraps of paper on which notes, translations of hymns and other details would be scribbled in ink of every hue. On one occasion he burst out of a hansom cab, shedding bundles of notes on the pavement at her feet.[30]

There is no doubt that Vaughan Williams did not undertake his task 'lightly or wantonly' but 'reverently, discreetly, advisedly, soberly'. His musical preface is a masterpiece which could well be given wider circulation in our present day. If heeded it would rid us of many of our current church music distortions and horrors. In his preface Vaughan Williams said that the *English Hymnal* Committee believed many clergymen and organists were beginning to realize their responsibility in providing tunes of dignity and appropriateness in divine worship. 'The task of providing congregations with familiar tunes is difficult', he said, 'because many tunes popular with congregations are quite unsuitable to their purpose.' He condemned the argument that favoured bad music on the grounds that, although fine tunes are musically correct, people want 'something simple'. 'Musically correct' has no meaning, he said, the only 'correct music' is that which is beautiful and noble. As we have seen, this is exactly the same line that Dearmer, inspired by Morris, took. Vaughan Williams, in his preface, declared that:

> It is indeed a moral rather than a musical issue. No doubt it requires a certain effort to tune oneself to the moral atmosphere implied by a fine melody; and it is far easier to dwell in the miasma of the languishing and sentimental hymn tunes which so often disfigure our services. Such poverty of heart may not be uncommon, but at least it should not be encouraged by those who direct the services of the church; it ought no longer to be true anywhere that the most exalted moments of a church-goer's week are associated with music that would not be tolerated in any place of secular entertainment.

Certainly, at this juncture, the Musical and the Literary editors of *The English Hymnal* could be said to have been literally engaged in that activity which, in contemporary society, is usually only regarded as a wearisome symbolic cliché: 'singing from the same hymn sheet'.

A comprehensive book?

During the process of compiling and designing the book no doubt there would have been many changes and alterations; many debates, discussions, and disagreements. No minutes of the meetings have survived and none of the participants left a record. The details of one interesting change have survived; Dearmer altered his preface. In the collated proofs, preserved in the Pratt Green Collection in Durham University Library, the first sentence of the preface is: 'Many have come to desire a Hymn Book that shall be as comprehensive as the English Church. This desire we have endeavoured to fulfil in the new Hymnal which is offered as a humble companion to the Book of Common Prayer.' In the event, the printed version commenced: *'The English Hymnal* is a collection of the best hymns in the English language, and is offered as a humble companion to the *Book of Common Prayer* for use in the Church.'[31]

Both versions go on to assert that it was not a party book 'expressing this or that phase of negation or excess, but an attempt to combine in one volume the worthiest expression of all that lies within the Christian Creed, from those ancient Fathers who were the earliest hymn writers down to contemporary exponents of modern aspirations and ideals. We therefore offer the book to all broad-minded men, in the hope that everyone will find within these pages the hymns which he rightly wants.'

The Preface boasted that a unique feature of the book was that it made 'complete provision for the liturgical requirements of Churchmen', a claim which meant the statement that it was 'not a Party book' must be taken with a fairly liberal pinch of salt. It was true that 'the liturgical requirements of Churchmen' were broadening every year at that time, but not everyone was happy about this fact. The very same year as the publication of the new hymnal saw published the report of the eagerly awaited Royal Commission on Ecclesiastical Discipline which had been set up to 'inquire into the alleged prevalence of breaches of neglect of the Law relating to the conduct of Divine Service in the Church of England and to the ornaments and fittings of churches; and to consider the existing powers and procedures applicable to such irregularities and to make recommendations as may be deemed requisite for dealing with the aforesaid matters'.

Between 16 March and 3 November 1905 the Royal Commission held one hundred and eighteen meetings, at which the average attendance of the commissioners was an amazing one hundred and ten. *Inter alia,* the use of hymns in the Church of England was discussed. It was acknowledged that, although they had no precise legal status, hymns were now widely accepted. One Diocesan bishop put it like this, which was received without demur from any of the members: 'The general use of hymns in all services, and at all sorts of unforseen points in the course of the service, is another instance of an irregularity which has found popular acceptance, but for which, so far as I am aware, no legal authority could be advanced.' His Lordship was highly suspicious of hymns. He realized their potency for evil as well as good. 'Much more false doctrine finds its way into people's minds through hymns than through sermons or other practices.'[32]

The prevailing situation as regards the regulation of worship in England was clearly one of the greatest confusion, mixed with prejudice, bigotry and

zealotry. In the recent past, priests had gone to prison rather than forgo performing the rites and ceremonies of the church in the manner they believed
right and proper. The hundreds of pages of evidence which precede the recommendations of the 1906 Royal Commission are mainly from snoopers and
interlopers spying on the liturgical 'goings on' in scores of churches up and
down the land. Putting aside all the legal and canonical arguments it was a
poisonous and unedifying atmosphere which never should be associated
with the worship of Almighty God.

Percy Dearmer had already, seven years earlier, in 1899, with the publication of his influential *The Parson's Handbook* attempted to 'help, in however
humble a way, towards remedying the lamentable confusion, lawlessness,
and vulgarity which are conspicuous in the Church at this time'. Dearmer
himself appeared before the Commission and, perhaps surprisingly, stoutly
defended many of the provisions of *The Book of Common Prayer*.

Yet, the spirit of *The English Hymnal* was very much in tune with the
conclusions and recommendations of the Royal Commission. The
Commissioners gave it as their opinion that 'the law of Public Worship in
the Church of England is too narrow for the religious life of the present
generation', and continued:

> It needlessly condemns much which a great section of Church people,
> including many of her most devoted members, value, and modern thought
> and feeling are characterised by a care for ceremonial, a sense of dignity in
> worship, and an appreciation of the continuity of the Church, which were
> not similarly felt at the time when the present law took its present shape.[33]

In 1906, then, those who were anxious about the future shape of Anglican
worship found they had a Royal Commission advocating a more relaxed
attitude towards additions and omissions. On hymns they specifically stated
that their singing was nowhere declared illegal and was a custom of long
usage, although they qualified the statement by quoting the legal dictum
that usage, though entitled to the greatest respect, 'cannot contravene or
prevail against positive law'. This was also the year in which the new
hymnal appeared, necessarily a work of private enterprise which had
neither sought nor received any kind of official approval or imprimatur. A
book which, its producers believed, would suit the needs of 'learned and
simple alike, and shall at the same time exhibit the characteristic virtue of
hymnody, its witness, namely, to the fact that in the worship of God
Christians are drawn the closer together as they are drawn more closely to
the one Lord'.

The English Hymnal appeared on Ascension Day 1906 with its characteristic
green cover displaying its tooled Arts and Crafts design. The chi-rho (the first
two Greek letters of *Christos*) was at the centre. It was wrapped in a very plain
brown cover with no more than the words '*The English Hymnal*' in a ruled

panel together with the information : Oxford. Printed at the University Press. London : Humphrey Milford Amen House. On the title page additionally there was the name of the co-publisher: A R Mowbray & Co. Ltd. of 28 Margaret Street, London, W. Is it too fanciful to suggest that the cover design was the work of Dearmer's book-designing artist wife?

'Not a Party book,' Dearmer had claimed in his Preface. 'The hymns of Christendom show more clearly than anything else that there is even now such a thing as the unity of the Spirit.' As hinted earlier there were those who believed, as Bishop Knox did, that more could be inculcated through hymns than many other ways, and detected in this new hymnal insidious signs of such a campaign of insidious propaganda.

Controversy arises

It would seem that there had already been warning shots across the bows of the Hymnal Committee. But apparently they had chosen to take no notice of warnings they had received from Henry Frowde, the publisher at Oxford University Press. For instance, a year before publication (30 June 1905) Frowde had written to Dearmer:

> My referee has gone carefully over your Hymn Book and has sent me a preliminary and final report of which I enclose copies. You will see that, while he is generally in favour of the book, he considers that it contained a few things that would prove fatal to its success in the Church as a whole.
>
> The only other person who has seen the MS is the Dean of Christ Church, and he fully endorses all my referee's objections, and is of the opinion that some of the Bishops would inhibit the book if it appeared in its present form.
>
> I shall be very glad if you can see your way to elikinate (sic) from the copy such pieces and portions to which objection is taken.[34]

Frowde could not have made things clearer; in its present form the book would attract severe criticism, and risk inhibition unless modified. The Dean of Christ Church (T B Strong) who had expressed this opinion now wrote to Frowde again on 24 July 1906 and stated: 'I am quite sure that the hymns on S Mary and some of the Saints will cause great trouble. You will remember that in the Report of the [Royal] Commission the Bishops are recommended to use much more care in dealing with Hymns and Anthems than they did. They can hardly authorize some of these.' It was true, number three of the ten Recommendations of the Royal Commission commenced: 'In regard to the sanction to be given for the use of additional and special services, collects, and hymns, the law should be amended as to give wider scope for the exercise of a regulative authority.' In other words: regulation by the Bishops. By return of post Frowde explained the difficulty of his position to the Dean:

We did everything in our power, short of throwing up the contract, to exclude the extreme Hymns which were likely to cause trouble, and nearly all those to which we objected were abandoned but there remained two or three which Mr. Dearmer and his Committee absolutely refused to forgo, even if they had to find another publisher. The Rev C F Rogers (who was originally recommended to me by Dr Sanday) acted for me in the matter, with very good results. If pressure from the Bishops should bring the Committee to reason and they should consent to change or rewrite one or two of the offending hymns I should be very glad. I enclose a copy of a letter just received from the Bishop of Oxford, and am at a loss to know whether it is the hymns to S Mary to which he objects, or those taken from Sankey's Songs and Solos.

The letter from the Bishop of Oxford which Frowde mentions is brief and much to the point:

Let me thank you sincerely for your kindness in sending me a copy of *The English Hymnal*. In binding and in printing the volume seems to me, if I may say so, well worthy of the great Press from which it comes.

Perhaps I should end here: but I should not feel quite frank in my acknowledgement of your kindness if I did not add that there are parts in the contents of the book which seem to me open to some serious criticism.

Dean Strong was a high churchman who, incidentally, had taught Dearmer at Christ Church and would seem to have introduced him to a style of churchmanship somewhat different to that of his rather stiff evangelical home. Therefore he was not an implacable enemy, just a realist. He wrote to Frowde:

I don't think the Bishops will do anything yet, and of course the Hymnal was published and compiled in ignorance of what the Commission was likely to say. The Bishop of Oxford is a very severe critic of hymns. I am sure he dislikes those containing Invocations of Saints, and I do not think he would look with sympathy on Sankey's effusions or the like.

In the event the balloon went up not in Oxford but in Bristol. On 16 October the sixth annual meeting of the Bristol Diocesan Conference was held in the Chapter Room of the Cathedral. In his address the Bishop of Bristol (the Rt Revd George Forrest Browne) referred to the newly published Report of the Royal Commission, in particular to the evidence he had himself given to the Commission, which had been in favour of liberalization and a return to the standards of the 1549 Prayer Book.

Bishop Browne was an old-fashioned high churchman who previously had a distinguished career at Cambridge both as an academic and administrator. Immediately before going to Bristol he had been one of Frederick Temple's

Suffragan Bishops in London. Browne was something of a pedant when interpreting rubrics and canons; he also felt the burden of stabilizing the diocese of Bristol which, only nine years earlier, had been re-established as a separate identity from the Gloucester diocese.[35] He was anxious to eliminate any false or heretical doctrines but on his appearance before the Commission he told them: 'I would just legalise a number of things which are done by people who are true and staunch supporters of the Church of England and of that side generally against the Church of Rome. My tremendous fear is, that if you try to puritanise it all, those people will have to say that, much as they dislike any changes at all, if you really force them to consider and make a choice between this and that, they will go to that and not stay with us.'[36] On 16 October 1906 having assured his Diocesan Conference that he did not intend to repeat the evidence he had given to the Commission he neverthe-less swung into attack against what he believed was an insidious influence. The Bishop said, 'It must be evident to all who have a considerable acquain-tance with hymnody that under poetic inspiration the writers of hymns sometimes use phrases which go beyond calm and exact statement of doc-trine. To myself and I know many others, there has been a good deal of anxiety about the extent to which this fervour of poetic expression has been showing itself.'[37]

Bishop Browne then got down to particulars and identified the collection of hymns which contained hymns which 'go beyond calm and exact' doc-trinal statements. 'In my judgement, the recent issue of a book called "*The English Hymnal*" has made it necessary for me to speak in public of my anxiety.' In a side sweep he added, 'I should say, in passing, that except in the case of well-known hymns by well-known writers, I could not think of applying the epithet poetic to a book which in many cases is far removed from any claim to the possession of that character.' He then returns to his main point and says that his particular objection is to the 'direct attempt to introduce into the services of the Church of England, under the cover of hymns, requests addressed to Saints on our behalf'.

He then quoted at length from the hymns 'Hail O Star that pointest', 'Ye who own the faith of Jesus' and four Saints' Days office hymns. His conclu-sion is unambiguous: 'I cannot reconcile it to my conscience, or to my historical sense, to do less than prohibit a book which would impress upon the Church of England tendencies so dangerous to our access to the one only Mediator between God and man.' It would be practically useless, he realized, to prohibit the use of certain parts of the book while allowing the book itself to be used in the public service. His only course was to prohibit entirely the use of *The English Hymnal* in the public services of the Church in the diocese of Bristol.

The report of the Conference's proceeding was, of course, red-hot news. Within forty-eight hours Dearmer was writing, somewhat ingenuously, to Frowde. 'I think the Bishop of Bristol will do good. I had nine interviewers yesterday and I think the Public will resent his interference with their liberties. This I think is the line to take – that the Bishop's attack savours of the Papacy. It is a good thing that he did it and not anybody else, because he has done things of this kind before.'

Frowde was obviously more worried than Dearmer and wanted an urgent meeting: 'I don't think the Bishop of Bristol's prohibition will make very much difference one way or the other, but it will be a serious matter if he is followed by other Bishops as I learn may possibly be the case. If you are this way this afternoon and can spare the time I shall be glad if you will call in so that we may talk the matter over. I suppose if the Committee would allow the hymns in question to be relegated to a supplement which could be omitted or included at will that would remove the difficulty.'

The Dean of Christ Church had also read the newspaper accounts of the Bristol Conference and he quickly wrote to Frowde: 'I see that the Bishop of Bristol has prohibited *The English Hymnal* in his diocese. I am not altogether surprised, and I think other Bishops may follow his example. I have always thought that some of the Saints' day Hymns would produce this effect, for they go far beyond anything that has ever been openly used before. But I do not think we can do anything. I expect the Editors will have great objections to meeting any change.'

It would seem that Dearmer rather enjoyed the notoriety that the hymn book had achieved and the fact that 'nine interviewers' had hastened to his Vicarage in Chalcot Gardens, England's Lane to question him on the Bristol inhibition. To the *Daily Chronicle* he said, 'The Bishop is simply setting himself against freedom.' The paper commented that it was evident that Mr Dearmer was in no way alarmed by the episcopal thunders. He remarked that 129,000 copies of the Hymnal had already been sold (that is in four months).[38]

The reporter from *Daily News* said that Mr Dearmer expressed his views on the matter with great frankness and with a calmness that might almost have been indifference. 'It has been a recognised principle of the Church of England always,' he said, 'that there should be no "index" of forbidden books, and no attempt to revive the method of the Inquisition. No hymn book has ever been prohibited in the Church of England. The choice of hymns has always been a matter left to the discretion of the minister, and it is quite certain that neither the clergy not the laity of the Church will submit to this new tyranny, so that the matter does not really concern us very much. No doubt most of the Bishops will be actuated by a higher sense of justice.'

The newspapers drew Dearmer's attention to the Bishop of Bristol's objection to the verse:

For the sick and for the aged
For our dear ones far away,
For the hearts that mourn in secret,

All who need our prayers today,
For the faithful gone before us,
May the Holy Virgin pray.

On this, the paper reported, Mr Dearmer asked,

> Does the Bishop think we should sing 'May the Holy Virgin not pray'? It is
> ridiculous. Every Nonconformist and every Churchman believes that all
> God's saints pray. The Bishop takes the old fashioned conservative view,
> and any phrase that is new to him sounds shocking. That hymn is written
> by Mr V S S Coles, Principal of Pusey House, Oxford, one of the most
> respected and trusted clergymen of the Church of England. I suppose that
> a hundred years ago the Bishop would have put Mr Coles in prison, or
> three hundred years ago would have burned him.[39]

Would other Bishops join Bishop Browne's campaign, that was the crucial
question? Dearmer thought not. In a letter to Frowde he said:

> It seems important for us just now to do nothing and to say nothing so far as
> the contents are concerned; to show ourselves anxious to make concessions,
> might draw the enemies' fire. Meanwhile we have done a good deal quietly
> to let other Bishops see that this sort of attack will be found impossible.
> Today I think one is able to say that the attitude of the *Times* and *Guardian*,
> show that a Bishop would not get sufficient backing to encourage any more
> attacks. I should think that even the Bishop of Bristol has an inkling by now
> that he made a mistake, and that others are not likely to follow his example.
> My greatest fear was about the Bishop of Oxford, but this danger also seems
> to be past.

Dearmer was wrong, very wrong, and he did not have to wait long before his
misplaced optimism was completely shattered. Whereas the Bristol Diocese
was one of the smallest in the country, the next salvo of opposition came from
the Primate of All England no less. In a message to the clergy of his diocese the
Archbishop of Canterbury (Randall Davidson) stated that, after careful examination of *The English Hymnal*, he felt bound to express his strong wish that it
should not be adopted in any church in the diocese of Canterbury. His Grace
is reported as saying, 'The book contains hymns which appear to express doctrines contrary to the spirit and traditions, or even to the express teaching of
the Church of England.' The danger, he considered, lay specially in certain of
the hymns relating to the Holy Communion, to the faithful departed, and,
most markedly, to the hymns for use on saints' days. Fast on the archiepis-
copal heels came reports that the Bishop of Exeter (Archibald Robertson) and
the Bishop of Winchester (H E Ryle) had also refused to sanction the use of the
book.

In the face of such weighty opposition, some wondered if the next thing would be a charge of heresy brought against the Compilers. The Archbishop hastened to say he had no intention of imputing heresy against them. Commenting on that statement the *English Hymnal* editors noted: '(1) That your Grace has not thought the matter one that calls for your intervention as Archbishop of the province; (2) that you in no way charge us with heresy; (3) that your letter is only advice personally given to the clergy of your diocese respecting the adoption of a particular book in their churches.'

Seeking a compromise
Not surprisingly Oxford University Press was beginning to get worried about the situation, no doubt believing that their reputation was at stake. It is at this point that Henry Frowde first broaches the idea of an expurgated edition. He realizes that he is going to have considerable difficulty in persuading Dearmer and his colleagues to agree to this. In a letter to Dearmer of 19 October:

> Another Bishop has asked me confidentially today whether a few hymns which are regarded as objectionable can be cut out, and I am aware that several Bishops, Oxford among the number, are not happy about two or three. In cases where the omission of certain Hymns threatened to mitigate against the adoption of our book you are aware that I am arranging to supply supplements, but instances are far more numerous where the inclusion of 5 or 6 hymns bars the way to its use and seriously limits its sale. What would you say to me if I were to consent to print cancels to order for a particular church so as to remove a few hymns, leaving blanks or substituting hymns as required by the Rector? Of course I am not doing so.'

At the same time, unknown to the *English Hymnal* Committee, Frowde attempted to organize a flanking movement on them. He decided to enlist the aid of his friend the Dean of Christ Church and wrote to him on 5 November,

> I wonder whether you will help me, through Canon Scott Holland or any others, in an endeavour to bring Mr Dearmer and his co-editors to reason? The Archbishop of Canterbury and the Bishops of Winchester, Exeter, Bristol and Oxford have inhibited the book in its present form, and the Bishops of Winchester and Exeter point to the remedy. The former says, in his monthly letter to the diocese, 'It is true that the number of hymns to which such objection may be made is, comparatively speaking, insignificant. I could greatly wish that the hymns, to which loyal members of our Church must take exception, could even now be removed from the book, so that its public use might "be attended with no cause for offence" and the latter says the collection has 'much merit in very many respects; but certain features, unless they are removed in future editions, seem to me to be

incompatible with the use of the book in public worship by those who take their guidance from our formularies'. If the Editors could only be persuaded to permit me to issue a Revised Edition from which the objectionable hymns were removed, and hymns acceptable to the Bishops substituted, I believe the trouble would be over. About 66 churches have already adopted the book, but some of these would no doubt be willing to fall into line. The original edition would only be supplied when specially asked for, and I suppose there could be no objection to its sale for private use. There are already two editions of both *Hymns Ancient & Modern* and *The Hymnal Companion* being sold side by side. I shall be exceedingly thankful for any help and advice that you can give me.

Dean Strong replied that he would write to Canon Scott Holland, as Frowde requested, but he believed that such a scheme as he had outlined was already before the editors and they were proving difficult to persuade.

This was indeed very true. On 8 November Frowde met with Hanbury-Tracy, the chairman of the *English Hymnal* Committee, and requested permission to issue an alternative edition with some substitutions or omission 'just sufficient to make it available for use in those churches which would not under any circumstances use the original edition or which would be deterred from doing so by the inhibition of their Bishops'. The two editions would command a very large sale, 'while it would not in any way injure the sale of the original edition'.

Without any real hesitation, the day after that meeting Hanbury-Tracy wrote to Frowde: 'I think I should make it quite clear that I find it is our unanimous opinion that this is a time when any talk of concession would be fatal to the Hymn Book. If any one tries to bring pressure upon you, you might tell them that we shall take our stand upon our legal rights in the matter. I only put this forward to help you. The Committee is entirely convinced that the Delegates of the Press will not in the 20th century attempt any interference with that liberty of "Unlicensed printing" which Milton defended in a work I believe already republished by you.'

Hanbury-Tracy encloses with his letter an embargoed copy of an extraordinary open letter to the Archbishop of Canterbury from the *English Hymnal* committee. It does not seem calculated to make peace with Lambeth. On the contrary the *English Hymnal* committee are clearly deeply incensed by the accusation of heresy made against them.

> It becomes our painful duty to reply publicly to the most serious charges which you have brought against us, the editors of *The English Hymnal*, which charges have been communicated to your diocese. These charges amount to a distinct accusation of heresy. We feel that we cannot ignore such an accusation when made by one in your Grace's exalted position. Your Grace objects to some hymns in the book as putting forward doc-

trines contrary to the express teaching of the Church on the Holy Communion and the faithful departed, the censure applying especially to the hymns for use on Saints' days. With the utmost respect we repudiate this charge, the most serious that could be brought against a body of churchmen lay and clerical. Maintaining, as we are bound to maintain, the recognised rights and liberties of churchmen, we beg leave to point out that when such a charge is made, it is incumbent on the accuser to indicate the particular expressions to which objection is taken as erroneous, and also the particular declarations of the authoritative formularies of the Church which they are said to contravene. If your Grace will do this we are pre-pared to vindicate the orthodoxy of the hymns which we have collected for the use of our brethren, on the basis of the Prayer Book and the Articles and that teaching of ancient and godly Fathers to which the Church of England uniformly appeals.

When the Dean of Christ Church read this letter he described it as 'ingenious but monstrous'. Meanwhile the Committee continued to meet to monitor the situation. They wrote to Oxford University Press to ask how far sales had been influenced by the publicity. Have any new churches adopted the book since the Archbishop's first pronouncement? Have any since his correspon-dence with us has been published? Have any more incumbents asked you to take their books back? How many have done this in all? What has been the general sale of the book during the present month? 'We should be grateful if you could give us information on these points,' they asked.

In a letter to Frowde, Dearmer expressed the opinion that the Bishops' utterances were improving, citing the Bishop of Lichfield who 'apparently assumes the book will be in use in the Diocese, and only warns the Clergy against certain hymns not specified'. Indeed the Committee complained that any decision regarding recommendations they might make was being ham-pered by the fact that the Bishops would not specify exactly the hymns to which they took objection.

Meanwhile the statistical news from the Press was not good. Since the Archbishop's pronouncement sales had averaged 250 copies a week as compared with 1000 copies a week just previously. The falling off would have been still greater if the action of the Bishops had not created con-siderable curiosity as to the contents of the book. For several days after the pronouncement orders for single copies of the words edition were very numerous. Applications for free copies of the music edition had dropped from twelve or fifteen per week to three. Frowde says that quite a number of booksellers had returned copies: 'probably they got frightened'. Frowde now tries a different tack, a little flattery, hoping to mollify the Committee:

The English Hymnal is undoubtedly the best Church Hymn Book that has ever been compiled, and if you give me permission to issue an alternative edition it will call forth more episcopal commendation than any Hymn Book has hitherto received. The Bishops naturally shrink from specifying hymns, and if they were to do so they would probably ask for too many changes. The substitutions or omissions should be extremely few.

The abridged version

By the end of November the Committee is beginning to consider modifying its hard-line stance. Dearmer says that Canon Scott Holland and Canon Newbolt are in discussion with the Bishop of London (Arthur Winnington-Ingram) and that he believed 'slight omissions in five cases would be sufficient, and if they were offered, the Committee would agree to such an edition'. Frowde breathed a sigh of relief because the sales position was becoming desperate. 'The drop in sales has been so complete that I have been obliged to stop an impression of the book with music.'

On 6 December 1906 came the breakthrough. Hanbury-Tracy wrote to Frowde saying the committee had accepted the Bishop of London's proposal for the omission of five hymns, together with the alteration of small points in others. 'We shall therefore ask you to publish such an edition abridged "at the request of the Bishop of London",' writes Dearmer. He adds that Canon Holland tells him that the Bishop of Southwark (E S Talbot) and the Bishop of Birmingham (Charles Gore) concur in this arrangement. Both Bishops were significant high churchmen. 'We are not likely to hear of more objections,' Dearmer says with confidence.

The designing of the abridged edition is a typographical triumph. The Committee insisted that there would be no alteration in the numbering of the hymns nor should there be gaps and blank pages. This is achieved by redistribution of the number of verses on the pages either before or after the omitted hymns.[40] It is an ingenious piece of typographical 'invisible mending'. The omitted hymns were taken out of the indexes and the list of 'hymns arranged for Sundays and Holy Days'. This additional note was added at the end of the preface: 'At the request of the Bishops of London and Southwark, the editors issue this abridged edition of the English Hymnal, which it is hoped may be found useful by those who desire an alternative to the complete edition.'

There was only one further slight piece of unpleasantness before the abridged edition was published. In January 1907 the Bishop of London wrote to Dearmer saying that as a friend of the Committee he hoped that the original book would be taken off the market and the abridged edition put in its place. Dearmer replied that the Committee never had any intention of withdrawing the complete edition, and that they could not under any circumstances agree to it. Hanbury-Tracy was of the opinion that the other Bishops were using London 'as a cat's paw with a view to securing the withdrawal of the old book and the issue of the new one amended according to their ideas, and they are advising him not to sanction anything less than this'. The Committee were having none of this. The amended version appeared and the full edition continued to be widely available.

The result of all this feverish activity was that the abridged edition never took off. Indeed copies of the book are extremely rare and successive re-printings of the original book bear no traces of these controversies. There is a copy in the Colles Library of the Royal School of Church Music and one in the Pratt Green Collection at Durham University Library, otherwise they seem to have disappeared. There is no copy in the Bodleian Library in Oxford. Oxford University Press archives does not possess a copy and expressed complete ignorance of its existence until apprised of its history through this research.

Schedule of changes in the abridged edition

Hymns omitted:
  185, 195, 208, 213, 350

Hymns altered:
  184 verse 7
  Wherefore made co-heirs of glory,
  Dwelling now with Christ on high,
  May they by their supplications
  Help us as for grace we cry.

  200 verse 5 line 2
  for 'Queen of Grace' 'full of grace'.

  218 The refrain 'Hail Mary, full of grace' omitted throughout.
  Verse 7 omitted.

  253 Verses 11 and 12 omitted, verse 13 altered to 11.

The tunes to the five deleted hymns were printed in the appendix of the music edition taking Appendix numbers not their original numbers.

A 'Catholic' supplement

There are stalwarts of the High Church tradition in the Church of England who would confidently claim that they, like the poor, have always been with us. One of the tradition's historians claims, 'It is arguable that there is a continuous, distinguishable High Church tradition in the Church of England throughout the period from the Reformation to the late twentieth century.' But he then goes on to add a note of caution, suggesting that all those individuals, groups and movements were not necessarily participating in a continuous process and a single evolving Christian tradition but rather responding to the peculiar circumstances confronting them in their day. They may contain links with past manifestations of high churchmanship or seem

to anticipate things to come, but there have always been 'various and sometimes strong currents and cross currents, divisions and antagonisms which
may cause doubts about the identity or oneness of such a tradition'.[41] No time
was more full of such divisions and antagonisms than the period after the
opening of the Oxford Movement.

Put simply, the first stage of the Oxford Movement was between the years
1833 and 1845, the latter date being the year of Newman's secession to Rome.
In the main, the post-1845 heirs of the original Tractarians were moderate
men, not fanatics or extremists, but by the 1860s there was the definite change
of tone among an increasingly large body of Anglo-Catholics.

It has been said that a Church of England worshipper of the 1660s would
have noticed few liturgical changes in his parish church if he returned in the
1840s, whereas sixty years later, in many places, he would have found it hard
to believe that the services had any relationship whatsoever with those autho-
rised by *The Book of Common Prayer*. After the influence of the Ecclesiologists
came the second wave of the Anglo-Catholic, Tractarian, High Church
Movement, the emergence in the 1860s of the Ritualists, which revolutionized
Anglican worship in scores of churches.

This radical change in the appearance and content of high church Anglican
worship was not of a uniform style, but at the turn of the century it could be
definitely divided into two camps. There were two types of parishes: 'Sarum'
and 'Roman'. The first had its most detailed outworking in Percy Dearmer's
The Parson's Handbook (1899), in the Alcuin Club (1897) and the advocacy of
the English Use. The second centred, in the main, around the Society of St
Peter and St Paul, founded in 1911 to co-ordinate its activities. The division
between the two groups was wide.[42] Peter Anson said, '*The Parson's Handbook*
was regarded by extreme Anglo-Catholics as little short of heresy.' It was
'British Museum Religion' whereas SSPP was to be not 'a return to the past,
but as a resumption of arrested development'. In other words the object of the
Society was not to return to the pre-Reformation period, but to advance
towards what the Church might have been if the Reformation, in its most
destructive aspects, had never occurred.[43]

The result was back to Baroque; an undisguised policy to transform the
externals of Anglican worship into the closest possible resemblance to those
of seventeenth- and eighteenth-century Continental Roman Catholicism. It
was a campaign to confirm the worst fears of the 1906 Commissioners. It was
all that Dearmer and the 'English Use' advocates hated the most.

As regards ceremonies and décor these Anglo-Papists had plenty of
models and exemplars from Roman Catholic sources, but what could they do
about hymns and hymn books? Here was a dilemma. Many, though certainly
not all, were urban parishes where the congregation wished to sing in
English. The answer was that they gritted their teeth and adopted *The English
Hymnal*, despite its connection with Dearmer, Athelstan Riley, T A Lacey and
other 'unsound' Anglican Catholics. They figuratively crossed their fingers

and took into church with them *The English Hymnal* – and a little book of their own designing entitled *The English Catholic Hymn Book*.

The preface states that 'this Hymn Book is intended as a supplement to the older hymn-books already in existence, and especially to *The English Hymnal*'. In order to mark the supplementary character of the present book the hymns were numbered from 801 onwards and the repetition of hymns easily available elsewhere was avoided. It generously acknowledged that *The English Hymnal* 'constituted a rich store-house of the finest hymn tunes' so that it only appeared in a words-only edition with recommendations for the appropriate *English Hymnal* tune.

The English Catholic Hymn Book was first published in the late 1930s by Talbot & Co., the publishers for *The Catholic Literature Association*, whose objects were 'the spreading of knowledge of the Catholic Faith and the issue of literature of Catholic doctrine and devotion'. W Knott & Son, who also produced *The English Missal* and that essential *vade-mecum* used in SSPP and similar parishes, *Ritual Notes*, published a revised and augmented edition in 1955 and the last printing of the hymn book was in 1973. The English edition of the revised Roman Missal became available in 1975 and W Knott & Son went out of business soon after.

Services for young and old

In 1914 Oxford University Press produced an edition of *The English Hymnal* containing 'Services for Young and Old'. These comprised 'A Little Psalter' and 'Short Services for Missions, Schools and Catechism'. The psalter was indeed small, containing only twelve psalms together with three canticles, Te Deum, Magnificat and Nunc Dimittis. Other outline services were entitled 'First Prayers', 'Last Prayers' and 'A Short Service for Adults'. The material for the Catechism included two orders for ordinary occasions and an 'Order for a Catechism Festival'. There was also a 'Short Service for a Holy Day' and 'A Little Service for Lent'. The book also contained opening and closing services for Sunday School and a special order for Kindergarten.

The book's prefatory note states that in the first place this special edition is intended for churches 'with no choir or but few choristers so that easily sung hymns may be seen at a glance'. To this end, such hymns are marked with an asterisk. In the main, these hymns are those contained in the 'List of Simple Hymns' which the main hymn book included until 1933, and intended for 'Mission Services, for use at Sea, for Catechisms, Schools and Institutions'.

As regards the other services in the book, a note explains that 'in some churches a simple popular service is wanted for Sunday evening or in others weekdays'. Of the forms of service for young people it is claimed that they 'are everywhere wanted'. Furthermore, 'the new Kindergarten method necessitates a carefully drawn-up order'.

The particular provision made for the Catechism of young people ensures that there is no doubt about the main proponent of this special edition. 'The teaching of children and young people had been an important part of Percy's work from quite early years,' wrote his wife Nan Dearmer.[44] In each of his curacies he had founded a successful Catechism based on the method made famous by Bishop Felix Dupanloup at S. Sulpice Paris and adapted for Anglican use by Spencer Jones.[45] Dearmer's *The Parson's Handbook*, which pre-dates the hymnal, contains these same detailed instructions as those in the 'For Young and Old' edition of *The English Hymnal.*

'The Prayer Book', wrote Dearmer, 'knows nothing of Sunday Schools, which became a necessity owing to the want of "diligence" on the part of the clergy.'[46] That is, failing in their duty of catechizing. Dearmer made his views very clear:

> It is a pity that this rubric should have fallen into such abeyance. It is true that the use of gas, and other modern customs, have put Evensong so late that it is sometimes inconvenient to take the children during the service. But in the country it would be thought that the parson would often do more good by catechising before his people than by exhausting his powers in a second sermon. 'He that preacheth twice a day prateth at least once,' said Bishop Andrews.[47]

No doubt Dearmer was equally forceful in persuading his fellow committee members to include, as part nine of *The English Hymnal*, a section entitled 'At Catechism' which contains twenty-seven hymns suitable for young people. Subsequent printings of the 1906 book, and of the new edition of 1933, all add notes at the end of the Catechism section which refer to the 'For Young and Old' edition of the hymn book.

The 1933 revision

The 1906 edition of *The English Hymnal* lasted unchanged and unrevised for twenty-seven years. In 1933 a new edition was published in which the changes were almost entirely musical. The exceptions to this were the inclusion of the words of Blake's 'Jerusalem' and 'in rare instances a few words have been altered at the request of the authors'. These were on stylistic rather than theological grounds.

No tune found in the 1906 edition was omitted in the revision, but over a hundred tunes were added. This was achieved, in the first place, by removing a number of cases where there were duplications and also by placing a number of tunes in an appendix and replacing them with new tunes in the main body of the volume. Vaughan Williams commented that congregations would not be affected by the changes, but choirs would have the opportunity of enlarging their repertory, while they could still, if it was preferred, sing any particular hymn to the former tune.

For the revised book J H Arnold totally re-edited the plainsong tunes and wrote a new preface to that section, replacing the one by W J Birkbeck in the original edition. Vaughan Williams added an extra note to his musical preface in which he thanked those who had assisted him in the revision, particularly mentioning Martin Shaw. Shaw (at one time organist at Primrose Hill) had been very much involved with Dearmer and Vaughan Williams in the production of *Songs of Praise* in 1925, as he was also in preparing *The Oxford Book of Carols* in 1928. Encouraged by the initial success of *Songs of Praise* an enlarged edition was produced in 1931. In the preface to *The English Hymnal* Dearmer had given it as his aim not to produce a party book. He now went further in *Songs of Praise* and said his intention was to produce 'a national collection of hymns for public worship'. The book was enthusiastically adopted by the newly emerging, but not over-large, Modernist party within the Church of England. Otherwise it did not seriously affect the sales of either *The English Hymnal* or *Hymns Ancient & Modern*, although it remained popular in its schools edition long after it had pretty well disappeared from the pews.

Hymnal for Scotland

The Church of England has never had an official hymnal; parishes are free to choose from what, in recent years, has been an increasing range of books in various shapes and styles. Other parts of the Anglican Communion have treated the matter differently. In 1950 the Episcopal Church in Scotland, the Anglican province 'north of the border', decided to authorize a *Hymnal for Scotland*. The book comprised *The English Hymnal* in its entirety, together with fourteen additional hymns, numbered 745 to 759.

Many of the hymns, words and music, have a distinctly 'celtic' flavour, deriving from Scotland, Wales and Ireland. There are hymns commemorating Saints Kentigern, Columba, Ninian and Queen Margaret, four additional eucharistic hymns and six other hymns.

Ralph Vaughan Williams was involved in the process, being asked to supply a hymn for St Margaret. The words were written by Ursula Wood, later to be the second Mrs Vaughan Williams. The tune *St Margaret*, he said, is to 'the metre of *The Charge of the Light Brigade*'.[48] Thus Vaughan Williams concluded nearly fifty years of magnificent hymn tune composition, which had contained such gems as *Down Ampney*, *King's Weston* and *Sine Nomine*.

English Hymnal Service Book

It was almost thirty years after the 1933 revision before any further substantial book emerged from the *English Hymnal* stable, but in 1962 Oxford University Press published *The English Hymnal Service Book*. It was not intended that this new book would supersede *The English Hymnal*, but rather that it would provide in a single volume a core selection of hymns from that hymnal together with all the music that both choir and congregation would need 'in the corporate use of the Prayer Book services of Mattins, Holy Communion and Evensong'. There were 298 of the 657 hymns in the original book together with 38 hymns and carols not in that collection. New features included the Preces, Versicles and Responses from Mattins and Evensong, a pointed Psalter, and the Merbeke setting of the Holy Communion.

The aim of *The English Hymnal Service Book* was to enable congregational participation in the spirit of the Liturgical Movement, which in the Church of England meant the growth and spread of the Parish Communion.[49] The unsigned Preface said: 'It is not enough to be edified and uplifted by the words and actions of others: worship is an activity and a work in which all present have a positive part to play. This book has been compiled in order to assist congregations to take their full part in the worship provided for in *The Book of Common Prayer*.'

In order to make the book especially useful in Parish Communion parishes particular attention was given to eucharistic hymns, while also commending some familiar hymns which it believed 'take on a new significance when sung at various junctures in the Eucharist'.

English Praise

The *Service Book* was followed in 1975 by *English Praise*. This was described as 'A Supplement to *The English Hymnal*'. The editors (Christopher Dearnley, Howard Hollis, Arthur Hutchings, Cyril Pocknee and George Timms) stated that at first it was intended to produce a complete revision of *The English Hymnal*. In that revision hymns which had been little used would have been omitted and replaced with 'a number of classic hymns which have since become established in popular favour' and were not included in 1906, together with some good hymns written since then and now in widespread use.

In the event no such root and branch revision took place. Instead *English Praise* provided a supplementary selection of 106 hymns and carols together with eight responsorial psalms (music by Dom Gregory Murray). The hymns were 'some which have already proved their worth elsewhere, some are modern hymns which show signs of becoming established, others are new ones written for this collection', wrote the editors.

Interestingly the St Mary's Primrose Hill connection continued strongly among the editors of *English Praise*: Hollis and Timms were both at one time Vicars there.[50] Pocknee, like Dearmer, was a long-serving member of the Alcuin Club committee. The editors hoped that while trying to preserve the high standard set by the words and music editors of *The English Hymnal*, they had produced a supplementary collection which would be useful in contemporary Anglican worship.

New English Hymnal

Eleven years later the task which the *English Praise* editors had originally in mind was completed – a full-scale revision of *The English Hymnal*. *The New English Hymnal* appeared in 1986 to warm and wide welcome. The 1906 and 1933 editions of *The English Hymnal* as well as *The English Hymnal Service Book* and *English Praise* were published by Oxford University Press. The new book was produced by Canterbury Press Norwich as the new publishers to The English Hymnal Company Ltd.

The editors (of which George Timms was the chairman – the Dearmer connection went on) were very much aware of the daunting task that they had undertaken in producing, after nearly eighty years, a successor to *The English Hymnal*, knowing that the 1906 book had 'set new standards in words and music for Anglican worship in the twentieth century'. In all due humility the 1986 editors presented their work 'in the hope that it may be used to give greater glory to God in his people's offering of the sacrifice of praise'. There can be no worthier aspiration for hymn book editors than that.

Notes

1 Donald Gray, *Percy Dearmer: A Parson's Pilgrimage*, Norwich, Canterbury Press, 2000, 33.

2 Percy Dearmer, *Art and Religion*, London, SCM Press, 1924, 29.

3 Gray, *Dearmer*, 29.

4 Pamela Todd, *The Arts and Crafts Companion*, London, Thames and Hudson, 2004, 11.

5 Gray, *Dearmer*, 30.

6 Jill Shefrin, *"Dearmerest Mrs Dearmer"*, Toronto, The Friends of the Osborne and Lillian H Smith Collections Occasional Papers Series, 2, 1999, *passim*.

7 Stephen Paget, ed., *Henry Scott Holland*, London, John Murray, 1921, 246; Alan Wilkinson, *Christian Socialism: Scott Holland to Tony Blair*, London, SCM Press, 42ff.

8 A H Fox-Strangways and M Karples, *Cecil Sharp: His Life and Work*, 3rd ed. rev. M Karples, London, Routledge & Kegan Paul, 1967, *passim*.

9 Janet E Grenier, in C S Nicholls, ed., *The Dictionary of National Biography, Missing Persons*, Oxford, OUP, 1993, 595.

10 Karples, *Sharp*, 46–7.

11 *Ibid.*, 115.

12 Ursula Vaughan Williams, *RVW : A Biography of Ralph Vaughan Williams*, London, OUP, 1964, 29.

13 Ralph Vaughan Williams, *The First Fifty Years: A brief account of The English Hymnal from 1906 to 1956*, London, OUP, 1956, 2.

14 Ralph Vaughan Williams, *National Music*, London, OUP, 1934, 4.

15 Karples, *Sharp*, 199.

16 Percy Dearmer, *The Art of Public Worship*, London, Mowbrays, 1919, 48.

17 *Ibid.*, 49.

18 Horton Davies, *Worship and Theology in England*, vol. 3, London, OUP, 65.

19 J R Watson, *The English Hymn*, Oxford, Clarendon Press, 1997, 333ff.

20 Gray, *Dearmer*, 62–3.

21 Anselm Hughes, *The Rivers of the Flood*, 2nd ed., London, Faith Press, 1963, 136.

22 Erik Routley, 'That Dreadful Red Book' in *The Hymn Society of Great Britain Bulletin*, vol. 8, 5, 1974, 80ff.

23 John Barnes, *George Ratcliffe Woodward 1848–1934*, Norwich, Canterbury Press, 1996, 87.

24 Draft article in Oxford University Press archives, NRA 27790 OUP (OUP/PUB/30).

25 Ursula Vaughan Williams and Imogen Holst, *Heirs and Rebels: Letters written to each other and occasional writings on music by Ralph Vaughan Williams and Gustav Holst*, London, OUP, 1959, 38–9.

26 Watson, *Hymn*, 511.

27 Catherine Phillips, *Robert Bridges*, London, OUP, 1992, 162.

28 *Ibid.*, 164.
29 Routley, 'Red Book', 83–4.
30 Nan Dearmer, *The Life of Percy Dearmer*, London, The Book Club, 1941, 180.
31 Pratt Green Collection, University of Durham Library, X 783. 9 FO ENG.
32 Bishop of Manchester (E A Knox), *Royal Commission on Ecclesiastical Discipline,* Cd. 3071, vol. iii, 19954.
33 *Ibid., Report*, 399.
34 This and all subsequent correspondence between Frowde, Dearmer, Strong and others are from OUP archives NRA 27790 OUP (OUP/PUB/30).
35 G F Browne, *The Recollections of a Bishop*, London, Smith, Elder, 1915, 364ff.
36 *Royal Commission*, vol. iii, 155229.
37 *Bristol Times Mirror*, 17 October 1906.
38 *Daily Chronicle*, 18 October 1906.
39 *Daily News*, 18 October 1906. In the face of Episcopal condemnation Stuckey Coles declared himself 'honoured that my two hymns on the Blessed Virgin Mary and the Blessed Sacrament have been singled out for disapproval by those to whom the Catholic Tradition means little'. (J F Briscoe, ed., *V S S Coles, Letters, Papers, Addresses, Hymns and Verses with a Memoir*, London, A R Mowbray, 1930, 261.) As a result of this criticism five hundred of Coles' friends, including twenty-four bishops, presented an address to him praying God 'that you may be spared for many years to continue your great work, and to maintain the battle for the Faith in the anxious days which seem to lie before the Church of England' (*ibid.* 109–11).
40 For instance: 186 is spread over two pages to fill the gap caused by the omission of 185; 193 and 194 are given separate pages to fill the 195 gap.
41 Kenneth Hylson-Smith, *High Churchmanship in the Church of England,* Edinburgh, T & T Clark, 1993, ix–x.
42 Nigel Yates, *Anglican Ritualism in Victorian Britain 1830–1910*, Oxford, OUP, 1999, 336–8.
43 Peter Anson, *Fashions in Church Furnishings 1840–1940*, 2nd ed., London, Studio Vista, 1965, 316.
44 Nan Dearmer, *Life*, 158.
45 Spencer Jones, *The Clergy and the Catechism*, 6th ed., London, Skeffington, *passim*.
46 Percy Dearmer, *The Parson's Handbook*, 4th ed., London, Grant Richards, 1903, 391.
47 *Ibid.*, 387.
48 Ursula Vaughan Williams, *RVW*, 281.
49 Donald Gray, *Earth and Altar: The Evolution of the Parish Communion*, Alcuin Club Collections 68, Norwich, Canterbury Press, 1986, *passim*.
50 Francis Stephen, ed., *St Mary's Primrose Hill – A Guide and History*, London, St Mary's, 1972.

'FAIR WAVED THE GOLDEN CORN': TAKING STOCK AT THE JUBILEE

Simon Wright

In the summer of 1956 Geoffrey Cumberlege retired as Publisher to the University of Oxford, then one of the most exalted posts in the British book trade. In prestige it was matched only by its Oxford University Press printing counterpart, the Printer to the University (at that time Charles Batey). Having revitalized the Oxford University Press editorial and distribution operations in India, and then North America, Cumberlege succeeded Sir Humphrey Milford as Publisher in 1945, and presided over his famous list (which included *The English Hymnal*, *Songs of Praise*, *The Oxford Book of Carols*, the Tudor Church Music series, Oxford 'Companions', Bibles, and prayer books) from OUP's elegant Amen House office in the shadow of St Paul's Cathedral. *The English Hymnal*, from the beginning, had come under OUP's London list: although it and many other London books were printed in Oxford, titles published there (under the Clarendon Press imprint) were exclusively scholarly and academic, and treated apart from the 'trade' titles put out by London. London's titles traditionally carried the Publisher's personal imprint, and thus *English Hymnal*s printed between 1945 and 1956 took the legend 'Geoffrey Cumberlege: Oxford University Press' on their full-title page.[1] The year 1956 would see not only Cumberlege's retirement, but also the Golden Jubilee of *The English Hymnal*, one of his best-selling books. As both devout churchman and canny publisher, Cumberlege saw an opportunity to take stock and celebrate the achievement of a great book over its fifty years of Christian mission and proselytizing for hymnody, as well as simply to increase sales: ' "The first-ripe ears are for the Lord, / The rest he gives to man" '.

Thus it was that in the spring of 1955 Cumberlege (taking a personal and executive interest in a marketing project that would be unusual at his level today) began to draw up plans to celebrate fifty years of *The English Hymnal*. That this was no mere commercial gesture, but an act of heartfelt devotion to a cause in which Cumberlege fervently believed, became evident after his retirement, when he became first a director, and then Chairman, of the English Hymnal Company.

From 1953 *The English Hymnal* had come under OUP's new Hymn & Service Book Department, with Guthrie Foote in charge. Foote, a conductor and music arranger in his own right, established a department which, in its work, floated somewhere between OUP's Music and Bibles publishing: under his remit came *Songs of Praise* and its derivatives, *Prayers and Hymns for Use in*

Schools, and *The Daily Service*, as well as *The English Hymnal*. Foote was prompt to issue a 40-page prospectus, *Characteristic Hymns from 'The English Hymnal' Suitable for Congregational Practices, Festivals, etc.*, which sold at two shillings. 'With the publication of the *English Hymnal* in 1906 a new era in hymnody was begun, as is now recognized by all authorities on the subject,' proclaimed the Preface. The booklet was designed to promote the hymnal into churches, not only through a 'sampler' of twenty-six carefully chosen hymns and tunes reproduced from the 1933 edition of the book itself, but also in an essay giving guidance on introducing *The English Hymnal*, even in situations where there might be opposition. 'The obstacles should first be removed' is the advice given. Taking as read that instructions to clergy 'to preach sermons about hymns' would be followed, the problem of congregational resistance is then addressed and demolished. 'Some people do not like the trouble of buying new hymnals. Therefore it is much the best plan to obtain at grant rate from the Oxford University Press sufficient books for the congregation, and to place these in shelves at the end of the church ... This only costs a few pounds, according to the size of the congregation; and it will be found that the people will at once, of their own free will, begin to buy books, so that in a few years they will have copies of their own ... Also, copies of the *English Hymnal* should be given as Sunday School and Catechism prizes.' The essay continues with a controlled programme for introducing the hymns in the context of a service, and even offers a 'demonstration-practice' (today this would be called a workshop) from OUP itself.

In 1953 many churches would still have been using the original 1906 or 1907 editions, and so the booklet's Preface gave details of what it called the 'Amplification' in 1933: the revision of the plainsong accompaniments, and the addition of about one hundred new tunes, accomplished without the removal of any of the existing ones. That the original 1906/7 numbering had been retained in 1933, despite these changes, was highlighted: although not stated, this was because *The English Hymnal* had learned from the serious mistake of *Hymns Ancient & Modern*, which failed to do this in its 1904 edition, one of the reasons for its infamous limited success. The *Church Times* (13 July 1956) in covering this point in its Jubilee reporting said that 'the revisers [of A&M] had changed the numbers, Number 60 masqueraded as Number 62, a trick which, more than any other, rouses the exasperation of conservative critics'.

The principal 'obstacle' to introduction was of course *The English Hymnal*'s old rival, that very book, *Hymns Ancient & Modern*, which, by the 1950s, had sold in its tens of millions, and was found in almost every Anglican community worldwide. However, for at least part of its first fifty years *The English Hymnal* shared its printer and distributor with *Hymns Ancient & Modern*'s. The OUP General Catalogue of 1920 lists various editions of *Ancient & Modern*, printed on Oxford's exclusive India paper and bound with Oxford prayer books, as well as words only and music editions bound with *Oxford*

Helps to the Use of the Hymns. The two hymnals found common ground in the annual almanac compiled by Percy Dearmer, which in the 1920 catalogue was listed as *A Kalendar of 'Hymns Ancient & Modern' and 'The English Hymnal' for the Year of Grace 1920*, but then, mysteriously, *Twenty-fourth year of issue.*

The University Printing House in Oxford, which OUP's London business had at its disposal, was a magnificent resource of printing, design, paper-making, and binding skills and expertise, and for fifty years London played to this advantage in exploiting *The English Hymnal* (and all its Bibles, prayer books, and other hymnals) to the full. By 1920, OUP's catalogue listed a vast range of sizes and binding styles for the 'Tunes' and 'Words only' editions, plus a number of hymns available as offprints at 1*d.* or 2*d.* each. And already, a prototype of Foote's 1953 leaflet, *Hints on the Introduction of 'The English Hymnal' and the Improvement of Congregational Singing*, had been introduced (6*s.* per 100 copies). By 1931, when OUP issued its first Music Catalogue, the spin-offs had proliferated, with an *English Hymnal* book of organ accompaniments, a subject index, a *Transition Tune-Book* (fifty-two *English Hymnal* tunes to be sung to familiar words), and a book of hymns suitable for congregational practices. The 1933 revision of course saw further industry along the same lines.

By the mid-1950s the number of editions and binding styles was at something of a zenith, and the back cover of Foote's leaflet detailed these. The choice was bewildering, and those type sizes, bindings, and formats, another fifty years on, are simply redolent of a great printing house, now disappeared. The Music Edition (Crown 8vo) and the Melody Edition (Small Crown 8vo) were both available in a range of simple or 'superior' bindings, while the Words Edition came in Crown 8vo and Long Primer 8vo (various bindings), and as Minion 48mo, Ruby 32mo, Nonpareil 32mo, Beryl 32mo, and Pearl 32mo, in standard bindings. There was a Sunday School Edition, and a range of publications 'based on *"The English Hymnal"* including *A Subject Index of Hymns in 'The English Hymnal' and 'Songs of Praise'*, *The Nine Sequences of 'The English Hymnal'*, a special edition entitled *Hymnal for Scotland*,[2] and books of descants and communion hymns, introits and antiphons. Prices ranged from the standard Music at 11*s.* 6*d.* to Words (Pearl) at 1*s.* 9*d.* Superior binding prices, presumably, were upon application.

It was to a new brochure that the thoughts of Cumberlege and Foote turned when they met to consider the Jubilee in the spring of 1955. 'I have been thinking further about the idea of a booklet telling the story of EH,' wrote Foote to the English Hymnal Company on 24 May;[3] but, 'I fear that all the people concerned in the original production on the words side are now dead ... Fortunately we have Dr. Vaughan Williams with us still ...' Foote not only expressed concern to capture memories and facts, but was also conscious of the book's greater purpose: 'The longer I preach the gospel of EH the more I realize how valuable such a story would be.'

Fifty years had indeed removed most of those involved in the book's compilation, and Foote had to write instead to families and friends for recollections. Percy Dearmer's widow, now Lady Sykes, responded with an informative letter,[4] which told how Dearmer was forced to leave the 'hobgoblins' out of 'He who would valiant be' (402) because, in 1906, they 'would never have been accepted for inclusion in a hymn book. It was revolutionary enough to make a hymn at all from Bunyan's original.' Martin Shaw, though not an *English Hymnal* 'original', was written to, and supplied an anecdote[5] about a lady in a congregation where the book had recently been introduced. She was 'greatly shocked because, having A&M bound up with her prayer book, she thought it part of the Church service, & therefore regarded EH as a kind of heresy to be stoutly resisted by the faithful'. Ralph Vaughan Williams, naturally, was approached, and promised Foote that 'I will do my best to provide some comic relief for your booklet'.[6] In the absence of any other substantial material, 'Some Reminiscences of the English Hymnal' by Vaughan Williams was eventually to form the introductory section to Foote's booklet, itself entitled *The First Fifty Years: a Brief Account of 'The English Hymnal' from 1906 to 1956*.

Through the autumn and winter of 1955 Foote continued to track down anecdotes and information. Vaughan Williams delivered his 'comic relief' on 12 March 1956. Foote privately noted[7] that 'I fear it will require a certain amount of editing', although eventual intervention was light. Production of the brochure occupied Foote throughout April and May, and in June he was able to send a draft to Cumberlege, who was enthusiastic. 'This seems to me very good indeed. Perhaps at the end when "opposition" to it is touched on, we might say that this quickly died down and of the controversy which then seemed so acute nothing is now heard – or something to that effect. We should give the impression that it has ceased to be an issue.'[8] Foote then submitted the typescript to the English Hymnal Company, and Vaughan Williams.

The Vaughan Williams reminiscences provided a valuable and characteristically wry gloss on the book's compilation, understandably concentrating on the music, but opening by recalling his first meeting with Dearmer (Roger Lloyd, in his *Manchester Guardian* article of 24 September 1956, called this famous first exchange, with Dearmer arriving by cab and announcing himself as he burst through the door of the composer's study, a 'pleasantly Sherlock Holmes touch'). At an early stage, Vaughan Williams remembered, he had determined that 'besides being a compendium of all the tunes of worth which were already in use, the book should, in addition, be a thesaurus of all the finest hymn tunes in the world', even if this meant Dearmer writing or finding texts to fit tunes to which no English words were available, this being the origin, for example, of Riley's 'Ye watchers and ye holy ones' (519), which was written for Vaughan Williams' fine harmonization of *Lasst Uns Erfreuen*. Of plainsong, Vaughan Williams was adamant: 'On this subject I was really ignorant, so I refused to touch it.' He acknowledged a debt to Robert Bridges' *Yattendon Hymnal* (1899, and incidentally the first hymnal printed by Oxford

University Press), but reiterated his determination that, in editing the music of *The English Hymnal*, he 'would not follow the careless, slipshod methods of earlier hymnal editors'. The article concluded with a spirited defence of his adaptations of folk tunes, criticisms of which in some quarters evidently still rankled with him fifty years on: 'but this is', he wrote, 'surely an age-old custom'.

The remainder of the booklet ('A Short History of *The English Hymnal*') was compiled by Foote from information in files, from anecdotes collected, and from personal knowledge. In five pages he moves from the poor standard of hymn singing prevalent at the turn of the nineteenth century, through an account of Dearmer's informal collection *English Hymns* and its metamorphosis into *The English Hymnal*, glances at the book's wide geographical and historical spread ('the compilers cast their nets far and wide'), praises the work of Vaughan Williams ('It is doubtful if any other hymn book (except *Songs of Praise*) has ever had as its Music Editor a musician of such calibre'), and eventually gives account of the book's reception on publication. Cumberlege's anxiety about the controversy resulting in the 1907 'emergency' abridged edition is neatly dealt with: 'Any initial opposition quickly died down and the intrinsic worth of the new book carried it into every part of the English-speaking world. As the Church of England has wakened to her rich heritage of worship she has found in *The English Hymnal* unique provision for her growing needs.'

The printing estimate from Oxford was received on 3 August 1956, and the booklet went to press (17,000 copies). Ready in September, *The First Fifty Years* was mailed to all religious and musical papers, all Anglican incumbents, and many college and school chaplains. It was widely acclaimed, and remains valuable as a picture of the perception and value of *The English Hymnal* after fifty years.

The booklet was issued just after Cumberlege's retirement, but in time to coincide with the Jubilee project in which he had taken the greatest personal interest, a celebratory BBC radio programme. Cumberlege, and indeed OUP, had long been used to collaboration with the BBC (the Company, as it first was, and OUP's Music Department had been founded within months of each other), and a direct approach from him to the BBC's Religious Programmes Department seemed natural. After all, Cumberlege himself had seen to publication in 1951 *The BBC Hymn Book* after a long and difficult gestation of fourteen years, a delay caused mainly by the War. This book, designed 'for use in studio services, and particularly at the Daily Service', contained, incidentally, thirty *English Hymnal* copyright hymns or tunes, a sure sign of the older book's growing influence and worth as a resource for other hymnals (the administration of these copyrights became an important part of the work of OUP's separate Hymn Copyright Department, also based in London).

Cumberlege, Foote, and the BBC met on 19 January 1956.[9] At this stage a 'feature broadcast during which recordings of typical *English Hymnal* hymns' would be performed, followed by a liturgical service, was the idea under discussion. The meeting notes record two suggestions, both sadly to come to nothing. John Betjeman's name was proposed (but eventually rejected) as a writer and narrator for the script; and amongst ideas for musical performance was that one hymn should be 'sung by members of the Trans-Antarctic Expedition'.

Along with the successful assault on Everest, the Commonwealth Trans-Antarctic Expedition was one of the great neo-Elizabethan scientific and exploratory enterprises, with Vivian Fuchs and Sir Edmund Hillary between 1955 and 1958 leading the first land crossing of the Antarctic. The expedition carried copies of *The English Hymnal*, and OUP was detailed to secure a tape recording of hymn singing by its men.[10] On 28 May Foote was able to report to the BBC: 'As promised, I send you the tape-recordings of the *Pilgrim Song*[11] made by the Antarctic Expedition... They were made while the ship was nosing its way through the ice and one can hear the noise of the engines.' Although the same hymn was eventually to open the broadcast, it was in a straightforward performance with organ, and the recording by Fuchs' 'merrie men' (Foote's words) was not used. Vaughan Williams, in particular, would surely have savoured the rougher version, truly in the missionary spirit of the book, and with the sound of the ship's engines pushing inexorably toward the unknown region.

Entitled *The Glory of the English Hymn*, and with much material supplied by OUP, the programme was broadcast on the Home Service on 7 October 1956 at 7.45 in the evening, and lasted about twenty minutes. Perhaps because of the BBC's policy of non-commercial endorsement, the programme as broadcast had moved subtly away from the planned celebration of *The English Hymnal* itself, and had become a 'programme about hymn singing on the occasion of the Jubilee of *The English Hymnal*'. This was a disappointment to some, given that at least half the programme was devoted to the history of 'the hymn', with actors playing the roles of figures prominent in hymnody (the modern term would be 'docu-drama'): Elizabeth I, Rochester, Watts, John and Charles Wesley, Keble, and others. Words spoken by Charles Wesley ('... I shall weary you indeed were I to tell you of all my 7,000 hymns') characterize the pedestrian mood of the script, and when it came to it the *English Hymnal* coverage seemed scant.

An actor played Dearmer but Vaughan Williams himself ('very much alive'), in two recorded gramophone inserts, spoke on behalf of the otherwise deceased editorial team. The programme covered *The English Hymnal*'s compilation, skirted even more adroitly than Foote around the 1906–7 prohibition crisis ('There was some criticism that the new Hymnal had a High Church look about it'), and stressed Vaughan Williams' achievement as he 'restored tunes to their original freedom of life, pitching [them] within the vocal range of mixed congregations'. Amongst the hymns included, sung by the BBC Singers with George Thalben-Ball at the organ, were 'He who would valiant be' (402), 'Glory to thee, my God, this night' (267), 'Love's redeeming work is done' (135), and 'Lead, kindly Light' (425). After the final Vaughan Williams spoken contribution, the broadcast concluded with 'For all the Saints' (641), to his tune *Sine Nomine*, specially written fifty years earlier, for the hymnal itself. The programme was followed with a (non-liturgical) Act of Thanksgiving, conducted by the Dean of Lincoln, the Rt Revd Colin Dunlop.

While Vaughan Williams was clearly a true progenitor of *The English Hymnal*, there was subtle reciprocation, the child eventually becoming the father of the man in terms of the influence the book and its contents were to have over Vaughan Williams the composer, until the end of his life. Working with OUP meant that when the Press set up its own music publishing department in 1923, it seemed natural for Vaughan Williams to join their new list of composers: OUP remained Vaughan Williams' publisher until his death, and this was a connection born of *The English Hymnal*. At an obvious level, the tunes he had assembled for the book were used as a 'repository' of material, later worked into a variety of compositions. The tunes *Bryn Calfaria* (319), *Rhosymedre/Lovely* (303), and *Hyfrydol* (301) appeared in *Three Preludes Founded on Welsh Hymn Tunes* for organ (1920, and published by Stainer & Bell); and *Five Variants of 'Dives and Lazarus'* for harp and strings, written for the 1939 World Fair, is based on *Kingsfold* (574). But, deeper than this, Vaughan Williams' immersion in hymnody is sensed less literally throughout certain works dating from as early as the *Fantasia on a Theme by Thomas Tallis* (it was first performed in Gloucester in 1910, with Elgar waiting in the wings to conduct *The Dream of Gerontius*), quintessentially English in its rich string sound and modal language (the theme in question is embodied in *The English Hymnal* as *Third Mode Melody* (92)), and in many other hymn-like movements, such as the 'Romanza' of the Symphony in D major (1943). Throughout his life, Vaughan Williams, almost as a pilgrim himself, developed music on the theme of Bunyan's *The Pilgrim's Progress*, culminating in his great 'Morality', performed at Covent Garden in 1951. His involvement with Bunyan was manifest first in 1906, the year of *The English Hymnal*, with incidental music written for a dramatization at Reigate Priory. Amongst other hymns, Vaughan Williams included in his score 'He who would valiant be' to *Monks Gate* (402), and the 'Alleluyas' from *Sine Nomine* (641). In the vast Morality itself, hymnody, modality, and folk-song are gloriously melded in a unique and somehow inevitable soundscape peculiarly Vaughan Williams' own, yet on English music of the twentieth century, profoundly influential. It was a soundscape that was also *The English Hymnal*'s, and which developed in parallel with the book's first fifty years, and was part of its (unexpected) legacy. It was, in a sense, to vanish when Vaughan Williams died in 1958.

Vaughan Williams, as the sole 'original EH survivor', had been much in demand as a speaker throughout the Jubilee year, despite his increasing deafness and advanced age. Ill-health almost prevented his appearance at the special 'English Hymnal Jubilee' conference of the Hymn Society of Great Britain and Ireland, held at Addington Palace on 12–13 June 1956. But appear he did, to great applause, speaking on his work as Musical Editor. The Literary Editorship was covered by Professor Arthur Hutchings who, in comparing *The English Hymnal* with Palgrave's *Golden Treasury*, noted of the compilers their 'artistry, scholarship, wide knowledge, tolerance, understanding of other men's needs, sincere religious experience, and the shrewdness to tell when the expression of that experience rang true and when it did not'. At this conference, it was only unfortunate that the special hymn sheet for use following the lectures printed the original (1906) version of the plainchant accompaniment (in minims) to 'Let the round world with songs rejoice' (176), rather than its 1933 (crotchet) replacement. Although spotted before the event, it was too late to reprint. The mistake did not, of course, matter in performance.

Thanks in the main to Foote's efforts, the Jubilee received the broadest possible press coverage; the reviews and features he secured together provide a considered view on the standing of *The English Hymnal* in 1956. The very extent of the coverage, for example in national daily papers, gives a clear picture of the progress to musical, ecclesiastical, and publishing icon that this early twentieth-century book had achieved by mid-century. The *Church Times* (18 May) observed that the book 'has become an indispensable part of Eucharistic worship in countless parishes. It is, in the true sense, a hymn book of the Church.' However, the same reviewer could not resist a jibe against 'the weakness for airy-fairy folk tunes, and an occasional lapse into doggerel'. *The Times* (13 June) covered the book's genesis, the discontinued 1907 edition, and the 1933 revisions; in a counter to the *Church Times* complaint, Vaughan Williams' use of folk melodies was praised. The *Church Times* was softer on 22 June when, in its reporting of the Addington Palace conference, the whole issue of folk tunes was overlooked in favour of Vaughan Williams' statement that he had shaped *The English Hymnal* as 'good, honest, and thorough'. In a large feature on 13 July, the *Church Times* covered a lecture in Oxford at which Erik Routley had robustly defended Vaughan Williams' work of selection and arrangement, calling *The English Hymnal* 'a pivotal book as a standard of taste'.

The Hymn Society's own Bulletin covered the Jubilee, with consecutive issues (Volume 4, numbers 75 and 76 – both entitled 'Summer, 1956') devoting space, respectively, to an editorial on *The English Hymnal*, and a transcript of Hutchings' conference lecture, and other reporting. The editorial called *The English Hymnal* 'an honoured part of the English landscape', and reflected in particular on 'what the Oxford Press [*sic*] achieved in setting a new standard of clarity and pleasantness in its type'. However, the book was criticized for favouring the introduction of new (musical) material above 'proper exploration of the existing repertory'. And this sin was compounded in the 1933 edition, its own new tunes resulting in 'quite preposterous collocations...along with a vast inflation of the Appendix'.

A E F Dickinson, in the *Musical Times* (August 1956), having heard Vaughan Williams' lecture at Addington Palace, put his *English Hymnal* work in the context of Vaughan Williams' composing career: 'For R. Vaughan Williams an advance hymnal critique has been a significant preliminary to a like career of probing creative work, habitually downright and, if liable to spasms of routine, yet singularly lacking in horrific lapses.' Dickinson also covered the hymn singing at Croydon, opining that 'a pompously "final" rallentando' somewhat marred that 'greatest of folk-tune reconstructions (Monksgate) [*sic*]'.[12]

The *Methodist Recorder* (9 August) observed that *The English Hymnal*, in its two main editions, 'has so far outlived two normal hymn-books – the average life of a hymn-book being about twenty-five years'. Methodists were reminded that the inclusion of Charles Wesley's original 'Hark, how all the welkin rings!' (23), as well as the restoration of the verse commencing 'His dying crimson like a robe' in the Watts hymn 'When I survey the wondrous Cross' (107), were particularly appealing features.

In an earlier *Musical Times* article ('Some thoughts about *The English Hymnal*', May 1956), A E F Dickinson claimed that the book's rich content, and material drawn from 'many frontiers of belief and period and nation-state', led it to be ' "the spiritual man's companion", and a fresh invocation to unity'. But the universal and enduring success of *The English Hymnal* was best summed up by Roger Lloyd in the *Manchester Guardian* (24 September 1956), who wrote,

> The editors went to hymnody to find a moral code, and what they found and applied is very simple. Those who habitually sing sentimental tunes tend to become sentimental people. Those who sing in worship trite words, platitudinous words, or enervating words will find these weaknesses built into their characters. Those who impiously alter the words or tunes of great artists dead and gone have no artistic conscience. Good music is always moral music wherever it comes from, and several of the tunes in the English Hymnal come from folk-song and sea-shanty. Such were the moral principles which they built into their hymn-book, and every congregation which has adopted it has come to feel that it is an anthology not only good in itself but one which subtly conveys throughout the fact that it is planned and principled. In fact it is hardly too much to say that the English Hymnal judges the church which uses it, and its members know that it does... The fact is that the local parson, organist, choir, and people are the final judges and there is no superior court of appeal for any hymn-book. They have judged the English Hymnal now for 50 years, and all that time its popularity has steadily increased, and still does. There is some dead wood in it: with 744 hymns how should there not be? But there is marvellously little of it.

Almost as an afterthought, *The First Fifty Years* had included on its final page a graph of *English Hymnal* church adoptions from 1951 to 1955. Geoffrey

Cumberlege was enthusiastic about this graph, as publishing managers always are, particularly when they progress in an upward direction, as this one did. Unfortunately the vertical axis failed to include any figures at all, so the graph is meaningless – the only flaw in an otherwise admirable publication. Far more informative is a file note from OUP's accounts people.[13] In the laconic tone common to memoranda from all such departments it notes, 'English Hymnal. Sales from Publication to 31 March 1956. <u>All editions</u>. 4,897,762'. Fair waved the golden corn, indeed.

Notes

1 This practice ended at Cumberlege's retirement: anonymity came to be viewed as preferable to individuality. However, the Printer's personal imprint continued to appear, full-title verso, on books printed at Oxford until the University Printing House closed in 1989.
2 This book, produced in 1950, was effectively the 1933 edition of *The English Hymnal*, with fourteen additional hymns specially approved for use in the Episcopal Church in Scotland bound in after (but not included in) the index.
3 All quotations from correspondence to and from OUP are taken from documents in OUP's file 'English Hymnal Jubilee' (OUP/PUB/30/3/7). Material is quoted by kind permission of the Secretary to the Delegates of the Oxford University Press.
4 Letter, Lady Sykes to OUP, 21 June 1955.
5 Letter, Martin Shaw to OUP, 28 June 1955.
6 Letter, Ralph Vaughan Williams to OUP, 1 July 1955.
7 Letter, OUP to Colin Dunlop, 28 March 1956.
8 Memorandum, Cumberlege to Foote, 11 June 1956.
9 Agenda and meeting note in OUP/PUB/30/3/7.
10 The meeting note records: 'This is the second time that <u>E.H.</u> has been taken to the Antarctic. The previous time was with the British Grahamland Expedition 1935-7. It also went to the Arctic with the British Arctic Air Route Expedition 1930-1.'
11 i.e., 'He who would valiant be' (402).
12 *Monks Gate* (402).
13 25 May 1956.

ENGLISH HYMNAL REVISION FROM 1950 TO THE PRESENT DAY

Martin Draper

'It was with an awareness that they had set themselves a daunting task that the editors undertook to produce a successor to the *English Hymnal*,' wrote George Timms in the preface to *The New English Hymnal* in 1986, before going on to explain that the original book had not been revised, 'save for a new music edition in 1933', for almost eighty years.

Producing a new edition of any hymn book is a massive task, and was particularly so in what now seem the far off days of the first half of the 1980s. Personal computers were unheard of, and the text of each hymn had to be typed and its tune or tunes written out by hand, before a final manuscript could be given to a publisher. But a new hymn book is also an important investment for any congregation. A large number of copies need to be purchased and the lifetime habits of a congregation altered, as unfamiliar numbers begin to appear on the hymn boards.

It is perhaps not surprising, then, that the two mainstream Anglican hymn books, which have now been around for at least a hundred years, have not produced a completely new edition of their titles very frequently. The first attempt to do so by *Hymns Ancient & Modern* in 1904 was not a great success and an alternative method of adding supplements to the main book served, in the end, from 1861 until the completely new edition of 1950. Similarly *100 Hymns for Today* and *More Hymns for Today* supplemented *Hymns Ancient & Modern Revised* and were incorporated whole into an abridged edition of that book in 1983. Only in 2000, fifty years after 'AMR', was a completely new book published.

We can see this same pattern in the work of the editors of *The English Hymnal*. Its first 'revision' in 1933 was restricted to the music, though Percy Dearmer, some of whose theological positions had changed since 1906, took the opportunity to make subtle changes to the text of two of his own hymns thinking, perhaps, that no-one would notice. The provision of forty completely new tunes was a not insignificant addition to an existing book, though the attempt to persuade congregations to sing unfamiliar tunes to practically every evening hymn was almost doomed from the start in an age when Evensong was still a popular service.

The compilers of *Hymns Ancient & Modern* began planning a major revision of their book in 1938, a work that was taken up again after the Second World War, and the minutes of *English Hymnal* meetings show that similar thoughts occupied its directors' minds. But nothing was done until almost ten years after the publication of *Hymns Ancient & Modern Revised* in 1950, and the next step proved to be in a different direction altogether.

The minutes of the meeting on 2 July 1958 state:

> Following a meeting between the Directors and the Oxford University Press, it was considered the time had arrived for the publishing of a shortened form of *The English Hymnal* to include from 300 to 350 hymns, together with pointed psalms and a simple setting of the Communion service.

The book was to be called the concise or shorter *English Hymnal*, though finally the name *The English Hymnal Service Book* was chosen. This was because the book proved to be rather more than a shorter version of the main book. A number of carols, not in *The English Hymnal*, were added. The responses and canticles for Morning and Evening Prayer were included as well as Merbecke's setting of Holy Communion, so that congregations could find everything they needed for each service within a single book. There were even proposals for the new *Revised Psalter* to be included once it was published, as well as the Collects, Epistles and Gospels. But these ideas were, in the end, left for the future.

The book was published in February 1962 but did not sell well: around 25,000 copies a year in the first two years, whereas *The English Hymnal* was still selling 100,000 copies a year during the same period. Nor did the idea of a complete revision go away, and in 1966 the minutes of a meeting actually speak of *settling* 'the procedure for appointing editors and consultants for the proposed revision of the English Hymnal book'.

It was perhaps surprising, then, when in 1969 a directors' statement was released via the Oxford University Press, saying:

> Contrary to rumour, the Directors of the English Hymnal Company Ltd have no plans for the issue of a revised edition of that hymnal for the foreseeable future.

The directors gave the current experimental state of the Church's liturgy as the reason for not proceeding with a complete revision and then went on to speak of their hope of publishing 'within the next year or two' a small supplementary book 'for use with *The English Hymnal* or any other hymn book that may be in use'.

The first supplement to *Hymns Ancient & Modern Revised* also appeared in 1969 and it turned out to be an enormous success. Thus the *English Hymnal* committee urgently got to work quickly on their own supplementary book, called provisionally *Hymns New and Old*, which, say the minutes, 'was to be sent to the publishers by the autumn of 1970'. Yet publication was delayed again and again. Minutes of June 1971 speak of the material 'being in the publisher's hands' to be published the following year, those of 1972 speak of it 'being sent to outside advisors for comment', those of 1973 of the publishers 'beginning to do the costing', while in 1974 the price of the book is still said to be under discussion!

English Praise, for that was its new name, was finally published in November 1975 and it was clearly meant to be a temporary book. No hard cover edition was produced and the Chairman was already stating that 'a complete revision of *The English Hymnal* might be undertaken in about five years time'.

In 1978 and 1979 special meetings were held to discuss the future policy of the company and in a letter to Cyril Taylor at *Hymns Ancient & Modern* George Timms wrote:

> As we look ahead it has occurred to me and to other members of the committee of *The English Hymnal* to wonder whether, in the future, there is really room for two major 'non-evangelical' Church of England hymn books.

Clearly the compilers of *Hymns Ancient & Modern* were also thinking about their next step too. Their second supplement *More Hymns for Today* was completed and published in 1980, the same year as *The Alternative Service Book* with the prospect of a period of liturgical stability at least until the end of the century.

Meetings took place between the two committees and there was a clear desire to work together. It was interesting, however, that it was a trustee of *Hymns Ancient & Modern*, Canon Henry Chadwick, who was most concerned that the distinctive witness of *The English Hymnal* be continued, and the meetings concluded that both 'traditions' would continue to produce separate books.

Once the committee got to work on the revision it was clear that they imagined a sizeable volume, yet Oxford University Press, the publishers of *The English Hymnal*, were speaking of the need for a volume of only about 250 items, half from *The English Hymnal* and half from elsewhere. The directors were keen to preserve over 400 hymns from the original book and to add new material as well.

The new-found collaboration between *The English Hymnal* and *Hymns Ancient & Modern* was to resolve the dilemma. *Hymns Ancient & Modern* had decided that their next step was to be a more modest one than a full revision. They envisaged producing a volume containing roughly half the contents of *Hymns Ancient & Modern Revised* together with its two supplements in their entirety. But they were more than happy to publish the complete revision of *The English Hymnal* on which the directors were working *as well*, even creating a new publishing house, Canterbury Press, to guarantee the independence and distinctive character of the book.

Continuing collaboration ensured that the editors of both books allowed and encouraged each other to draw freely on the others' work, particularly in the matter of tunes. Thus for the first time 'the EH tune' and 'the A&M tune' to a hymn often appear on the same page: the bringing together of two traditions without sacrificing either.

The New English Hymnal was published in January 1986, almost eighty years after the original book. It was an immediate success. Within six months it had been adopted by 231 churches, one third of which had previously used one of the editions of *Hymns Ancient & Modern.* Even by 1993 it was still being introduced into 120 *new* parishes a year. One or two reviewers criticized the book for being too conservative a revision and for not including sufficient hymns from the 'post-war hymn explosion', yet it has proved popular not only in former *English Hymnal* parishes but also in many which are new to that tradition. It is particularly encouraging to note that it is used in almost all the cathedrals and in many independent schools.

The continued authorization of *The Alternative Service Book* for a further ten years until 2000 and the fact that *The New English Hymnal* was in use in so many parishes absolved the editors from any immediate need to plan a further revision for a little while. But liturgical revision continued. The house of Bishops' seasonal material for Lent, Holy Week and Easter as well as that for the Christmas cycle of feasts had been published too late for the liturgical section of *The New English Hymnal* to take account of it. Thus, though that section is widely used on such occasions as Candlemas and Holy Week, only 'traditional language' text has been provided. From 1995 onwards the committee of *The English Hymnal* was aware that something would need to be done once new liturgical material was produced after 2000.

In the meantime *Hymns Ancient & Modern* had decided that the new century was an appropriate time for a complete revision of their book – the first for fifty years – and accordingly *Common Praise,* to accompany *Common Worship,* was published in 2000.

For the directors of The English Hymnal Co. Ltd, the year 2006 loomed ahead. As the centenary of *The English Hymnal* it would certainly be cause for celebration, but it also seemed to be the right moment to consider the question of future revision. The publishers were clear that, in spite of overhead projectors and service leaflets, two 'traditional' hymn books for use in the Church of England made commercial sense and encouraged us to think in terms of a new book. There was talk of a centenary edition.

Our first concern was faithfulness to the churches and schools which had adopted *The New English Hymnal*. First of all, we asked ourselves, what would such communities want from a new hymn book if, as it appeared, they were already extremely happy with the book they were using? The answer appeared to be: more of the same. More of the new tunes and hymns which look as though they are going to remain favourites for years to come, yet which had appeared too late for inclusion in 1986; more responsorial psalms;

more liturgical material for new liturgical occasions; and even, in one or two cases, the return of old favourites.

It was also clear that many churches would not wish to introduce yet another new book so soon after *Common Worship*, but would still wish to enjoy access to this same new material. But it would have to be in a way that would be compatible with the existing book.

Thus 2006 loomed, and with it 'that daunting task'. Could we really, only twenty years after the appearance of *The New English Hymnal*, produce a book which would replace it, and which, given that it would be published exactly a century after *The English Hymnal*, might be expected to be a similar 'landmark in English hymnody'?

The directors are of the opinion that while there is certainly enough material that they would wish to make available to those who have adopted *The New English Hymnal* – and perhaps to others besides – it is still too early to attempt a complete revision of the 1986 book. Indeed, final texts of the very liturgical material for which we might wish to make provision in a new book are *still* not available as I write.

So we shall continue that venerable tradition, common now to both *The English Hymnal* and *Hymns Ancient & Modern,* of providing a supplement to the present book and we shall publish it, as part of our centenary celebrations, during 2006. It will contain a mixture of the items listed above. Roughly fifty hymns new to *The English Hymnal*, some new but already established tunes to existing words, more than twenty responsorial psalms and canticles, and liturgical material, both old and new.

A supplement to *The New English Hymnal* rather than a complete revision of it is, somehow, a relief from that 'daunting task'. We are free to include in a supplement hymns which are popular at the moment, but which we might have hesitated to include in such a definitive-sounding tome as a centenary edition of *The English Hymnal*. We are also free to include in it, without creating an impossibly large book, liturgical items which are no longer easily available elsewhere.

There will be one important difference between our supplement and those which have been produced in recent years. The numbering of the items will begin at, or above, the point at which *The New English Hymnal* ended. Not only will that ease a congregation's use of two books, it will also enable the production of a complete *New English Hymnal* in a single volume if such a book proved to be the next stage in the history of *The English Hymnal*.

The English Hymnal has sometimes been labelled 'a party book' by some, on the grounds of its use in the majority of what used to be called Anglo-Catholic parishes. Yet *The New English Hymnal* has been adopted by hundreds of churches which would not apply that label to themselves. And if one is hardly likely to come across the book in churches which prefer 'choruses' to traditional hymns and, indeed, leaflets and overhead projectors to any hymn book at all, the various editions of *The English Hymnal* are enormously valued wherever ordered worship helps fulfil human beings' desire to adore and praise Almighty God.

The *English Hymnal* tradition, from that first 'landmark' edition in 1906 down to its latest modest supplement a century later, claimed and claims 'to be "a humble companion" to the common prayer and worship of the Church of England'. Indeed, we might add that it has become an integral part of prayer and worship in many churches elsewhere in the Anglican Communion and even beyond it. As the present committee celebrates that tradition with joy and gratitude we pledge ourselves to its continuance and development in the service of all those who 'worship the Lord in the beauty of holiness'.

THE INFLUENCE OF *THE ENGLISH HYMNAL* IN NORTH AMERICA

Paul A Richardson

Soon after the publication of *The English Hymnal*, texts and tunes first presented there were finding their way into books compiled west of the Atlantic. A century later, materials from this hymnal and its successors continue to appear in collections across a broad spectrum of North American Christianity.

Consideration of the contribution of *The English Hymnal* must take into account that 1906 book, *Songs of Praise* (1925), and its *Enlarged Edition* (1931). *The Oxford Book of Carols* (1928) also contributed to the body of literature available to compilers.

In relation to the *English Hymnal Songs of Praise* enterprise, an examination of hymnals published in North America suggests three generations. The first extends from 1906 until 1937. The demarcation is occasioned by three Anglican books that consolidated a large portion of this repertory in North America: *Songs of Praise for America* and *The Book of Common Praise*, both published in 1938, and *The Hymnal 1940*, issued in 1943.

The dividing line between the second and third generations is not as clear. *Lutheran Book of Worship* (US, 1978) is often cited as the first to take into account the changes in culture, particularly in the language of worship, of the 1960s and 70s. In the following two decades nearly every denomination produced a new hymnal that was noticeably different in content and tone.

The contributions that might be attributed to the EH-SP tradition are various. Most obvious are texts and tunes written for the volumes. Closely related are materials they altered or harmonized. The modesty of the editors in identifying these, particularly in 1906, has obscured this aspect of their work. There are also those items, first published elsewhere, that were presented to a broader public through these books. The works of Robert Bridges in his *Yattendon Hymnal* fall in this category. A special class consists of poetry that was not originally intended as hymnody but was conscripted for this cause in these volumes. Another important cohort of material consists of matches of text and tune, first made in one of the EH-SP volumes, that have endured. The settings of 'Immortal, invisible, God only wise' to *St Denio* and 'Let all mortal flesh keep silence' to *Picardy* are examples of this type.

One might conduct a thorough census of all items and their appearance in all hymnals, respecting whatever delimitations might be defined. This would entail considering such matters as whether a book including a tune harmonized by Vaughan Williams retained his harmony, accepted but altered his work, reverted to an earlier form, or drew on a later hand. Anyone with the patience and resources to do this should be granted the doctorate worthy of such a dissertation! The method of this study, similar in approach, makes no claim to exactness – though it aims not to mislead. Representative items have been selected and traced, both through the examination of several dozen hymnals[1] and the use of the *Dictionary of North American Hymnology*,[2] an invaluable resource that records (with the fallibility of volunteer labour) publication in collections up to 1978.

The first generation: early appearances

The earliest text from *The English Hymnal* in an American book appears to be Henry Scott Holland's 'Judge eternal, throned in splendour', found in *Fellowship Hymns*, published in New York in 1910 by the Young Men's Christian Association. In the following year, Dearmer's 'Father, who on man dost shower', set to Vaughan Williams' harmonization of *Quem Pastores Laudavere*, appeared in *The Hymnal* (US Presbyterian).

Three EH texts made their first North American appearances in *The Riverdale Hymn Book* (US, Fleming H Revell, 1912): Richard Baxter's 'He wants not friends that hath thy love'; John Bunyan's 'He who would valiant be'; and Isaac Watts' 'My Lord, my life, my love'. All of these had been modified from earlier English sources, the first two by Dearmer and the third by Bridges. *The Lutheran Hymnary* (US, 1913) includes 'Ah, holy Jesus'; whether this came directly from Bridges cannot be known, but the book has nothing else from EH. G K Chesterton's 'O God of earth and altar' made its American debut in *Social Hymns of Brotherhood and Inspiration* (US, A S Barnes, 1914).

No influence is evident in the Canadian Anglican *Book of Common Praise*, compiled in 1908. *The Hymnal* of 1916 (US Episcopalian) was the first to include Athelstan Riley's 'Ye watchers and ye holy ones'. The editors of its 1918 edition with tunes, known as *The New Hymnal*, apparently were not impressed with the musical repertory of EH. One of them, Charles Winfred Douglas, wrote *St Dunstan's*, a masterpiece, rather than use *Monk's Gate* for 'He who would valiant be'. William Henry Hall also set Dearmer's revision of Bunyan, composing the less-successful *Egbert*. In preference to the harmonizations of Vaughan Williams, Douglas prepared his own of *Agincourt*, while T Tertius Noble did the same for *In Babilone*.

Dearmer's translation, 'Father, we praise thee', had its first North American publication in the *Harvard University Hymn Book* of 1926. *Songs for Young and Old*, published in 1927 by the Religious Education Council of Canada, features the first borrowing of 'In the bleak midwinter', by Christina Rossetti.

H Augustine Smith drew significantly from the EH-SP repertory in *American Student Hymnal*, his 1928 book for Fleming H Revell. Not only did it include William Blake's 'To mercy, pity, peace, and love', claimed for hymnody in EH, but also a half dozen texts that had but recently appeared in the first edition of SP: Blake's 'And did those feet in ancient time'; 'All the past we leave behind', from the American poet, Walt Whitman; Dearmer's 'Book of books, our people's strength'; Laurence Housman's 'Father eternal, ruler of creation'; 'I vow to thee, my country', by Cecil Spring-Rice; and Briggs' 'Our Father, by whose servants'. Clifford Bax's 'Turn back, O man, forswear thy foolish ways' had its first American publication in *Middlesex Hymn Book* (US, F L Gilson, 1928).

The Methodist Hymnal (US, 1935) marked the first American publication of G A Studdert-Kennedy's 'Awake, awake to love and work'. A US Methodist children's collection of the same year, *Singing Worship with Boys and Girls*, included the first appearance of Dearmer's picturesque (and now embarrassing) missionary hymn, 'Remember all the people', which had first appeared in *Songs of Praise for Boys and Girls* (1929).

Hymnal for Boys and Girls (US, D Appleton Century, 1935) featured Eleanor Farjeon's 'Morning has broken'. Another notable writer enlisted by Dearmer for the *Enlarged Edition* was Jan Struther. 'Daises are our silver' became the first of her texts to make the Atlantic crossing when it appeared in *The Beacon Song and Service Book* (US Unitarian, 1935), where Cyril Alington's 'Good Christian men, rejoice and sing' also made its first American appearance.

Several of Struther's texts reached American hymnals in the next few years. *Hymns of the Spirit* (US Unitarian, 1937) included 'We thank you, Lord of heaven' and 'When Stephen, full of power and grace'. *New Church Hymnal* (US) of the same year brought the North American premieres of 'Lord of all hopefulness' and 'Sing all ye Christian people'. 'High o'er the lonely hills' is found in both books. These collections each contain one additional American debut: Bridges' 'All my hope on God is founded' in *Hymns of the Spirit*, and 'Lord Christ, when first thou cam'st to man', by Walter Russell Bowie, in *New Church Hymnal*. Bowie, it should be noted, was a US Episcopal priest whose hymn was solicited for SP31 by its compilers.

The second generation: consolidation and widening influence

Three books for the Anglican Communions of North America brought EH-SP items into wider currency. *Songs of Praise for America*, a supplement published in 1938 by Oxford University Press, was not widely used, but it certainly would have been known by those preparing *The Hymnal 1940*. Several Dearmer texts had first American printings in this collection: 'Jesus, good above all other'; 'Now quit your care'; and 'Sing alleluia forth in loyal praise'. George W Briggs' 'Christ is the king! O friends upraise', Housman's 'The saint who first found grace to pen', and Jan Struther's 'When a knight won his spurs' also had initial appearances here.

In the same year, the Anglican Church of Canada revised its *Book of Common Praise*, adding a substantial number of EH-SP items. Here is the first trans-Atlantic inclusion of T A Lacey's 'O kind Creator, bow thine ear'. Three texts not previously published in North America are in both *Book of Common Praise* and *Songs of Praise for America*: 'When Christ was born in Bethlehem' by Housman, and 'Unto us a boy is born' and 'Strengthen for service, Lord, the hands', both by Dearmer.

By the time *The Hymnal 1940* was issued in 1943, much of the EH-SP repertory had appeared in North America. This book assembled an impressive quantity of this legacy and influenced subsequent collections in various traditions. It also marked the first adoption of the set of processional hymns, 'Hail thee, festival day', set to Vaughan Williams' magnificent *Salve Feste Dies*. Also here for the first time for American worshippers are 'From glory to glory advancing', in C W Humphreys' EH translation; the EH version of 'Christians, to the paschal victim'; and 'Christ, the fair glory of the heavenly angels', reworked by the editors of *The Hymnal 1940* from the EH text.

The first North American publications of a few texts occurred in other books of this same period. *Mennonite Hymnary* (US, 1940) provides Briggs' 'Come, risen Lord, and deign to be our guest' and Dearmer's 'Thou true vine that heals'. Dearmer's translation, 'Father most holy, merciful and tender', appears in *The Lutheran Hymnal* (US, 1941).

A few EH-SP texts did not appear in North American hymnals until after 1950. *The Children's Hymnal* (US Lutheran, 1955) was first to print 'On Christmas night, all Christians sing', collected by Vaughan Williams and included in *The Oxford Book of Carols*. *Pilgrim Hymnal* (US Congregational, 1958), obviously influenced by *The Hymnal 1940*, contains a strong cadre of EH-SP materials. It also introduced Dearmer's 'Ah, think not the Lord delayeth' and 'The whole bright world rejoices now', from OBC. Another translation from that book, J M C Crum's 'Now the green blade riseth', now found in many collections, did not appear in American books until *The Methodist Hymnal* (US, 1966).

The peak of the EH-SP tradition in North American books may be seen in certain collections of the early 1970s: *Hymnbook for Christian Worship* (US Baptist and Disciples, 1970), *The Hymn Book of the Anglican Church of Canada and the United Church of Canada* (1971), *The Hymnal* (C Baptist, 1973) and *The Hymnal of the United Church of Christ* (US, 1974). Though the actual numbers of EH-SP items do not reach those of *The Hymnal 1940* or *The Hymnal 1982*, their proportion in these books is high. Dearmer's 'Draw us in the Spirit's tether', whose only previous North American appearance was in *Songs of Praise for America*, is paired in *Hymnbook for Christian Worship* with *Union Seminary*, a tune drawn from Harold Freidell's 1957 anthem. This match has been widely accepted.

The third generation: refinement and reduction
The Hymnal 1940 was succeeded in 1985 by *The Hymnal 1982*. Its refinement of repertory exemplifies general patterns from the second to third

generation of this study. The total number of EH-SP texts is smaller, but there are additions as well as deletions. The tune repertory changed similarly, with, for example, the addition of three Vaughan Williams tunes against the loss of five. Two of his better-known tunes found wider application, with *Forest Green* now setting three texts versus one in the former book and *Lasst Uns Erfreuen* (called *Vigiles et Sancti* in H40) employed for two rather than one. Gustav Holst and both of the Shaws saw their contributions diminished in the newer book. Episcopalians got Vaughan Williams' *Randolph* for the first time in the 1997 supplement, *Wonder, Love, and Praise*, along with another iteration of *Lasst Uns Erfreuen*, setting Dearmer's doxology, 'From [originally, 'through'] north and south and east and west'.

The Anglican Church of Canada followed a different path to a similar place. Its cooperation with the United Church of Canada in the 1971 *Hymn Book* necessitated some compromise in repertory. When the Anglicans published *Common Praise* in 1998, there was further reduction of EH-SP texts. The representation of Dearmer, for example, went from eight in 1938 to six in 1971 to three in 1998. However, as with *The Hymnal 1982*, there were additions, including 'Morning has broken', admitted to both these books only in their most recent editions. At the same time there was an increase in EH-SP tunes, including some restoration of tunes from 1938. Those by Vaughan Williams dropped from 1938 to 1971, then increased markedly in 1998.

Conservative non-denominational hymnals show minimal inclusion of EH-SP texts but small, steady use of tunes from Vaughan Williams. For example, *Hymns for the Family of God* (US, Paragon, 1976) has nothing by Dearmer or Struther. Only 'Morning has broken' represents EH-SP, and its presence is likely the result of popularity stemming from Cat Stevens' 1972 recording. There are single uses of *Forest Green, Kingsfold, King's Weston, Lasst Uns Erfreuen, Picardy* and *Sine Nomine*. *Hymnal for Worship and Celebration* (US, Word, 1986) also has 'Morning has broken' as its only EH-SP text and single printings of *Kingsfold, Lasst Uns Erfreuen* and *Sine Nomine*. Its successor, *Celebration Hymnal* (1997), has no EH-SP texts, uses *Kingsfold* and *Sine Nomine* once each and *Lasst Uns Erfreuen* three times.

More liberal traditions have discarded many texts because their language is deemed no longer appropriate. For example, *The New Century Hymnal* (US United Church of Christ, 1995) deleted 'Father eternal, ruler of creation'; 'Good Christian men, rejoice and sing'; 'He who would valiant be'; 'Judge eternal, throned in splendour'; 'Lord Christ, when first thou cam'st to men'; 'Thou judge by whom each empire fell'; and 'Turn back, O man'; all of which appear in *The Hymnal of the United Church of Christ* (1974). At the same time, groups on the left of the theological spectrum continue the use of parts of the EH-SP repertory whose strengths are more poetic than doctrinal, though these have been largely discarded by others. *Singing the Living Tradition* (US

Unitarian Universalist, 1993), for example, contains 'Can I see another's woe' and 'To mercy, pity, peace, and love', both by Blake.

Two US Presbyterian collections of 1990 illustrate more typical, but divergent, approaches to the EH-SP corpus. *Trinity Hymnal* was prepared by the Orthodox Presbyterian Church and the Presbyterian Church in America, groups avowedly conservative in theology and liturgy. It includes no texts by Dearmer or Struther and only a small number reflecting the EH-SP heritage. *The Presbyterian Hymnal* serves The Presbyterian Church (USA), the more liberal branch of the tradition. It also lacks Struther texts, but has two by Dearmer, 'Draw us in the Spirit's tether' and 'Father, we praise thee', and a longer roster of others with EH-SP connections. The books make nearly the same use of tunes from Vaughan Williams, sharing *Kingsfold*, *Forest Green*, *King's Weston*, *Picardy*, *Sine Nomine* and *Randolph*. *Trinity Hymnal* also has *Sussex Carol*, while *The Presbyterian Hymnal* adds his harmonizations of *Helmsley* and *Song 1*, as well as two tunes tied to texts not found in the more conservative tradition, *Salve Feste Dies* and *Down Ampney*.

Southern Baptists, the largest non-Catholic body in the US, show by their limited incorporation of EH-SP materials that they are more kin to conservative than mainline denominations. Indeed, it was not until the *Baptist Hymnal* of 1956 that any EH-SP items appeared, and these were limited to *Lasst Uns Erfreuen* and *Picardy*. In 1975 were added 'Awake, awake to love and work'; 'Good Christian men, rejoice and sing'; 'He who would valiant be' (an artifact of Baptist heritage); 'Morning has broken'; and 'When Stephen, full of power and grace'. *Forest Green*, *Kingsfold*, *King's Weston* and *Sine Nomine* were included for the first time in this tradition. When *The Baptist Hymnal* (1991) was compiled, only 'Morning has broken' survived. *Iste Confessor* was deleted, though *Picardy* was restored. *Forest Green* now set four, rather than two, texts, but *Kingsfold* and *King's Weston* were reduced to single appearances.

An unusual feature of US Lutheran hymnals has been their slow adoption of the folk tunes introduced by Vaughan Williams. As late as the *Lutheran Book of Worship* (1978), *Forest Green* and *Kingsfold* are not found. *Forest Green* makes one appearance in *Lutheran Worship* (1982), and both it and *Kingsfold* are in *Christian Worship: A Lutheran Hymnal* (1993). The largest Lutheran group, the Evangelical Lutheran Church in America, introduced these tunes in *With One Voice* (1995), the supplement to the 1978 book.

Collections for Roman Catholics in North America have gradually introduced some EH-SP materials. As Vincent Higginson noted, *Lasst Uns Erfreuen*, which comes from a 1623 German Catholic source, had appeared in earlier American Catholic books, but its current use must be attributed to its reclamation by Vaughan Williams.[3] Among the various books available to Catholic worshippers in the US, the editions of *Worship* from GIA have drawn most from Protestant hymnody. The first of these (1971) includes 'Ah, holy

Jesus'; 'Father, we praise thee'; 'Hail thee, festival day'; 'Unto us a boy is born'; and 'Ye watchers and ye holy ones'. By the third edition (1998), the content of EH-SP items was comparable to the books of mainline Protestants. The most recent Canadian Catholic hymnal, *Catholic Book of Worship III* (1994), has about a half dozen texts, but more than a dozen tunes, from EH-SP.

African-American hymnals have not adopted EH-SP materials. Neither *The New National Baptist Hymnal, 21st Century Edition* (US, 2001) nor the non-denominational *African American Heritage Hymnal* (US, GIA, 2001) contains any EH-SP texts. Both include *Sine Nomine*, but neither has *Forest Green* or *Kingsfold*. The harmonization of *Lasst Uns Erfreuen* in both collections is by Norman Johnson.

Repertory studies

Two studies of North American hymnic repertory offer insights regarding the importation of EH-SP material. In 1976, the Consultation on Ecumenical Hymnody developed a roster of 227 texts together with recommended tunes.[4] Fourteen of the texts on the list trace their parentage to EH-SP. More than twenty tunes (the listing makes precision difficult by referring not to specific versions but to the books that contain them) are also from this line.

In 1997, Michael Hawn examined 40 hymnals in use at the time and derived a list of material appearing most frequently.[5] Thirteen EH-SP texts appear at least ten times each. A second list, which records the settings of the more common texts, includes 21 EH-SP tunes. *Amazing Grace*, an anthology of hymn texts for devotional use compiled in 1994 by The Hymn Society in the United States and Canada, includes 13 EH-SP hymns.

Conclusions

The text repertory derived from EH-SP has diminished in the last generation of North American hymnals. Anglican bodies have retained the most, while mainline groups, which added in the second generation, have reduced their numbers. More conservative theological traditions adopted few.

The enduring part of the musical legacy is substantially the work of Vaughan Williams. Two of the English folk tunes that he harmonized, *Forest Green* and *Kingsfold*, have become ubiquitous. Similarly, it is rare to encounter a hymnal without his versions of *Hyfrydol* and *Lasst Uns Erfreuen*. It is not unusual to find any or all of these three times in a given collection. (Hope Publishing's 2001 hymnal, *Worship & Rejoice*, appears to have the record with its five settings to *Kingsfold*, though the United Methodists in the US may win on a technicality, as this tune is used three times each in *The United Methodist Hymnal*, 1989, and its 2001 supplement, *The Faith We Sing*.) *Sine Nomine*, though not so often repeated, is found in nearly as many books. His other original tunes from 1906, *Down Ampney*, *Randolph* and *Salve Feste Dies*, appear with the texts for which they were written. *King's Weston* is also widely printed. Other tunes, made better-known through RVW harmonizations, are now found both in versions by him and by others. With the enlargement of the carol repertory in many hymnals, *Sussex Carol* is being used more widely, as are Martin Shaw's harmonizations of *Besançon* and *French Carol*. A few tunes created by others for EH-SP, such as Holst's *Cranham*, John Ireland's *Love Unknown*, and Geoffrey Shaw's *Langham*, are found wherever the texts for which they were written are included.

Across the century since its initial publication, *The English Hymnal* and its siblings have enriched the singing of congregations in North America. The endurance of more than a dozen texts and the increasing use of Vaughan Williams' tunes suggest that this inheritance will continue to be a vital part of the hymnic repertory.

Notes

1 I acknowledge, gratefully, the superb assistance provided by the inter-library loan service of WorldCat through the Harwell G Davis Library of Samford University.
2 *Dictionary of North American Hymnology: Comprehensive Bibliography and Master Index of Hymns and Hymnals Published in the United States and Canada 1640–1978*. Compiled by Leonard Ellinwood and Elizabeth Lockwood; edited by Paul R Powell and Mary Louise VanDyke. Boston, The Hymn Society in the United States and Canada, 2003. CD-ROM.
3 J Vincent Higginson, *History of American Catholic Hymnals: Survey and Background*, [Springfield, Ohio] Hymn Society of America, 1982, 10.
4 'Hymns and Tunes Recommended for Ecumenical Use', *The Hymn*, 28/4, October 1977, 192–209. The project is described by Ford Lewis Battles and Morgan Simmons in 'The Consultation on Ecumenical Hymnody', *The Hymn*, 28/2, April 1977, 67–8, 87.
5 C Michael Hawn, 'The Tie that Binds: A List of Ecumenical Hymns in English Language Hymnals Published in Canada and the United States since 1976', *The Hymn*, 48/3, July 1997, 25–37.

THE LITURGICAL SECTION OF *THE ENGLISH HYMNAL*

Michael Thompson

The English Hymnal is a liturgical book. Everything about its structure and compilation is dictated by the needs of the liturgy. This is true of both the original and its successor of 1986, and in each to a much more marked degree than other earlier major collections. It follows such High Church compilations as *Hymns Ancient & Modern* in furnishing hymnody to enrich the Christian year and to accompany the rites and offices of the Anglican Liturgy, but carries such principles further. Whereas other hymnals had sought to provide for the restoration of, for example, office hymns, as enrichments to the official services, here something more fundamental may be discerned. Wholesale addition to the official liturgies is provided for and an actively participatory liturgy is envisaged.

Bernarr Rainbow, Hutchings[1] and others have shown how the cathedral tradition and its revival had been seen as an exemplar for the whole church. It was a major inspiration to musicians and clergy active in the liturgical and musical development of nineteenth-century parish music. *The English Hymnal* is different; it is something of a watershed.

For example, the extensive espousal of Gregorian chant melodies in itself suggests the more active participation of all the faithful in the singing of texts not simply seen as additional to the liturgy, but utterly part of it. Here is an English manifestation of the liturgical movement which was growing across all of western Christendom and finding expression in the revival of chant, the Caecilian Moment and, for the Roman Catholic Church, leading via the *Moto Proprio* on Sacred Music by Leo XIII to a culmination in the documents on liturgical and musical renewal promulgated under the authority of the Second Vatican Council.

How delicious it is that so evidently Sarum and English a compilation as *The English Hymnal* can be seen to be so thoroughly in the main stream of western liturgical thinking. This would not have outraged the compilers, although there is no doubt that the editorial committee was dominated by the proponents of the English Use within the anglo-catholic movement. Dom Anselm Hughes gives rich insights into the tension between the various schools of thought, not least in the matter of liturgical music, in his works *Rivers of the Flood* and *Septuagesima*.[2] Almost invariably, the compilers of the hymnal favoured the local over the Roman in the selection of texts, tones and melodies. In this the principle of subsidiarity was anticipated. Nonetheless it can fairly be said that no other major Hymnal, Anglican or Roman, equipped the laity to participate so fully and actively in the liturgy.

Most astounding of all are the inclusion of the scriptural propers for each Sunday and great feast taken from the Sarum Missal. That they are numbered separately made it evident that they were available for use by all. Previously such provision had been found only in such peripheral books as the *New Office Hymn Book*[3]; now they are envisaged as mainstream.

It is not certain that the compilers envisaged the *active* participation of the bulk of the people. Re-set to the rich Gregorian melodies by Dr Palmer and lavishly produced by the Sisters at Wantage, some accomplished choirs no doubt attempted them. But the demands of the chant would defeat most untrained singers. Francis Burgess recognized the complexity of these melodies and the consequent problems of congregational performance. His second edition of the *English Gradual*[4] set them afresh to simpler psalm tones (and these in staff notation). So it was that well into the 1970s entire congregations could be heard not simply singing at mass, but singing the entire mass, Ordinary and Propers, with the further addition of seasonal hymnody. From the seventeenth century liturgists had looked back with fondness to the Rite of 1549. The Introit psalms included by Cranmer (not always chosen with a clear seasonal purpose, it should be said) had continued to commend themselves for use. Devotional manuals, companions to the altar and amplified altar service books had reprinted the introit or entrance psalmody of the Sarum, Roman and other Uses. In like manner, the remnant of psalmody which was the gradual or tract[5] and the Alleluia (or Alleluya as the compilers of *The English Hymnal* insisted[6]) together with the Scriptural Offertory and post-communion sentences is found in full in *The English Hymnal*, and there can surely have been no other part of Christendom where these seasonal sections of the Church's worship were restored to the congregation. A similar provision is found in *The New English Hymnal*, the fragments of psalmody having been restored to substantial sections and the participation of the people provided for in the collection of responsorial psalms by a Roman Catholic Benedictine liturgical musician, the late Dom Gregory Murray. Modal in flavour, they are heavily influenced by chant.

Throughout both books this preference for liturgical music which, although newly composed or arranged, evidently flows from an earlier source is clearly more than one of musical taste. The books are profoundly traditional, in the sense of handing on and making new pre-existing forms. This gives a durability and extraordinary stability to both, but it can also make them feel a little quaint and proper. Perhaps it was because of this that the tunes of the appendix and some hymns, not of the editors' choice, forced themselves into each book as a sort of leaven. Even if a little staid, the responsorial psalms are easily acquired by congregations and bear repetition. At a time when general music skills in public singing have been in decline and the nuances of, for example, Anglican chant have been lost to many, they provide a ready vehicle for psalm singing at the Eucharist and the office. It is even possible to put settings for a simple congregational evening office together by using responsorial or metrical psalms. The pointed chant canticles, *Magnificat* (NEH504) and *Nunc Dimittis* (NEH506) or two fine hymn versions, *Tell out my soul* (NEH186) and *Faithful vigil ended* (NEH44) fill out the uncomplicated structure of the older forms if desired.

Sequences, extended seasonal poetic texts originally expansions of the Gradual Alleluya, to be sung before the Gospel on greater festivals and at requiems, are an important feature of both *English Hymnals*. Here again no slavish emulation of the Latin Church was made. Many more Sequences, all from the pre-Reformation English liturgies, are provided.[7]

Processions, of which *The Book of Common Prayer* 1662 envisaged only that of the bier from the churchyard as the Clerks sang the sentences, and perhaps at the Litany and Rogations, are lavishly provided for. There are in each book responses and collects at various stations on the way. Yet again these, found mainly in two sections; 'Processions' and 'Suitable for use in procession' in *The English Hymnal*, generally find their way to the liturgical section in the NEH. The rubric of the original book 'At the Procession' and the existence of those two groupings seem to presuppose such a ceremony. Certainly so generous a resource did much to lead to their widespread espousal well beyond the incense-laden confines of the anglo-catholic movement and in even moderate parishes and cathedrals they were in living memory much in use. Dramatic and colourful, they could seem perhaps somewhat pompous and pointless. Would that the rubric in the newer book commending them as 'a token pilgrimage' which 'should not begin at the altar' but 'be a means of arriving at the sanctuary' had been universally taken to heart.

It is in the augmentation and supplementation of the official liturgical provision that both books have been most radical and influential. The inclusion of the Reproaches will have done nothing to discourage the reintroduction of some form of the veneration of the cross and other aspects of the ancient liturgies. *Benedictus* (741) and *Agnus Dei* (742) are furnished to enrich the 1662 texts well in anticipation of the proposed book of 1928, and the inclusion of the then requiem *Agnus* (743) and requiem propers (733) among introits and anthems takes us to a liturgical theology much more explicit than that of the then existing funeral offices.

The New English Hymnal takes this further and provides for the blessing of candles and the liturgical procession into the church. Somewhat curiously the antiphons which accompany the imposition of ashes on the first day of Lent are not found in either book. Perhaps the complexity of the chants put them too far from the competence of the people and at a time when rather than singing they were participating in a religious sacramental. It could hardly be said that either book leaves wanting suitable music for congregational use at this time, should such be desired. The Lent prose with its easy refrain and fairly simple verses had, and perhaps still has, extensive usage. (Only the refrain, one suspects, of the other prose, that of Advent, would be suitable congregationally.) For the last Sunday of Lent, Palm Sunday, each book makes provision for the procession. *The New English Hymnal* provides the text of the antiphons at the actual blessing of the palms. This volume also makes extensive provision for Maundy Thursday, envisaging the blessing of oils at a Chrism Eucharist with *Blest by the sun, the olive tree* (NEH512).[8] The *mandatum* or washing of feet, stripping of altars and altar of repose are all envisaged and provided for. The resources for Good Friday and the veneration of the cross stop short of mentioning the mass of the pre-sanctified. In this way, resources for a vastly amplified range of seasonal and Holy Week liturgies are placed into the hands of the people and priest alike. They foreshadow much of the later official provision.

The most extensive provisions in the liturgical section of *The New English Hymnal* are those dealing with the *tridium*. Its importance lies not just in the texts and music thus made available. Throughout, the rubrics are a ready guide to liturgical best practice; ideals that are too often swamped in Anglo-Catholic circles and beyond with the unchallenged accrual of half-remembered custom and misplaced inventiveness. A good example is the rubric after the procession of Palm Sunday: 'The theme of the Eucharist which follows (the palm procession) is that of the Passion'. This in a brief statement lucidly interprets the progression of that day.

The words only editions are careful to point the psalms used for the stripping of the altars for congregational singing. Later, in the text for the Easter Vigil, two psalms and two Old Testament canticles are pointed for Gregorian and responsorial psalm alternatives indicated. Throughout the melody edition (a true hymn book, not simply a poetry anthology which might be sung) the Gregorian melodies are rendered in staff notation for greater ease of use by the greatest number of worshippers. The active engagement of the whole church in the offering of the liturgy is paramount. Certainly the chant is favoured, but such gems as the Jesuit James Quinn's translation and versification of *Ubi caritas* give these gracious texts to the widest number and in their own tongue.

Better yet, even in the words only edition, the whole assembly is offered the Ordinary to sing.[9] For the traditional Anglican texts the setting is by Merbecke with various realizations of the *Kyrie*. The Lord's Prayer is included. For those, the majority no doubt, using more contemporary language there is the all too little used setting based on a composition by Ernest Warrell for King's College, London as revised by George Timms. This elegant, durable modal setting deserves much greater currency.

Neither book has been short of critics and on many grounds, not least their 'English' titles in an age when English-speaking Anglicanism has far outgrown England. As a liturgical resource, however, each has had few critics. Such criticism as there is and has been reflects the dissatisfaction of those who find the undeniable conservatism of the ethos too constricting and those simply out of sympathy with the theological tenor.

Each book is unashamedly Catholic and self-consciously Anglican. Why would it not be? The personality of the early Dearmer dominated the first hymnal; that of Timms the second. Doubtless both books suffered some limitation as a result but there is a strong sense of purpose and cohesion.

Under each, a collection of talented liturgists, fine poets and superb musicians combined to produce a work utterly at the service of God in the liturgy and with a constant eye to the fullest place of the People of God caught up into that offering. That is no unworthy achievement.

The first book in particular attracted early on some considerable official opprobrium mainly centred around devotion to and invocation of our Lady. The rights and wrongs of that debate must be dealt with elsewhere. If contemporaries thought the projects dangerous because of moderate Marian devotion, they missed the true potential for change they offered. What I hope has become clear is their radical, opponents might suggest even subversive, liturgical nature. Everything which lies behind these books speaks of the tradition, of the essential sacramental and catholic nature of the Anglican Church. It is assumed that abrogated rites and ceremonies will be restored and renewed. Not only that; there lies behind both projects the implicit belief that in facilitating this renewal and restoration the Anglican tradition will not be swamped or distorted, but that it will be made more fully perfect. Whether or not this is correct, it must surely be admitted that the liturgical life of the English-speaking Anglican church in general, and the Church of England in particular, was profoundly altered in no small part as a consequence of the publication of the first book.

The New English Hymnal like the original fed the same river of liturgical renewal which saw the revised Eucharistic rites of the last forty years: *Lent, Holy Week and Easter* and the other compilations of seasonal liturgies. Indeed it was the principal engine of change.

Notes

1   Arthur Hutchings, *Church Music in the Nineteenth Century*, London, 1967.
2   Anselm Hughes, *Septuagesima*, London, Plainsong and Mediaeval Music Society, 1959, and *The Rivers of the Flood*, London, The Faith Press, 1961.
3   *New Office Hymn Book* W. Knott Holborn 1905.
4   Francis Burgess, ed., *The English Gradual,* 2nd ed., London, Plainchant Publications Committee, 1920.
5   The Tract replaced the Gradual with its Alleluya from the third Sunday before Lent until Easter and at funeral liturgies.
6   A quirk of spelling remarked upon in a contemporary review in the Jesuit periodical *The Month* (September 1906). That such a journal should take note of an Anglican hymnal at that time is in itself of interest.
7   Only five were retained by the Council of Trent and two by the Second Vatican Council. *The New English Hymnal* alone has seven in the designated Liturgical Section and *The English Hymnal* many more spread throughout the book.
8   A version of an early Latin hymn by Father Richard Rutt, b. 1925, sometime Bishop of Leicester.
9   *Kyrie* or response to the commandments, *Gloria, Credo, Sanctus-Benedictus and Agnus.*

THE INFORMATORY *ENGLISH HYMNAL*

Kenneth Trickett

There were widely divergent views about *The English Hymnal* on its appearance, but there is no doubt that it was a *different* book. It was strikingly different in appearance, presentation and content from any of those recently published, such as the 1890 edition of *The Hymnal Companion to the Book of Common Prayer*, the 1903 edition of *Church Hymns*, both of which, like many Nonconformist collections, gave the name of the composer with the tune but not the author of the words, and the 1904 'New Edition' of *Hymns Ancient & Modern* which gave neither. *The Yattendon Hymnal*, produced by Robert Bridges, had indeed broken new ground in 1899 by providing critical notes on every hymn. A small booklet, undated, entitled *Hymns selected from The English Hymnal as suitable for occasional use and in Congregational Practices in Singing, with Tunes*, was marketed (Price Fourpence net) in order to acquaint the public with some of the book's features – 'many strong and original features' according to a tribute from the *Church Times* printed on the back cover. For instance, its first hymn, Laurence Housman's 'The maker of the sun and moon' from the section entitled 'Christmas Eve', carries a foreword 'Suitable till Candlemas'. Another inclusion, 'Ye sons and daughters of the King', is headed 'Easter-Day: Evening Procession' and the tune *O Filii et Filiae* is given in two versions; the first is the *Proper melody (Solesmes version)* harmonized by E W Goldsmith, Mode ii, whereas the second is the *Proper melody (modern version)* as given in Webbe's *'Motetts or Antiphons'* 1792. The words are *'Ascribed to 17th cent. Tr. J.M.Neale'* and are to be followed by the *Collect for Easter Even*. Instructions continue. *'In returning up the Nave, Ps. 115, Non nobis Domine, may be sung by Chanters and People in alternate verses, with Alleluya at the end of each verse. At the Chancel step all may stand, while verse 15, Ye are the blessed of the Lord, to the end of the Gloria Patri is sung, followed by:* V. Tell it out among the heathen. R. That the Lord hath reigned from the Tree. Alleluya.'

 The English Hymnal itself begins with extensive prefaces dealing respectively with the words, the music and the plainsong melodies; then there is a detailed table of contents starting with Part I: The Christian Year; Part II: Saints' Days and Other Holy Days; and concluding with Part XII: Introits, &c; Appendix; and Indexes, &c. But these sectional headings are not to be rigidly observed; at the end of most sections there is given a list of other suitable hymns by number and first line, and sometimes further information, as at the end of Part IX: At Catechism, where a footnote states that 'the simpler hymns in other parts of the book are also suitable for use at Catechism, and should be freely used in addition to the hymns in this part'.

 A consideration of the first hymn, 'Creator of the stars of night', exemplifies some principles observed throughout the book. Thus, plainsong melodies and their accompaniments are given in minims, with neumatic notation of the melody placed above in a four-line stave with an indication of the ecclesiastical mode. If no modern tune is supplied, there is a suggestion of a suitable one to be found elsewhere in the book. Office hymns for Saints' Days are so designated, with a letter E or M denoting Evensong or Mattins respectively. The words of translated hymns are headed by the first line of the original language. Ascriptions of authorship are given for both the original and its translation, often with dates of births and deaths. Then follow the words in numbered verses, a full point being printed after the number of the last verse.

Moving on to the third hymn and beyond, it will be seen that tunes other than plainsong are given in either minims or crotchets, according, as the preface says, to whether the hymn is 'solemn, or of a brighter nature'. Above the notation are placed the name of the tune, its metre, and an ascription of its source or composer, with dates. Descriptions of speed are given together with a suggested metronome mark; however, this is admittedly 'believed to indicate the proper speed in a fairly large building with a congregation of average size', and 'absolutely strict time' is not encouraged. Pause signs and commas are sometimes used to designate short breaks in the sound. The authorship of the hymn is given, with dates, with often an indication of appropriate usage of a hymn placed either opposite its authorship or as a postscript, while alternative settings or additional information sometimes suggest variety; thus at Hymn 323, 'O, most merciful', 'As this hymn consists of one verse only it is suggested that it be sung twice; once by the choir alone and again by choir and people in unison. It may also be used as a short motet for unaccompanied singing by the choir', and at Hymn 612, 'Who is he, in yonder stall', 'The first part of each verse may be sung as a solo'. At Hymn 30, 'While shepherds watched their flocks by night', *Winchester Old* is given as in *Este's Psalter*, 1592, and as in *Ravenscroft*, 1621, the latter in a footnote being recommended for 'the Choir alone, or with the people singing the melody (prominent in the tenor part), to verses 2, 3, and 4'. A further footnote says that 'it is impossible to print all the tunes which are traditionally sung to this hymn. The tune often used in Cornwall is printed in the Appendix'. This tune turns out to be *Northrop*, the first of the 'additional tunes which do not enter into the general scheme of the book'. Tunes suggested as alternatives to those set are cross-referenced, sometimes being the same melody presented with a different harmonization, as *Vater Unser*, 462 and 539, or in a different key.

Some of the ascriptions of authors and composers are incomplete or incorrect. For instance, 'Blest are the pure in heart' (370) is credited entirely to J Keble, whereas verses 2 and 4 are in fact by other hands; and the alteration of Keble's 'cradle' to 'dwelling' in verse 3 is not noted. *Bryntirion* (248) is marked 'H.Roth(?)', which is a pseudonym of A H T Lutteroth, the composer. The attribution of *Nun Freut Euch* (4) to Martin Luther is without any evidence. Some tunes marked only 'Welsh Hymn Melody' should be credited to their composers, such as *Llanfair* (143) to Robert Williams, *Caersalem* (397) to Robert Edwards, and *Meirionydd* (334, 473) to William Lloyd.

There are several informative indexes at the end of the book. The *Table of Office Hymns for Saints' Days* lists all the principal feast-days month by month throughout the year, beginning with St Andrew's Day, 30 November, and concluding with St Catherine's Day, 25 November, with corresponding numbers of appropriate hymns. The lists of *Hymns arranged for Sundays and Holy Days* begin with those for Advent Sunday, proceeding to the Last Sunday after Trinity, and concluding with hymns for Dedication Festivals and some Saints' Days. The hymn numbers for each respective Day are given in order, designated M for Mattins, G for General, P for Procession and so on. There is a *List of Simple Hymns*, comprising 'suitable hymns for Mission Services, for use at Sea, for Catechism, Schools and Institutions', arranged under seasonal headings. The numbers of hymns suitable for both young people and adults are printed in heavy type: 'these hymns, together with those in Part IX (i.e. 'At Catechism', 586–612), will thus form a *School and Catechism Hymn Book'*. Then follow metrical and alphabetical indexes of tunes, indexes of composers and of authors (without, however, dates of birth and death which are found with the individual hymns), an index of original first lines of translated hymns, and a 'General Index' of first lines with corresponding set tunes.

The second edition of *The English Hymnal* published in 1933 had an outward appearance similar to the 1906 edition, but there were important modifications. Part VIII: FOR MISSION SERVICES was additionally subheaded *Not for ordinary use*. The indexes were necessarily extended to accommodate the material added to this edition, but the 1906 *List of Simple Hymns* was omitted.

The English Hymnal Service Book (1962) has a quite different Table of Contents from that which was necessary in the 1906 version. Whereas in 1906 the hymns were arranged alphabetically in each subsection of the twelve separate parts, in 1962 the entire repertory, considerably reduced in number to 298 hymns, is printed in alphabetical order, covered by the single heading 'Hymns'; the words of each hymn, however, have a heading indicating their appropriate season or usage. Next comes a 'Supplement of Hymns and Carols, comprising hymns which have proved their usefulness since 1906', and 'a small selection of carols for use at Christmas, Epiphany and Easter'. The succeeding headings indicate additional 'Service' material: there are nineteen 'suggested collects for Processional Hymns'. There is a comprehensive Subject Index, and alphabetical Indexes of Tunes and of First Lines, but no Metrical Index and no Indexes of Composers or Authors, omissions at variance with the rest of the *English Hymnal* corpus.

English Praise, A Supplement to the English Hymnal (1975) follows the 1906 pattern with the hymns and carols set out according to seasons and occasional rites, but the table of contents adds the headings 'Praise and

Thanksgiving', 'Christian Unity' and 'Social Justice'. The list of acknowledgements immediately following the Preface concludes respectively with details of tunes harmonized, and of non-copyright texts altered, by the editors.

The New English Hymnal (1986) is closely modelled on the 1906 book. The editors are sparing in their performance directions by comparison with the directions given in 1906 for every modern tune. They restrain themselves to occasional 'Slow', 'Majestically' or 'Dignified', and certainly give no metronome marks. The first of the indexes at the end of the book gives lists of 'hymns suggested for Sundays and some Holy Days according to the New Lectionary'. For each Day there are hymns for the Eucharist, followed by hymns which could be substituted, or selected for a second service. These contain 'many general hymns unrelated to any lectionary, the use of which will enable a congregation to enjoy a large and varied selection during the course of a year'. A counsel of perfection indeed!

THE MUSICAL TYPOGRAPHY OF *THE ENGLISH HYMNAL*

Andrew Parker

In 1906, when Oxford University Press came to produce *The English Hymnal,* the printing of any forms of music, let alone complete hymn books, was a relatively new venture for them. The lists of Henry Frowde, Printer to the University, show that only in 1898 had OUP started hymn-book production, with the publication of the *Church Hymnary* for the Church of Scotland, while there had also been some much smaller projects in the 1890s consisting of occasional hymns for college or University use. Perhaps this should not surprise us. The setting of musical type was a very intricate process which, unlike working in exotic fonts such as Greek or Coptic – already a speciality of OUP – would ideally have required a greater depth of understanding of music than could, perhaps, normally have been expected from a compositor. For this reason the printing of hymn books had been the domain of more specialized firms such as Novello & Company, or William Clowes. But to understand quite how involved this process of typesetting could be, it is appropriate briefly to consider the antecedent methods of representing music on the printed page.

It should be appreciated that, unlike letterpress, musical notation presents some very particular problems to the typographer. Whereas text in almost any script can have characters standing adjacent to one another, the only complications being kerned accents or diacritical marks, such as the breathings in classical Greek, music has to be represented superimposed on a staff, and so the majority of symbols have to show the stave lines along with the notes or rests. The earliest printed music represented polyphony, with one voice-part to a separate part-book. When, in 1501, the quasi-incunabulist Italian printer Ottaviano dei Petrucci created his first publications, the task was to imitate the high calligraphic standard of contemporary musical manuscript. This he achieved to very great effect by multiple impression. He would print stave lines, musical notation, text and woodcut block initials in separate phases of presswork, and it is illustrative of his technical artistry that he was able to achieve superlative accuracy of register in the process.

Such methods, however, were not commercial, in the sense that so much press time was absorbed in a single page. The answer to this was 'moveable type', a system where each note or rest was exhibited as a sort (an individual piece of type) already superimposed on its stave. In this period of part-book printing, with no concept of representing a complete score, it was thus a relatively straightforward matter to compose successive sorts of bar-lines, notes and rests, with lines of text for vocal underlay, and so achieve an acceptable result. But the artistry which Petrucci had displayed was lost. Conventional letterpress could be inked evenly by using the inkballs in a circular motion from all sides; but the music type, standing edge-to-edge, could frequently miss being inked at the extremities, and the straight-line portions of it were also far less tolerant of wear and tear. The result was that the stave lines thus formed by the rows of music sorts rarely looked anything like continuous. The system also had the severe disadvantage that, unless one were to modify individual sorts to butt them together vertically, it was impossible to represent chords.

The changes of musical style in Italy during the last part of the sixteenth century, and subsequently through continental Europe, brought new demands on the techniques of music printing. With the emphasis changing from discrete polyphony to monody with instrumental accompaniment, as well as the increasing demand for editions of keyboard music, there was a need for a printing method which could notate chords, beams and slurs. So it was that engraved plates formed the printing medium of many editions of music for the next several centuries. Once again, as in Petrucci's period, it was possible for the graphical result to be artistic, the pewter plates being testimony to the engraver's art, and the method was therefore capable of representing almost anything which could be written in manuscript. Pewter, however, is a soft material, so that relatively few impressions could be taken off any one plate before it would degrade significantly. In general, in the days of sixteenth-century moveable type, where we know of edition sizes the numbers of copies seem to have been only a few hundred. In England, during the engraved plate era, most music publications were funded by subscription, each issue being intended as self-financing, and the lists of subscribers in the frontispiece of such editions give us a fairly precise indication of the minimum number printed. It seems there was no immediate expectation for engraved plates to produce more copies than they might physically be capable of, but, by the middle of the eighteenth century, this limitation was to begin to restrict the more enterprising publishers.

In the early 1750s it occurred to Johann Georg Immanuel Breitkopf, the Leipzig publisher whose firm continues under his name to this day, that a new form of moveable music type could be created from fragments of the stave, rather than the sixteenth-century version with each sort requiring a complete 5-line stave to be attached. If each note had merely its immediate neighbouring portion of a stave line, then it would be possible to build up chords. In a similar fashion, a small slur or tie could also be created with the image of a stave-line fragment, and the same could be done with beams and rests. In 1754 Breitkopf produced his first volume by this method. It had the additional advantage that the musical type could easily be combined with letterpress, so enabling music to be printed in textbooks and, important for our purposes, hymn books. So successful was the new complex typography that by 1769 Breitkopf was using engraved plates only on a small scale, the majority of pages now being composed with the new moveable type. The presswork, on the other hand, still depended on keeping the type standing while all the impressions needed could be taken from the formes, so that edition sizes initially were no larger than when printing from plates. The solution to this problem was not forthcoming until the invention of the stereotype towards the end of the eighteenth century. This involved a papier-maché mould (a flong) being made from the standing type, which, when hardened and coated, could be filled with type-metal, thus making a complete image of the page as a single plate. The original type could then be distributed and used for subsequent pages. Thus, once a page had been proof-read and passed, it could be captured on a flong and stored. The wear on the type was, therefore, minimal, and the impressions obtainable would thus keep crisp. If the stereo plate wore in the press, provided the flong had been kept, a new plate could be made — otherwise the page would have to be re-composed.

As well as a publisher and innovator Breitkopf was also a type-founder, and it is said that he sold his products around the world. It is not surprising, therefore, to observe in 1785 that William Caslon, the famous London type-founder, was exhibiting samplers with music fonts, in two sizes, for one of his printing specimens (*Example 1*). When William Clowes began his publishing firm, with the acquisition of a small business in a yard at the west end of the Strand in 1801, he quickly established himself as a printer of music, as well as producing more general work.

The early nineteenth-century examples in England of music printed by complex moveable type are, perhaps inevitably, somewhat crude. In 1823 the

Example 1: An excerpt from Caslon's sampler of c1785

proprietors of the first British music periodical, *The Harmonicon*, seized the opportunity to combine music and copious text for which the new moveable types were ideal. However, a sample of chord progressions from the first issue shows either how unrefined the font was, or how unskilled the labour may have been. There was no discrimination between semibreve and minim noteheads, for example, the latter being achieved by placing stems immediately to the right of the white note (*Example 2*). There is reason to believe the fault was with the particular font design, for there are several examples of piano notation in this same issue of *The Harmonicon*, which are reasonably competently executed. An oddity would seem to be the placement of the key signatures on the treble stave.

It was in 1847 that Alfred Novello, the founder of what became, in effect, the mainstay of nineteenth-century British music publishing, proposed improved methods of moveable type. Having previously had a 'right-stemmed' font (that is, a font where both upward and downward stems are to the right of the noteheads), from mid-1847 he introduced a version which accords much more with our current usage. In a pamphlet that year Novello implied he had expanded the range of sorts, with the addition of new symbols, and he stated he had commissioned the new font from the Soho Type Foundry. With this moveable type he was able to increase vastly his output of vocal music scores, and, in 1861, to print the first edition of *Hymns Ancient and Modern*. However, the graphical appearance of plate-engraving was superior to that of moveable type, and when, in the late nineteenth

Example 2: Two samples of the right-stemmed fonts from The Harmonicon *of 1823*

century, it became possible to make electrotypes of the engraved plates, thus effectively duplicating them, the inferior method was reserved by Novello and other music publishers for hymn books or journals. From 1855 the London typefounding company of J H King, which two years later became the Patent Type-Founding Company, produced music fonts. When this firm's Scottish manager, Peter Shanks, bought the company in 1881 it became for years synonymous with the two sizes of the Gem and Diamond music fonts, and it is no surprise to find that these were the designs used by Oxford University Press to print their first hymn books in the 1890s.

Let us now observe the fonts in use in *The English Hymnal*.

Example 3 is from the opening of the tune *Repton* (in the 1933 edition) at hymn 383. The large dissected note is to demonstrate the different components for the first e-flat in the melody. The longer example has had the joins between the type sorts exaggerated, so it can be seen how many individual components were necessary. Notice how the first two notes use stem pieces which are only half the width of the notehead, whereas those on subsequent notes use full-width stem segments. The individual stave lines are composed of an interwoven series of line-segments, the length of each being a multiple of half a notehead.

You will see how the first bar-line is, in fact, a sort intended equally for the right-hand end of a stave line. Observe that the beam is designed to overlap the descending stem segment on the second note, and that the rudimentary slur is severely compromised in design by needing to cross the stave line from the middle of the upper space to the middle of the one below — an interval of a third. The noteheads beneath, meanwhile, are on adjacent scale steps.

Example 3: Enlarged notation from hymn 383 (second edition)

Example 4: Hymn 133 and Appendix 13 – settings of 'Easter Hymn'

Next we see a comparison of the two designs of font at the larger and smaller size, by examining the final bars of the first line of *Easter Hymn* at 133 and, a tone higher, at Appendix 13 (*Example 4*). The minim and semibreve noteheads are computed as one and a half times the width of the black notehead, but at the smaller size their design is out of scale with the line width, perhaps in a bid to aid clarity, and this gives them a very squashed appearance. Two of the ties in the larger version are almost elegant, as they are single sorts for that purpose which taper appropriately. The longer phrase marks are, however, awkwardly managed, each being composed from several segments. In the D major version, the tie in the alto is entirely missing! Another striking feature is that the stems are too short. Ideally, unless they are projecting outside the staff, they should all be another scale-step longer. This is not a design problem with the font, since a stem could be composed of the requisite segments to give exactly the length required. How much, one wonders, was this shortening a time-saving exercise, since it was simpler to use longer stave-line pieces instead? There is also a tendency for all slurs (and beams, although not visible in this example) to be too steep for the notes adjoining. A good rule is that a beam or a slur has half the slope of the interval of the notes. This font, however, makes the beams identical in slope to the notes, and it forces the short slurs to be twice as steep.

So far we have observed the music font being used much in accordance with the intentions of its design. But sometimes the symbols would not fit. Then it was necessary for the compositor to modify the type sort. This happened most often with accidentals. Example 5, from the final cadence of tune 92ii, shows the competition for space faced by the soprano f' sharp. With a

Example 5: Hymn 92ii

slur above (which ought to be in the space above, not crossing the stave line – such sorts did exist for use outside the stave, after all) and the stem-down minim in the alto, the compositor had no option but to maul the type sort and knock off most of the verticals.

Whereas these 'modified types' might have been stored separately in the case for use in such instances, or where it was wished to avoid putting accidentals in two columns on chords, an example (*Example 6* on page 72) from tune 101 shows a correct usage in the second line, and then the wrong type reused where there was no need for it. Incorrectly used modified accidentals occur frequently in this manner, for example in many key signatures.

The automatic inclusion of the stave line was not without its problems. Note, in the same example, the tenor c' sharp in the second half of the same bar. In normal circumstances when on a ledger line an accidental does not require an extension of that line through itself. Unfortunately, with the Gem and Diamond fonts, that simply wasn't possible, and the effect can make some chords appear unbalanced graphically.

When the book was revised for the 1933 edition it is perhaps surprising that there was relatively little resetting of the music. Where possible the image was left to stand as it had been in 1906, but, as the plainsong accompaniments were all reworked and renotated in smaller note-values, all accompanied plainsong had to be replaced typographically. In many cases this could be accomplished in the same space, but occasionally, where there were two tunes for a hymn, and one of them had been plainsong, this resetting while leaving the other material untouched could cause an imbalance of page layout. For example, at hymns 14 and 17 the cramped text layout of the later verses was improved by resetting, at hymn 49 verses 7 and 8 were reset, and at 65 there could be much improvement following the excision of the plainsong Amen; but at hymn 50 the Amen, which in the resetting now appeared at the end of the plainsong melody itself, left a gap on the right-hand page after its removal, and at 66 the original text block for verses 3 to 5 was left stranded once the reason for its placement so high on the page had been eradicated. A similar, though lateral, cramping of the text appears in similar circumstances on the following page, at number 67.

Example 6: Hymn 101

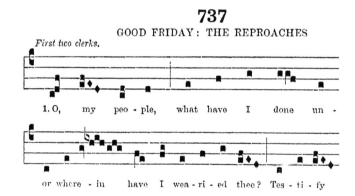

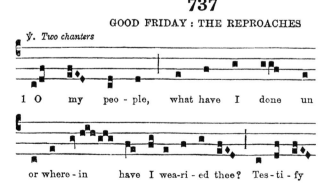

Example 7: The two settings of hymn 737 from 1906 (top) and 1933 (below)

It is very likely that the Gregorian font for the plainsong had enjoyed a less stressed life than that for the metrical notation. Turning to the Good Friday Reproaches at 737 (*Example 7*), the typographical result is immediately more elegant. The general absence of stems means far fewer potential breaks in the stave, and so straight away the type shows a far better fit, with all the components satisfactorily butted together and locked in the forme. Although this is unaccompanied plainsong, with no organ part to be revised, it is interesting that it, too, was reset in 1933. One cause was a change of style in the abolition of the left-hand barline to all plainsong staves. Another is more curious in its effect, for the essential B flats of 1906 (and the Solesmes versions) have been removed. Was this to accord more closely with perceived Sarum practice?

The presentation of the plainsong chant is equal to the high standard which was achieved in the Benedictine *Graduale Romanum* and *Antiphonale Monasticum* published at Solesmes, but I think we should be slightly surprised at the less happy fit of the *English Hymnal* main body of notation. The only other major project from the same font – the large-size organ music edition of the *Church Hymnary* of 1898 – is a very clean example of typesetting and printing, and the smaller Gem music edition is almost as good. Had that type deteriorated so much in the following few years? Could it be that when we examine the first two hymn books from Oxford University Press in 1898 and 1906 we are not comparing like with like, and that the typesetting was not necessarily carried out by the same establishment? It would be very hard to believe that such a large printer was running sheets off the original cold type on a flat-bed press, and thus inflicting damage on it, but some of the small Diamond font in *The English Hymnal* appears to have endured a very hard life.

All of this might seem to imply that the typography of *The English Hymnal* was, in some manner, substandard. Even if the methods imposed by the design of the font make it hard to achieve the highest quality, it has to be said that such work would have required considerable dedication by the compositors, which it is easy to overlook today. The overall result compares very favourably with hymn books produced by the same methods for years afterwards, and there simply wasn't an expectation of high art in such utilitarian typography. Perhaps OUP themselves felt the fonts available for hymn books to be lacking in distinction, which is why they created and cut a new music font, by scaling-down punches cut in Oxford by Peter de Walpergen around 1683, which they had already used full-sized in the *Yattendon Hymnal* of 1899. This distinctive smaller design was used for the *Oxford Hymnal* 1908. But it was not more legible than Gem or Diamond — indeed, its odd stem-positioning towards the centres of noteheads, and its resemblance to manuscript, give a confusing appearance.

If we might nowadays see the imperfections of the nineteenth-century music fonts, it is perhaps only because we now enjoy the advantage of automated methods to achieve a much higher standard of graphical image and control of minute detail. There are some who feel regret that the precision and the continuously variable spacing which can be achieved by computer have undermined the art of the craft engraver, who, by being committed to a horizontal spacing grid if he was a plate engraver, or to notehead-width scaling if he worked with music fonts, nevertheless produced a result which can frequently be pleasing to the eye. Whatever the technology we possess today, the compilers of *The English Hymnal* were undoubtably well served by Oxford University Press a century ago.

CHARLES WESLEY IN *THE ENGLISH HYMNAL*

J Richard Watson

'*THE ENGLISH HYMNAL* is a collection of the best hymns in the English language.' So begins the Preface of 1906; like many sentences in prefaces, it has a significant and challenging sub-text. It does not say – 'we think that these are the best'; it is more assertive than that. It pretends to authority. It also challenges the reader to assent (or perhaps dissent), and in the process it demands a judgement. It calls up a critical faculty, by which the opening words can be tested: are these the best hymns in the language? The sentence requires the reader to refine judgement.

It also suggests that the reader should rejoice in the possession of such a book. This has the best hymns in the language (unlike other books). This new hymn book, the first sentence affirms, is the best: better than successive editions of *Hymns Ancient & Modern*, the last edition of which has been so badly received; better than *Church Hymns with Tunes*, or Monsell's *Parish Hymnal*, or Thring's *Church of England Hymn Book*, or any of the books by various Methodists, or the Church of Scotland, or the Congregationalists. This is better than any of these: better even than the *Yattendon Hymnal*, because that was so selective (100 hymns) and so dominated by local conditions for which it was produced and the taste of the editor.

In this best book, who are the authors of these best hymns? The chief of them is 'Anon.', whose work appeared in Breviaries or as Office Hymns; then there is John Mason Neale, as translator, with 62 translations and 9 hymns; and then comes Charles Wesley, with 20. Percy Dearmer and Athelstan Riley feature with translations and hymns (Dearmer with 18, Riley with 12), and others such as Heber, Keble and Lyte have their own contributions (Heber 11, Keble 10, Lyte 5). Isaac Watts and James Montgomery, from the Nonconformist tradition, have 10 each. But Charles Wesley is pre-eminent among modern writers, and pre-eminent among those who are not translators.

The word 'modern', of course, has a particular significance in hymnody. As the Preface continues, EH is 'an attempt to combine in one volume the worthiest expressions of all that lies within the Christian Creed, from those "ancient Fathers" who were the earliest hymn-writers down to contemporary exponents of modern aspirations and ideals' (p.iii). So, although the title 'Ancient and Modern' had been taken, and the compilers were setting their work over against the A&M tradition, the hymns divide quite distinctly into 'ancient' and 'modern'. Those which were translated by Neale, or by others such as John Chandler and Edward Caswall, have about them a recognizable tone, which comes from the affirmation of straightforward and incontrovertible doctrine.

After the Reformation, hymns begin to reflect the problems of a post-Renaissance world, a world which Matthew Arnold had written about just fifty years before, contrasting the ideal world of the Greeks with that of his own time:

> The calm, the cheerfulness, the disinterested objectivity have disappeared; the dialogue of the mind with itself has commenced; modern problems have presented themselves; we hear already the doubts, we witness the discouragement, of Hamlet and of Faust. (Preface to *Poems*, 1853)

Mutatis mutandis, I know of no quotation which better describes the difference between the early hymns of EH and those of the four centuries before 1906. The dialogue of the mind with itself has commenced, in John Mason ('but who am I?') or in Henry Francis Lyte ('I need thy presence every passing hour'). The disinterested objectivity ('O come, O come, Emmanuel') has disappeared. Beside this vast change, the primary shifting tectonic plates of hymnic geology, the movements of the transient decades, such as the Evangelical Revival or the Oxford Movement, appear as minor alterations in the landscape.

It is in the context of this modern hymnody in EH that Charles Wesley becomes all the more prominent. He is the writer whose work most frequently expresses the post-Reformation truths of modern Christianity, the relationship of human beings to the divine seen in the context of the dialogue of the mind with itself. It is possible that the compilers recognized Charles Wesley as the writer in whom these things are kept in perfect balance, which is why he is such a great hymn writer; but his pre-eminence in the 'modern' side of EH is owing to more than just his poised equilibrium between self-knowledge on the one hand and an awareness of the divine on the other.

We may approach the subtleties of Charles Wesley's appeal by returning to the Preface. The book was clearly Anglican, because it was 'offered as a humble companion to the Book of Common Prayer for use in the Church'; but it was also offered 'to all broad-minded men, in the hope that every one will find within these pages the hymns which he rightly wants'. From the 'broad-minded' hint, the Preface then moves onward, groping towards an ecumenical vision:

> In the worship of God Christians are drawn the closer together as they are drawn closer to the one Lord. In Christian song Churches have forgotten their quarrels and men have lost their limitations, because they have reached the higher ground where the soul is content to affirm and to adore. The hymns of Christendom show more clearly than anything else that there is even now such a thing as the unity of the Spirit. (p.iii)

From its clearly Anglican origin, the book stretched out its hands towards the whole Christian community, if only because the church divided was a scandal. In 1906, the compilers of EH could look back across a century which in spite of all the expenditure of Christian energy had been a major disaster for the church. They were not just gesturing towards ecumenism: they were calling loudly for a new and better religion, in which the needs of the world would be addressed by practical action linked to the beauty of holiness:

> We have attempted to redress those defects in popular hymnody which are deeply felt by thoughtful men; for the best hymns of Christendom are as free as the Bible from the self-centred sentimentalism, the weakness and unreality which mark inferior productions. The great hymns, indeed, of all ages abound in the conviction that duty lies at the heart of the Christian life – a double duty to God and to our neighbour; and such hymns, like the Prayer Book, are for all sorts and conditions of men. (p.v)

In this it is not difficult to discern the thought of Percy Dearmer as General Editor. Dearmer had been a member of the Guild of St Matthew, founded by Stewart Headlam, in which a fundamental principle was that 'we are social-ists because we are sacramentalists'; and he joined the Christian Social Union while an undergraduate at Oxford, and worked in the East End of London during the dock strike of 1889. A contemporary in the Guild, Joseph Clayton, wrote of him: 'Socialism for P D meant more than economic change. It meant opening the kingdom of art and beauty to all.' The inclusion of John and Charles Wesley was part of that ideal. With it went a dissatisfaction with the church of his age which led him to draw a parallel with the eighteenth century. 'The Clergy seem naughty folk . . . I think we want a Wesley,' he told Henry Scott Holland. It is in this context that we must see the pre-eminence of Charles Wesley in EH, and also the fleeting presence of John Wesley, who appears twice, as the co-author with Isaac Watts of 'Eternal Power, whose high abode' (635), and as the translator of Tersteegen's 'Gott ist gegenwärtig', 'Lo! God is here! Let us adore' (637), both in the 'Dedication Festival Procession' section.

The treatment of Charles Wesley begins with the Advent section, in which 'Lo! He comes with clouds descending' (7) is described as being by 'C Wesley (1758) and J Cennick (1750)'. The only lines by Cennick are the last two, in which Wesley's 'Jah, Jehovah, / Everlasting God, come down' is replaced by Cennick's simpler 'O come quickly! Allelujah! Come, Lord, come!' Cennick needed a mention (the compilers would have had access to the entry on the hymn in Julian's *Dictionary of Hymnology* (1892)); the EH text also indicates a preference for the straightforward rather than the arcane (also found in Percy Dearmer's re-writing of 'He who would valiant be').

This hymn had appeared in A&M, and in many other nineteenth-century books, often in altered forms but always recognizably the hymn by Wesley/Cennick. Its inclusion in the section for Advent was also well estab-lished, if only because it refers to the coming in glory of the second part of the

Advent Collect – '. . . that in the last day, when he shall come again in his glorious Majesty to judge both the quick and the dead . . .'. Much more surprising is the next hymn by Charles Wesley, 'Hark, how all the welkin rings!' (23), printed to a tune called *Dent Dale* in its original four-line verses (77.77), omitting only the two final verses ('Adam's likeness, Lord, efface'. . . 'Let us Thee, though lost, regain'). The eight verses that remained were faithful to Wesley's original, in spite of the public disapproval which had greeted the first lines in the 1904 A&M. George Whitefield's emendation to 'Hark! The herald angels sing' had become so generally accepted that the original version had been relegated to the status of a curiosity. Its inclusion here suggests a certain defiance of popular opinion, although the compilers were astute enough to add the Whitefield text, in three verses to *Mendelssohn*, as the next hymn in the book (24). The 'welkin' text is evidence, in all probability, of the compilers' estimate of the poetic superiority of Wesley's first version, and their determination to keep it before the public eye, including such couplets as 'Universal nature say / 'Christ the Lord is born to-day', which is so much more imaginative, and metrically secure, than the literal (and badly rhyming) 'With the angelic host proclaim / Christ is born in Bethlehem.'

The picture that emerges from these first two (three) hymns is of a preference for simplicity, authenticity, and figurative verse. The last of these is in evidence in the next hymn, 'O for a heart to praise my God' (82), which includes the original verse 6:

> My heart, thou know'st, can never rest
> Till thou create my peace;
> Till of my Eden repossest,
> From self, and sin, I cease.

This verse was known to Methodists, but omitted from A&M. Its inclusion here was a tribute to Wesley's metaphorical theology. More striking still is its placing in EH, as a hymn for the season of Lent which gives the hymn a specific direction and point: in A&M it had been among the 'General Hymns', headed 'A perfect heart'. The EH placing is a reminder of the hymn's origin as a rendering of Psalm 51:10: 'Create in me a clean heart, O God; and renew a right spirit within me', though now the Lenten experience ends in a vision of love.

From Lent we pass to Easter and Ascension-tide, represented first by 'Love's redeeming work is done' (135), Charles Wesley's 'Hymn for Easter-Day' from *Hymns and Sacred Poems* (1739). This omits the first verse of the original, 'Christ the Lord is risen today', perhaps because it was so close to 'Jesus Christ is risen to-day', printed two hymns before. The tune is *Savannah* (*Herrnhut*), which leaves out the 'Alleluia' at the end of each line. What is preserved in EH are the finest couplets, the first in the original verse 2 (EH verse 1):

> Lo, our Sun's eclipse is o'er!
> Lo, he sets in blood no more!

The second is in the following verse:

> Death in vain forbids his rise;
> Christ has opened Paradise.

The EH text shows an astonishing boldness in retaining the final verse, which had been lost to Wesleyan Methodists (though not to Primitive Methodists):

> Hail the Lord of earth and heaven!
> Praise to thee by both be given:
> Thee we greet triumphant now;
> Hail, the Resurrection thou!

The second of these hymns is 'Hail the day that sees him rise' (143), seven verses with 'Alleluias', described as by 'C Wesley and T Cotterill (1820)'. It was another of the hymns for the great festivals of the church's year in the 77.77 metre from *Hymns and Sacred Poems* (1739), here in the altered version made by Thomas Cotterill for the ninth edition of his *Selection of Psalms and Hymns* (1820).

This had already become a well-known hymn for Ascension-tide. A&M had printed an innocuous version, described as 'altered by..?'. On the basis of 'the welkin rings', one might have expected a return to Wesley's version, with its splendidly accurate classical vocabulary – 'Ravished from our wishful eyes', 'There the pompous triumph waits', 'Prevalent he intercedes'; but the compilers once again went for simplicity: 'Glorious to his native skies', 'glorious triumph' and 'His prevailing death'. But they retained the precise 'harbinger' – 'Near himself prepares our place, / Harbinger of human race' – and the final verse (omitted in A&M):

> There we shall with thee remain,
> Partners of thine endless reign;
> There thy face unclouded see,
> Find our heaven of heavens in thee.

Wesley's soaring imagination takes the Collect for Ascension Day, but transforms it into a vision of the risen soul 'finding itself' both literally and metaphorically in the presence of Christ, unclouded, seeing no longer through a glass darkly but face to face.

The next two hymns by Charles Wesley adjoin one another, as they do in A&M. They are 'Christ, whose glory fills the skies' (258) and 'Forth in thy name, O Lord, I go' (259), in the 'Times and Seasons – Morning' section. The first, that perfect representation of morning light becoming inward light, is found in its usual form. The second prints a pithy verse ignored by Methodists and omitted by A&M:

> Preserve me from my calling's snare,
>   And hide my simple heart above,
> Above the thorns of choking care,
>   The gilded baits of worldly love.

This wonderfully complicates the hymn, turning it from a prayer about dedicated life and work to a meditation on the place of work in relation to religion. How much should we devote ourselves to our careers rather than to God? How far into worldly success can hard work be allowed to take us? In the context of EH we can see this question as originating with Charles Wesley but integrating with the concerns of the Christian Social Union. Commenting on the verse many years later, Percy Dearmer described it as striking 'just the notes of social duty and avoidance of anxiety that are prominent in modern religion':

> Indeed the nineteenth century, with its powerful and pious wealth-makers, is being rather fiercely attacked at the present day [1933] for not having avoided the 'calling's snare'.

Behind this mild comment can be glimpsed the Dearmer who had worked in the East End of London, and who tried to unite socialism and sacramentalism. It may have been Dearmer who unearthed this verse: it is certainly one of the moments in which the beauty of EH is linked to a pressing concern with contemporary problems.

The next three hymns by Charles Wesley are in the section 'Sacraments and other rites'. Two are for Holy Communion: 'Author of life divine' (303) and 'Victim divine, thy grace we claim' (333). Both had been in A&M, so there is nothing unexpected in their inclusion. In the second, EH omits a verse about sacrifice, which probably sounded too unmodern:

> God still respects Thy sacrifice,
> Its savour sweet doth always please;
> The Offering smokes through earth and skies...

The third was for Confirmation: 'O Thou who camest from above' (343). As with 'O for a heart to praise my God', the placing sharpens the hymn while at the same time limiting it. It is indeed a superb hymn for Confirmation, with the word 'Ready' in the last verse finding a resonance on that occasion which makes it even stronger than usual. The compilers of EH might have found the hymn in the 1904 edition of A&M (earlier editions did not include it) but went back to Charles

Wesley's original in verse 2 ('With inextinguishable blaze' instead of 'With ever-bright undying blaze' in A&M) and preferred the original 'my sacrifice' in the final line, as opposed to 'the sacrifice' of John Wesley and succeeding editors.

The hymns considered so far were all in specific sections. Part V, containing the 'General Hymns' (361 to 519), has the following selection of Charles Wesley's work:

Come, O thou traveller unknown (378)
Jesu! Lover of my soul (414)
Let saints on earth in concert sing (428)
Love Divine, all loves excelling (437)
O for a thousand tongues to sing (446)
Rejoice, the Lord is King (476)
Soldiers of Christ, arise (479)

There are no surprises here, either in the selection or in the verses chosen. 'Come, O thou traveller unknown' has four verses (A&M 1904 had five); 'Jesu, Lover of my soul' has four; 'Let saints on earth in concert sing' is the rather ordinary but popular version of Wesley's much finer 'Come, let us join our friends above' (from A&M 1861 onwards). The second verse of 'Love Divine' has 'Let us all thy life receive', as Charles Wesley wrote it, and not John Wesley's 'grace', and the hymn is in three eight-line verses (to *Moriah*) and not six four-line verses (to *Love Divine*). 'O for a thousand tongues' has six verses, following A&M; 'Rejoice, the Lord is King' also follows A&M in having four verses, and missing the change in the final refrain; and 'Soldiers of Christ, arise' borrows W H Monk's tune *St Ethelwald* from A&M and has five verses, ending 'And stand entire at last' (A&M has 'A crown of joy at last', followed by a doxology).

Two hymns remain. The first is 'Gentle Jesus, meek and mild' (591) in the section 'At Catechism'. The compilers of EH could have found this in the *Baptist Church Hymnal* of 1900 or in the *Primitive Methodist Sunday School Hymnal* of 1901. They divided it into three short parts, presumably to suit a child's attention span, and used two tunes, *Farnaby* and *Lew Trenchard*, with a reference to Martin Shaw's *Gentle Jesus* as an alternative. The second is 'The church triumphant in thy love' (639) in the section 'Saint's Day Procession'. This is a three-verse hymn selected from Charles Wesley's 'Happy the souls to Jesus joined', omitting the first verse. The omission can hardly have been a dislike of the word 'happy' as an opening, because EH has 'Happy are they, they that love God', but it must be admitted that 'The Church triumphant in thy love' makes a very splendid opening line, as part of a magnificent hymn.

What conclusions can be drawn? The first is the confirmation of Charles Wesley's supreme excellence as a modern hymn writer. There was nothing new in this: there had been over 50 Wesley hymns in Edward Bickersteth's *Christian Psalmody* as early as 1833. But the presence of 20 of his hymns in EH is evidence of his relevance to the troubled religious conscience of 1906. This was beautifully recognized and handled: an accurate placing sharpens their meaning, and the joy of their precise original language is balanced with care against a need for simplicity. And finally, the printing of specific verses, and in one case of a largely forgotten hymn, is evidence of a remarkable vigilance in looking for the best in religious poetry, for that which most profoundly places the concerns of the time into the hands of God.

THE SONGS OF DAVID AND THE METRICAL PSALTERS

Paul Iles

Looking back after fifty years, Vaughan Williams remembered how he had conceived his task when unexpectedly he was asked to be the music editor of *The English Hymnal*. He wrote, 'I determined to do the work thoroughly, and that, besides being a compendium of all the tunes of worth that were already in use, the book should, in addition, be a thesaurus of all the finest hymn tunes in the world.'[1] He knew the relative poverty of the hymnody in use in English churches at the time from his own experience at St Barnabas Pimlico, where he had been organist for four years.[2] As he searched for music to match the language of the Prayer Book he turned to the historic psalters of the sixteenth and seventeenth centuries which were becoming better known at the time and which he had begun to research in some depth.

At the turn of the twentieth century, two new hymn books were published which had already made good use of tunes from the metrical psalters. *The Yattendon Hymnal* edited by the poet Robert Bridges (1899) and *Songs of Syon* (1904) edited by G R Woodward (who had been assistant priest at Pimlico) contained no less than thirty-nine French metrical psalms together with metrical versions of the Ten Commandments and the Song of Simeon (Nunc Dimittis). Another book which may well have both influenced and informed Vaughan Williams was *The Psalms in Human Life* by R E Protheroe (1903) which included a good deal about the background to the metrical psalters. Previously, about twenty tunes from the psalters had been included in the first edition of *Hymns Ancient & Modern* (1851) and another handful added in the 1904 edition although, as is to be expected, these were mostly from the English psalters. Vaughan Williams was particularly interested in the Genevan and the Scottish psalters.

In the new hymn book Vaughan Williams included his own selection of psalm tunes: sixteen from the famous Geneva psalters of 1542, 1543, 1551, and 1562; thirteen from the Scottish psalters of 1615 and 1635; and over twenty-five from the English psalters. Altogether he discovered not only the extent of the musical repertory of the psalters but also their wide and established popularity during the Reformation.[3] Here was a treasury of popular people's music ready to be pressed into service again. The many hymn tunes derived from metrical psalmody which are sung by English-speaking congregations today are known largely through the pioneering work of Vaughan Williams in *The English Hymnal*.

The development of metrical psalmody began as a result of the sixteenth-century Reformation. Three factors came together which led to the production of a large number of psalters which were used in worship both on the continent and in England. First, the use of the vernacular in liturgy gave the whole congregation an opportunity for the first time to sing together during the church services. The custom grew up that a psalm should be sung by everyone present at least at the end of a service. Second, the rapid development of printing presses made possible a wide circulation of books both of music and texts from which these congregational psalms were sung. The quantity of psalters printed and sold between 1500 and 1700 is remarkable. Third, since a central focus of the Reformers was the Bible obviously this included the psalms of David which had been an essential ingredient in Christian worship from the beginning. The psalms were used to great purpose in the daily offices of the monastic liturgies and what was required now, to extend them beyond the exclusiveness of the cloister, were new translations and new methods of singing them. When the Reformers produced their translations of the psalms, therefore, they were paraphrases of the biblical text put into metre.

The first metrical psalms to appear in print originated in an unexpected context: two royal households. Clément Marot, a *valet de chambre* to Francis I, included a versification of Psalm 6 in a book of verse dedicated to the king's sister, Queen Marguerite, published in 1533. Quickly his attractive version of the psalm text became extremely popular. It was easy to sing and practical to use. Encouraged, Marot went on to translate more psalms. In 1542 he published a total of thirty psalms in a single volume. His book did not include music but, to facilitate singing, it provided a metrical index which matched psalm words with suitable well-known contemporary tunes, usually secular in origin. In the same year, Marot was attacked by the ecclesiastical authorities in France and he fled to Geneva where he made an enlarged collection of fifty psalms which was published in 1543.

A psalter had been published in Strasbourg in 1539 by John Calvin, another Frenchman, who renounced his allegiance to the Catholic Church in 1534. In 1537 he was called to Geneva to lead the Protestant reformers there. However, it proved not to be an easy task and a year later he fled in fear of his life. From Geneva he went to Strasbourg where he settled happily and published his psalter containing seventeen psalms. He included twelve of Marot's texts and added five of his own translations. He commissioned the organist of the Minster Church in Strasbourg, Matthäus Greiter, to provide and arrange the tunes. *Psalm 68* (544) and *Nostre Dieu* (233) are tunes Vaughan Williams used from Calvin's psalter.

Calvin returned to Geneva in 1541 at roughly the time when Louis Bourgeois (c1510–61) was appointed Cantor at St Peter's Church. Bourgeois was born in Paris and was a Hugenot.[4] Calvin recruited him to be musical editor of the sequence of psalters produced in Geneva after 1543 which steadily increased the number of psalms available in French. In church services, the psalm tunes were sung in unison but Bourgeois also harmonized and arranged them in parts primarily for private use at home, where they were sung and could be played on instruments. He died in 1561 before the whole psalter had been completed. Calvin persuaded Theodore Beza (1519–1605), a theologian with a reputation as a scholar who also wrote Latin poetry, to make the remaining translations. The completed psalter was finally published in 1562. Although the work of Calvin and Bourgeois in producing the Genevan psalters is concerned with psalmody, nevertheless, it is fundamental to the development of all later hymn singing. In Erik Routley's words, 'we owe the poise and simplicity of our best hymn tunes to John Calvin; and of the Genevan psalm-tunes the finest and the most universally known is the *Old 100th* (365); not far behind it is the *Old 124th* (352)'.[5]

About the same time in England, Thomas Sternhold (? – 1549), a member of the royal household of Edward VI with a modest talent for poetry, versified nineteen psalms which were published in a collection dated 1549. Sternhold seems to have held a position at the English court similar to Marot's place in the French court. He is described as a 'grome of ye kynge's Maiesties roobes'. A second, enlarged, edition with eighteen more psalms translated by Sternhold and seven translated by John Hopkins (? – 1570) was published later in the same year, just after Sternhold's death.

Further editions of this psalter were published between 1551 and 1553 until during Mary's reign (1553–8) many English Protestants also fled to Geneva taking their English psalter with them. There they were greatly impressed with the Genevan psalter which was being used, partly because of the greater variety of metre which it employed in the psalm texts and also because the music was so attractive and singable. Compared with the Genevan psalms, English psalmody was rather plain and simple. In 1556 an edition of Sternhold's English psalter was published in Geneva with music. Each psalm was given a different tune, mostly in eight-line double common metre. The tunes, printed without harmony, were fairly obviously imitations of the French Genevan tunes which were so well liked. This method of setting a particular tune to a particular psalm produced what later came to be called 'proper' tunes.

Returning home after 1558, the exiles brought some Genevan texts and psalm tunes with them which helped to expand the musical vocabulary available for psalm singing as it continued to develop in English churches. Gradually more translations were added to the collection of Sternhold and Hopkins by John Norton, William Whittingham and William Kethe until in 1562 *The whole book of Psalms collected into English Metre* was published by John Day (1522–84). This book became known as 'The Old Version' or simply 'Sternhold and Hopkins'. It contained no music at the time of publication but the psalms were being sung to a number of tunes which by now were in regular use. Deliberately the tunes maintained simplicity and dignity so that all could take part.[6] Later some composers would supply more elaborate music settings but at this stage psalmody was uncompromisingly the people's music.

Elizabeth I, in her injunctions to the clergy of 1559, instructed that the custom of singing a psalm at the beginning or the end of services (sometimes both) was not only permitted but should be encouraged.[7]

> And yet nevertheless, for the comforting of such as delight in music, it may be permitted, that in the beginning or in the end of Common Prayer, either at morning or evening, there may be sung an hymn, or such like song, to the Praise of Almighty God, in the best melody and music that may be conveniently devised, having respect that the sentence of the hymn may be understood and perceived.

John Day held a licence to print music as well as books and, following the 1562 publication of the psalter, the next year he issued an edition which included music arranged in four parts. Day's harmonized versions of the tunes are presented so that they may be sung and played on instruments. This psalter was a most beautiful printed-book and it is the start of the long tradition of printed psalters which Vaughan Williams used to the full. It was issued in four volumes or part books.[8] The tune was given to the tenor part (if there were any trebles they joined in with the tenors) and there was a bass part and two contratenor parts. Any accompaniment would have been played on the organ or whatever instruments were available. The tunes were mostly in double common metre, an eight-line stanza; some tunes were new but the majority were either from the Genevan psalters or derived from Geneva and some were survivals from the earlier ballad tradition. In attempting to adapt the Genevan psalm tunes to English translations they often became awkward and clumsy. One solution was to reduce the tune from eight lines to four, which then became known as common metre and eventually was preferred.

Day may have used William Parsons (c1515 – ? after 1563) to edit the music in his psalter since eighty-one out of one hundred and forty-one of the tunes are arranged by Parsons. Of the remainder, twenty-seven are by Thomas Causton (? – 1569) and it is very probable that others are by Tallis, Tye and possibly Taverner. Vaughan Williams included at least four tunes from this psalter in *The English Hymnal*: *Old 25th* (149), *St Flavian* (161), *Old 22nd* (163), and Tallis' *Lamentation* (235).

In 1579 William Damon published a psalter with music but strangely he quickly withdrew it probably because he seems not to have wished to own the musical settings. Only after his death was a second edition of his work published. The publisher was Thomas East (? – 1609) who had become the leading music printer after Day's death in 1584. East issued his great psalter in 1592 with the title: *The whole book of Psalmes with their wonted tunes, in four parts,* suggesting that the link between texts and tunes was becoming reasonably established and accepted. This psalter was issued in two volumes. In one the tune was given to the tenor part while in the other it was given to 'the highest part'.[9] The composers who arranged and harmonized the tunes were a group of ten leading musicians of the day – John Farmer, George Kirbye, Richard Allison, Giles Farnaby, Edward Blancks, John Dowland, William Cobbold, Edmund Hooper, Edward Johnson, Michael Cavendish. The book lasted well and was one of the first to print the tunes in score. Also, East was the first to adopt the custom of giving names to tunes to help identify them, some probably derived from the places and localities where the tunes were sung. In *The English Hymnal* Vaughan Williams selected six: *Winchester Old* (30), *Cheshire* (109), *Old 22nd* (163), *Old 120th* (209), *Old 44th* (211) and *Old 77th* (461).

Even more influential was the psalter published in 1621 by Thomas Ravenscroft (c1590 – c1633). He was a chorister at St Paul's Cathedral and later music master at Christ's Hospital. His book gathers up and uses much that had gone before and illustrates the extent to which psalmody had developed since the 1530s and how widely it had spread through Europe. Ravenscroft claims in the psalter's title that his book is the first to include tunes sung *in England, Scotland, Wales, Germany, Italy, France and the Netherlands* (six French, three German, two Dutch and one Italian). The tunes were now mostly in four-line common metre marking a definite shift away from double common metre, helped no doubt because double common metre was unwieldy and the longer tunes were not always easy to memorize. Ravenscroft did most of the musical arrangements himself although the list of composers who contributed is further extended and in his psalter he named all the tunes for easy reference.

The development of psalmody in Scotland also interested Vaughan Williams. An early Scottish psalter with tunes was published in 1564. Still mostly in double common metre, the tunes were derived from Geneva. *Old 107th* (493) is an example which illustrates well the rhythmic variety of the type of melody which was usual in Geneva.[10] In 1615 a new psalter was published in Edinburgh, edited by Andro Hart, from which Vaughan Williams took four tunes: *Dundee* (43), *Dunfermline* (64), *67th Psalm* (291), and *York* – the stilt tune – (472). Included in this psalter, for the first time, is a group of common tunes printed at the back which were composed to be sung generally, to any psalm. As the double common metre tunes steadily went out of use, more common metre tunes appeared and, following the habit of East, these common tunes were given names to enable singers to identify which tune was to be sung to which hymn. In the 1615 psalter there were twelve common tunes but when the 1635 psalter was published the number had increased to thirty-one, although the book also tried to stem the tide of change somewhat by including a few 'proper' tunes, one or two newly composed. Vaughan Williams includes no fewer than eight tunes from this psalter: *Windsor* (332), *Wigton* (354), *Caithness* (445), *Martyrs* (449), *Culross* (525), *Melrose* (451), *Old 117th* (637) and *Newtoun* (cf 394).[11]

Three other collections of metrical psalms which Vaughan Williams drew on for *The English Hymnal* provided him with tunes written by several notable

Elizabethan and Jacobean composers: Thomas Tallis (c1505–85), Orlando Gibbons (1583–1625) and Henry Lawes (1596–1662).

Archbishop Parker's psalter was written while he lived in quiet retirement in Suffolk during Mary's reign. Elizabeth made Parker Archbishop of Canterbury in 1559 and, some time after, his psalter was printed but curiously not distributed by publication. Musically it is valuable because the book includes an appendix containing nine tunes composed by Thomas Tallis. Unusually the attribution to the composer is clearly stated. The best known of Tallis' tunes is the eighth, written in canon and widely used (267). Another, the *Third Mode Melody* (92), was to become particularly famous when Vaughan Williams used it as the basis of his *Fantasia on a theme by Thomas Tallis* for strings.[12] While Vaughan Williams was editing *The English Hymnal* he had yet to become an established composer of orchestral and choral music but it is not too much to claim that his editorship of the book had an impact on English music generally, helping to break down some of the barriers between religious and secular music which produced a revolution in church music during the twentieth century.[13]

Orlando Gibbons provided tunes for a collection published in 1623 by George Wither, *Hymns and Songs of the Church*. Some suggest that this is the first attempt at an Anglican hymn book. The metrical biblical paraphrases in the book are not limited to psalmody, some being from the New Testament.[14] Unfortunately, in spite of royal patronage, the publication was not successful and the fifteen tunes of Gibbons mostly disappeared with it. Only the famous *Song 34* known as *Angel's Song* (259) was later rescued in a four-line version.[15] By including eleven tunes by Gibbons in *The English Hymnal*, Vaughan Williams restored another significant corpus of musical excellence to hymnody.

For a collection published in 1637 by George Sandys entitled *A Paraphrase upon the Divine Poems*, Henry Lawes wrote twenty-four tunes which are, as he describes in the title, 'for private devotion'. Their character is distinctive and almost experimental. Lawes used the technique of seventeenth-century song writing and provided his striking melodies with 'a thorow bass'. Probably they were not sung by a congregation at the time, but Vaughan Williams included five of Lawes' tunes in *The English Hymnal*. The best known and the only one which remains in regular use is *Farley Castle* (217). The others are *Falkland* (21) *Whitehall* (234) *Battle* (432) and *Psalm 32* (505).

During the Civil War the Cromwellians sang metrical psalms as their battle songs. Then, during the Interregnum, while psalms continued to be sung, no new psalter appeared although several notable music books were published, especially by John Playford (1623–86/7). After the Restoration in 1660, there was a period of decline in psalm singing.[16] Some congregations had always refused to sing them for reasons of conscience.[17] Fashions in music and art as well as in devotion and prayer were changing. Playford made a genuine attempt to prevent the loss of the psalm tunes and arrest the decay of the tradition. In 1671 he published an experimental psalter with tunes set in three parts, perhaps because at the time three-part writing for men's voices was popular while the tradition of using boy trebles in choirs had yet to be recovered, following their disuse during the Commonwealth. The book was quickly seen as a failure but in 1677 Playford published another version with the more usual four parts which by contrast was a great success and had considerable influence, being reprinted regularly until some time in the nineteenth century. His aim was to popularize the existing tunes, re-establishing them at a time when their idiom was becoming dated. This earned him the nickname 'the improver'. To his credit he rescued Gibbons' *Angel's Song* (although unfortunately he appears to have been responsible for mangling it) and, also, *St Mary* (84) from Prys' Welsh psalter, 1621. His adaptation of the Scottish psalm tune *Newtoun* was renamed *London New* (394).

Before the end of the seventeenth century even 'The Old Version' began to receive criticism which led to the production of 'The New Version' of 1696 to take account of changing times.[18] Famously, the poet laureate of the day Nahum Tate (1652–1715) cooperated with Dr Nicholas Brady (?1659–1726) in its production. The book was never meant to replace the older version but to stand alongside it as an authorized alternative. Only nine tunes were provided for the whole book which inevitably meant more tunes came to be provided in the *Supplements* which followed in 1700, 1702, 1704 and 1708. William Croft (1678–1727) is thought to have been the musical editor who included at least four tunes which are now classics: *St Anne* (417), *Hanover*, which he may have composed (466), *St Matthew* (526) and *Alfreton* (189).

In *English Praise* three more tunes are from the metrical psalters. *Coverdale* (EP 60) is from the earliest attempt at a metrical psalter in England, *Goostly Psalmes, c1543*, and two – *Schutz* (EP72) and *This joyful Eastertide* (EP37) – are from Holland (*Psalmen Davids*, Amsterdam, 1661 and 1685).

The New English Hymnal loses some of the metrical tunes which had been set to words which are no longer required. Most of them had also proved to be more difficult to sing than the ones which the editors have retained. However, in *The New English Hymnal*, there is one significant experiment in psalm singing worthy of Vaughan Williams' spirit of exploration. Among the most recent developments in ways of singing congregational psalms is the method developed by the French priest, Joseph Gélineau, which has become much used in France and among the protestant Taizé community.[19] Its popularity in England has been nurtured by Dom Gregory Murray. Twelve Responsorial Psalms with music by Dom Gregory are included in *New English Hymnal*. Totally different in atmosphere from the metrical psalm tunes, they fall somewhere between a plain chant and an Anglican chant. They are easy to sing and the ancient tradition of singing antiphons with the psalms has been revived. This makes possible imaginative use of singing the psalms with various combinations of soloists, choir and congregation. There is great potential in this attractive new music. Well rehearsed and sung with

strength and conviction, they are both flexible and energetic. As all congregational psalm singing should, they make an impressive contribution to the
people's music in worship.

Notes

1 Ralph Vaughan Williams, *The First Fifty Years: A brief account of the English Hymnal,
   1906–1956*, London, OUP, 1956.
2 The vicar of the church was Hanbury-Tracey who led the first group who produced *The
   English Hymnal*. Vaughan Williams had a dispute with him over making his communion
   which led to his resignation. An account appears in Donald Gray, *Percy Dearmer: A Parson's
   Pilgrimage*, Norwich, Canterbury Press, 2000, 64.
3 Charmingly described in Protheroe, op. cit. and in Horton Davies, *Worship and Theology in
   England*, Princeton, 1970, I., 384 & 385.
4 Bourgeois had a colourful life, including a spell overnight in prison sent there by the City
   Council for having 'without leave' altered some psalm tunes. He was supported and
   rescued by Calvin. He fared better after his practical recommendation that a printed list of
   the psalms to be sung should be displayed publicly in the churches.
5 Erik Routley, *Hymns and Human Life*, London, John Murray, 1952, 39.
6 The psalters often included a section of instruction on learning to sing.
7 John Jewel testified to the popularity of metrical psalms in a letter he sent to Geneva in
   1560. '*Religion is now somewhat more established than it was. The people are everywhere exceedingly inclined to the better part. The practices of joining in church music (the psalms) has very much
   helped us. For as soon as they had once begun singing in public, in only one little church in London,
   immediately not only the churches in the neighbourhood, but even in the towns far distant began to
   vie with each other in the same practice. You may sometimes see at St Paul's Cross, after the service,
   six thousand persons, old and young, of both sexes, all singing together and praising God.*' From
   Davies, *Worship and Theology*, I., 386.
8 To issue music in part books rather than score was the usual way for music to be circulated
   in Elizabethan England.
9 In one psalter, the tune is given to the top line throughout. Richard Allison produced his
   psalter in 1599 and it provides a lute accompaniment indicating the likelihood of at times
   solo performances.
10 Vaughan Williams takes his version from the 1635 Scottish psalter.
11 Playford 'improved' the tune in his psalter and renamed it *London New* (see pp. 88–9).
12 The piece was commissioned for the Three Choirs Festival in Gloucester in 1910. Coupled
   with the grandeur of the occasion (the first performance preceded Elgar's Gerontius conducted by the composer) it was among the seminal influences which transformed English
   music in the 20th century.
13 The purpose of *Songs of Praise* 1931, also edited by Vaughan Williams, was deliberately to
   produce a hymn book for use outside and beyond the church.
14 A note must be made about the additional texts printed in many of the psalters. These are
   known as the Evangelical Hymns, meaning songs from the Gospels and paraphrase versions of the Lord's Prayer, the Ten Commandments, the Creeds, and the Prayer to the Holy
   Spirit (Veni Creator)
15 Erik Routley points out that the EH version is incorrect (Erik Routley in *The Music of
   Christian Hymnody*, London, Independent Press, 1957, 66). Many prefer the version in AMR
   336. The six-line version is in *Songs of Syon* 410a.
16 In his 1671 Preface, Playford mentions the dire situation and, incidentally, gives an excellent summary of metrical psalmody over a period of one hundred and fifty years. 'For
   many years, this part of divine service was skilfully and devoutly performed, with delight
   and comfort, by many honest and religious people; and is still continued in our churches,

but not with that reverence and estimation as formerly: some not affecting the translation, others not liking the music: both, I must confess, need reforming. Those many tunes formerly used to these psalms, for excellence of form, solemn air, and suitableness to the matter of the Psalms, were not inferior to any tunes used in foreign churches; but at this day the best, and almost all the choice tunes are lost, and out of use in our churches; nor must we expect it otherwize, when in and about this great city, in above one hundred parishes, there is but few parish clerks to be found which have either ear or understanding to set one of these tunes musically as it ought to be: it having been a custom during the late wars, and since, to choose men into such places more for their poverty than skill or ability; whereby this part of God's service hath been so ridiculously performed in most places, that it is now brought into scorn and derision by many people.'

17 Davies, *Worship and Theology*, II, 272ff.
18 The book was not widely accepted. Cf. C S Phillips, *Hymnody Past and Present*, London, 1937, 142–3.
19 A useful description of this method may be found in Erik Routley, *Twentieth Century Church Music*, London, Herbert Jenkins, 1964, 108ff.

POETRY AS HYMNODY

Elizabeth Cosnett

In treating this subject one faces awkward questions. What is a poem? What is a hymn? Who is a poet? Who is a hymn writer? How does a text originally written with a different purpose and/or in a different form become a hymn in any sense recognizable by the modern church-goer? May this process of becoming a hymn alter in some way the original artefact even if the words remain the same, which is not always the case? 'God be in my head' exemplifies many such questions. The text, but not the tune, is of fourteenth-century liturgical origin, taken into *Songs of Praise* from *The Sarum Primer* by way of *The Oxford Hymn Book* (1908). It has something in common with folk literature in that it appears in differing French and English manuscript versions. Taken out of context it embodies no specifically Christian doctrine and could be sung by non-Christians though not by atheists. In a church context, however, it would appear unequivocally Christian. Unlike most hymns its form is that of free verse or a prose poem, themselves question-begging terms. Inclusion in *Songs of Praise* may have disseminated the words and brought them to the notice of later editors but nowadays they are usually partnered by Sir Henry Walford Davies' eponymous tune which was composed for the Temple Church in 1910 and entered mainstream hymnody via *The Methodist Hymn Book* of 1933. In short, we cannot classify the text, say whether or in what sense its author was a poet or decide how much of its success as a modern hymn is due to Percy Dearmer.

There is of course an overlap between hymnody and poetry. Helen Gardner rightly included Charles Wesley's *Wrestling Jacob* in *The New Oxford Book of English Verse* (1972). Isaac Watts wrote 'When I survey the wondrous cross' as a congregational hymn but it is nonetheless poetry of a high order.[1] Conversely a few devotional poems have been highly successful as hymns. One example is Christina Rossetti's 'In the bleak mid-winter' which as a hymn we owe to *The English Hymnal* (25) and as a carol to *The Oxford Book of Carols*. Another is George Herbert's 'Teach me my God and King'. John Wesley first saw its hymnic potential and included it, with considerable alteration and an additional verse, in a collection he published in America in 1737. Pearcy Dearmer rediscovered it and restored Herbert's original wording but omitted one verse. A few writers such as William Cowper had success in both genres and were quite clear which was which. Some are now remembered mainly for their hymns. Mrs Alexander, a great hymn writer, published poetry for adults which few but scholars read today. On the other hand Wordsworth's only hymn, written in 1834, entitled 'The Labourer's Noonday Hymn' and intended to complement the well-known morning and evening hymns of Bishop Ken, has now fallen out of use.[2] In this case the one hymn by an eminent literary figure seems to have entered *The English Hymnal* (263) toward the end of its useful life.

Authorial intention is not always quite so clear. Dearmer notes John Donne's use of the word 'hymn' in the title of his poem beginning 'Wilt thou forgive that sin where I begun' (515) and also that it was sung by the choir at St Paul's while its author was Dean, but this does not necessarily make it a hymn in the modern sense. Donne may have used the word slightly differently and the congregation's experience may have been more like listening to an anthem than joining in a hymn. Joseph Addison's hymns were introduced into various of his *Spectator* essays. The context makes it clear that he appreciated the beauty as well as the spirituality of the psalms and that he wished to produce English versions of high aesthetic quality. He uses equally the words 'poetry', 'ode' and 'hymn'. He may have envisaged their use in public worship, especially as they are psalm paraphrases, although freer, more ornate and more literary in style than those current in his time. George Wither in the early seventeenth century and Robert Bridges in the late nineteenth certainly intended their work for congregational use and hoped it would become popular precisely because they wished to raise the standards of worship, by which they meant literary and aesthetic standards.[3]

Much good religious poetry is unsuitable for congregational singing and the majority of good hymns are not the most intense poetry but there is a body of material which includes consciously literary hymns alongside other devotional or occasionally secular work which has hymnic potential. This potential is released by selection, the context in which it is sung, a match with the right tune and by judicious editing, which sometimes involves considerable rearrangement and alteration. Percy Dearmer was pre-eminent among such editors in the twentieth century although he freely acknowledged his debt to others, especially Robert Bridges, whose *Yattendon Hymnal* provided thirteen texts for *The English Hymnal,* and William Garrett Horder, who introduced selections from nineteenth-century American poets such as John Greenleaf Whittier to English Nonconformists, especially Congregationalists and Unitarians.

The sequence of *The English Hymnal* (1906), *Songs of Praise* (1925) and *Songs of Praise Enlarged* (1931) shows an increasing introduction of highly literary material but only a small proportion of the final total was retained in 1986 by the editors of *The New English Hymnal*. Of this reduced amount much appeared first in the 1906 edition, is of very high quality and also occurs in comparable, current books such as *Hymns and Psalms* (Methodist 1983) and *Rejoice and Sing* (United Reformed Church 1991). There is considerable variety of period, style and purpose. 'Most glorious Lord of Life' (283) is taken from *Amoretti* by Edmund Spenser. Like many Elizabethan sonnet cycles this one contains a narrative element based on a fictional situation in which a lover pleads with an unattainably and highly romanticized mistress to show him favour. The style is ornate and the setting involves both natural and church seasons. The mistress is freely compared with the saints and the aspiration of the lover with religious devotion. Classical deities are also featured. This sonnet initially addresses Christ,

> Most glorious Lord of life, that on this day
> Didst make thy triumph over death and hell,

but divine love is used as an argument to persuade the mistress to accept the lover's very earthly advances. In the final couplet, the climax of a good sonnet, the man turns toward his human 'dear Love' with the plea,

> So let us love, dear Love, like as we ought:
> Love is the lesson which the Lord us taught.

Some modern worshippers might be horrified to know the original meaning of a sonnet which they understand very differently in the context of a Christian hymn book. One psalm paraphrase, 'The God of love my shepherd is' (93), and three poems, 'King of glory, King of peace' (424), 'Teach me, my God and King' (485) and 'Let all the world in every corner sing' (427) by George Herbert made very successful hymns. The last named appeared in the 1875 edition of *Hymns Ancient & Modern* and is described by Dearmer as 'The only hymn of George Herbert that partly escaped the neglect of the 19th century books'. Herbert entitled it *Antiphon* and marked the lines,

> Let all the world in every corner sing
> My God and King

as 'chorus'. He may have imagined the work being sung, probably by a soloist and choir. The 'chorus' appeared only once in the middle of the text. In modern hymn books it is repeated in order to make two metrically identical verses for congregational singing. Other seventeenth-century poems making use of the conceits or elaborate metaphors fashionable at the time are 'Drop, drop, slow tears' (98) by Phineas Fletcher and 'How shall I sing that majesty' (404) by John Mason.

John Bunyan wrote 'Who would true valour see' as a fictional song within a prose story, where it refers to the character of Mr Valiant-for-Truth. The editors of *The English Hymnal* were looking for 'cheerful and manly hymns' and 'this one sprang to mind'. Dearmer adapted it to produce 'He who would valiant be' (402). His main changes are intended to replace the lines,

> Hobgoblin nor foul fiend
> Can daunt his Spirit

on which he commented, 'no-one would have been more distressed than Bunyan himself to have people singing about hobgoblins in church'.[4] William Blake's text, 'To Mercy, Pity, Peace and Love' (506), produced varied reactions. In the *New Supplement* (1907) to Julian's *Dictionary of Hymnology* occurs the understandable comment, 'It is certainly difficult to call it a hymn at all.' Yet Dearmer saw it as 'so incisive for the very centre of Christianity'. It makes no use of what Dearmer calls 'the vernacular', the traditional language of Christian doctrine, and it concentrates exclusively on the gentler virtues with no mention of justice, whether human or divine. This is typical of Blake's distaste for what he saw as 'Nobodaddy', the God of the Old Testament. One could argue, however, that the concepts behind the Christian narratives of creation and incarnation are very strongly implied throughout. As a poem its title, *The Divine Image*, points the reader initially toward a Christian interpretation and is itself a part of the meaning. As a hymn this clue is unfortunately lost.

From the mid-nineteenth century come 'Strong Son of God, immortal Love' (483), taken from Tennyson's *In Memoriam*, Christina Rossetti's 'In the bleak mid-winter' and Oliver Wendell Holmes' 'Lord of all being, throned afar', shaped by its American author's career as a scientist and man of letters with a deep interest in theology. A minor poet, Dorothy Gurney, wrote 'O perfect love, all human thought transcending' (346) for her sister's wedding in 1883 and it is still popular today.

The book includes two outstanding texts by contemporaries of Dearmer, G K Chesterton's 'O God of earth and altar' (562) and Rudyard Kipling's 'God of our fathers, known of old' (558). The former is still in use today. It is a strange but powerful mixture of romanticized mediaevalism and down-to-earth modernity. Its prayer for industrial Britain that God will

> Tie in a living tether
> The prince and priest and thrall

is quite bizarre albeit seductively alliterative. By contrast its second verse is highly relevant to our twenty-first-century world of terrorism, propaganda, abuse of human rights, scandals about arms deals and apathy in the face of human suffering:

> From all that terror teaches,
> From lies of tongue and pen,
> From all the easy speeches
> That comfort cruel men,
> From sale and profanation
> Of honour and the sword,
> From sleep and from damnation
> Deliver us, good Lord.

Kipling's text is no longer usable in worship. Ironically its earlier great success as a hymn may have contributed to its being misunderstood and unfairly criticized as a poem. Its overall theme is the responsibility of empire and the tone is penitential. The last verse deals with the wrong reliance on military power instead of on God and here Kipling's metonymy of 'reeking tube and iron shard' is more convincing than Chesterton's 'sword'. The words, 'heathen heart', refer not to foreigners but to Britons and 'valiant' is not used as a term of unqualified praise but in a context where it indicates the limitation of courage without prayer. In *The English Hymnal* the two starred verses are those beginning, 'The tumult and the shouting dies' and, 'Lo, all our pomp of yesterday', presumably because they referred to a specific occasion, the naval review celebrating Queen Victoria's diamond jubilee. In *Songs of Praise* the one starred verse is number four because of the words, 'lesser breeds without the law', which even Dearmer felt obliged to justify in *Songs of Praise Discussed*. With hindsight the original starred verses could have real meaning for today. Britain has lost an empire but,

> Still stands thine ancient sacrifice,
> An humble and a contrite heart.

As a poem this text is a fine 'recessional' for an empire already beginning to make its exit from the world stage:

> Lo, all our pomp of yesterday
> Is one with Nineveh and Tyre.

The literary tone of the whole collection was created not only by the new introductions named in this brief survey but also by many works which already had varying degrees of currency due to inclusion in earlier hymnals, and by a few which fell out of use. The former group includes translations and psalm paraphrases by Milton, Addison, Dryden and Robert Bridges, poems by Richard Baxter and Samuel Crossman and hymns by Cowper and Whittier. Other literary figures are represented by just one text, Francis Turner Palgrave by 'O thou not made with hands' (464), Charles Kingsley by 'From thee all skill and science flow' (525) and James Russell Lowell by 'Once to every man and nation' (563).

Ebenezer Elliott's early nineteenth-century protest song, 'When wilt thou save the people' (566), with its repeated 'God save the people', is a good example of the way in which context affects understanding, especially when texts written for other purposes are requisitioned as hymns. Elliott may have alluded ironically or even subversively to the national anthem and his intended readers could have made the link easily. In my mid-twentieth-century schooldays I sang both from *Songs of Praise* without ever doing so.

There are few complete failures but Donne's 'Wilt thou forgive that sin where I begun' (515) is an example of a fine poem which is unsuitable as a hymn because, like much metaphysical verse, it is both too clever and personal in the wrong way. The pun on the poet's name, 'When thou hast done thou hast not done', displaces the worshipper's own penitence from the centre of the text and turns attention toward the obtrusive figure of the writer. Despite the current fashion for 'we', good hymns may be very personal. 'He wants not friends that hath thy love' (401) movingly reflects Baxter's sense of isolation as a result of standing by his principles[5] but the expression is sufficiently general for others to identify with it and make it their own. Herbert's conceit,

> A man that looks on glass,
> On it may stay his eye,
> Or, if he pleaseth, through it pass,
> And then the heaven espy

is acceptable because of its clarity, relative simplicity and regular rhythm. People can grasp it without having to stop and refer back to previous verses. There are no sudden changes of mood, startling contrasts or abrupt shifts of perspective. The same applies to John Mason's,

> Thou art a sea without a shore,
> A sun without a sphere;
> Thy time is now and evermore,
> Thy place is everywhere.

These are exceptions however. Most metaphysical poetry is essentially private rather than communal. It demands to be studied at the changing pace of each individual reader. All the more credit is therefore due to editors who notice the hymnic gems.

The 1931 *Songs of Praise Enlarged* contains a further six texts by Whittier, five by Christina Rossetti, three by Herbert, two each by Herrick, Milton and Tennyson, and one each by Bunyan, Mason, Crossman, Wordsworth, Kingsley and Lowell. Newly introduced writers include from the early period Shakespeare with the sonnet, 'Poor soul, the centre of my sinful earth', Thomas Campion, Thomas Heywood, Francis Quarles, Henry Vaughan, George Wither and Sir Henry Wotton. From the eighteenth century comes Pope, with a cento from a lengthy and uninspiring paraphrase of the Lord's Prayer originally appended to the poem, *Essay on Man*, and also Christopher Smart with four contributions, although these do not include what may now be his most popular hymn, 'Where is this stupendous stranger?', three verses of which were introduced by Francis Bland Tucker into the American Episcopalian book, *Hymnal 1940*. It did not enter the *English Hymnal* tradition until 1986 (NEH 41). Major nineteenth-century figures include Shelley, Anne and Emily Brontë, Browning and Coleridge. Rather less well known today are

Jean Ingelow, Arthur Hugh Clough, George Macdonald, A C Swinburne, Arthur Shaughnessy, Francis Thompson and the Chartist and Christian Socialist, Gerald Massey. America is further represented by Sidney Lanier with 'Into the woods my master went' (SP126) and Walt Whitman with 'All the past we leave behind' (304). Among Dearmer's contemporaries were Laurence Binyon and Thomas Hardy, the latter with an extract from *The Dynasts* which it is hard to imagine any congregation singing with fervour.

Much of this material, especially that from the earlier period and from the very well known names, is unsuitable because it is too complex as poetry. This applies particularly to extracts from long narrative or dramatic poems such as Coleridge's *The Ancient Mariner* or Browning's *Rabbi Ben Ezra*. The material by relatively minor nineteenth-century writers tends to be simpler and more singable although it sometimes errs in the opposite direction and becomes banal. Some texts were useful in their day but have not stood the test of time. This will always be the fate of many hymns, literary or not, and is no discredit to authors or to editors. Moreover, although *Songs of Praise* and selections from it appealed greatly to schools and other groups it never really supplanted traditional denominational books in the churches. It particularly emphasized non-traditional and non-doctrinal language. Later editors of books for church use would naturally reject what were to them moral or aspirational songs rather than true Christian hymns. Poems celebrating the beauty of nature were popular in the nineteen-thirties but today we are more concerned about its protection and more aware of its darker side. Many worthy expressions of social concern have become dated because changing perceptions, which perhaps they helped to bring about, have made their language appear sexist or unduly nationalist. Geoffrey Studdert-Kennedy's 'whirl of wheels and engines humming' (SP698) hardly represents British industry in the computer age. *Songs of Praise* did, however, introduce two notable successes. Eleanor Farjeon and Jan Struther were invited by Dearmer to contribute because he was already acquainted with their writing. Many of their texts were for special occasions such as weddings or for children but 'Morning has broken' (SP30), written for the tune, *Bunessan*, and 'Lord of all hopefulness, Lord of all joy' (SP565), written for *Slane*, have gained general acceptance and exemplify the thoughtful simplicity which can be achieved when a competent and sensitive versifier writes with the requirements of worship and of music specifically in mind. Both are retained in *The New English Hymnal*.

The Oxford Book of Carols reflects the catholicity of Dearmer's taste and the particular stress he laid on joy as a key element in Christian life and worship. He makes it clear in the preface that although there is some overlap the carol is a genre distinct from the hymn and with its own history. As regards content therefore, the carol book stands somewhat aside from his other work. In particular it contains a huge amount of late mediaeval material. Some of this is translated or fairly freely paraphrased from other languages and some is English with modernized spelling and varying degrees of adaptation. Much is of popular origin and would not have been seen as literary in its own day although we now call it 'folk poetry' and enjoy the archaism which would not have been there for its intended audience. Some is fine writing by any standards although the names of individual authors, if they ever were recorded, are lost to us. Unlike most hymns these pieces may be in ballad or dramatic form, are frequently jolly and sometimes secular. Some are doggerel but singable and enjoyable doggerel brought to life by the music. One of the finest is 'I sing of a maiden' (OBC183). To enjoy this fully, however, a modern singer or listener needs to acquire some understanding which would have come naturally to its first performers. The word, 'makeless', for instance applies to Mary in two senses. She is 'without a mate', virgin and also 'without an equal', matchless. Following verses involve very delicate repetition and variation,

> He came all so still
> Where his mother was,
> As dew in April
> That falleth on the grass.
>
> He came all so still
> To his mother's bowr,
> As dew in April
> That falleth on the flower.
>
> He came all so still
> Where his mother lay,
> As dew in April
> That falleth on the spray.

This does more than set the virgin against an attractive natural background. Fifteenth-century readers would immediately associate dew with grace and in particular the dew which fell on Gideon's fleece with the word of God coming to Mary, and would understand the rods of Aaron and of Jesse which miraculously bore fruit as prefiguring her bearing of Christ. For them the 'coming' of the poem would be at least as much about the annunciation as about the birth of Jesus. The eucharistic imagery in other examples such as the closely related texts, 'Down in yon forest there stands a hall' (OBC61) and 'Over yonder's a park, which is newly begun' (OBC184) require a similar kind of understanding.

Among named poets *The Oxford Book of Carols* introduces Chaucer, with a roundel to welcome Summer taken from *The Parlement of Foules*, the Scottish poet William Dunbar, Ben Jonson, Robert Southwell, Robert Graves and Walter de la Mare, with a mock ballad exploring the idea of the redemption of Judas. Many poets represented in *The English Hymnal* and in *Songs of Praise* reappear but in most cases with different work. Laurence Binyon has a typical Georgian nature poem, 'Down in the valley' (OBC161), while G K Chesterton in 'The Christ child lay on Mary's lap' (OBC143) juxtaposes an idealized picture of Christ's birth with parentheses expressing a sense of world-weariness. An interesting but not particularly successful example of Dearmer's editorial methods is 'On Christmas Eve the bells were rung' (OBC189). Couplets are taken at widely spaced intervals from the introduction to Canto VI of Scott's *Marmion*, made into two stanzas and sandwiched together with a traditional refrain. The effect is greatly to dilute the atmosphere of the original poem, most of which would not suit modern taste. Many carols are lullabies, addressed either to the imagined baby Jesus or to a contemporary infant whose situation is compared with his. Fine examples include Wither's 'Sweet baby, sleep' (OBC185), Watts' 'Hush, my dear, lie still and slumber' (OBC130) and Blake's 'Sweet dreams, form a shade' (OBC196) from his *Songs of Innocence*, another instance of a poem remaining attractive and singable but losing much of its subtlety when taken from its context.

One could discuss many more examples but a pattern is already emerging. The editors of the three books under consideration were hugely influential in raising standards and in extending the general perception of what constitutes a hymn. They did this not just as individuals but by their unique combination of talents and the dedication to a shared aim which enabled them to offer English speaking worshippers a resource from which we still benefit today. This resource includes texts written as hymns by people who are as well or better known for their poetry or other writings and also hymns made from poems. Particularly in the latter case adventurous experiments were made and an increasing proportion of the later ones were unsuccessful. Some, however, were outstanding and we owe these triumphs to the editors' risk-taking approach. In 1933 Dearmer himself noted one indicator of success. 'There was a sentence by Mr Winston Churchill in the popular *Sunday Graphic* for Dec. 28, 1932 "Without an equal growth of Mercy, Pity, Peace and Love, science herself may destroy all that makes life majestic and tolerable". It was in 1906 that we brought Blake's poem ... into common and familiar use: nothing could illustrate better than a casual sentence like this how it is already sinking into the national consciousness.'[6] The poem referred to here is probably less well known now, certainly as a hymn, than it had become between 1906 and 1933 but there are later examples. Toward the end of the twentieth century the Anglican liturgist, Donald Gray, entitled a scholarly book *Earth and Altar* while a New Zealander, Shirley Irena Murray, separated from George Herbert by half a world and more than three centuries, called a collection of her own hymns *In Every Corner Sing*. Early in the twenty-first century the first verse of 'Morning has broken' to *Bunessan* was used as background to a television advertisement for Warburton's bread. Because of its association with the Women's Institute, Blake's poem, *Jerusalem,* to Parry's tune has featured in the film, *The Calendar Girls*, and, perhaps more significantly and poignantly, in March 2004 the complete hymn was sung during the opening sequence of *Who Killed PC Blakelock?*, a BBC documentary about the Broadwater Farm riots of October, 1985. It was hard to tell whether it was intended ironically or not as it introduced such a shameful story, but this element of ambiguity was in keeping with Blake and made it an excellent choice.

Dearmer himself regretted that in previous centuries so few great poets had been involved in providing the church and the nation with hymns and hoped that things would be different in the future but this seems to me unlikely for several reasons. Most obvious is the demands made by the traditional hymn tune in an age when poets tend to reject strict rhyme and metre. Even where poetry is in metrical stanzas it often contains rhythmic irregularities, sudden changes of mood or tone, ambiguities and subtleties of meaning which are a vital part of the poetic effect but make it unsuitable for congregational singing. As already noted, much poetry is either too cerebral or too narrowly personal for liturgical use. Music also presents another less obvious difficulty. Because it often intensifies the way in which the words are experienced emotionally it requires texts which allow it to do this and are therefore not too intense in themselves. Such relatively relaxed poetry was popular in the eighteenth century but much contemporary work is fractured, intense, ambiguous and concerned with private rather than public experience. This distinction may help to explain why writers who are good versifiers rather than great poets often produce extremely worthwhile hymns. Although religion is still dealt with today and Christian imagery is used poems are often moral and spiritual rather than specifically doctrinal, and religious experience is rarely presented in a way which makes it easy for others to make their own in worship. Devotional verse is still being written but in a secular age it is no longer a natural part of the wider literary scene as once it was and in a multicultural society Christianity is no longer the assumed default position. For all these reasons it seems unlikely that Dearmer's hopes will be fulfilled in the foreseeable future, which is all the more reason for us to treasure what he and his fellow-editors have already given us.[7]

Notes

1   For further insight into the craftsmanship of this hymn see J R Watson, *The English Hymn: A Critical and Historical Study*, Oxford, Clarendon Press, 1997, 160–70.
2   There is an extended note including the poet's own reflections on this hymn in Percy Dearmer, *Songs of Praise Discussed: A Handbook to the Best Known Hymns and to Others Recently Introduced*, London, OUP, 1933, 24. Stanzas from Wordsworth's *Ode to Duty* appear in *Songs of Praise Enlarged* (647) but do not make a good hymn.
3   Bridges held deeply considered, if occasionally eccentric, views on hymnody. They may be explored in the notes to *The Yattendon Hymnal*, Oxford, 1899, in an essay entitled *Some Principles of Hymn-Singing* and in a letter to Lady Mary Trefusis. The two last named are published in M M Bridges, ed., *Collected Essays and Papers of Robert Bridges*, London, 1935,

21–73. A note on page 52 states, 'When one turns the pages of that most depressing of all books ever compiled by the groaning creatur, Julian's Hymn-dictionary, and sees all the thousands of carefully tabulated English hymns, by far the greater number of them not only pitiable as efforts of human intelligence, but absolutely worthless as vocal material for melodic treatment, one wishes that all this effort had been directed to supply a real want.'

4 Michael Baughen, *Sing Glory: Hymns Psalms and Songs for a New Century*, Kevin Mayhew Ltd, 1999 contains a further re-write by Michael Saward beginning 'Who honours courage here'. The 'manly' language is modified to avoid sexism. There are no hobgoblins but the devil features prominently.

5 He lost his living as a result of the Act of Uniformity of 1662 and later became a Nonconformist minister.

6 Dearmer, *Songs of Praise Discussed*, xxiii.

7 For further information about Dearmer's life and thought see Donald Gray, *Percy Dearmer: A Parson's Pilgrimage,* Norwich, Canterbury Press, 2000.

CHILDREN'S HYMNS IN THE *ENGLISH HYMNAL* TRADITION

Ian Sharp

At Catechism: 1906

The hymns 'At Catechism', Part IX of *The English Hymnal*, are fully representative of the standards and style of the whole book, and their influence on liturgical and educational practice has been considerable. This part of the book consists of 27 hymns, which, together with the one children's litany, 654, makes up under 4% of the total contents. Additionally, the editors were conscious that much of the rest of the book should be suitable for children and young people. The use of the word catechism implies the use of instructional material within the established life of the church. In practical terms this meant that a hymn book which was used by congregations on Sundays and week-days could also be handled by those, usually of younger years, who attended catechism classes. The aims of the catechism class were, then, clearly related to the teachings of the church. Dearmer's children were passing through a cate-chistic stage and would enter into full, eucharistic, membership of the church, which would then open up for them the full range of 'adult' hymns in *The English Hymnal*. Dearmer's decision to emphasize the catechism class, rather than the Sunday School, was symptomatic of his parochial experience.[1] Some other denominations had considerable experience of using catechism hymns. Within the Lutheran tradition catechism songs were in regular use, with J S Bach including organ chorales on catechism hymns in his *Clavier-Übung* (1739). The first comprehensive collection of English hymns for children, Isaac Watts' *Divine Songs* (1715), was designed not for liturgical use as such, although the author hoped that all children, 'baptised in infancy or not', would join together in his songs. The editors of the *The English Hymnal* were well acquainted with the legacy of children's hymns, both that of individual writers and of books such as Mrs Carey Brock's *The Children's Hymnbook* (1881). The standard hymnals of the time had sections designated 'For the Young', for instance in *Ancient & Modern* from 1861 onwards, so there were plenty of precedents for including material of this nature in Dearmer's new book.[2]

What then, was new about these catechism hymns in *The English Hymnal*? Above all, the editors were concerned about the value of what people were given to sing. Vaughan Williams had strong views about the morality of singing tunes which, although popular with congregations, were, he claimed, quite unsuitable for their purpose. Certain tunes, he stated, were 'positively harmful to those who sing and hear them' and, in the context of what consti-tutes a 'fine melody', he writes:

Children at all events have no old association with any particular tune, and incalculable good or harm may be done by the music which they sing in their most impressionable years.

Vaughan Williams' concern for excellence was shared by others. In secular education, those who had responsibility for the national curriculum were determined that songs of a music hall type should not be sung in schools. The unsigned preface of the *Song-book for Schools* (1884), edited by C V Stanford, stated that 'a sound basis of musical feeling can alone be obtained from genuine folk-songs, which have grown up along with the development of the country itself'.[3] The Board of Education's *Handbook of Suggestions for Teachers* (1905) was unambiguous over the question of standards: 'That children should only hear what is intrinsically good is the fixed principle which should govern the use of music in Elementary Education.' Stanford's *National Song Book* (1906) was an anthology of the best songs, but not hymns, of the four British nations, and as such was a model of good taste and well-crafted musicianship. Dearmer and Vaughan Williams were, then, not alone in believing that children should be taught nothing but the best.

The hymns in Part IX of EH are arranged alphabetically, starting with 'Advent tells us, Christ is here' (586), a hymn that typifies the approach of the editors. It presents the seasons of the Christian year in the same order as in the rest of the 'adult' book with a text that is instructional and clear in tone and language. The set tune is from the seventeenth century, the folk-like *Keine Schönheit hat die Welt*. Both text and tune first appear in this book, and so would have been new to catechism teachers and their pupils. This hymn sets the tone for the remainder of this section, which, being clearly headed 'At Catechism', is intended for those who, in the words of the BCP Catechism, are of 'competent age'. That is, they can 'say, in their Mother tongue, the Creed, the Lord's Prayer, and the Ten Commandments'. Of course, if the members of a Catechism Class, whether 'Children, Servants or Prentices', really had to answer searching questions put to them by a Bishop before being confirmed, surely the learning and singing of a hymn such as 'Advent tells us, Christ is here' would have come as light relief![4]

There are five hymns by Mrs Cecil Frances Alexander in this section, starting with 'All things bright and beautiful' (587; without the 'rich man in his castle'), set, in 1906, to the inoffensive tune *Greystone*, but in 1933 to the traditional English melody, *Royal Oak*. This hymn, as with many in the section, is marked 'suitable also for adults', a clear indication that the catechism hymns were not to be regarded as exclusively for the young. Indeed, what better commentary on the Catechism could one have than Mrs Alexander's hymnic companion to the Creed. The selection of her hymns continues with 'Do no sinful action', which paints wickedness in rather pastel colours compared with the songs of previous generations. Holiness rather than damnation is her theme. Here are the third and last verses of Mrs

Alexander's hymn, written to expound the first baptismal promise, 'to renounce the devil and all his works'. They can then be compared with the dire warnings of the second and last verses of Isaac Watts' Song XI on 'Heaven and Hell'.

> There's a wicked spirit
> Watching round you still,
> And he tries to tempt you
> To all harm and ill.
>
> Christ is your own Master,
> He is good and true,
> And his little children
> Must be holy too. (Alexander, 589)
>
> There is a dreadful hell,
> And everlasting pains;
> There sinners must with devils dwell
> In darkness, fire, and chains.
>
> Then will I read and pray,
> While I have life and breath;
> Lest I should be cut off to-day
> And sent to eternal death. (Watts, *Divine Songs*, 1715)

Mrs Alexander refers in this hymn, as so often in early Victorian writing, to 'little children'. Does this term imply a romanticized view of early childhood with implications of the innocence of the very young? It is more likely that the expression, 'little children', was just a turn of phrase, a mannerism of the time, with no pejorative associations.[5] There is even one hymn in this catechism section which uses the word 'little' seven times in six verses, without mentioning 'children' once: Mrs J A Carney's 'Little drops of water' (600). Mrs Alexander, both before and after she was married, had personal experience of the living conditions of children, whether in orphanage or country rectory. Her style was not to talk down to children; rather, she talked with them, and helped them, as individuals on their own Christian journey. So 'We are but little children poor / And born in very low estate' (610), significantly *not* marked as 'suitable for adults', concludes with an affirmation of what even small and weak children can do for Jesus.[6]

> There's not a child so small and weak
> But has his little cross to take,
> His little work of love and praise
> That he may do for Jesu's sake!

If there is anything incongruous about this hymn it is that it is set to the tune *Puer Nobis Nascitur*, composed or adapted by Praetorius and harmonized by G R Woodward. In *The Cowley Carol Book* (1902, No.21) it makes sense as a translation of the Latin, where it is set to the words, 'The Son of God is born for all / At Bethlem in a cattle stall'. The second verse of Mrs Alexander's hymn refers to the Holy Innocents, so there is a somewhat tenuous link between those particular young children and the general concept of 'little children poor'. However the match between the words and printed tune seems somewhat forced, particularly when the melody sweeps upwards at the words 'very *low* estate'. The more humble *Alstone*, of *Hymns Ancient & Modern* vintage, makes for a better pairing. This, then, is a typical instance of the educational aspirations of the editors of EH overriding the functional requirements of the catechism class.

This section of the book contains two other hymns by Mrs Alexander. 'Once in royal David's city' (605) is, quite correctly, classed as a children's hymn which is 'suitable also for adults', and so, logically, appears here with the Catechism hymns. The other is 'Every morning the red sun / Rises warm and bright' (590). This hymn uses imagery from nature, morning and evening, spring and autumn, to extol the delights of heaven. 'There's a land we have not seen, / Where the trees are always green'. (But why 'green'? Not the happiest of images, one feels.)

The range of catechism hymns in EH extends from the eighteenth to the twentieth century. Charles Wesley's 'Gentle Jesus, meek and mild, / Look upon a little child' (591), arranged here as eight verses in three parts, is set, somewhat optimistically, to *Farnaby*, adapted from an English traditional melody, or to *Lew Trenchard*, another English traditional melody. Not for the editors of EH the tune *Innocents*! These verses are the best of Wesley's writing for children, with the final verse giving expression to a child's personal faith. The hymn is theologically and educationally sound, and, with its choice of simple lines and rhymes, remains in the memory.

> I shall then show forth thy praise,
> Serve thee all my happy days;
> Then the world shall always see
> Christ, the holy Child, in me.

Moving on to the nineteenth century, Jane Taylor's 'Lord, I would own thy tender care' (601), is paired, imaginatively, to the English traditional melody, *Eardisley*. Here the child is given a short litany of thanksgiving. The Angels are 'kind' and we note that 'My health and friends and parents dear / To me by God are given'. What a contrast with Isaac Watts at his sternest!

> Have you not heard what dreadful plagues
> Are threaten'd by the Lord,

To him that breaks his father's law,
Or mocks his mother's word?

What heavy guilt upon him lies!
How cursed is his name!
The ravens shall pick out his eyes,
And eagles eat the same.
(vv. 2 and 3 from 'Obedience to parents', Song XXIII, Watts, 1715)

Understandably, the editors of a hymn book for Edwardian society and Edwardian children wanted none of that! Perhaps as a reaction to what they might well have remembered from their own school days they were more inclined to the gentler forms of expression and instruction. Mary Duncan's 'Jesu, tender Shepherd, hear me' (599), to *Shipston* and Jane Leeson's 'Loving Shepherd of thy sheep' (602), to *Buckland*, both use the image of the child as a (little) lamb, to be taken at last to heaven.

Take me, when I die, to heaven,
Happy there with thee to dwell. (Duncan)

Till before my Father's throne
I shall know as I am known. (Leeson)

Chatterton Dix provides a hymn particularly appropriate to a child's daily experience. His theme of 'In our work, and in our play' (596), could be promising, but by the second verse the meaning becomes somewhat tortuous. Presumably these lines are meant to state that Jesus was a carpenter!

Thou didst toil, O royal Child,
In the far-off Holy Land,
Blessing labour undefiled,
Pure and honest, of the hand.

The catechism section contains two hymns by Sabine Baring-Gould. 'Hail the Sign, the Sign of Jesus' (592), is a worthy attempt to teach about the cross of Christ. 'Now the day is over' (603) is deservedly well-known, especially when sung to *Eudoxia*. (But surely not at the snail's pace of the marked speed of minim = 63!) Each of the eight verses is succinct and eminently memorable. Here is verse six, a prayer for the night.

Through the long night watches
May thine Angels spread
Their white wings above me,
Watching round my bed.

A similar theme is also addressed by William Canton's 'Through the night thy Angels kept /Watch beside me while I slept' (609). Bishop Christopher Wordsworth's 'Heavenly father, send thy blessing / On thy children gathered here' (593), is carried by its attractive tune, *Pleading Saviour*. There are two 'story' hymns, which appear together and are both devotional in character. Although they are set to English traditional melodies, Emily Miller's 'I love to hear the story' (594) surely cries out for H J Gauntlett's *I Love to Hear the Story*. Mrs Jemima Luke's 'I think, when I read that sweet story of old' (595) is, by today's standards, sentimental, with rather too much made of the 'dear little children'. Much the same could be said of Albert Midlane's 'There's a friend for little children / Above the bright blue sky' (607). Its theology is questionable; for is heaven really 'above the bright blue sky', as we sing in each of the six verses, and why do Angels 'know not Christ as Saviour'? But one can understand its popularity (but not to *Ingrave*, the tune set in EH). The repetitive structure is simple and the message direct. It is a comforting hymn, and one which, in speaking of the act of singing, sows the seeds of its own success.

> There's a song for little children
> Above the bright blue sky,
> A song that will not weary,
> Though sung continually ...

There are a few of the catechism hymns which could equally well have been placed in other sections of the book, although they undoubtedly have value in the catechism class. 'There is a happy land, / Far, far away'(608) and 'Who is he, in yonder stall' (612) come into this category. A poem by Laurence Housman, 'When Christ was born in Bethlehem' (611), presumably features in this section because of its reference to the Holy Innocents. But as it appears to be speaking about childhood and not with or for children, one wonders why it was not designated 'suitable also for adults'.

> Lord Jesus, Christ, Eternal Child,
> Make thou our childhood thine;
> That we with these the meek and mild
> May share the love divine.

Dearmer's catechism class are also provided with material for special occasions. 'O dearest Lord, by all adored' (604) is designated 'For the Close of a Festival', with a new text by M F Bell to the melody of the Bohemian brethren, *Mit Freuden Zart*. No.654 gives us a sixteen-verse Children's Litany, which has some reference to the childhood of Christ. The editors set this to *Farnaby* (see also 591) but they acknowledge the reality that any of the 7.7.7.7 metre (more tuneful) tunes could be adapted to the litanies.

Jesus, Saviour ever mild,
Born for us a little Child
Of the Virgin undefiled:
Hear us, Holy Jesu. (v.2)

By thy birth and early years,
By thine infant wants and fears,
By thy sorrows and thy tears,
Save us, Holy Jesu. (v.12)

I have left discussion of three of the catechism hymns to the end, because I feel that they embody the best of the EH tradition in this genre. R S Hawker's 'Sing to the Lord the children's hymn' (606) is child friendly and didactic ('children of the font'), with just one mention of the proverbial 'little child'. Its success is underlined by the English traditional melody, *St Hugh*, singable and straightforward. Bishop William Walsham How's 'It is a thing most wonderful' (597) is far more memorable than his 'Behold a little Child, / laid in a manger bed' (588). First published in *Children's Hymns* (1872), 'It is a thing most wonderful' is a model of a catechism hymn, personal and instructive at the same time. 'That God's own Son should come from heaven, / And die to save a child like me' (v.1). Set to the traditional English melody, *Herongate*, this has become one of the best known children's hymns of its type.

It is most wonderful to know
His love for me so free and sure;
But 'tis more wonderful to see
My love for him so faint and poor. (v.6)

And yet I want to love thee, Lord;
O light the flame within my heart,
And I will love thee more and more,
Until I see thee as thou art. (v.7)

Percy Dearmer's own 'Jesu, good above all other' (598), beautifully matched to the folk carol, *Quem Pastores Laudavere*, and marked 'suitable also for adults', is surely one of the gems of the collection.[7] Written for the book, this is everything that a member of the catechism class could want. Direct, memorable, theologically impeccable ('Jesu, for thy people dying, / Risen Master, death defying') it inspires and teaches in equal measure.

We'll go on with thee beside us,
And with joy we'll persevere! (v.5)

It is significant that the editors of EH did not limit their hymns for children to the 28 hymns already mentioned. There is a rubric stating that the simpler hymns in other parts of the book are also suitable for use at Catechism, and, more specifically, the List of Simple Hymns, for 'Mission Services, for use at Sea, for Catechisms, Schools, and Institutions' extends to over half the hymns in the book! The user of the book was left in no doubt that the editors took the task of providing words and music for those of catechism years very seriously. Indeed, it is stated that the simple hymns so marked were intended to form a *School and Catechism Hymn Book*.

The **Songs of Praise** *tradition*

With *Songs of Praise* (1925) the educational zeal of the editors, Percy Dearmer and Vaughan Williams, now joined by Martin Shaw, was undiminished. As the Preface puts it:

> It is hoped that this book will be found specially suitable for young people and may prove not unacceptable to those who bear the responsibility of our national education ... Even young children ... should be brought up on the standard hymns, and it is supremely important that they should know and love the best simple hymns and tunes that are sung by adults.

The original book had moderate success in schools, but, as Erik Routley has noted, 'its small derivatives, under the astute guidance of Canon Briggs, had an enormous popularity and reached astronomical figures in sales'.[8] One of these derivatives, *Songs of Praise for Boys and Girls*, came out in 1929, consisting of 113 hymns. Its preface states that the collection is broadly intended for those between the ages of seven and seventeen. But no attempt at grading can be final as 'some quite young children will show a remarkable understanding of adult hymns' and, on the other hand, 'some children's hymns are now among the most popular of adult hymns'. The stance taken by *Songs of Praise*[9] was quickly adopted by many County Education Authorities, and its contents were used as the basis of many books of prayers and hymns for children and young people. So, for instance, *Songs of Praise for Little Children* (1932) which consisted of 53 hymns and six prayers set to music, together with prayers for little children, was, as a compilation, 'the copyright of the County of Leicester'.

What, exactly, constitutes a 'children's' hymn? One sung and cherished by children over the years, and not necessarily to be found in the children's section of a book. Lizette Woodworth Reese's 'Glad that I live am I' (SP499), set to Geoffrey Shaw's delightful *Water-End*, has become a hymn loved by generations of children, but it appears among the 'general' hymns. The test of time would surely place Eleanor Farjeon's 'Morning has broken' (SP30), set to Martin Shaw's arrangement of the old Gaelic melody, *Bunessan*, among the most popular of hymns remembered from childhood. The reception history of this hymn demonstrates that there is often no hard and fast line to be drawn between hymns of childhood and those of adulthood. Many readers will find that their own recollection of hymns from their school days will, in fact, take them back to *Songs of Praise*. In the following brief discussion the examples are taken from those children's hymns which appear in the 1931 edition of SP, where Part VI, 'For Children', consists of 34 hymns. Many of the organizational features already in EH are repeated here. There is the insistence that the hymns in the section are not intended for older children, but for the youngest, with the hymns designated for young people being marked up in the index. Catechism hymns as such were not needed, although most of the hymns are well suited to use in educational institutions. In fact, 11 out of the 28 EH catechism hymns do appear in SP. The short section of SP marked Sunday Kindergarten consists of just one hymn, arranged, somewhat bizarrely, in six parts (SP386). The verses were 'made' by Percy Dearmer for *Song Time*: a book of rhymes, songs, games, hymns and other music for all occasions in a child's life, which he edited in collaboration with Martin Shaw in 1915. 'We wish you many happy returns of the day', to Martin Shaw's *Birthday*, is functional song at its best and as such has given pleasure to hundreds of thousands of young singers, their teachers and their families. To be both healthy and moral, this is what is wished for children, with the invocation of God's blessing almost as an optional extra.

> We wish you many happy returns of the day!
> We hope you may be healthy and strong all the way:
> Strong to do right, slow to do wrong,
> And thoughtful for others all the day long. (SP386, v.3)

The preoccupation with educational standards shows, even in small details. 'Praise him, praise him, all his children praise him' (SP386: v), is 'consciously modified from Carey Bonner's original to make the lines inclusive of grown-up people'. Martin Shaw supplied a new tune, *Manor Street*, which preserves the rhythm of Carey Bonner's *Praise Him* without, however, substituting a melody of equal charm.

Editors can always be allowed some idiosyncrasies! Percy Dearmer's fondness for the word 'oversea', which then can be rhymed with 'nations free', is found in his 'Remember all the people / Who live in far-off lands' (SP369), a hymn which is remarkably inclusive for its time. It captures the imagination, with children wading through rice-fields and apes swinging to and fro in sultry forests.

Another curiosity, even a kindness, of editorial practice is the inclusion of Stainer's tune, *In Memoriam* (SP373). This appears with the words 'The wise may bring their learning (SP373) and not to 'There's a Friend for little children' (words at EH607). The editorial note explains how the tune may be sung 'to the words for which it was originally written'.

As might be expected in a book entitled *Songs of Praise*, the themes of nature and creation feature strongly in the material for children. 'Winter creeps, Nature sleeps' is well suited to the Welsh traditional melody, *Suogân* (SP380). Sarah Rhodes' Sunday school hymn, 'God who made the earth, / The air, the sky, the sea, / Who gave the light its birth, / Careth for me' (SP358), is set to a new tune, *Platt's Lane* by Evelyn Sharpe. Canon G W Briggs supplies both the words and tune, *Springtime*, of 'Hark! A hundred notes are swelling / Loud and clear. / 'Tis the happy birds are telling / Spring is here!' (SP360). He is probably at his most felicitous in 'I love God's tiny creatures' (SP361) where his words are set to Gordon Slater's original and folk-like tune, *Bilsdale*, written especially for the enlarged *Songs of Praise* of 1931. What a catalogue of creation, and what a shame that recent changes in the overtones of language make the final rhyme of the first verse unacceptable to today's singers.

> I love God's tiny creatures
> That wander wild and free,
> The coral-coated lady-bird,
> The velvet humming-bee;
> Shy little flowers in hedge and dyke
> That hide themselves away:
> God paints them, though they are so small,
> God makes them bright and gay.

The editors' experience of working on the *Oxford Book of Carols* (1928) shows in the inclusion of several suitable carols for children, notably Isaac Watts' Cradle Song, 'Hush! My dear, lie still and slumber' (SP382), to *Northumbria*, an English traditional melody arranged by Martin Shaw.

The book contains some poems previously not used as hymns, for example verses by Christina Rossetti, 'The shepherds had an angel' (SP372), to *Berwick Street*, a rather nondescript tune by Martin Shaw. The combined effect adds little of significance to the canon of children's hymnody. However, it is in this children's section of SP where we find two of the hymns which have achieved great popularity over the years. Both are by the poet, Jan Struther, and are characterized by language that is dignified, eloquent and memorable. She has the happy knack of being able to put language into the heads and hearts of children without talking down to them. In both hymns the successful match of tune to text is nothing less than inspired: 'Daisies are our silver' (SP454), to Kenneth Finlay's pentatonic *Glenfinlas*, and 'When a knight won his spurs, in the stories of old' (SP377), to the English traditional melody, *Stowey*. Magical verses such as these remain in the memory!

> Make us bright as silver;
> Make us good as gold;

Warm as summer roses
Let our hearts unfold. (SP354, v.5)

Let faith be my shield and let joy be my steed
'Gainst the dragons of anger, the ogres of greed;
And let me set free, with the sword of my youth,
From the castle of darkness the power of the truth. (SP377, v.3)

The popularity of *Songs of Praise* and its associated books for schools was considerable. Indeed, the 1931 edition of *Songs of Praise* is still in print in 2005. Hymns which children learn at school often remain with them for life. So it is that there are adults, in the twenty-first century, who can still sing, from memory, 'When lamps are lighted in the town, / The boats sail out to sea; / The fishers watch when night comes down, / They work for you and me'; the words by M M Penstone and the music, *Butler*, Martin Shaw's arrangement of an English traditional melody (SP378). The language of this hymn is not particularly distinguished, and its imagery represents an age long past, but there is something about it which attracted teachers and through them their children. Such can be the power of children's hymns and such is the responsibility of those who write, edit and select songs for children.

Epilogue: **The New English Hymnal** *(1986)*
Of the original 28 catechism hymns in the 1906 EH only five survive in *The New English Hymnal* (1986). Four of these are predictable: 'All things bright and beautiful' to *Royal Oak*, 'It is a thing most wonderful', 'Jesus, good above all other' and 'Once in royal David's city'. Laurence Housman's 'When Christ was born in Bethlehem' also appears. There is no separate section for children in the 1986 book, nor indeed any index of material suitable for children. One can only assume that either, the children who attended churches which used the 1986 book sang the hymns intended for adults, or, that the churches obtained material from elsewhere.[10] It would be unreasonable to expect much of the material selected for Edwardian children to last more that a couple of generations. But the omission of newly commissioned material (not even one hymn) which could have marked a renaissance of children's hymnody within the Catholic tradition was surely an opportunity missed. The editors of the 1906 *English Hymnal* had a different view of their task, for not only did they include a Catechism section which was full enough to provide teachers with suitable material for much of the year, but they also went out of their way to show which 'adult' hymns were appropriate for children to sing. These views were shared by the editors of *Songs of Praise*. By maintaining a high standard for the selection and presentation of words and music Dearmer and his colleagues ensured that those coming to the 'years of discretion' were not to be offered childish fare, either in church or in school.

Notes

1 The hymns in the Catechism section of the book were intended for use in a particular setting. A collection such as Carey Bonner's *Child Songs* (1908), which were written 'for the primary departments of the Sunday School and Day School and for Home Singing' was intended to reach a larger audience.

2 For general surveys of the history of children's hymns see:
Songs of Praise Discussed, compiled by Percy Dearmer with notes on the music by Archibald Jacob, London, OUP, 1933, 195–209;
Lionel Adey, *Class and Idol in the English Hymn*, Vancouver, University of British Columbia Press, 1988, 93–157;
Erik Routley, 'Hymns Written for Young People', in *Hymns and Human Life*, London, John Murray, 1952, 250–62;
Erik Routley, 'Children's Hymns', in *Hymns Today and Tomorrow*, London, Darton, Longman and Todd, 1964, 77–87;
Ian Sharp, 'Childhood and the Christian Hymn', in *Hymn Society Bulletin*, No.199, April 1994, 38–48.

3 Quoted in: Bernarr Rainbow, *Music in Educational Thought and Practice: a survey from 800 BC*, Aberystwyth, Boethius Press, 1989, 271.

4 'Advent tells us, Christ is here' was used in a Children's Festival in Liverpool Cathedral in March 2004. Several teachers commented favourably on its suitability for use in collective worship today.

5 For discussion of the 'littleness' of children see:
Elizabeth Cosnett, 'A (Female) Bookworm Reads Some Hymns', in *Hymn Society Bulletin*, No.205, October 1995, 177;
Ian Bradley, *Abide With Me. The World of Victorian Hymns*, London, SCM Press, 1997, 133.

6 In *Hymns Ancient and Modern* (1868, No.363) the inscription heading this hymn emphasizes a more profound connotation of being little, and indeed serves as the inspiration of the hymn: 'If thou hast little, do thy diligence gladly to give of that little.' This text does not appear in EH.

7 The first two verses are derived from J M Neale's translation of Adam of St. Victor, found at *Hymns Ancient and Modern Revised*, No.456. Neale gives us a snippet; Dearmer a hymn!

8 Erik Routley, 'Percy Dearmer, Hymnologist', in *Hymn Society Bulletin*, No.111, Winter, 1967, 174.

9 'A book of songs for Christians to sing, and especially for young Christians.' *Ibid*.

10 Perhaps from the hugely popular and influential *Come and Praise*, London, BBC, 1978, which, in the words of Geoffrey Marshall-Taylor, the compiler and producer of the radio programmes, embodied the principle that 'songs in assembly should be enjoyed, not endured'.

THE AMERICAN CONTRIBUTION

Alan Luff

It is readily apparent that there are a number of hymns in EH that are of American origin. The number increased greatly in SP and was reduced in NEH. The table below shows the extent and the pattern of the usage. I have included three hymns in the Mission Services section of EH (marked * in the list) which were not needed in the other books.

Writing in SPD (8) Dearmer quotes Dr F M Bird writing in Julian's *Dictionary of Hymnology*: 'In Great Britain the noblest forms of American hymnody are known to the few', and goes on to say,

> In fact, while English compilers and translators were ransacking the material of the Dark Ages, and adding translations from hymns of the Counter-Reformation to those of Medieval origin, the modern American school was hardly consulted – if at all – by Anglican compilers; and, as it happened, it was just in America that the best hymns, and those which are most in accord with the convictions of the present age, were being written.

The exception to this was William Garrett Horder (1841–1922) who edited many collections for the Independents and Congregationalists, including in 1896 *The Treasury of American Song*, and in 1898/1905 *Worship Song*, which Dearmer readily acknowledges in SPD as a source for many of his American selections. It is clear that twenty years after EH he was even more convinced that American hymnody had a great deal to contribute to his new kind of hymn book. So whereas there were 15 in the main body of EH there were 50 in SP.

Hymns of American origin

Author	*First line*	EH	SP	NEH
Alstyne, Frances J Van 1823–1915	*Safe in the arms of Jesus	580		
Anon. Pub. 1885	Away in a manger		353	22
Bliss, Philip Paul 1838–76	*Ho! My comrades, see the signal	570		
Bowie, Walter Russell 1882–1969	Lord Christ, when first thou cam'st to men		562	
Brooks, Phillips 1835–93	O little town of Bethlehem	15	79	32
Bryant, William Cullen 1794–1878	O North, with all thy vales of green	550		

117

Burleigh, William Henry 1812–71	Lead us, O Father in the paths of peace		102	
Carney, Julia Abigail 1823–1908	Little drops of water	600	365	
Chadwick, John White 1840–1904	Eternal ruler of the ceaseless round	384	485	355
Coxe, Arthur Cleveland 1818–96	Saviour, sprinkle many nations	551		
	Who is this with garments gory	108		
Doane, George Washington 1799–1859	Fling out the banner	546		
	Thou art the way, by thee alone			464
Duffield, George 1818–88	*Stand up, stand up for Jesus	581	646	453
Everest, Charles William 1814–77	Take up thy cross, the Saviour said	484	119	76
Gannett, William Channing 1840–1923	The Lord is in his holy place		655	
Hartsough, Lewis 1828–1919	*I hear thy welcome voice	573		
Holmes, Oliver Wendell 1809–94	Lord of all being, throned afar	434	564	403
	Our Father, while our hearts unlearn		620	
Hosmer, Frederick Lucien 1840–1929	Father, to thee we look in all our sorrow	538	347	
	Made lowly wise, we pray no more		575	
	Not always on the mount may we		589	
	O beautiful my country		322	
	O light from age to age the same		192	
	O thou in all thy might so far	463	614	429
	Thy Kingdom come! On bended knee	504	680	500
Howe, Julia Ward 1819–1910	Mine eyes have seen the glory of the coming of the Lord		578	
Johnson, Samuel 1822–82	City of God, how broad and far	375	468	346
Larcom, Lucy 1826–93	I learned it in the meadow path		531	

Longfellow, Samuel 1819–92	I look to thee in every need	406	532	
	Holy Spirit, truth divine		520	
	Life of ages, richly poured		559	
	The summer days are come again	288	8	
	'Tis winter now, the fallen snow	295	16	
	O life that makest all things new		602	
	When my love to God grows weak		134	
Lowell, James Russell 1819–91	Men, whose boast it is that ye		306	
	Once to every man and nation	563	309	
Merrill, William Pierson 1867–1954	Rise up, O men of God		635	
Palmer, Ray 1808–87	Jesus, thou joy of loving hearts		549	292
	Jesus, these eyes have never seen	421	550	389
	Lord, my weak thought in vain would climb		536	
	My faith looks up to thee	439	580	72
Rankin, Jeremiah Eames 1828–1904	God be with you till we meet again	524	334	
Scudder, Eliza 1821–96	Thou long disowned, reviled, oppressed		673	
Sears, Edmund Hamilton 1810–76	It came upon the midnight clear	26	76	29
Smith, Eleanor	In another land and time		362	
Whitman, Walt 1819–92	All the past we leave behind		304	
Whittier, John Greenleaf 1807–92	All as God wills, who wisely heeds		438	
	All things are thine, no gift have we	173	189	
	Dear Lord and Father of mankind	383	481	353
	I know not what the future holds		530	
	Immortal love, for ever full	408	536	378
	O brother man, fold to thy heart thy brother		307	
	O Lord and master of us all	456	603	

	O sometimes gleams upon our sight	610		
	Sound over all waters, reach out from all lands	327		
	Thine are all the gifts, O God	331		
	When on my day of life the night is falling	697		
Willis, Love Maria 1824–1908	Father, hear the prayer we offer	385	487	357

One of the earliest of these hymns to appear regularly in modern books is Ray Palmer's 'My faith looks up to thee', written in his early twenties as he looked forward to his work as a Congregationalist minister. He came from an orthodox background whereas many of the best American hymns are from Unitarians. They do not flaunt that aspect of their theology in their hymns and so their work can easily be used in the context of so thoroughly Trinitarian a book as EH. One of the finest is Samuel Johnson's 'City of God, how broad and far', which moves with weighty and well-judged rhetoric to the final line, indeed to the final word, 'The eternal city stands'. He published his work with Samuel Longfellow, whose 'Holy Spirit, truth divine' is widely used, but is not in EH or NEH (where indeed none of Longfellow's hymns are to be found). EH much appreciates his nature verse and uses two hymns for Summer and Winter.

Another Unitarian was Oliver Wendell Holmes, whose prose writings were much beloved on both sides of the Atlantic. His 'Lord of all being, throned afar' which has commended itself to many editors uses imagery that expresses the belief, widespread among American hymn writers, that all natural phenomena may speak to us of God, and not only of his beauty but of the seriousness of sin. Dearmer clearly finds a sympathetic voice in Hosmer, again a Unitarian. His 'Thy Kingdom come! On bended knee' is a noble expression of Christian hope and longing for a better world, though without any indication of how that might be achieved or at what cost.

In strong contrast there is a more stern expression of that hope in Lowell's 'Once to every man and nation'. Lowell wrote this as a poem at the time of the war with Mexico, which he considered unjust. From its 180 lines Garrett Horder produced these 32 lines that face the evil of the world with realism and conviction.

Two Christmas hymns are mentioned in the general survey of EH. Sears (another Unitarian) wrote 'It came upon the midnight clear' in 1849, with its conviction that the world was about to turn to ways of peace. He was disappointed by the outbreak of the Civil War ten years later, and as we sing it we likewise must often find its hope hollow. 'O little town of Bethlehem' was written for his Sunday School by the Anglican clergyman, Phillips Brooks, who became Bishop of Massachusetts. Its high moral hopes, so typical of American hymnody, are more modestly expressed than in Sears' hymn, and all the more effectively. Little known in Britain before its inclusion in EH, it is now essential to any major book.

An Anglican bishop totally opposed theologically to Phillips Brooks was Arthur Cleveland Coxe. His 'Saviour sprinkle many nations' shows the wide vision typical of American hymns, and has appeared in a number of other books, but 'Who is this in garments gory' is lurid in its imagery, and favoured by no other British editors. It is fortunate that the splendid Welsh tune *Ebenezer* did not die with it. One wonders what Dearmer really thought of it.

During the Civil War Chadwick (another Unitarian) wrote one of the noblest expressions of the American view of life, 'Eternal ruler of the cease-less round'. He looks at the order of the natural world and moves to pray for such order in our lives as we dedicate ourselves to the overcoming of wrong. Another Unitarian, Bryant, described as the first American poet, begins in 'O North with all thy vales of green' with a call to the four corners of the earth to praise God, and continues in much the same vein as Sears, to see a better world approaching as all seek to do God's will. It is unusual to find a hymn addressed to 'Truth' as is Scudder's 'Thou long disowned, reviled, oppressed'. It is only in SP and no other editors have found it convincing. Similarly it was SP that found a place for Howe's 'The Battle Hymn of the Republic'. This is the only hymn in our books that reflects in any way the fight for the emancipation of the slaves. It is not explicit about this, but the constant repetition of the word 'free' shows what was in mind.

The most important name in the list is that of Whittier (another anti-slavery campaigner). It is usually said that he never wrote a hymn as such since, as a Quaker, he had no use for them. But there are a few pieces in his collected works with 'hymn' in the title. 'All things are thine; no gift have we' was written for the opening of a church. But it is true that most of his words that we use as hymns are quarried from his poems, which as J R Watson puts it in *The English Hymn* (p. 497) display 'a high moral purpose, a love of nature, and a certain unbounded-ness, so that Whittier is the supreme American poet of the love of God "for ever flowing free"'. The quotation is from 'Immortal love, for ever full', one of the two hymns from Whittier to survive in NEH, and a hymn that now appears in a huge number of books. Editors make different selections ('O Lord and master of us all' is one such) from its 38 stanzas, some of which are in fact quite polemical against traditional kinds of Christian worship.

Similarly a selection had to be made to bring 'Dear Lord and Father of mankind' into being as a hymn. It is the final section of a poem entitled 'The brewing of Soma', which depicts under the guise of pagan worship the noisy ecstatic Christian worship of the kind that Whittier abhorred. This text is widely loved especially to the noble tune by Parry. Like many fine hymns, it does not say all that there is to be said about the Christian life, but brings a salutary emphasis for many today.

'O brother man, fold to thy heart thy brother' is still a useful text in the context of prayer for peace. The first line is far too masculine for present taste but can be readily amended without damage to the whole. It appears in the Social Service section of SP, which is headed by a much more unlikely choice, a selection of lines from Walt Whitman's 'Pioneers, O Pioneers'. Introducing the section in SPD Dearmer points out that SP is intended for use in places other than churches, but also says that this, which is much more a choral song than a hymn, was being used at Ordinations.

Some of the hymns from American sources do not strike us as being different in spirit from those from British authors. It may surprise to find that 'Thou art the way, by thee alone' and 'Take up thy cross, the Saviour says' are from America, but this is a tradition of what may be called classic hymn writing in America that has been continued by F Bland Tucker (1895–1984), two of whose texts appear in NEH (284, 335). There are, however, hymns from America that do have a quite individual contribution to make to our worship, and it is to be hoped that at least the NEH selection remains fairly constant in future books.

TURNING THE PAGES OF *THE ENGLISH HYMNAL*

Picking up some loose ends

Alan Luff

The editorial committee of *The English Hymnal* did not need to agonize over the order of the hymns as has to be done for some non-Anglican books. It was to be 'a humble companion to the Book of Common Prayer' (p.iii). Thus its prime purpose was to serve the liturgy of the church. The various editions of *Hymns Ancient & Modern* begin with 'Times and Seasons'. EH begins straight in with Advent. I shall look at the hymns provided for this season in a little detail, hoping to show how the principles enunciated by the editors are carried out, in the hope that this will throw light on the whole book, which it is impossible to examine in such detail.

Advent

In the seasonal parts of the book the Office Hymns are placed first, followed by the other hymns in alphabetical order. John Harper deals with the two Office Hymns in his chapter. So we come at No.3 to 'Behold the Bridegroom cometh', a rather dull translation by G Moultrie from a Greek text which moralizes rather heavily on the servant waiting for the arrival of the bridegroom. One may suspect that it is used to accommodate the Tallis *Second Mode Melody*. Other texts also appear in the book where the purpose is similarly musical. The principle may seem to be rather shaky, but some excellent hymns have come into being in this way, notably 'Ye watchers and ye holy ones' (519) written by Athelstan Riley for Vaughan Williams' version of *Lasst Uns Erfreuen*. This Advent hymn however was unsuccessful. No other book took it up.

Modern hymnody makes its appearance at No.4 with 'Great God, what do I see and hear!', a composite text from the early nineteenth century. It is difficult to see how the aim of the editors, of which they make much in the Preface, to print the hymns 'as their authors wrote them', (Preface, p.iv) can be applied here. It appears that the first and last verses may be translations from sources difficult to trace, while verses two and three were jointly written by William Collyer and Thomas Cotterill. Nevertheless it is a fine, if sombre, hymn based on New Testament pictures of the End. It has not commended itself to many other editors.

At number 5 is another translation, this time by Edward Caswall from the Latin, 'Hark! A herald voice is calling'. There is alteration here but only the first line, altered from Caswall's original 'Hark an awful voice is sounding'. SP however produced a radically altered version, 'recast' says Dearmer in *Songs of Praise Discussed* (SPD) 'in the hope of bringing out that which is nearest the truth for thoughtful people in the present century'. It is difficult to see why with this in mind in v.3 'the Lamb' has to become 'the Power', though the alterations in favour of a picture of love coming as a merciful judge in v.4 are more to be commended. NEH remains faithful to EH. This hymn is clearly one that arouses much interest but little agreement since Julian lists over two dozen translations.

With number 6 we come to a classic English text by Doddridge, 'Hark the glad sound! the Saviour comes', with the usual selection of four verses from the original seven. SPD warms to 'its manly strength and hopefulness'. Here the editors follow their rule and in v.3 print 'To enrich the humble poor' in place of A&M's 'To bless ...' which is easier to sing. NEH recognizes the problem and drops the 'To'.

Another English classic follows at No.7, 'Lo! He comes with clouds descending'. Again the question of what is original arises. John Cennick wrote a hymn in 1750, beginning

Lo! he cometh, countless trumpets
Blow before his bloody sign!

and continuing in the same vein, with much that is from the New Testament's more extreme pictures of the Second Coming. Charles Wesley produced a version in 1758. All editors now have to make a choice of what to make of this hymn. SPD explains that EH and SP give a cento of Cennick and the Charles Wesley version. It is close to what appears to be the modern received text of the hymn. SP has minor changes from EH, but the main one is in the last line, where SPE goes with A&M and prints 'Thou shalt reign, and thou alone', while EH and SP have the more striking 'Alleluya! Come, Lord Come!' which NEH retains.

The great classic Advent hymn 'O come, O come, Emmanuel!' is at No.8. EH uses a new translation by T A Lacey, which is not noticeably superior to the J M Neale version that is, with revision, generally accepted in most hymn-books. Indeed there are some marked infelicities: in v.2 'From nether hell, thy people save' is obscure; in v.4 'The royal door fling wide and free' is a little mystifying; in v.5 to ask a congregation to sing 'Adonai' as four syllables causes problems. SP nevertheless reprints this version without alteration as does NEH.

Another translation from the Latin appears at No.9 with 'On Jordan's bank the Baptist's cry'. These seventeenth- and eighteenth-century Latin hymns from France were once thought to be ancient and were seized upon eagerly in the early nineteenth century by English translators wishing to enrich the repertoire with 'Hymns of the Primitive Church', as Chandler entitled his publication of 1837. Some have proved to be excellent hymns, as is this by

Charles Coffin, though most hymn books have much altered Chandler's original. EH retains it, but perhaps not wisely, as SPD comments. Verse 4 in the original has clear reference to healing the sick and to beauty, but EH (with Chandler) has:

> Once more upon thy people shine,
> And fill the earth with love divine.

The A&M version gives some sense to the Latin 'decor' with:

> Shine forth and let thy life restore
> Earth's own true loveliness once more.

SP goes further with:

> Show us the glory of thy face
> Till beauty springs in every place.

No.10 is a plainsong hymn. No.11 is another hymn by Coffin that has been widely received in hymn books and equally widely revised. EH provides a completely new version by Henry Putman (1861–1935). Strangely in v.4 'awful light' is here acceptable. NEH prefers 'dazzling'. Dearmer in SPD says in a rather charming note, 'as we are not bound to re-echo the theology of Paris in the reign of Louis XIV, [the editor] has modernized it rather freely ...'

'Wake, O wake! With tidings thrilling', No.12, is one of the greatest of the Chorales (see Bernard Massey's chapter). EH has a fine translation by F C Burkitt, which has found acceptance in many books, including NEH and the latest book from A&M, *Common Praise*, though there are also many others in circulation. SP produced a new one, and SPD gives an interesting insight into the preparatory work on the book, saying that 'we were compelled by our advisory committee to attempt yet another so as to transfer the phraseology more evidently to the present day'. It is difficult to see however how contemporary is a word like 'tryst', or 'cressets' in place of 'torches'.

The last hymn in this section, No.13, 'When came in flesh the incarnate Word', is by the brilliant scholar and poet J Anstice who tragically died at the age of 27. It is a strange mixture of traditional Advent imagery and more modern ideas. It has reappeared in a small number of books including AMR 1950. They were prepared to retain 'The awful pomp' in v.2, but NEH felt it necessary to change this to 'The judgement light'.

All too many of those who choose hymns tend to see a hymn labelled 'Advent' as suitable only for that season. So the decision on what hymns to place in an Advent section and what to place in a more general section, with perhaps a reference to them at the end of the seasonal hymns, is a difficult one. EH decides that 'Ye servants of the Lord', 'The Lord will come and not be slow' and 'O quickly come, dread Judge of all' should be later in the book, while NEH keeps all three under Advent. SP has removed 'Wake, O wake!' from the Advent section. Neither EH nor SP have Wesley's 'Come, thou long-expected Jesus', but EHS finds it such a loss that it is included in the Supplement in that book and it is in EP and NEH.

Looking through the book – the shock of the General

Were one to leap to the General section starting at 361 and to try (per impossibile) to give the same treatment as that given to Advent, the first six hymns would produce bewilderment. They are together, of course, simply because each section is arranged alphabetically. So 'A few more years shall roll' (361) comes first. Bonar's words take us back to the sentimentality of the nineteenth century and the tune by G W Martin nails us there with five repetitions of the first chord. Next come the splendours of 'A safe stronghold' (362) in Carlyle's craggy translation and the tune in full Bachian splendour with a storm of passing notes and marked 'Very slow and solemn'. Then 'Abide with me' (363), seen by some as the very epitome of what is wrong with the nineteenth century, but recognized by Dearmer writing in SPD as 'This beautiful poem' and as a hymn for one in illness and not an evening hymn. What Vaughan Williams thought about *Eventide* may be another matter, for his descant version in SP is one of the most extravagant of the genre, and one suspects a 'send up' to use a later twentieth-century expression. 'All hail the power of Jesu's name' (364) sees us on firm ground. Dearmer called it 'magnificent' (SPD440), and it is clearly a manly and vigorous tune such as VW demanded. The *Old Hundredth* (365) sees the book back on the bedrock of English hymnody. But with 'Art thou weary, art thou languid' we are again on uncertain ground, with a hymn than J M Neale had to admit was not, as he had claimed at first, a translation from the Greek but almost entirely his own. Perhaps the last word of the first line prejudices the mind against the rest of the hymn, but it is a very self-centred piece. There is a reference to a tune in the Appendix, but it is not the expected one from A&M. Clearly, because the editors had to consider popular demand as well as their own very high standards, there are many hymns in EH whose inclusion today surprise us. One must suppose that the judgement was that, at the time, they were needed. It does leave us as we go through the book with a kind of roller-coaster ride of highs and lows.

Christmas and Epiphany

Even in the short Advent section it is clear that the editors were unable to go very far along the lines of their declaration that they would print hymns 'as their authors wrote them'. They did have to add in the Preface (p.iv) 'wherever possible'. One of the many joys of SPD is that Dearmer from time to time between the notes on the individual hymns writes a general note, and after the discussion of 'Hark! the herald angels sing' he heads one such note

'Improvement or Mutilation', and, having quoted John Wesley on the subject, says,

> The fact is that we cannot include some hymns at all unless they are altered; many a good hymn would have to be rejected because of an unsingable line, or some word that had changed its meaning or syllabic value, or some really impossible *gaffe*.

The discussion of this great Christmas hymn is relevant because one of the points on which critics of the 1904 edition of A&M centred was the editors' reinstatement of Wesley's original first line 'Hark, how all the welkin rings'. It helped towards the failure of the book. Now, faced with the same problem the EH editors print both versions (23, 24), the original in four-line stanzas and the more familiar version to the familiar tune. SP follows this.

Two American hymns considerably enrich the Christmas sections, 'O little town of Bethlehem' (15) and 'It came upon the midnight clear' (26), but the hymns from this source are sufficiently important to merit a separate chapter. One misses 'Angels from the realms of glory'. It made a fleeting appearance only in EPS. Not until NEH did Smart's 'Where is this stupendous stranger' appear. At the time of EH there seems to have been a clear distinction in editors' minds of the difference between hymns and carols. *The Oxford Book of Carols* by this same editorial group shows the reverse operation of this principle in that it includes no Christmas hymns. After OBC however a number of carols did appear in SP. EPS had a supplementary section of seventeen carols. NEH ventures no farther than to include 'God rest you merry, gentlemen', though by that date most hymn books were including a selection of carols. They do also have 'Silent night'. It is interesting to conjecture what the EH editors would have thought of that, even in G B Timms' interesting new paraphrase.

SPD notes the reluctance of earlier Anglican hymn book editors to take up Monsell's 'O worship the Lord in the beauty of holiness' (42), which EH includes under Epiphany, and which is now very much part of the standard repertoire. SPD makes a suggestion of how to avoid the extra syllables at the beginning of the first and fifth verses, but SPE itself does not follow that up, and nor does NEH.

Lent to Trinity

The Lent section is generally unremarkable, except that it perhaps exemplifies Vaughan Williams' *bon mot* when writing about Beethoven's Ninth Symphony, which is true also of words,

> It is admittedly harder to write good music which is joyful than that which is sad. It is comparatively easy to be mildly dismal with success.

One wonders whether Addison's 'When rising from the bed of death' (92) would have been included but for the magnificent *Third Mode Melody*, of which Vaughan Williams was to make such good use. Watts' 'Nature with open volume stands' does not appear until EP, whence it came into NEH. His even greater classic on the passion, 'When I survey the wondrous cross', is given its full five verses in EH (107).

One of the glories of the SP and SPE selection for Passiontide is Crossman's 'My song is love unknown', which EH missed although it had been in *The Anglican Hymnbook* 1868. SP was the means by which it became popular with the magnificent tune *Love Unknown* by John Ireland. For Whitsuntide 'Come down O love divine' (152) is another magnificent text, now made known by the great Vaughan Williams' tune new in EH.

By the time of EH one would have thought that much of the rather earthy vocabulary of earlier hymn writers had been excised, but Faber's hymn on the Trinity (161) is allowed to begin 'Have mercy on us, worms of earth'. (SPD has a note on 'The Hymnic Worm'.) The 1933 edition marks verse 1 as being a section on its own, with the implied suggestion that we should begin the hymn at verse 2, 'Most ancient of all mysteries'.

The Saints
The Preface to NEH notes that 'Ordinary hymns proper to particular saints' days have rarely been noted for their high quality'. The editors felt it necessary to revise or rewrite many of these. This whole section is certainly a low point in EH, lit up by Watts' delightful 'Give me the wings of faith to rise' (197), alongside 'I bind unto myself today' (212) and 'Forsaken once, and thrice denied' (227). For the Transfiguration EH (236) and NEH have ''Tis good, Lord, to be here!' to which NEH felt able to add the only Brian Wren text it thinks worthy of inclusion, 'Christ upon the mountain peak'.

Evening
Now comes 'Times and Seasons', with seventeen hymns for Evening. This would be astonishing in a contemporary book, but for some time up to that point, and for over half a century afterwards, the evening service in many churches was the best attended. It had its own atmosphere, which, in a note on 'Abide with me' in SPD, Dearmer mocks by writing of '. . . the custom, then extremely common, of being sentimental at the Evening Service; . . . the people did not notice much what the words were, so long as the tune suited their mood.' Two notable contributions from the *Yattendon Hymnal* appear in this section, 'O gladsome light, O grace' (269) and 'The duteous day now closeth' (278).

Sacraments and other Rites
The Sacraments and other Rites section was clearly important to the editors, though not uniquely so, since it must be remembered that A&M in fact orig-

inated in that same Oxford Movement as EH. The 1904 edition of A&M provided 25 hymns for the Eucharist. EH gives 35, with the two books overlapping in half their provision. EH adds such treasures as 'Deck thyself, my soul, with gladness' (306), 'From glory to glory advancing' (310), and 'Let all mortal flesh keep silence' (318), which Dearmer radically re-wrote for SP; subsequent editors have preferred his 1906 choice of the Moultrie translation. Neale had translated a prose prayer from the Syriac of the Liturgy of Malabar; C W Humphreys produced a metrical version; Dearmer modified this to create the magnificent 'Strengthen for service, Lord, the hands' (329) to fit the tune that Vaughan Williams wished to use. By such means sometimes a great hymn can come into being. It is surprising to find Cowper's 'There is a fountain filled with blood' (332) since by the time of SP Dearmer will have none of it (see note at SPD125), or any such mention of blood.

The General Hymns

In the General Hymns section there are a number of the hymns that EH introduced to congregations. In looking for 'some cheerful and manly hymns' the editors came upon Bunyan's 'Who would true valour see', the song about Mr Valiant-for-truth. A quarter of a century later Dearmer writing in SPD finds it necessary to write a long article to defend his famous re-writing of this text as 'He who would valiant be' (402). He concentrates on how impossible it would have been to ask congregations to sing about 'hobgoblins'. What he does not point out is that he in fact changed the whole tenor of the piece into a song of personal resolve and self-dedication, and it is this that makes it more suitable as a hymn. In the end, of course, it was the magnificent tune, adapted by Vaughan Williams from a folk-song, that made the hymn widely successful in whatever version it is now sung, though it is interesting to note that the Americans have an equally successful tune in Charles Winfred Douglas' *St Dunstan's*.

From the same century and used in EH for the first time as a hymn came John Mason's 'How shall I sing that majesty' (404), a text that uniquely explores the notion of the majesty of God. SP and NEH have been loyal to the text even though it has not had its ideal tune until very recently with *Coe Fen*. Another hymn about God is 'Immortal, invisible, God only wise', made popular by its inclusion in EH (407). One of its many splendours is the powerful imagery of the last line, ''Tis only the splendour of light hideth thee'. It is astonishing how many editors baulk at this.

National

The 'National' section is a strong one, though, necessarily, one has to say, dated, since any such section can only refer to the situation at the time at which the editors are working. Kipling's 'Recessional' (strangely without the title that explains much of the meaning), was written after the great naval and military reviews to celebrate Queen Victoria's Diamond Jubilee in 1897, and is a genuine prayer with its repeated plea for forgiveness (558). Equally penitential but much more swashbuckling in its expression is G K Chesterton's only hymn, 'O God of earth and altar' (562). One would be hard put to explain the sense of every line, but it is marvellously effective. Equally sombre is 'Once to every man and nation' (563), discussed with other American hymns. Ebenezer Elliott's 'When wilt thou save the people?' (566) comes from as far back as 1850, but remains a strong, even bitter plea for the welfare of ordinary people. The section also refers to 'Judge eternal, throned in splendour' (423), seemingly the only hymn by Henry Scott Holland, which appeared in 1902, was taken up by EH and has been used a good deal in books since then. Even in SP the final verse could read 'Cleanse the body of this empire', though by NEH this had to be amended to 'nation'.

Mission Services
There is a section in EH of hymns for 'Home and Foreign Missions'. But there is also a section headed 'Mission Hymns'. This was not the first time that the heading had appeared. *Church Hymns* had such a section, but with only one hymn in it. By contrast A&M1904 had 33 under this heading. EH provides 14, only agreeing with A&M over four. There may be some ambiguity about the use of the word 'mission' in this context. In *The Parson's Handbook* (ninth edition p.524) Dearmer has a single index reference to 'a "mission" service', and that is for a non-liturgical service at 8 p.m. on Good Friday, clearly of a rather popular nature, since he mentions the use of pictures. His use of inverted commas shows that he has a particular kind of service in mind. There was a tradition of parish missions, which would be often be taken by a visiting preacher, with services every evening of the week for the purpose of teaching or in some other way grounding the congregation more deeply in the faith. Some of the hymns in A&M1904 and EH seem clearly to be intended for such occasions, since they are standard church hymns. One indeed, 'Evensong is hushed in silence' (569) seems to be explicitly for a weekday evening. Indeed, in the A&M selection some are so standard (e.g. 'Fight the good fight'; 'Souls of men! why will ye scatter') that there might be some confusion about where to find them for normal use. Although the EH selection has some standard hymns, such as 'O Jesus, I have promised' (577), often used at Confirmation Services, and 'I heard the voice of Jesus say' (574), there are also some that have the ring of the other kind of popular mission service of the time, those led by such visiting Americans as Sankey and Moody. Five have definite American connections, 'Ho! My comrades' (570) by Philip Bliss, 'I hear thy welcome voice' (573) by Lewis Hartshough, 'Safe in the arms of Jesus' (580) by Frances J Van Alstyne (Fanny Crosby), 'Tell me the old, old story' (583) by Kate Hankey, and 'There were ninety and nine that safely lay' (584), the text by the English Elizabeth C. Clephane, but the tune by Ira D Sankey. There is another text by Elizabeth Clephane, 'Beneath the cross of Jesus' (567), and one by the American George Duffield, 'Stand up, stand up

for Jesus' (581), both of which have been widely taken into British hymn books, and so do not carry with them the same flavour of the public mission service. The EH editors welcomed a considerable influx from America, but these under the 'Mission' heading may perhaps have been seen as of a lower standard, though necessary owing to popular demand. Only the last mentioned hymn survived into SP and NEH.

Final musings
Turning the pages of EH leads one to a great number of fine standard hymns that are now to be found in any hymn book, often in interesting versions, and to a number of others distinctive of the book. But in the end it is not for the words so much that EH is valued, as for the tunes. With SP the situation is different, since, with a different agenda, a large number of texts are put forward for our consideration that serve a different view of what worship should be and where the church might be heading. NEH returns to the task of serving the liturgy that EH had set itself, but without the flair or crusading zeal of the first editors. By the time of its preparation it was clear that a revival of hymn writing was in progress. As always, of the many hundreds of texts written only a few reached a really high standard, and not all of these were on subjects of such general interest as would merit inclusion in a hymn book. But the editors of NEH overstate their case when they say:

> The post-war surge in hymn-writing has not been ignored, but we regard much of it as poor in quality and ephemeral in expression. In particular, while the social gospel is an important element in Christian teaching, its translation into verse can be so contemporary that it quickly becomes dated ... we have not overlooked the social duty of Christians, but we believe that its application to immediate needs can often be better expressed in sermon and prayers than in hymnody. (Preface p.vi)

There is new song writing that entirely answers their description. But there is also a body of serious work of high quality, beyond the fourteen texts by the Chairman of the Editors, George Timms, by no means all of it on social issues. Even if some of it has a life limited to a single generation, not to include it in a new book is to deny its constituency the benefit of valuable hymnody. The phenomenally long life of EH cannot be assumed for any book brought out today. There are still those who use at least the 1933 edition. As late as 1950 there was a demand for a special new edition for Scotland. In the present state of hymnody in the churches, NEH is unlikely to live that long but its success in many churches shows that there are many who wish to carry on the tradition begun by Dearmer and his colleagues, while shedding many things that are no longer needed by the church at the beginning of the twenty-first century.

THE MUSIC OF *THE ENGLISH HYMNAL*

John Bawden

When in 1904 Ralph Vaughan Williams accepted the Reverend Percy Dearmer's invitation to edit the music of *The English Hymnal* he evidently had some doubts about the wisdom of taking on such a task, with the prospect of having to suspend his own composing during the two years that would be needed in order to do the job properly. He later remarked, 'I wondered if I was wasting my time. But I know now that two years of close association with some of the best (as well as some of the worst) tunes in the world was a better musical education than any amount of sonatas and fugues.'[1]

The need for a completely new hymn book had arisen primarily because of growing dismay at the increasing mediocrity of successive editions of *Hymns Ancient & Modern*. The first edition, edited by H W Baker and W H Monk[2] and published in 1861, had been an admirably eclectic volume containing plainsong melodies, metrical psalmody, chorales and new tunes by Monk, Ouseley,[3] Dykes[4] and others. It quickly became a huge success, a national institution even, and only seven years after its publication the first of a series of supplements and revisions appeared.[5] With the production of the 1889 edition it became the unofficial standard hymn book of the Church of England (there never was an official one), with over 75% of churches using it, according to an 1894 report.[6] Consequently A&M became the dominant medium for the propagation of the music of the national Church.

But as time went by and revised and expanded editions kept appearing, criticism grew of the ever-increasing quantity of third-rate material within its pages, which with the 1889 edition had reached alarming proportions. Amongst the most prominent of A&M's critics was the Reverend Percy Dearmer,[7] Vicar of St Mary's Primrose Hill. He and a group of friends had already started meeting together with the intention of producing a words-only supplement to *Hymns Ancient & Modern*, to be called *English Hymns*. However, it soon became clear that nothing less than a completely new hymn book was called for.

Dearmer and his colleagues set about finding a suitable music editor for *The English Hymnal*, as the new book was to be called. Dearmer consulted Cecil Sharp and Canon Scott Holland, both of whom, independently, came up with the same name – Ralph Vaughan Williams. Cecil Sharp was the leading collector of folk-songs and Scott Holland was a Canon of St Paul's Cathedral. The choice of Vaughan Williams as editor was a surprising one for two reasons. Firstly, he was at the time little known. There were other musicians who were on the face of it far better qualified and far better known amongst the musical establishment. Secondly, he was a professed atheist. It says much for the vision of Dearmer's group that Vaughan Williams was nevertheless regarded as the right person for the job.

And so began a collaboration between Vaughan Williams and the Reverend Percy Dearmer that was to last some 30 years. Together they edited not only *The English Hymnal* (1906) but also *Songs of Praise* (1925), *The Oxford Book of Carols* (1928) and *Songs of Praise Enlarged* (1931). In addition to these four principal volumes there were some ten lesser collections that were mainly derived from one or other of the parent volumes. Dearmer's and Vaughan Williams' work was underpinned by a common aim of setting new standards of excellence, and by their shared commitment to a revivalist agenda. This extract from Dearmer's Preface to EH clearly reveals his underlying philosophy:

> The ENGLISH HYMNAL is a collection of the best hymns in the English language, and is offered as a humble companion to the Book of Common Prayer for use in the Church. It is not a party-book, expressing this or that phase of negation or excess, but an attempt to combine in one volume the worthiest expressions of all that lies within the Christian Creed, from those 'ancient fathers' who were the earliest hymn-writers down to contemporary exponents of modern aspirations and ideals ... these ancient hymns ... in their Scriptural simplicity and sober dignity represent the deep Christian experience of more than a thousand years ... we have attempted to redress those defects in popular hymnody which are deeply felt by thoughtful men; for the best hymns of Christendom are as free as the Bible from the self-centred sentimentalism, the weakness and unreality which mark inferior productions.[8]

Dearmer's bold claims immediately suggest that the editors were intending *The English Hymnal* to be regarded as nothing less than a new benchmark of hymnodic excellence. Ancient and contemporary are conjoined in language calculated to invite the reader to regard both as manifestations of all that is finest.

But the real crux of Dearmer's message is to be found in the second part of this extract, with its contrast between the admirable qualities of ancient hymns and the inferiority of popular ones. There is a striking similarity between his language here and that of Vaughan Williams a year or two earlier. In a lecture on the history of folk-song he underlined the universal connection between folk-song and the church, seen at its most obvious in the words and music of the Christmas carol. He then went on to say:

> In this country the old tunes, which had served our forefathers so well, lasted well into the last century. The village band which, with all its shortcomings, was a definite artistic nucleus in the parish, was superseded by a

wheezing harmonium played by an incompetent amateur, or in more ambitious churches a new organ was set up ... The organist had usually developed his technique at the expense of his musicianship, and his taste was formed on the sickly harmonies of Spohr, overladen with the operatic sensationalism of Gounod; and the church hymns had followed suit ... in the original edition [of *Hymns Ancient & Modern*] there appeared a quantity of these exotic and languorous tunes which could be nothing but enervating to those who sang and heard them; and in later editions the element of maudlin sentiment has grown alarmingly until at last the bad has almost driven out the good. National music should represent the people. Will anyone dare to say that the effusions of the Barnby school represent the English people? Hard-working men and women should be given bracing and stimulating music, not the unhealthy outcome of theatrical and hysterical sentiment.[9]

As with Dearmer, the language used here by Vaughan Williams is heavily laden. The band – no comment is made about the quality of its instruments or its performing capabilities other than a vague reference to 'its shortcomings' – apparently possessed 'a definite artistic nucleus'; on the other hand the 'wheezing harmonium' was played by an 'incompetent amateur'. Those churches ambitious enough to afford an organ would, according to Vaughan Williams, usually find that the organist had sacrificed musical taste in the cause of improved technique.

His value judgements about the music itself are equally trenchant. The implication is clear – this sort of music, based as it is on inferior foreign models, should no longer be deemed acceptable. To be truly representative of the 'hard-working' English people the music of our hymn book needed to be 'bracing and stimulating', just like the 'old' tunes of 'our forefathers'.

From this and other pronouncements it becomes evident that Vaughan Williams saw the music of hymnody as a vital part of a wider national music, which he unequivocally linked to a revivalist agenda. Clearly, the underlying philosophies and objectives of the two editors were remarkably similar.

Vaughan Williams made it quite plain that wholesale change in the hymn-tune repertoire was not only desirable but essential:

The task of providing congregations with familiar tunes is difficult; for, unfortunately, many of the tunes of the present day which have become familiar and, probably from mere association, popular with congregations are quite unsuitable to their purpose. More often than not they are positively harmful to those who sing and hear them.[10]

The heart of the matter, though, is this statement:

It is indeed a moral rather than a musical issue. No doubt it requires a certain effort to tune oneself to the moral atmosphere implied by a fine melody; and it is far easier to dwell in the miasma of the languishing and sentimental hymn tunes which so often disfigure our services. Such poverty of heart may not be uncommon, but at least it should not be encouraged by those who direct the services of the Church.[11]

What is revealed by these two statements is the benevolent didacticism which lay behind much of his ethical and artistic beliefs. Vaughan Williams' high moral tone shows that, whilst holding perfectly good musical justifications for change, he sought to lend his reforms added primacy by the invocation of a higher authority.

Vaughan Williams clearly saw that his role as Music Editor of *The English Hymnal* was to 'show the way' and to lead Anglican congregations out of the musical morass into which they had fallen. This would be achieved by re-connecting the music of the hymn book to the cultural roots of England through a commitment to an explicitly revivalist agenda and a determined quest for musical excellence. At the same time, reforming the music of the hymnals constituted a fundamental and vital part of his wider mission to establish a new national music for England.

In compiling the music for *The English Hymnal*, one of the first decisions facing Vaughan Williams was to resolve the competing musical claims on the hymn territory made by choir and congregation. He could not have been more explicit about this:

> The music is intended to be essentially congregational in character ... Fine melody rather than the exploitation of a trained choir has been the criterion of selection ... The pitch of all the tunes has been fixed as low as possible for the sake of mixed congregations ... the choir have their opportunity elsewhere, but in the hymn they must give way to the congregation.[12]

Vaughan Williams also introduced a much greater variety and interest in the arrangements and accompaniments. There were several hymns with special unison arrangements for one or two of the verses, some with descants, and many more intended entirely for enthusiastic unison singing, with strong, supportive organ parts. Amongst these were a number of French 'church melodies' which became widely used in France during the sixteenth and seventeenth centuries. These were adaptations of older, 'unmeasured' plainsong melodies and traditional secular airs, regularized into conventional barred rhythms. Particularly fine examples are *Deus Tuorum Militum* ('Eternal Monarch, King most high', 141) and *Orientis Partibus* ('Christ the Lord is risen again', 129) (*Example 1*).

Example 1: Orientis Partibus

There were a number of equally stirring arrangements of traditional tunes such as *Kingsfold* ('I heard the voice of Jesus say', 574) and the ancient Irish melody called *St Patrick* ('I bind unto myself today', 212), later to be renamed *St Patrick's Breastplate*. These were strong unison arrangements that congregations could quickly learn. Fine as these arrangements undoubtedly are, it was in three of his own great tunes, *Down Ampney* ('Come down, O Love divine', 152), *Salve Festa Dies* ('Hail thee, Festival Day!', 624) and *Sine Nomine* ('For all the saints', 641) that Vaughan Williams really excelled himself. In order to highlight the originality of which he was capable within the modest framework of the hymn tune, it is worth looking a little more closely at *Salve Festa Dies* (*Example 2*).

The musical construction is unusual. It is in three sections; the first is in G, the second in A minor and the third begins in C, modulating to E minor. The alternation of these three sections provides a constantly changing harmonic context, ensuring that musical interest is maintained throughout this lengthy hymn. The rhythmic variety of the melody is further enhanced by the use of a syncopated figure, first heard at the end of the third bar, and a triplet figure used in the C major / E minor section. These features are thrown into relief by the steady crotchet beats of the 'walking bass', which is itself varied by the

STRENGTHEN FOR SERVICE

SALVE FESTA DIES (2) Irregular — R. Vaughan Williams 1872–1958

Example 2: Salve Festa Dies

subtle introduction of minims in the third section. Vaughan Williams' innovative use of melodic, harmonic and rhythmic elements reveals his total mastery of the hymn-tune genre, and his instinctive understanding of what kind of setting would inspire enthusiastic congregational singing.

His approach to selecting the music for *The English Hymnal* was typically thorough and scholarly:

> I determined that my collection should contain the finest version of each tune, not necessarily the earliest, but if the earliest version were not used the fact should be duly noted; in the case of an altered version of the tune, that alteration should also be recorded. I was determined that I would not follow the careless, slipshod methods of earlier hymnal editors.[13]

Vaughan Williams was aided by several colleagues, notably Gustav Holst and Nicholas Gatty, a composer and fellow-student at the RCM and assistant to Fuller Maitland in the editorship of the second edition of Grove's *Dictionary of Music and Musicians*. Others who provided advice and assistance were William Harris, Edward Goldsmith, Thomas Dunhill and John Ireland. The plainsong tunes were assigned to a specialist in this field, W J Birkbeck.

The musical sources listed in the musical preface to *The English Hymnal*

Musical sources consulted for *The English Hymnal*

German
> Lutheran chorale tunes from the 16th and 17th centuries
> Tunes from the 16th and 17th century Catholic song books
> Tunes of the 18th century, chiefly by Bach and Freylinghausen
> Modern German tunes
> German traditional melodies

French and Swiss
> Tunes from the Genevan Psalters of the 16th century
> Ecclesiastical melodies from the paroissiens of various French uses (chiefly those of Rouen and Angers)
> French and Swiss traditional melodies

Italian, Spanish, Flemish & Dutch
  Ecclesiastical, traditional, and other melodies from these countries

American
  Lowell Mason's tunes, certain tunes from *Sacred Songs and Solos*[14] and a
  few 'Western melodies' in use in America as hymn tunes

British
  a) Irish
    Irish traditional melodies
    Tunes by Irish composers
  b) Scottish
    Melodies from the Scottish Psalters of the 16th and 17th centuries
    Melodies from the Scottish tune-books of the 18th and 19th centuries
    Scottish traditional melodies
  c) Welsh
    Archdeacon Pry's Psalter
    Welsh traditional melodies
    Tunes by 18th and 19th century Welsh composers
  d) English
    Tunes from Day's, Damon's, Este's, Ravenscroft's, and Playford's
    Psalters of the 16th and 17th centuries
    Tunes by Tallis, Gibbons, Lawes &c., from their own collections
    Tunes from 18th century books – especially those by Jeremiah Clark and
    William Croft
    English carol, and other traditional melodies
    Tunes by 19th and 20th century composers[15]

(Source: *The English Hymnal* 1906, xvi–xvii)

---

provide some idea of the wide range of music that was researched, and from
which Vaughan Williams made his final selection, as the table below.

Of course, in drawing upon many common sources there was much that
The English Hymnal shared with its close contemporary, *Hymns Ancient &
Modern*. However, when the contents of EH and A&M1889 (the edition most
widely in use at the time) are compared, the remarkable increase in the range
of musical period and style contained in *The English Hymnal* becomes clear, as
in the following table.

Contents of A&M and EH compared

	Number of entries in A&M 1889 edition with First Supplement (779 hymns in total)	Number of entries in EH (744 in total, + 23 further hymns in the Appendix)
Victorian Composers		
Barnby, J	15	1 (+2)
Dykes, J B	60	10 (+2)
Gauntlett, H J	22	7
Goss, J	5	1
Hopkins, E J	11	2
Monk, W H	57	9 (+3)
Ouseley, F A G	13	1
Selby, B L	10	0
Smart, H	18	4
Stainer, J	32	0
Stanford, C V	7	0
Steggall, C	7	2
Wesley, S S	20	5
Early Psalters		
Day's Psalter	0	9
Divine Companion	0	5
Genevan Psalter	0	16
French Church Melody	2	27
German Psalters	15	42
Scottish Psalter	7	16
16th to 18th century German		
Bach, J S	1	33
Luther, Martin	3	8
Praetorius, M	0	4
English & Welsh Traditional		
English	0	47
Welsh	0	16
Tudor & Restoration		
Gibbons, O	7	16
Lawes, H	0	7
Purcell, H	0	3
Tallis, T	6	8

American
  Various   0   6 (+ 1)

Note: In the interests of conciseness the above comparison lists only those entries where there is a distinct difference between the two books. Entries that are broadly similar are not included.

(Sources: A&M1889; EH1906)

While *Hymns Ancient & Modern* focused disproportionately on Victorian composers, *The English Hymnal* employed relatively few. In fact, some of these were only included in the Appendix in order to accommodate prevailing sensibilities.[16] Despite some notable exceptions the Victorian repertoire in A&M was dominated by a dull, four-square style, typified by this Barnby tune (*Example 3*).

Example 3: St Joseph of the Studium

Here, the almost exclusive use of minim beats in all four parts, and the unadorned repetition of the two semibreves at the end of alternate lines of the eight-line text, gives the music an unrelievedly heavy rhythm. The presence of the dotted figure in exactly the same place each time only serves to emphasize this. The stolid harmony consists almost entirely of common chords, and though a brief modulation to D flat at the end of the third line of music brings some harmonic and melodic interest, it then degenerates into weak chromaticism, collapsing onto an unimaginative pedal B flat in the final phrase.

In *The English Hymnal* the same words are set to a melody by Melchior Vulpius,[17] adapted by Bach (*Example 4*).

Although the basic rhythmic pulse is very similar to the Barnby tune, the liberal use of suspensions and passing notes avoids any hint of rhythmic dullness. The rich harmony is characterized by carefully judged chromaticisms, a rising bass line which underpins the halfway close of the hymn in the mediant major, A, and a brief transition to the subdominant in the penultimate phrase. Harmonic interest and momentum is thus maintained throughout. The contrast between these two settings could scarcely be greater, epitomizing some of the changes that Vaughan Williams was seeking to bring about. He considered that the second-rate dullness of Barnby and others was intolerable and should be replaced by settings of the finest musical quality, such as this Bach arrangement.

By far the most radical innovation, however, was the introduction of a large number of English and Welsh traditional sources – tunes adapted by Vaughan Williams from folk-songs – of which there were 63, a subject that merits an entire chapter.

A further difference between the two hymnals was the much more extensive use that was made of music from the early psalters; the comparison above shows 115 such hymns in *The English Hymnal* as against 24 in *Hymns Ancient & Modern*. Early German tunes also offer an illuminating comparison; there are only 4 in A&M as compared with EH's 63. The enhanced presence of Bach chorales, 33 of them, again dealt with in a separate chapter, is worth noting, and testifies to Vaughan Williams' enormous admiration for Bach's music and its universality.

In addition, within *The English Hymnal* were now to be found the strong individuality of Purcell, Gibbons and others, and the distinctive character of the early French church melodies. This early music was balanced by the modern idiom of Vaughan Williams and his contemporaries and the unfamiliar modal harmony of the folk-song adaptations. Without question *The English Hymnal* signified a sea change in the musical language of the hymn book.

Example 4: Weimar

The principal features of Vaughan Williams' editorial policy may now be summarized as follows:

- The adaptation of a significant number of English folk-songs as hymn tunes
- The revival of many Tudor and Restoration composers
- The rejection of large numbers of second-rate Victorian tunes
- The rejection of almost all foreign composers active later than the eighteenth century
- The inclusion of exclusively English modern composers

From this it can be seen that Vaughan Williams was not only seeking to improve the general musical quality of the new hymn book; he was deliberately expunging the Victorian bias of *Hymns Ancient & Modern* and its associations with recent German musical dominance, replacing it with music that emanated primarily from unequivocally English and early continental cultural sources. Later, in *Songs of Praise* and *The Oxford Book of Carols*, he employed the same policies, developing them still further.

These editorial practices closely corresponded with the underlying currents of the wider English musical renaissance, which sprang from a number of influences, at the heart of which were the firm rejection of recent Austro-German dominance, the rediscovery of English music of earlier periods, and the realization of the crucial relationship between the English verbal language and the English musical language. Much of the impetus that sustained the early decades of the English musical renaissance was centred on choral and vocal music, which in turn drew upon the rich vein of English poetry and literature. In its content, its style and its musical language, therefore, *The English Hymnal* directly reflected these wider principles.

In 1925 *Songs of Praise* was published. Once more Vaughan Williams and Percy Dearmer collaborated on the project, but this time with the addition to the team of Martin Shaw, who was engaged as joint music editor. This was to prove an important move. Martin Shaw (1875–1950) and his younger brother, Geoffrey, shared a deep interest in folk-song and church music. Martin was organist at St Mary's Primrose Hill, London (1908–20) (where Percy Dearmer was vicar until 1915) and then of St Martin-in-the-Fields, 1920–24. His brother Geoffrey succeeded him as organist of St Mary's. He was also a Senior Inspector of Schools. Both were extremely influential in the development of church and school music.

Though its contents drew heavily on *The English Hymnal*, *Songs of Praise* went even further in its declared intention of providing a national collection to include English poets and musicians of whatever faith. Its aim was to appeal to an even wider social spectrum, particularly through schools and colleges.

Soon after the publication of *Songs of Praise*, Dearmer, Vaughan Williams and Shaw began work on a new carol book. The situation with carols was very similar to the one encountered with *The English Hymnal* in 1904. The many books currently available were dominated by mediocre Victorian material. Some contained only a few traditional carols, often in spurious or mutilated versions of the originals. Carols had been suppressed by the Puritans in the seventeenth century and consequently became neglected and largely forgotten, other than as a vernacular tradition. It was the publication in 1871 of Bramley and Stainer's *Christmas Carols New and Old* that was mainly responsible for the nineteenth-century revival of the carol. The collection included thirteen traditional carols and twenty-four modern ones though, regrettably, both the words and the music of the old carols had been subjected to Victorian bowdlerization and most traces of their traditional association with the dance removed. Another book which provided impetus to the carol revival was G R Woodward's *Cowley Carol Book*, probably the most popular carol book in circulation until *The Oxford Book of Carols* came on the scene. This was only a slim volume eventually numbering 100 in the enlarged edition of 1919, and pre-dated the work of Cecil Sharp and others in rescuing traditional folk-songs, which of course included many carols, from oblivion.

There was obviously an overwhelming need for a new, comprehensive carol book based soundly on thorough research and scholarship, just as *The English Hymnal* had been. Editing *The Oxford Book of Carols* therefore required much the same approach as for EH; namely, going back to original and traditional sources and eliminating the second-rate Victorian material.

As with the team's previous productions, no effort was spared in preparing the words and music of *The Oxford Book of Carols*. Dearmer was assisted by a number of distinguished writers, including G K Chesterton, Robert Graves, A A Milne and Walter de la Mare. Vaughan Williams and Shaw arranged much of the music, which also included carols collected by Cecil Sharp and others. The modern composers represented included Rutland Boughton, Armstrong Gibbs, Holst, Ireland, Warlock and Rubbra. This combination of prominent national literary and musical figures of the time contributed significantly to the book's identity as an authoritative repository of national Christmas music. The contents comprised traditional carols from the British Isles and from France, and other carols from mainland Europe and Scandinavia dating from the seventeenth century or earlier. Once again traditional sources predominated, foreign sources were all ancient, very few nineteenth century carols were used, and new carols were all written by English composers. The book therefore espoused a purposefully revivalist nationalist policy, which, together with the firm move away from Germanic tonic-dominant harmony and the expansion of musical idiom and style, applied the principles that had been pioneered by *The English Hymnal* to the carol repertoire.

In the meantime *Songs of Praise* had proved to be such an immediate and overwhelming success that, in 1931, in response to popular demand, *Songs of*

Praise Enlarged was published, only six years after the initial version. The same sources were employed but this time tunes arranged from folk-songs and new tunes or arrangements by living composers figured even more prominently. The predominance of these traditional and modern English sources in *Songs of Praise Enlarged* represented a further advance in the policy that had been so soundly laid down in *The English Hymnal*.

In 1933 a revised music edition of *The English Hymnal* was published. There were two principal changes. Firstly, new accompaniments by Dr J H Arnold were provided for all the plainsong melodies. Following current practice these accompaniments were much lighter and more flexible than those in the 1906 edition. Secondly, a significant number of tunes that had first appeared in *Songs of Praise* were incorporated into the new book. These included three tunes by Vaughan Williams, one by Geoffrey Shaw and nine by Martin Shaw, including *Royal Oak* ('All things bright and beautiful', 587) and the splendid *Marching* ('Through the night of doubt and sorrow', 503) (*Example 5*).

Example 5: Marching

This cross-fertilization between successive hymn books was highly significant. Individually the hymnals each made their own major contribution; collectively they acted as inter-related agents in the development of a national music for the Church. *The English Hymnal* was the first and most important publication, setting new standards of scholarship and excellence, and introducing a clearly conceived musical policy. In *Songs of Praise* a more explicitly national identity was pursued, whilst *The Oxford Book of Carols* applied the principles of its two predecessors to the carol repertoire. In *Songs of Praise*

Enlarged this policy was carried even further, with traditional and modern English sources accounting for nearly a third of its contents. This liberation from the German-dominated musical style of the nineteenth century and its replacement by a specifically English idiom gave *The English Hymnal* and its successors a distinctive musical character that was all the stronger for its direct cultural link with the wider English musical renaissance.

At first *The English Hymnal* had been viewed as a controversial publication, its combination of scholarly revivalism and startling innovation appealing more to high church inclinations than to the ordinary parishes. Consequently its initial reception was distinctly mixed, but the reservations expressed about it quickly subsided so that from being regarded as a revolutionary development it soon became part of the musical and liturgical establishment. By the time that it celebrated its golden jubilee in 1956 EH had sold over five million copies. Although the shrewd judgement and promotional strategies of the Oxford University Press played an important part in this impressive achievement, there can be little doubt that the widespread and continuing success of the various publications was primarily due to the scholarship, vision and determination of the editors. Because of its rather specialized appeal it never seriously challenged the overall pre-eminence of the more populist *Hymns Ancient & Modern*. However, the fact that EH was taken up by cathedrals and high churches meant that from the beginning it was ideally placed to influence many senior figures within the Church hierarchy and it therefore achieved a recognition at the highest level which was a major factor in its eventual acceptance.

In due course the far-reaching influence of *The English Hymnal* was acknowledged, as for example by this commentator:

> In the past, churches have fostered the musically intolerable or spineless, either by using a bad book or by cherishing the worst in what they have, instead of bringing out hidden treasures. Today this is no longer a true generalisation; and fifty years after publication it seems undeniable that 'The English Hymnal' has been largely responsible for the improvement.[18]

EH had revolutionized the whole concept of the hymn book, setting new standards of musical and literary excellence. Its scholarship and artistic integrity established the criteria by which later hymnals would be judged, and many of these reprinted selections of its finest hymns.[19]

Through the huge commercial success of the hymnals, the radical reforms pioneered by *The English Hymnal* in 1906 were disseminated across a wide cross-section of society and over a considerable period of time. To begin with, this was through the wider Anglican community, comprising millions of individuals in Great Britain and overseas. With the advent of *Songs of Praise* the focus shifted to the nation's schools and colleges. SP became the BBC's standard hymn book for its many regular and occasional religious broadcasts

until 1951, when *The BBC Hymn Book* was published. An important consequence of this was that SP and its music was lent further authority through
the BBC's status as the cultural voice of the nation. The influence of *The
Oxford Book of Carols* was more diffuse. Its importance lay in its value as a
choir book, and as such it found its way into churches, schools, colleges and
choral societies.

Although the smaller offshoots of *Songs of Praise* contained little or no new
material, their importance should not be underestimated. These ten lesser
volumes were largely aimed at children and were the logical extension of an
emerging trend. There had been twelve children's hymns in *Hymns Ancient &
Modern* in a section 'For the Young', and twenty-seven in *The English Hymnal*
under the somewhat austere heading of 'At Catechism'. Both *Songs of Praise*
and *Songs of Praise Enlarged* contained a proper children's section of between
thirty and forty hymns. However, the new children's hymnals ran to over one
hundred entries in each. They were published at regular intervals between
the wars, and continued to be used extensively for some years after.

Thus at different stages the principal publications involved in what might
be called 'the *English Hymnal* project' – *The English Hymnal*, *Songs of Praise*,
The Oxford Book of Carols and *Songs of Praise Enlarged* – established themselves
at an influential level in three of the nation's principal cultural institutions –
the church, the education system and the BBC, and in so doing played a vital
part in changing the nation's perceptions of the music of the hymn book by
re-connecting them with the roots of English musical culture. As a result,
ordinary people became thoroughly familiar with the English folk-song heritage, with the music of Purcell, Tallis, Gibbons and others – composers who
were far less familiar in the early decades of the twentieth century than they
are now – and with a number of modern English composers. At the same
time there was a liberation from the long period of subservience to German
musical styles.

In 1975 a supplement to *The English Hymnal* was produced, called *English
Praise*. The Music Editors were Christopher Dearnley, organist of St Paul's
Cathedral, and Arthur Hutchings, a noted academic and authority on church
music. *English Praise* was a slim volume comprising 120 hymns. Nevertheless,
it represents another important milestone in the continuing development of
The English Hymnal. It contained a significant number of contributions by the
Music Editors, such as Arthur Hutchings' arrangement of the fine Irish traditional melody, *Dun Aluinn* ('Walking in a garden at the close of day', EP38),
and *Southwold* ('Hail, Easter bright, in glory dight!', EP30), a traditional
Suffolk melody arranged by Christopher Dearnley. There were several
modern tunes that, despite having been in print for some while, had reached
a wider audience largely through their inclusion in *Songs of Praise*; tunes like
John Ireland's *Love Unknown* ('My song is love unknown', EP27) and the
lovely *Slane* ('Be thou my vision', EP75). Also included were two contemporary hymn tunes that had become immensely popular and which are now

widely regarded as amongst the finest examples of the twentieth century, and perhaps of any century. These were Herbert Howells' *Michael* ('All my hope on God is founded', EP73), first published in *The Clarendon Hymn Book* in 1936, and Cyril Taylor's *Abbot's Leigh* ('Sing we of the blessed Mother', EP48), first published in the *BBC Hymn Book* in 1951.

It says much for the shrewd judgement of Percy Dearmer and Ralph Vaughan Williams that eighty years passed before a completely new edition of *The English Hymnal* appeared. However, the time eventually came when a wholesale revision was indeed called for, and so in 1986 *The New English Hymnal* was published. The new book was much reduced in size, from 816 entries in the 1933 edition down to 542. There were two principal changes. There was now a new Liturgical section comprising 42 entries, including a number of responsorial psalms with musical settings by Dom Gregory Murray, organist of Downside Abbey and one of the leading authorities on Gregorian chant.

The major change, though, was a general pruning of tunes that had proved to be little used, in order to make way for some 100 additional ones from both old and new sources. These included a number of new arrangements of some of the old French church melodies, such as *St Venantius* ('Why, impious Herod, shouldst thou fear', NEH46), and a number of fine tunes by Parry, Stainer and Stanford, which for copyright reasons had not hitherto appeared in any edition of *The English Hymnal*. The folk-song element was well rep-resented, with several new arrangements of well-established traditional melodies such as *Londonderry* ('O Christ the same through all our story's pages', NEH258), Michael Fleming's re-harmonization of the wonderful Irish tune popularly known, in England at any rate, as the Londonderry Air.

Of the new hymn tunes, particularly noteworthy are Arthur Hutchings' *Dolphin Street* ('Beyond all mortal praise', NEH340) and Michael Fleming's *Palace Green* ('Sing praise to God who reigns on high', NEH447).

Other recent composers represented were Kenneth Finlay, Bryan Kelly, Henry Ley, Wayne Marshall, Gordon Slater, George Thalben-Ball and David Willcocks. (Curiously, despite the emergence of numbers of first-rate female composers during the course of the twentieth century, the composition or arrangement of hymn tunes appears to be very largely an all-male preserve, judging by the fact that only three women are listed in the NEH music index.)[20]

Just as with the 1906 edition, *The New English Hymnal* contained plain-song melodies, the music of the early psalters, French church melodies, German chorales, English music from the Tudor and Restoration periods, traditional airs from various parts of the British Isles, and new tunes by recent and modern composers. *The New English Hymnal* was an anthology of the very best of *The English Hymnal*, *Songs of Praise* and *English Praise*, together with many new arrangements and the finest hymn tunes from other sources.

PALACE GREEN   87 87 887   Michael Fleming b 1928

Example 6: Palace Green

The New English Hymnal, then, represents yet another stage in what was referred to earlier as 'the *English Hymnal* project'; that is to say, the succession of publications which shared and continued to disseminate the musical objectives pioneered by *The English Hymnal*. To date, this comprises sixteen volumes:

1906   *The English Hymnal*
1921   *Hymns Selected from The English Hymnal*
1925   *Songs of Praise*
1928   *The Oxford Book of Carols*
1929   *Songs of Praise for Boys and Girls*
1930   *Hymns for Sunday School Anniversaries and Other Special Occasions*
1931   *Songs of Praise Enlarged*
1932   *Songs of Praise for Little Children*
1933   *The English Hymnal* (Revised)
1933   *Songs of Praise for Children*
1936   *Songs of Praise: The Children's Church*
1936   *The Daily Service*
1951   *The Hymnal for Scotland*
1961   *The English Hymnal Service Book*
1975   *English Praise* (Supplement to EH)
1986   *The New English Hymnal*

It is a remarkable fact that the outstanding scholarship and unerring judgement of the very first editors resulted in a model that has stood the test of time for no less than one hundred years. As the distinguished hymnologist Erik Routley observed,

> [*The English Hymnal*] represented the most important single historical event in modern English hymnody ... No later editors of any musical pretension dared to ignore it.[21]

In its various guises and revisions the '*English Hymnal* model' has proved itself flexible enough to absorb the best music from a wide range of sources, yet robust enough to resist ephemeral musical trends. The policies set out with such clarity of vision in 1906 by Vaughan Williams and his colleagues provided the firmest of foundations for his successors – Martin Shaw, Arthur Hutchings, Christopher Dearnley, Michael Fleming, Anthony Caesar and others – who confidently built on the *English Hymnal*'s example, as future music editors will no doubt continue to do.

Notes

1 R Vaughan Williams, 'A Musical Autobigraphy', in *National Music and Other Essays*, London, OUP, 1963.

2 William Henry Monk (1823–89) was organist of various London churches as well as holding a number of academic appointments. Though a great deal of A&M's initial success was due to the overwhelming need for such a volume, its continuing popularity was largely due to the expertise of its two chief editors, Baker and Monk. The fact that so many of Monk's pairings of words and music are still regarded as the definitive versions says much for his musical judgement and skill.

3 Frederick Arthur Gore Ouseley (1825–89) was a major figure in the 19th-century revival of English church music and was closely associated with the production of A&M. The 1889 edition contains thirteen of his hymn tunes.

4 Of all the Victorian hymn composers, John Bacchus Dykes (1823–76) was by far the most successful. No fewer than fifty-six of the hymns in the 1875 edition of A&M are set to Dykes tunes, and a large number of his estimated 300 hymn tunes are still in regular use.

5 The editions that preceded the appearance of *The English Hymnal* were as follows:

1861	First full music edition	273 hymns
1868	First Supplement	113 extra hymns added
1875	First Revised Edition	473 hymns
1889	Second Supplement	165 extra hymns added
1904	Second Revised Edition	643 hymns

6 Following a survey it had undertaken, the 1894 report of the Convocation of Canterbury found that 10,340 churches used *Hymns Ancient & Modern*, 1,478 used *The Hymnal Companion* and 1,462 used *Church Hymns*. 379 churches used other hymnals. P Dearmer, and A Jacob, *Songs of Praise Discussed*, London, OUP, 1933, xxiv.

7 Percy Dearmer (1867–1936) served as curate in several London parishes before becoming Vicar of St Mary the Virgin Primrose Hill, 1901–15. In addition to his editing of the hymnals discussed, he was a prolific author. His seminal work, *The Parson's Handbook* (1899), ran to thirteen editions. Dearmer's passionate Christian socialism and advocacy of the ordination of women were considered revolutionary at the time. He produced many original hymns, translations and adaptations; NEH contains 17 entries by him.

8 P Dearmer, Preface to *The English Hymnal*, London, OUP, 1906, iii–v.

9 R Vaughan Williams, 'Religious Folk Songs', Oxford University Extension Lecture, Pokesdown Technical College, Bournemouth, 1902.

10 R Vaughan Williams, Preface to *The English Hymnal*, London, OUP, 1906, x.

11 *Ibid.*, xi.

12 *Ibid.*, x.

13 R Vaughan Williams, 'Some Reminiscences of the English Hymnal', in *The First Fifty Years: A Brief Account of the English Hymnal from 1906 to 1956*, London, OUP, 1956, 3–4.

14 A collection edited by Ira Sankey and published in London.

15 RVW contributed four new tunes. The other modern composers included were William Bell (2 tunes), Walford Davies (1), Thomas Dunhill (1), Nicholas Gatty (2), A M Goodhart (1), Gustav Holst (3), John Ireland (1), Walter Parratt (1) and Arthur Somervell (3).

16 Vaughan Williams later admitted that he had been forced to make some compromises in *The English Hymnal:*

> Whilst trying to include all the good tunes, I did my best to eliminate the bad ones. This was difficult, because I was not entirely my own master. My committee insisted that certain very popular tunes should be retained. The climax came when my masters declared that I must myself write a fulsome letter to a prominent ecclesiastic asking for leave to print his horrible little tune. My committee and I finally settled our quarrel with a compromise by which the worst offenders were confined in an appendix at the end of the book, which we nicknamed the 'Chamber of Horrors.'

'Some Reminiscences of *The English Hymnal*' in *The First Fifty Years: A Brief Account of the English Hymnal from 1906 to 1956*, Oxford, OUP, 1956, 3.

17 Melchior Vulpius (c1560–1615) – German composer and *Kantor*. He wrote nearly 200 motets, a setting of the Passion according to St Matthew, and about 400 hymn tunes.

18 A E F Dickinson, 'Some Thoughts About The English Hymnal', in *The Musical Times*, May 1952, 243.

19 See A E F Dickinson, *Vaughan Williams*, London, Faber, 1963, Appendix A, 488–93 for details of the considerable number of other hymnals that reprinted Vaughan Williams' original tunes and arrangements.

20 Lucy Broadwood (*Devonshire*, NEH326), Jessie Irvine (*Crimond*, NEH459) and Millicent Kingham (*Benson*, NEH495).

21 E Routley, *The Music of Christian Hymnody*, London, Independent Press, 1957, 139–40.

A MORAL ISSUE?

Anthony Harvey

In the Preface to the 1906 edition of *The English Hymnal* Vaughan Williams wrote of the choice of hymn tunes that 'It is indeed a *moral* rather than a musical issue'. This sudden intrusion of moral values into a question which would normally be discussed in terms of aesthetics, ease of performance and general suitability was unexpected and not particularly characteristic – I have been unable to find anything in his published writing which develops the thought further. Yet it is clear that this was not a throw-away remark. Indeed he goes on in the Preface to talk of the 'incalculable good *or harm*' (my italics) which might be done to children 'by the music which they sing in their impressionable years', and says that 'a tune has no more right to be dull than to be demoralizing'. Evidently it was a matter on which he felt very deeply; and he chose to express these feelings in specifically moral terms.

The notion that music can affect our attitudes and emotions is of course very ancient; it needs no demonstration that martial music, for instance, is intended to inspire valour in war and funeral music to express corporate grief. Similarly it is possible to judge whether music written to be performed in public worship has an appropriately 'religious' character: music can be flippant, jocular or sarcastic, and tunes which display these characteristics could well be judged unsuitable. But that music may actually play a part in forming *moral* character, and that a particular piece may be judged according to moral norms, is a view far less easy to defend. We have to ask what made Vaughan Williams express his judgement on Victorian hymn tunes in this way, and what was the origin of his (in the modern world, at least) surprising association of morality with musical composition.

The obvious place to look for a precedent is, of course, Plato, and there is no doubt that Vaughan Williams both read and pondered on Plato's work. At Charterhouse he learned Latin and Greek, and the score of *Sancta Civitas* (1926) is headed by a quotation from the *Phaedo*. His copy of the dialogues in F J Church's translation is heavily marked in his own hand.[1] And the influence of Plato's philosophy is clearly evident in his belief in an inner person or soul that is totally independent of physical attributes: 'Mind and memory play even a more important part than the ear in appreciating music ... let us hear music with the mind's ear only. Perhaps in future this will happen – a new art will be evolved in which the mind of the composer will be in direct touch with the mind of the audience. But this art will not be music ....'[2]

But was he also influenced by Plato's views on music? As is well known, these were highly theoretical, and it is impossible to derive an understanding of the music of Plato's time from his theorizing. Yet the theory is based on a keen appreciation of the power of music over the emotions and the character. 'Rhythm and harmony sink deep into the soul, resulting in grace of body and mind.'[3] Music has the potential to foster an evil character in human beings,[4] but properly controlled and selected it can contribute to the 'harmony' of the soul, a harmony which exists already in the cosmos and which should be aspired to both in the city state and in the soul of the individual.[5] Hence the banishing of certain modes from the ideal republic and the acceptance of others as wholesome influences on moral character.[6] But even if particular modes and rhythms could be regarded by Plato has having the power (at least by association) to exert a moral influence, this does not take us much further. The precise character and use of these elements is lost beyond recall, and there is no easy translation of Plato's categories into modern terms. Indeed, the irony is that the closest we can get to the Ionian mode, so disapproved of by Plato, is with the major scale,[7] and it would be absurd to suggest that Vaughan Williams or any other composer of diatonic music should have shunned major keys on moral grounds!

But if Plato can provide no more than a general background to Vaughan Williams' moral aesthetic, there may be a significant trail in some of the other language he uses. In the same context in the Preface he writes of *enervating* tunes, and even allows himself to speak of 'the miasma of . . . languishing and sentimental hymn tunes'. Language of this kind has of course often been used about these tunes: C H Phillips, for example, did not hesitate to call John Bacchus Dykes' tunes 'self-satisfied and unctuous' and to ascribe their character to 'the flight from reason, and from the tensions and controversies to which reason leads, which is the mark of Victorian England at its worst'.[8] But this kind of judgement verges more on the sociological than the moral. When Erik Routley speaks of Arthur Sullivan in his hymn tunes 'vacillating between vulgarity and glum monotony', and ascribes this to the 'fundamental security and complacency of Victorian churchmanship, defensive against those social forces etc',[9] he is bringing social and historical categories into his aesthetic in much the same way as Ernst Bloch, from his Marxist standpoint, found that the sonata form presupposes 'a capitalist dynamic' and the fugue 'a static, hierarchical society'.[10] But Vaughan Williams' use of such words as 'languishing' suggests that at the root of what he felt to be a moral influence lay something to do with vigour and movement. Just as Stravinsky objected to people listening to music with their eyes closed rather than watching the performers, because this 'allows them to abandon themselves, under the lulling influence of sounds, to vague reveries – and it is these they love, more than the music itself',[11] so Vaughan Williams' dislike of the 'false sentimentalism' of many hymn tunes may have something to do with tempo and lack of vigorous progression. It is true that he goes out his way in the Preface to warn against taking hymns too briskly: 'The custom in many English churches is to sing many hymns much too fast'; but if we compare the recommended tempo of some of his own hymns with that of those he displaced, we find that he clearly leans towards a more vigorous style. His *King's Weston*, for example, is marked 'With vigour', compared with the alternative tune, the mediaeval *Laus Tibi Christe*, which is marked 'Moderately slow, dignified'. Or again, *White Gates* is 'In moderate time', compared with J B Dykes' *St Aelred*, which is marked 'Very slow', and relegated to the Appendix. Was it, then, the sluggish pace and lack of musical energy that distressed him in some Victorian tunes and made him feel morally uncomfortable?

If so, we may perhaps look in another direction for an explanation of his preferences. His motivation will not, of course, have been primarily religious; as his most recent biographer has said, 'his mind was unclouded by any thoughts or scruples of religion'.[12] Yet he may well have been influenced by the strong tradition in Protestantism that congregational singing should be lively and invigorating. According to Luther, 'It is the function of music to arouse the sad, sluggish and dull spirit . . . The listless mind is sharpened and kindled, so that it may be alert and vigorous as it proceeds to the task.'[13] Hence the readiness of Protestant churches to adopt and adapt secular songs and dance-tunes for use in church, a tradition notably revived by Vaughan Williams himself in *The English Hymnal*. Similarly, Isaac Watts, speaking of hymns, 'strongly advocated a faster pace and a heartier manner of singing them',[14] and John Wesley followed in the same tradition when he adapted some secular tunes that were far from sluggish. But it could certainly be said that the influence of the immensely popular *Hymns Ancient & Modern* had tended in the other direction. Some of J B Dykes' tunes, among the most popular in the book, invited a lingering style of performance that continues to this day in many parish churches. We would hardly want to say that it is actually *immoral* to sing hymns in this way; but there is certainly something in the Protestant soul which may rebel against a 'languishing' performance, and it may be that we have here at least one of the roots of Vaughan Williams' aversion to such tunes, which he then articulated in moral terms.

But is this simply a matter of performance, or does it provide grounds for a judgement on the tunes themselves? Finding objective factors in a musical composition that account for particular reactions in the listener is notoriously difficult; but we may perhaps find help in the psychological approach adopted, for example, by Leonard Meyer and Hans Keller, who identify the elements of harmonic suspension and resolution as at least one of the means by which the composer works on our emotions and rouses us into active attention.[15] Certain Victorian hymn tunes (particularly those of W H Monk) are constructed with a succession of diatonic chords which have very little harmonic progression or activity in the inner parts. Consider this example from the Appendix to EH (*Example 1*).

ST PHILIP 777   W. H. Monk 1823–89

Example 1: St Philip

The lack of any harmonic tension in this simple rhythmic structure might well rile the Protestant soul that feels instinctively that hymn singing should have something invigorating about it; Vaughan Williams' word 'enervating' seems particularly apt in this instance. Compare the Crüger tune with which he replaced it (Example 2):

Here the rhythmic pattern is identical, but the modulation in the second bar takes one by surprise, and the inner parts move independently of the theme and create suspensions which (at least according to this theory) keep the listener in a state of emotional and psychological arousal. In this case at least, we can understand how the difference between the two tunes might be expressed in terms such as 'enervating' and 'vigorous', and might even suggest, to someone of Vaughan Williams' background and upbringing, a sense that *moral* values are involved.

And perhaps there is a further factor. It is well known that folk-song was a profound influence on Vaughan Williams. In the words of the Editor of *Music and Letters* (A H Fox Strangways), he 'talked folk-song as to the manner born'; and a feature of the folk-song idiom, in the words of the same writer, is that 'the melody swings boldly from pivot to pivot and does not employ the balances of "civilized" music. In its scale those pivots are fixed ….'[16] Vaughan Williams' own tunes certainly have this kind of rhythmic strength, and the connection which he saw between folk-song and a sturdy sense of national

Example 2: Heiliger Geist

identity (developed at length in his lectures of 1934 entitled *National Music*) could well have led him, once again, to express his criticism of what he felt to be 'languishing' tunes in moral terms.

Yet that is surely not the end of the matter. Religious music in general, and also hymn tunes in particular, are by no means only characterized by robustness and vigour. Alongside the Protestant emphasis on an active and even muscular Christianity (often associated with public schools such as that in which Vaughan Williams was educated), there is a tradition, particularly in Catholicism, of religious music as leading, not to action, but to contemplation. Such music will inevitably have a quieter, less obviously dynamic, character; and some hymn tunes must be judged successful precisely because they lead the mind and heart to stillness and silent adoration. It would be impossible to deny that this is a kind of music (whether or not consciously 'religious') in which Vaughan Williams also excelled: one has only to think of *The Lark Ascending* or certain passages in *Job*. And it is in this light that we should assess the fact that possibly the most enduringly popular of all his hymn tunes is *Down Ampney*, not least because it seems to capture perfectly, not only the unusual metre, but also the deeply contemplative character of a remarkable fifteenth-century mystical poem, of which Littledale's translation is in its own right nothing less than an inspired contemplative poem, 'Come down, O love divine'.

Notes

1 U Vaughan Williams, *RVW: A Biography of Ralph Vaughan Williams,* London, 1964, 163.
2 Ralph Vaughan Williams, 'The Letter and the Spirit', in *Music and Letters*, March 1920.
3 *Republic* 401d–e.
4 *Laws* 669b–670a.
5 *Timaeus, passim.*
6 *Republic* 522a, *Symposium* 215c.
7 I owe this observation, as well as much helpful advice, to my son-in-law Anthony Ingle.
8 *The Singing Church,* London, Faber, 1947, 157, quoted by Erik Routley, *The Music of Christian Hymnody,* London, Independent Press, 1967, 122.
9 Routley, *Christian Hymnody*, 125.
10 *Essays on the Philosophy of Music*, 1974 (ET Cambridge, CUP, 1985), 209.
11 Autobiography, quoted by V Zuckerkandl, *Sound and Symbol*, ET London, R&K Paul, 1956.
12 Simon Heffer, *Vaughan Williams,* Boston, North East University Press, 2000, 29.
13 *On Psalm 4*, LA 1043, quoted in Ivor H Jones, *Music, a Joy for Ever,* London, Epworth Press, 1989, 73.
14 Nicholas Temperley in *The New Grove*, 2nd ed., vol. 12, p. 31, sv, 'Hymns' 4.3.
15 Cf. Anthony Storr, *Music and the Mind*, London, Harper Collins, 1969, 84–8.
16 *Music and Letters*, March 1920, 85.

THE ENGLISH HYMNAL: LITURGICAL AND MUSICAL ROOTS, AND THE PLAINSONG HYMNODY

John Harper

The English Hymnal is a hymnal intended for liturgical worship – day by day, season by season, coloured by the feasts of saints and martyrs. The plainsong hymns for the office are central to that purpose. They are given pride of place at the beginning of each liturgical section (or subsection) of the book. Two related movements in the nineteenth century contributed to the corpus of plainsong materials found in the book, and are crucial to an understanding of its nature: the international revival of plainsong, which can be marked by the Mechlin editions of Roman chant in the 1830s, and the specifically English interest in connecting the post-Reformation, Protestant Church of England with its pre-Reformation traditions and practices.

Plainsong is readily accessible today, often used as calming background sound, or to engender a sense of the past or the sacred in film and television drama. It is hard to imagine that it was not part of the normative experience of Western music. It was not so in the nineteenth century. The mellifluous flow of plainsong melodies that we take for granted depended on a complete revaluation of its nature and style. The Mechlin editions brought plainsong to the fore, but its texts and performance were transformed in the review instituted by Prosper Guéranger, the re-founder and abbot of Solesmes (1833), and taken forward by succeeding generations of monks there.[1] It was part of a larger project to renew the monastic life, and specifically the Benedictine tradition, ousted and destroyed in the aftermath of the French Revolution. Publication of the editions of plainsong made at Solesmes began in 1880. In 1904 they were adopted as the authoritative texts of the chant of the Roman Catholic Church. They were revolutionary in their time because they were based on the earliest available mediaeval manuscripts, edited on rigorous scholarly principles, printed in a new font that followed the style of the late mediaeval manuscript notation, and performed in a new, flexible rhythmic style derived from the notation.

The nineteenth-century background: reconnecting with the pre-Reformation Church
The French Revolution that suppressed the monasteries in France also forced English monasteries that had been sustained on the Continent to return to England: these included the Benedictine houses now situated at Ampleforth, Downside and Stanbrook. The emancipation of Catholics in 1829 encouraged

161

new foundations (e.g. the Cistercian monastery at Mount St Bernard, 1835). At much the same time as this took place, the Church of England's spiritual life was stirred up by a series of movements, of which those emanating from Oxford and Cambridge are most relevant here: the Oxford Movement and the Camden Society (later the Ecclesiological Society, known as the Tractarians). One aspect of their agenda was the reconnection of the Church of England with its pre-Reformation past. Three outcomes are significant here: the building of new churches and the restoration of old ones in a 'Gothic' style, complete with chancel for a choir; the founding of new Anglican religious houses from the 1840s onwards; and the re-evaluation of Church of England worship, particularly with regard to ceremony, music and – above all – more frequent Eucharistic celebration.[2]

Part of the process of musical re-connection with pre-Reformation tradition was the re-instatement of plainsong. The greater part of the plainsong repertory had been made redundant by *The Book of Common Prayer*. Psalms, canticles, versicles and responses were chanted to simple plainsong tones in the cathedrals and a small number of other places, but these were often harmonized and then replaced by composed settings. The characteristically Anglican form of chanting lost its connection with the plainsong of which it was originally a decoration. Since only the words of Scripture and of *The Book of Common Prayer* were authorized, metrical psalms, hymns, songs and anthems had no place within the service. By the famous Royal Injunctions issued in 1559, the singing of such items before and after service was permitted 'for such as delight in music'. In fact, it is apparent from bishops' visitations that the rules were flouted in some churches even in the later sixteenth century, but for the most part the services were read, and metrical psalms were sung before and after the sermon that followed.[3]

The explosion of hymn writing in the eighteenth century raised the question of the use of hymns in services. In the context of the nineteenth-century Oxford Movement and the Tractarians, this was part of a broader issue of what should be sung, and how, especially in parish churches. A handsome edition of the Prayer Book, printed in two colours, with plainsong based on Merbecke's *Book of Common Prayer Noted* (1550), appeared in 1841, edited by William Dyce. Those who wished to enrich that English plainsong repertory further were faced with three questions: where to find the music, how to translate the texts, and how to print the music. There were two solutions to the music: foreign editions of chant, and the pre-Reformation Latin service books still preserved in some libraries. The texts were similarly available for translation. Printing required the acquisition of new music fonts; earlier efforts were rarely attractive. The most important advances were stimulated by the typography of the new Solesmes editions appearing from 1880 onwards.

In the mid nineteenth century the experience of liturgical music sung in Anglican parish services, and of plainsong in particular, was new and fresh.

Within that rediscovery of chanting, the ancient liturgical hymns, many with texts compiled in the early Christian centuries, formed a key part. It was in the plainsong hymns that the enthusiasm for hymn singing and the re-connection of the Anglican Church with its pre-Reformation roots could be brought together. While the compilers of the first books had to make use of such resources as could be readily available, both English and Continental, a rapid growth in scholarly study of Latin liturgy and its chants made available a far wider resource. In general, editions of texts came first, and only at the end of the nineteenth century were editions of the musical sources more readily available. The outcome was a greater awareness of what was distinctively English about the mediaeval tradition.

The mediaeval hymns of the Use of Sarum

Mediæval worship in Britain before the Reformation was dominated by one variant of the Western Latin rite: the so-called Use of Sarum, originally based on the practice of the cathedral church in Salisbury. There were related Uses of York and Hereford (and also monastic Uses), but Sarum was prevalent. In the Anglican Church in the second half of the nineteenth century precedence was increasingly given to Sarum texts and Sarum plainchant, because it was English, and not Roman. The adaptation of the texts and chants of the Use of Sarum were not a reconnection with a Roman Catholic pre-Reformation Church, but a reconnection with English roots, inseparable from the continuity and authority of *The Book of Common Prayer*. Englishness went beyond the language: the title of *The English Hymnal* is itself a proclamation of Englishness, and the plainsong hymns within it express those ancient English roots.

Those who wished to introduce ancient chants and texts into nineteenth-century Anglican worship faced three problems: the pattern of services, their structure and prescribed content, and the translation of Latin texts into English. The 105 plainsong hymns, sequences, processionals and other chants included in *The English Hymnal* form only a small percentage of the mediaeval plainsong repertory (less than 200 out of a total of more than 3,500 chants for the office alone).[4] The hymns were intended for the daily round of prayer – the office. In the mediæval liturgy this consisted of eight services (Matins, Lauds, Prime, Terce, Sext, None, Vespers and Compline): in the Church of England's *Book of Common Prayer*, there were only two (Morning and Evening Prayer, often referred to as Mattins and Evensong). The mediaeval liturgy was rich in detail and observance: this had been stripped out of *The Book of Common Prayer* by 1552. Not only did the mediaeval repertory provide hymns for more services, but – as already observed above – the hymns properly had no place in Anglican worship at all. Finally, there was the question of translation, coupled with the shaping of new English texts to old Latin metrical patterns. This is a matter discussed in greater detail below.

The repertory of Latin hymns was, by modern standards, very small; and it was treated in a particular way. The Use of Sarum included about 112 core texts[5] and 67 melodies. On the face of it, there are just under two texts for each melody. In practice their use was far more sophisticated. Some texts (e.g. those for Prime, Terce, Sext and None) were unchanging throughout the year; but the melody to which they were sung varied according to the day, the season or the feast. (The hymn for Prime, 'Iam lucis orto sidere' (EH254), could be sung to as many as 20 different melodies over the year.) Some melodies were associated with specific seasons or types of feast, but they were sung to several different texts, again according to the day, the season or the specific feast. The weekday melodies were associated with the time of day (Matins, Lauds, Vespers) but the texts followed a weekly cycle. In a few cases there is a combination of a single melody and text (e.g. 'Conditor alme siderum', EH1). Overall, this resulted in about 200 different combinations of text and melody over the year. This small repertory, used flexibly, meant that the hymns – and there was no more than one hymn in any mediaeval office – were imprinted in the memory. Their strength and durability was proven across the centuries. However, for the most part, the repertory of hymns in the Middle Ages was sung by the clergy in choir, and not by the people. The nineteenth-century revival of plainsong changed all that. These were intended as hymns for congregational use.

Contemporary influences on the plainsong hymns of The English Hymnal

The first two editions of *The English Hymnal* introduced plainsong office hymns from English mediaeval sources to a wide group of worshippers. They did so at a time when plainsong was in the ascendant. No longer the preserve of the Ecclesiologists, its use spread to a significant number of cathedrals, colleges, greater churches and parish churches. It spread forth on the crest of the musical practice developed in the newly founded High Church parishes and religious communities. It was invigorated by the scholarship, enthusiasm, energy and publishing of a relatively small group of musicians and dilettantes.

Two new London churches, established in the second half of the nineteenth century, are central to the network of people who influenced and shaped *The English Hymnal* and its related publications: St Barnabas Pimlico, and St Mary Primrose Hill. Both were important centres of plainchant singing.

St Barnabas Pimlico opened in 1850. It was for this church that the Revd Thomas Helmore (1811–90) and the Revd John Mason Neale (1818–66) compiled the first and influential plainsong hymnbook in English, *The Hymnal Noted*, in the 1850s. Later in the century, the Revd George Ratcliffe Woodward (1848–1934), plainsong scholar and editor of *Songs of Syon* and *The Cowley Carol Book*, was curate there. He encouraged a leading compiler and editor of Sarum plainsong in English, the Revd George Herbert Palmer (1846–1926), to direct the church's music. Vaughan Williams was organist at the church from 1895 to 1899; and his vicar was the Revd the Hon. A Hanbury-Tracy, a member of the editorial committee of *The English Hymnal*.[6]

St Mary Primrose Hill opened in 1872. The Revd Percy Dearmer became vicar in 1901, and his first choirmaster was G H Palmer, assisted by Francis Burgess – another important figure in the promulgation of English plainsong. If this was the extent of the link between the two churches for the first edition of *The English Hymnal* (EH), it was more influential in the second edition (EH2) as well as in *Songs of Praise* (SP) and *The Oxford Book of Carols* (OBC). Martin Shaw (1875–1958), who assisted Vaughan Williams with research of tunes for EH, became organist of St Mary's from 1908 to 1920: he was joint music editor of both SP and OBC. Martin Shaw's brother, Geoffrey (1879–1943), succeeded him as director of music, and he was assisted by John Henry Arnold (1887–1956), plainsong editor of EH2. Much later, the Revd George Timms (1910–97), vicar of the church 1952–65, was chairman of the editors of *English Praise* and *The New English Hymnal* (NEH). Michael Fleming (b1928), director of music at the church 1977–81, was plainsong editor for NEH.

Two other associations are significant. First, there were the new Anglican religious communities. Much of G H Palmer's work was associated with and printed by the Community of St Mary the Virgin, Wantage, founded in 1848. Neale himself had established the Society of St Margaret in East Grinstead in 1855. Woodward's *Songs of Syon* and *Cowley Carol Book* are both associated with the Society of St John the Evangelist (the Cowley Fathers), founded in 1866. At the Community of the Resurrection, founded in Oxford in 1892, but established in Mirfield from 1898, the Revd Walter Howard Frere (1863–1938) was already the superior. He was a leading church and liturgical historian, and a fine plainsong scholar. He was closely associated with *Hymns Ancient & Modern* from 1894, not least with the pioneering but unpopular edition of 1904, and the monumental *Historical Edition* of 1909.

The other group to consider is the Plainsong and Mediaeval Music Society (PMMS), founded in 1888 to promote the study and practice of plainsong.[7] It also published. The most vigorous years of publishing were between 1890 and 1930, including three major publications edited by Frere: the facsimiles of the *Graduale Sarisburiense* (1892, 1894) and *Antiphonale Sarisburiense* (1901–24), and the catalogue of early liturgical musical sources, *Bibliotheca Musico-Liturgica* (1894, 1901). In addition to scholarly publications, PMMS brought out a series of practical editions of plainsong with English texts, the most important of which are *The Ordinary of the Mass* and *Plainsong Hymn-Melodies and Sequences*, both published in 1896.[8] The signatures of Frere, Palmer, Woodward and Arnold all appear in the PMMS council attendance book.[9] So too do those of Athelstan Riley (1858–1945) and William John Birkbeck (1859–1916), who were among the eight founder members of the society. Both were also on the editorial committee of EH, and Riley provided the preface to the 1904 edition of Woodward's *Songs of Syon*. They were wealthy landed gentry, close friends from their times at Eton and Oxford together, and leading establishment laymen in the Church of England, passionate in building connections with the

Orthodox churches. Birkbeck's London house was within half a mile of St Barnabas Pimlico; Riley's London residence was in Kensington.[10]

The vigour of two new parishes, four recently founded religious communities, and a society balanced between practice and scholarship provides a considerable foundation for the formation of a new hymn book. It is also founded on the experience of its editors, and their experience of inherited practice and available hymnal resources. Three specific phases can be distinguished: the mid nineteenth century, the end of the nineteenth century, and the years 1904–6.

Plainsong hymnody in English from 1851 to 1906

By far the most significant early source is *The Hymnal Noted*, first published in two parts, and in two editions. It was a landmark publication in British hymnody, and it continued to be reprinted and expanded, with a reprinting in 1895. It remained current in some churches right up to the publication of *The English Hymnal*, and the balance of its contents undoubtedly informed editorial decisions. In its original form it comprised 105 English translations of Latin texts (mostly hymns), and their plainsong melodies. There was an edition with the text set out beneath the melodies (1851 and 1856). The other edition (1852 and 1858), in larger format, included the full Latin texts of the hymns with their versified English translation on the left-hand side of each opening, and the plainsong melody with separate four-part organ accompaniment on the right-hand side. The music was edited by Thomas Helmore, and the text by John Mason Neale, who contributed 94 of the 105 translations.[11] Thomas Helmore was master of the children of the Chapel Royal, and vice-principal and precentor of St Mark's College, Chelsea. John Mason Neale, one of the founders of the Camden Society, was at that time warden of Sackville College, East Grinstead.

Part One (1–46) of *The Hymnal Noted* (HN) consists of hymns for Sunday (first Evensong, Compline, Matins, Lauds, Prime, Terce, Sext, None, second Evensong, and Compline), the temporal (Advent to Whitsun), the dedication festival, and the Common of Saints, ending with the seqence, 'Dies irae'. Part Two (HN47–104) is more varied and less systematic in content. There is a series of Sarum hymns for weekday morning and evening prayer (HN54–64), followed by four Christmas hymns from the Use of York (HN65–8). This part of the anthology includes texts and melodies from the Sarum Gradual, a Spanish Gradual, the Roman Antiphonal, as well as the seven Advent Antiphons. In Part One, seasonal melodies are provided for the hymns at the Little Hours: 10 for Terce, 12 for Sext, 12 for None, and 10 for Compline. These are drawn mostly from the Sarum repertory, but of five melodies for Prime, four are taken from Guidetti's *Directorium Chori* (1582). In Part Two, there is often an alternative melody, sometimes associated with another text which is identified in the attribution.

While the use of *The Hymnal Noted* continued, there were, however, significant new plainsong hymn publications in the last two decades of the nine-teenth century. In 1883 the London Gregorian Choral Association (founded in 1870, and now known as the Gregorian Association) published *Sarum Hymn Melodies taken from the ancient MSS and early printed books in the British Museum*. It was the precursor of the more authoritative (and far more attractively printed) *Plainsong Hymn-melodies and Sequences* (PHS), edited by W H Frere and first published by PMMS in 1896. Both volumes consist only of melodies, but each has a list of office hymns (by Latin first line) and a table of liturgical use.[12] In the liturgical table of *Sarum Hymn Melodies* there is a cross-referenced index to four hymnals: *The Hymnal Noted* (1851, 1856), *The People's Hymnal* (1867), *The Hymnary* (1870), and *Hymns Ancient & Modern* (1861).

What distinguishes the anthology of *Sarum Hymn Melodies* from *The Hymnal Noted* is its far stricter adherence to English, and predominantly Sarum, melodies. It is a part of the movement to establish the authentic roots of Englishness within the Church of England, a church that since the Reformation had lacked its own liturgical song for the people. The movement was enabled by the liturgical scholarship that burgeoned in England in the second half of the nineteenth century, and which resulted in the publication of critical editions of the Sarum Breviary, the Sarum Missal, books of the Uses of Hereford and York, and English monastic books.

G H Palmer was the anonymous editor of *Sarum Hymn Melodies*. *Sarum Hymn Melodies* is often bound up with a book of plainsong Introits for Holy Communion (1883) adapted to English texts, also prepared by Palmer. At this stage, without access to an edition of the Sarum Gradual or the Solesmes editions, Palmer was reliant on the Mechlin edition of the Roman chant (1831). His later series of liturgical plainsong books, printed by the Community of St Mary the Virgin, Wantage, was based principally on early English sources, with some use of Solesmes editions. *The Hymner* (texts only, 1891), also edited by Palmer, and printed privately in Cambridge, shows particular rigour in its compilation. This second edition (a first edition has not been traced in the main copyright libraries) is meticulous in its comprehensive provision for and specific allocation of office hymn texts. Unlike *The Hymnal Noted*, the hymn texts are almost all from the English mediaeval repertory. (There is a greater range of sources in the choice of sequence texts in *The Hymner*.)

The third phase, at the beginning of the twentieth century, is marked by the rapid appearance of four books in three years: the radical new edition of *Hymns Ancient & Modern* (1904: A&M), the first edition of *Songs of Syon* (1904: SS), a new edition of *The Hymner* (1904: TH), and finally *The English Hymnal* (1906: EH). All four books contain a significant anthology of hymns, liturgi-cally ordered and allocated, and intended primarily to be sung to plainsong melodies. All benefit from recent plainsong scholarship and both A&M and EH employ handsome plainsong notation in the Solesmes style.

The new edition of *The Hymner* (TH) was published by PMMS, and was intended to accompany the volume of *Plainsong Hymn-Melodies and Sequences*

(PHS). It was different in ordering,[13] and more precise in its scope than the 1891 edition, including only Sarum hymn texts (and excluding those from Hereford and York), and limiting the sequences to 16 and the processionals to six. The use of two separate books, one with words and one with music, addressed the problem of matching texts that used different melodies at different seasons, and melodies used for several different texts. (The combination of texts and melodies is discussed further below. These books addressed a problem faced by the editors of *The Hymnal Noted* (HN) who printed the same text as many as 10 or 12 times to different melodies: see above.)

The extent of the translated Latin liturgical texts with plainsong in each hymnal is indicative. Overall, there are 76 texts with plainsong in A&M (12% of the whole book), and 107 in SS (25% of the enlarged 1923 edition). EH is closer to SS in number, with 105 plainsong items, but only a little ahead of A&M in overall balance (16%). Thus, the two books intended for wider, general use have a similar balance of plainsong, while SS – intended as a more specialized supplement to other books – has a greater proportion. A&M and EH offer both accompaniments for all and alternative tunes for almost all of the texts with plainsong melodies, while SS offers few alternatives and no accompaniments.

Where EH diverges from both A&M and SS is in its use of translations of Latin texts and melodies taken from mediaeval English secular Uses. Taking PHS as the benchmark for comparison, the extent of English materials in the three books shown in the table below. English mediaeval sources supply two-thirds of the chanted items in A&M and about three-quarters of those in SS; but they account for well over 90% of those in EH.[14]

What relationship do these books have to HN? HN includes 73 items concordant with PHS, including 61 Sarum hymn texts and 7 from the Use of York, 3 Sarum sequences and 2 from York. Overall, 35 items are concordant with HN in EH, A&M and SS. All 35 also appear in PHS and TH. These are

English mediaeval hymns, processionals and sequences with plainsong melodies, included in EH, A&M and SS and compared with HN

		EH	A&M	SS	HN
Hymns	Sarum	82	46	71	61
	York	2	3	3	7
Processionals		3	1	1	
Sequences	Sarum	4		4	3
	York			1	2
		91	50	80	73

Sunday hymns, hymns for the Christian seasons, for the Common of the Saints, and for just one specific saint's day – St Michael and All Angels. Only one other hymn text is found in all the books except EH: the form of 'Aeterna Christi munera' for martyrs, a York hymn.

In all three books there is liturgical ordering according to the Calendar. This follows the broad pattern of the mediaeval hymnals: hymns for use week by week (diurnal), for the Christian year from Advent to Trinity (temporal), hymns used on a number of different saints' days (the common of saints), and hymns used on specific saints' days and feasts (the sanctoral). The only significant distinction is the placing of the feast of the dedication of a church: some place it at the end of the temporal, others at the end of the common.

Practically, by far the most meticulous and straightforward book to use is TH, both in the 1891 and the revised 1904 editions. The book leaves nothing to chance: every hymn is specified by day and service. Where the hymn to be used is set for several feast days, the text is cross-referenced. The least straightforward is HN. The melody edition and the accompaniments appeared in two volumes. The second volume complements, rather than continues the sequence of the first volume. Only in a words-only edition of HN are they presented in a coherent liturgical order (with a second sequence of numbering). The appendix in the second volume of accompaniments lays this out in two lists: one by diurnal, temporal, common and sanctoral; the other identifying the Latin source of each hymn in nineteenth-century editions.

The selection of texts to be sung to plainsong melodies gives some indication of the commitment to authentic English tradition in each book, a feature that is strongest in EH. As the table below shows, the balance of diurnal, temporal, common and sanctoral provides further evidence of the liturgical emphasis in each book. Each collection has its own distinctive internal features. However, in general terms, there is generous provision in the temporal and diurnal. Except in TH the sanctoral is more modest. The book which follows the general pattern least closely is A&M, with its relatively small

Distribution of texts with plainsong melodies in the hymnals

	HN	TH1891	TH1904	A&M	SS	EH
Diurnal	27	38	36	11	27	21
Temporal	48	46	37	41	36	35
Common	12	17	18	11	21	11
Sanctoral	14	40	33	5	16	19
Dedication etc	4	4	4	1	3	3
Processions		6	6	1	2	7
Other				6	2	9
	105	151	134	76	107	105

diurnal and sanctoral: clearly this was intended primarily as a book for Sundays and principal feasts.

The liturgical selection of the plainsong hymns in The English Hymnal

The formation of EH, and its relationship to other publications, are part of a complex history of liturgy, music and church politics. The preface of EH includes a substantial apology for the inclusion of the office hymns. 'The need has long been felt of such a complete set of these ancient hymns, which in their Scriptural simplicity and sober dignity represent the deep Christian experience of more than a thousand years.'[15] Dearmer is confident about their inclusion for Sundays and major holy days, but defensive about hymns for lesser feasts outside the Calendar of *The Book of Common Prayer*. Office hymns for these days are included, 'although we recognize the fact that as there is no Office for such days in the Prayer Book they can have no Office Hymn in the strict sense of the word'.[16] Nothing is said about the inclusion of processionals, sequences, or other plainsong items included at the end of the book.

The desire to provide a comprehensive collection had to be reconciled with the practicalities of a pattern of two (rather than eight) services of daily prayer. (See above, p. 163.) The repertory needed to be comprehensive for use on Sundays and holy days. It also provided for those cathedrals, colleges, communities and parish churches (especially urban churches) that maintained a pattern of daily sung prayer. While it was acknowledged that 'There is indeed no need for all the hymns of all the ancient services,'[17] the editors nevertheless included hymns for Prime, Terce, Sext, None and Compline. Such was also the case in HN, TH, SS, and A&M. They were ancient hymns, and usable on their own merits. However, there was already significant movement to revise *The Book of Common Prayer*, and the generous provision of hymns for the evening office of Compline anticipates the re-instatement of that service in the revised *Book of Common Prayer*, rejected by Parliament in 1927 and 1928.

The editors designated 74 items as office hymns, specifying their appropriate use at morning and evening prayer. While not specifying a distinction between first and second evensong, this is implicit in the ordering of the hymns themselves, and in the explanatory title (i.e. E. M. means Evensong on the eve and Mattins on the feast day itself; M. E. means Mattins and Evensong on the feast day). Two hymns from the mediaeval office for Corpus Christi (a feast firmly excluded from *The Book of Common Prayer*) appear in Part IV of the book, for use at Holy Communion. There are also nine hymns from the repertory of the Little Offices. In all, 85 of 112 hymn texts from the Use of Sarum listed in PHS appear in EH.[18] There is also the single text from the Use of York.

The 27 Sarum texts omitted from EH were excluded in a systematic way. There was no need for the weekday hymns for Latin Matins (6), feasts not represented in the Calendar (6), and feasts for which there was already adequate provision (3 for Matins, 5 for Lauds). The hymns sung on ordinary Sundays at Lauds throughout the year ('Aeterne rerum Conditor', and 'Ecce jam noctis') were excluded, in favour of those for Matins, reversing the selection pattern for ordinary weekdays. Also omitted were the hymn used at Lauds and second Vespers on All Saints' day, the hymns for saints' days in Eastertide (2),[19] and two seasonal hymns for Compline.

Translation of office hymn texts is a challenge, because of a series of conflicts and constraints. The translation has to be true to the original, and yet reflect contemporary language and thinking; it has to be lucid, and yet is restricted to the metre of the original and its melody; it has to be sufficiently strong to be worthy of use, and yet not so strong as to stand out in the reflective nature of the office and of plainsong, or pall with regular repetition. Not surprisingly, few office hymns stand out, and many have become dated. The editors of EH had to make some key decisions about adoption, revision or replacement of existing Latin translations. By comparison with the editors of A&M, they opted more often for replacement rather than revision in those cases where wholesale adoption was not possible.

All of the Latin hymns and sequences included in EH had appeared in G H Palmer's edition of TH in 1891. The overall quality of the translations in EH is markedly better. Of the 96 hymn and sequence texts included in EH, 38 had appeared in HN and TH, and a further 6 only in TH. Ten were substantially rewritten or centonized. The dominant translator is J M Neale: 30 of his texts (all from HN) were taken over intact or with only very minor revision, and four (three from HN) were substantially revised or elided with translations by other writers (e.g. Caswall in 'Pange lingua' (EH326), and 'Verbum supernum prodiens, nec Patris' (EH330)). Neale's translations therefore account for over one third of the texts for plainsong, and for 34 of the 44 texts taken over from the earlier plainsong hymn books.

The other 52 hymn and sequence texts included four 'established' translations: Edward Caswall (1814–79), 'Aurora jam spargit polum' (EH174); John Ellerton (1826–93), 'A solis ortus cardine' (EH21); Bishop Richard Mant 1776–1848), 'Exultet caelum laudibus' (EH176), and Father Benson (1824–1915), 'Jesu, Redemptor omnium' (EH189). The last three also appeared in A&M. Five other texts were in print, but recent: Robert Bridges' (1844–1930) translations of 'Primo dierum omnium', 'Splendor paternae gloriae' and 'Veni, creator Spiritus' (respectively EH50, 52, 154) were first published in his *Yattendon Hymnal* (1900); and 'Nox et tenebrae et nubila' and 'Lux ecce surgit aurea' (EH54, 55) were taken from R Martin Pope's translation of the hymns of Prudentius (published 1905). The remaining 43 translations were undertaken for EH – 23 by the editors and 20 by others at the editors' request.[20] Of the editors, Birkbeck and Riley each contributed two, but the majority were by T A Lacey (1853–1931) (10) and Dearmer (9). Of the others who wrote specially for the hymnal Laurence Housman (1865–1959) contributed 8; the remaining 12 were shared between Maurice

Bell (3), Charles Bigg (1840–1908) (2), Gabriel Gillett (1873–1948) (3) and R Ellis Roberts (4).

Proportionately the largest provision of new translations is in the sanctoral (14, a section where Neale had made significantly fewer translations). However, the largest number of new office hymns overall is in the temporal (16), and there are significant numbers of new texts in the diurnal (9) and the common (7). The processionals are new, as is just one sequence: the other eight are adopted (with revisions).

Perhaps none of the new texts can match the strength and durability of Neale's translations of 'Urbs beata Jerusalem' and 'Angularis fundamentum' ('Blessed city' and 'Christ is made the sure foundation'). Those of T A Lacey seem more dependent on existing translations, often borrowing complete lines unchanged; those of R Ellis Roberts seem most mannered. Dearmer's stand out for their directness and immediacy, and Housman's for their technical accomplishment. Seventeen of the 43 new translations are of metres other than LM, including all the Sapphic metres in the book. It is in these that both Dearmer and Housman demonstrate their control of metre and language, meaning and image. Dearmer's versions of 'Nocte surgentes' and 'O Pater sancte' are both strong. Housman is at his best in 8.7.8.7.8.7, and the group of four hymns for the Visitation of the Blessed Virgin Mary and St Mary Magdalen are particularly notable.

One measure of the success of the new translations for NEH is their survival into *The New English Hymnal* (1986: NEH). Of the 55 texts translated from Latin and set to plainsong in NEH, 44 were taken over from EH and 11 were replaced (mostly by editorial compilations). As the table below shows, Neale remains dominant, but most revised.[21] Of the new translations in EH, those by Dearmer find greatest favour. Surprisingly, perhaps, those by the

Texts for plainsong in NEH carried over from EH

	Preserved	Revised	Replaced	Total
Bigg	1		1	2
Dearmer	6	1		7
Gillett	1			*1*
Housman	2		3	5
Lacey	3	1	2	6
Riley	2			2
Roberts			2	2
Yattendon			2	*2*
Neale	9	8		*17*
Other (old)	9	1	1	*11*
	33	**11**	**11**	**55**

poets Laurence Housman and Robert Bridges fared least well. (The texts in NEH that replaced their work may be more accessible, but are less technically competent, as discussed further below.)

W J Birkbeck and the plainsong melodies in The English Hymnal

The liturgical pattern of EH being established, and the translations settled, the remaining tasks were the selection of plainsong melodies and the provision of accompaniments. So far as the melodies were concerned this was a straightforward matter: the allocation of melodies was established according to the customs of the Use of Sarum, and reliable edited texts were already available. It is, perhaps, less surprising that the editors entrusted an 'amateur', W J Birkbeck, to undertake this task. Birkbeck's fame rests on his extensive contacts with Russia, and especially with the Russian Orthodox Church. Apart from his own passion for unity with the Orthodox Church, he was both envoy and ambassador for the Church of England on many of his visits.[22] Clearly his private income enabled him to follow his interests: his entry in the 1901 Census reads 'Occupation: none'.

Palmer or Woodward would have been stronger candidates to be plainsong editor, and both had been part of the group planning a new hymnal. Now each had his own commitments to publishing projects: Palmer to the new edition of *The Hymner*, as well as other plainsong publications, and Woodward to *Songs of Syon*. Frere, the obvious other candidate, was already deeply involved with A&M, notably the unpopular new edition to which EH was a reaction. Within the circles of St Barnabas Pimlico and the Plainsong and Mediaeval Music Society, Birkbeck may have been a natural choice, and he may have been put forward by his long-standing friend, Athelstan Riley, the chairman of the editorial board of EH.

As already noted, both were founder members of the Plainsong and Mediaeval Music Society. Riley subsequently published a competent (if opinionated) study of hymn tunes and sequences,[23] and Birkbeck had undertaken substantial studies of both plainsong and the organ after leaving Oxford. His wife's memoir records that 'in London he worked at the Royal College of Music, and had organ lessons with Sir Walter Parratt. Also for five years, from 1883 to 1888, he devoted himself to the study of plainsong, visiting Maredsous, a monastery in Belgium, and learning much from his friends the monks there, going also to Solesmes in France, the chief centres of continental study on the subject, and many other places.'[24]

Parratt was organist of Magdalen College, Oxford (1872–82) during Birkbeck's undergraduate years at the college (1877–81). Subsequently organist of St George's, Windsor, Parratt became the first head of organ studies at the Royal College of Music, which opened in 1883. Bishop & Son, the organ builders, apparently built a four-manual house organ for Birkbeck's London residence in 1883, incorporating stops from an earlier bureau organ by Snetzler (1760).[25]

Birkbeck's country home was in Norfolk. Following the death of his father in 1897, the family moved to Thorpe St Andrew (the place of his birth) and then to Stratton Strawless Hall in 1900.[26] Here there was a chapel in the house, at which the Bishop of Norwich assisted 'at our sung Mass' on 2 February 1903 (the feast of the Presentation).[27] Later that year, the American bishop Charles Grafton reported 'Mr. B. says for the family morning prayer, the young people singing an antiphon to the Benedictus, Mr. B. playing on the organ, and I celebrated daily.'[28]

Birkbeck had musical credentials, but he also had support. In the section of the preface that he wrote on the plainsong melodies, he concluded by expressing his 'obligations to Mr. W Phillips Mus. Doc. (Oxon.), organist of St Barnabas, Pimlico, for having harmonized nearly half of the plainsong melodies for which I was responsible, and also to Sir Walter Parratt for his constant help and advice throughout the whole undertaking'.[29] In the equivalent preface in EH2, J H Arnold (who had responsibility for the revision of the plainsong), expanded further: there was also 'Dr. G H Palmer, in close collaboration with whom Mr. Birkbeck carried out his work'.[30] Birkbeck was indebted to past and present musicians at St Barnabas Pimlico, as well as to his old organ teacher.

Birkbeck's task was straightforward. In most cases there was no choice about which melody to use. In all, 47 of the 67 melodies included in PHS were selected for use in EH. However, the version given in EH is not always concordant with PHS. As Frere pointed out in the preface to PHS: 'The MSS by no means shew ... uniformity of musical text ...'[31] Birkbeck describes editorial decisions regarding the readings, suppressing both quilisma and liquescent notes, though acknowledging that these could have been included in the Solesmes-style notation employed. (In the cruder form of plainsong typography before this time, they could not have been reproduced.) Where there are variants, Birkbeck's reading most often follows that of SHM (1883) – probably the edition with which he had been most familiar in his years of study in London. This is certainly the case with minor variants in the melodies associated with 'Annue Christe saeculorum Domine' (EH174), 'Iste confessor' (EH188), and 'Quem terra pontus aethera' (EH214). It is evident in the choice of melody for 'Hostis Herodes impii' (EH38) which follows SHM rather than PHS, and especially with 'Ave maris stella' (EH213) where the form of the melody is significantly different in the two books. Birkbeck does introduce a lengthening in the third line of the melody (not included in SHM), and here – as elsewhere – the notation of the neums is more sophisticated than the crude printing of SHM. The decision to prefer the readings of SHM to PHS is significant, for the 1904 edition of Palmer's *The Hymner* was both published by the Plainsong and Mediaeval Music Society, and – as Palmer specifically points out in a note to the preface – intended for use with the melodies of PHS.

The choice of melody for the feast of the Transfiguration differs from all the other printed books which include it: for 'Caelestis formam gloriae' (EH233) Birkbeck selects the melody associated with 'Veni redemptor gentium' (EH14), rather than the other Christmas melody allocated to the Transfiguration hymn in all the other books and lists of the time (that for 'Christe redemptor omnium', EH18). This may, perhaps, be a personal preference, since it is one of the finest of the Sarum melodies, and one which he uses for six hymns in all. Certainly, the link between the Incarnation and the Transfiguration is retained. That richness of theological association through the association of melodies with different texts (and vice versa), a key feature of the original pattern linking the mediaeval hymn texts and melodies, is mostly lost. For instance, the 'Pentecost' melody of 'Veni, creator Spiritus' (EH151) is one most often used for the Compline hymn, 'Salvator mundi Domine' ('O saviour of the world, we pray'), especially at Christmas but at many of the great feasts – thus linking the gift of the Son and the gift of the Spirit. The text of 'Veni, creator Spiritus' was sung daily at Terce, generally just before the main mass of the day; hence the convention that persists in some places of singing it as part of the preparation for the Eucharist.[32]

For the other items, not included in SMH or PHS, Birkbeck looked elsewhere. In the preface to EH he identifies the editions that were the source of the melodies of three of the sequences – two from the new Solesmes editions ('Veni, sancte Spiritus', EH155, and 'Dies irae', EH351) and one from the Ghent Gradual ('Lauda Sion salvatorem', EH317). Three other pieces came from the Sarum Gradual. About the other plainsongs he is imprecise, though from J H Arnold, we know that Palmer provided the editions of the Reproaches and 'Crux fidelis' (both EH737), in addition to his general support to Birkbeck already noted.[33]

Birkbeck's most substantial task was to provide the plainsong accompaniments, of which half were provided by the organist of St Barnabas Pimlico, Dr Phillips. They are very close in style and notation to those printed in HN 50 years before. The texture is four-part, the notation is principally in minims (like a conventional hymn tune of the time), and for some melismata the treble notes are joined by a beam. The impression is one of a heavy and dense accompaniment, and it is an indication of contemporary practice, even in an avant-garde hymn book. In spite of Birkbeck's encouragement in the preface to sing the chant with flexibility, it is hard to imagine that this was achievable. (A comparable style is found in A&M.) The affinity of the EH plainsong melodies with SHM rather than PHS, and the continuation of HN style in the accompaniments, suggests that, unlike other parts of the book, Birkbeck's editing was conservative, and based on his experience of plainsong at St Barnabas Pimlico in the 1880s.

With the growing influence of Solesmes, plainsong singing and accompaniment were transformed in the 20 years after the appearance of the 1933 edition. Not surprisingly, not one of the plainsong accompaniments in the first edition survived in the 1933 edition. The change is already apparent in the two books that appeared under the editorship of Dearmer and Vaughan Williams: *Songs of Praise* and *The Oxford Book of Carols*.

Other plainsongs and the French ecclesiastical melodies

Before turning to the plainsong contents of the later books, a further group of hymns merits special consideration. These are set to melodies that are modal. Some are plainsong, or related to it; but none reaches the standard of authenticity that allows them to be presented in plainsong notation in EH. However, they serve important purposes in the overall scheme of the book.

The success of EH was based upon its clear aesthetic, its quality, and its realism. It avoided the alienation caused by the 1904 edition of A&M, partly because it was new, but also because it took care to appeal to a broader constituency than many of its High Church predecessors. Unlike HN and TH (but as in A&M), the editors distributed the plainsong hymns throughout the liturgical parts of the book; and with very few exceptions, they offered alternative harmonized tunes to the plainsong melodies. Pragmatically, they included popular hymns that were acceptable, if not always of the quality they sought. As Athelstan Riley reflected, '*The English Hymnal*, with all its scholarship and musical excellence, contains at least fifty tunes, and, in my judgement, more than one hundred hymns, which are unworthy of the rest, but which must be included in any Church hymn-book if it is seriously intended to provide for the necessities of the day.'[34]

Notwithstanding the vigorous objections to specific texts discussed by Donald Gray in the opening chapter, the liturgical presentation of the office hymns is very careful with regard to both Corpus Christi and the feasts of the Blessed Virgin Mary. The editors avoided the issue of the observance of Corpus Christi (identified as such in TH, and in the tables of SHM and PHS) by placing the office hymns for that feast in Part IV: Holy Communion. Similar sensitivity was shown in the treatment of hymns for the feasts of the Blessed Virgin Mary: the Purification and the Annunciation are listed thus without reference to the BVM; the feasts of the Conception and Assumption are omitted; her Nativity (8 September) is only identified implicitly in the listing of Hymns for Sundays and Holy Days – St Mary (more daringly St Mary the Virgin in EH2) being placed immediately before Michaelmas (29 September).

For those with a love of the 'older' plainsong melodies, some of the forms of the Roman chant from the Mechlin editions were retained, including 'Pange lingua' (EH330), 'Veni, creator Spiritus' (EH154), and 'Verbum supernum prodiens' (EH2),[35] as well as 'Aeterna Christi munera' from Guidetti's *Directorium Chori* (1582).[36] 'Adoro te, devote' (EH331) and 'Ave verum corpus' (EH311) come from French diocesan plainsong sources of the seventeenth and eighteenth centuries.[37] They are distinguished from 'authentic' plainsong by the use of modern notation throughout. Three other 'late' chants are given in neums: the sequence 'Sponsa Christi' (EH253; Paris

Gradual, 1666), the Advent prose 'Rorate coeli' (EH735; *Officia Propria*, Paris, 1673), and the Lent prose 'Attende Domine' (EH736; Paris Processional, 1824).

Some of the other melodies found in HN were treated in other ways, and augmented by new materials from the later seventeenth- and eighteenth-century French *paroisses* – anthologies of plainsong-derived and pseudo-plainsong melodies intended for parish use in the French dioceses. These clearly caught Vaughan Williams' imagination. Taking advantage of their melodic and implicit rhythmic character, he transformed many of them into some of the strongest tunes for the unison, congregational singing that he promulgated in the music preface. Some of these diocesan melodies had appeared in the 1808 edition of La Feillée's *Méthode du plain-chant*, and were used by Helmore in HN. However, Vaughan Williams acknowledges his principal debt to J B Croft 'who has kindly placed his great knowledge and experience of French ecclesiastical melodies at his service'.[38] Athelstan Riley implies that Croft may have pressed his case hard: 'These [melodies] have been persistently brought to the notice of English choirs by the Rev. J B Croft, priest-organist of St Matthew's, Westminster . . .'[39] Although English translations of the hymn texts from the French diocesan collections had been made much earlier by Isaac Williams (1832–7), John Chandler (1837, 1841), and W J Blew (1852), most of the melodies appeared for the first time in EH.[40]

The ascriptions are general, and mostly undated, suggesting that the original sources were not directly available to the editors. It seems that Croft's versions came from nineteenth-century editions, by which time the melodies from some diocesan collections had spread to several other dioceses.[41] Cyril Pocknee's (1906–79) short study traces six of the melodies as far back as the Paris Antiphoner of 1681; the other 14 melodies come from a total of nine other sources, dating from 1689 to 1784.[42] In some cases Vaughan Williams made use of the later version of the tune transmitted by La Feillée (e.g. EH174, 465); in other cases he was evidently unaware of the earlier, datable sources.[43]

In the original books, the French church melodies are printed without accompaniment in notation typical of plainsong at that time, with just two forms of neum: *virga* (a square with a downward stem) and *punctum* (either a square or a diamond shape). In EH these melodies are treated in two ways. LM tunes are set in triple time, feeling towards one in a bar; those in Sapphic metre (and some other metres) are set firmly with two minims to the bar. The melodic effect is always robust, and the music is driven forward by Vaughan Williams' strong harmonies and earthy keyboard textures: there is no place for politeness here. The chords follow hand shapes boldly, sometimes regardless of internal voice leading.

The transformation effected by Vaughan Williams can be observed by comparing his version of *Annue Christe* with that of Helmore. The text of 'Annue Christe' (EH174) from the common of apostles is in a rare metre (12.12.12.12), used only for one other hymn for the feast of St Peter and St

Paul, 'Aurea luce' (EH226). With no available modern tune, the melody printed in La Feillée's handbook is therefore the means of providing an alternative to the authentic plainsong as a second tune. The same is true of hymns in Sapphic metre, a metre rarely used in vernacular hymnody except translations from Latin. In the absence of English tunes, and only a very small number of German chorales, the French diocesan melodies therefore offer the only alternative to new composition. Their modal nature and contours make them particularly suitable for use with texts based on mediaeval Latin. Six Sapphic melodies are used as alternative tunes to seven plainsong hymns.[44] A further two melodies are used for three other hymns without plainsong, of which one is the very powerful Rouen melody *Iste confessor*.[45]

Eleven of the French melodies are in LM. All serve as alternatives to plainsong. In some cases it is possible to discern the contour of the authentic plainsong melody. Such is the case with the melody for 'Lucis creator' (EH51). By contrast, the Grenoble melody for 'Deus tuorum militum' (EH181) sweeps up an opening arpeggio, and on to the third above. The contour of the arpeggio shapes the whole melody. (The same is true, though in a less strident manner, in the Sapphic *Christe sanctorum* from Rouen, EH165.)

There are the established melodies of *Veni, Emmanuel* and *O filii et filiae*, both of French origin, also the melody found in the mediaeval Latin liturgical dramas from Beauvais: the Prose of the Ass (*Orientis partibus*, EH129, 480). The borderline between church and popular melody is sometimes hard to discern. The wonderful melody of *Picardy*, for ever associated with the majestic and mysterious words from the Orthodox Liturgy of St James, 'Let all mortal flesh keep silence' (EH318) is a French Noel, while the jaunty melody of 'Daily, daily' (EH568) is identified as *paroissien*.

In the less liturgical context of *Songs of Praise*, the French church melodies are rather more comfortable with their surroundings than the less numerous plainsong melodies (for which six serve as alternative). Twelve melodies occur, eleven of which had appeared in EH. There is one new example, *O amor quam ecstaticus* (SP607), cautiously identified as French, and set by Basil Harwood (1859–1949). With the same caution, it made its way into EH2, replacing the rather four-square melody taken from La Feillée (*St Ambrose*) as the alternative tune to complement the plainsong melody of 'Quem terra pontus aetherea' (EH214).

Songs of Praise

The first edition of *Songs of Praise* (1925: SP1) contained just eight plainsong hymns, one of which is treated in two parts, and this small anthology forms a liturgical microcosm: three hymns for the diurnal (one for morning, in two parts with separate melodies, and two for evening), and five for the temporal (one each for Passiontide, Easter, Pentecost, Trinity and Dedication). That for Pentecost is the sequence, 'Veni, sancte Spiritus'. In the enlarged version of *Songs of Praise* (1931: SP2), five further plainsongs were included: one morning, one Passiontide, one processional, and two versions of 'Jesu, dulcis memoria' (as hymn and sequence).

In the first edition, all the texts correspond with EH, as do all but two of the melodies. The weekday evening melody is used for the first part of 'Splendor Patris', but the traditional morning melody is provided for part two (SP1 21; SP2 33).[46] The melody of the Advent hymn, 'Conditor alme siderum', is used for the evening hymn 'O lux, beata Trinitas' (SP1 35; SP2 51) – no doubt a pragmatic decision, given the complexity of the authentic melody (see EH164). Of the texts, one is a conflation (SP1, 105; SP2 190; EH169–70).

The five additions in 1931 include two texts not found in EH: a new version of 'Pange lingua' (SP2 129) – a conflation of 'Pange lingua' and 'Lustra sex'; and the second form of 'Jesu, dulcis memoria' (SP2 549), a translation by Roy Palmer first published in 1859. The version of the processional 'Salve, festa dies' is part conflation, and part newly written. The melodies of all five are those traditionally associated with the Latin texts. One text is replaced: the 1670 translation of 'Vexilla regis prodeunt' displaces that by J M Neale (SP2 130; cf EH94). One is amended and shortened in the enlarged edition (SP2 148; EH124), and another omits the doxology (SP2 44, EH49).

All the hymns follow the Sarum melodies as given in EH, though that of 'Salve, festa dies' follows the slightly altered version of EH2 (cf. SP2 389; EH/EH2 624). The main differences are in the notation and in the accompaniments. None of the melodies is printed in neums: the melodies are all printed at the top of a short score, mostly in separately stemmed quavers. J H Arnold wrote all the accompaniments in the first edition, and three of

---

Comparative numberings of the two editions of *Songs of Praise* and of *The English Hymnal*

SP1	SP2	EH	Latin original text	Metre
29	44	49	Deus creator omnium	LM
21	33	52	Splendor paternae gloriae	LM
21	33	52	Mentem gubernet et regat	LM
85	130	94	Vexilla regis prodeunt	LM
	129	95	Pange lingua ... Certaminis	878787
92	148	124	Sermone blande	LM
101	180	156	Veni sancte Spiritus	*sequence*
103	186	160	O Pater sancte	Sapphic
35	51	164	O lux beata Trinitas	LM
	28	165	Nocte surgentes	Sapphic
105	190	169	Urbs beata	878787
	548	238	Jesu, dulcis memoria	*sequence*
	549	238	Jesu, dulcis memoria	LM
	389	624	Salve festa dies	irreg

the five in the enlarged edition. They provide the first examples of his published hymn accompaniments. The remaining two accompaniments in the enlarged edition are by Martin Shaw. All the accompaniments are markedly different from those of EH. The influence of the Solesmes school of accompaniment is pervasive, and the style prefigures the new versions of the plain song accompaniments in EH2. Arnold used the three accompaniments he contributed to the 1931 edition of SP2 in EH2 (SP2 348, 548, 549; EH2 624, 238, 17), but revised the others. In the original edition of EH the accompaniment was consistently four-part in texture, mostly with a change of chord for each change of note. This new style is far freer. The texture moves flexibly from two to four parts, as required, and the chord changes are far slower and freer. Furthermore, in the first edition only, there is an alternative accompaniment, written entirely in the treble clef, and 'useful for verses allotted to boys or women, or to chanters'.[47] These were abandoned in the enlarged edition, except for the chanters' verses of 'Salve, festa dies' where a second alternative was added in EH2 624.

The Oxford Book of Carols

There is just one plainsong item in *The Oxford Book of Carols* (1928): the processional 'Qui creavit caelum', the only plainsong item in Dearmer's books to be given in Latin, and without translation. It is taken over from John Wickham Legg's edition of the Processional of the Nuns of Chester.[48] The music is presented in modern notation, rather than neums, and J H Arnold provided an accompaniment in the style characteristic of Solesmes. The last two notes of each phrase of the melody have extended values, another feature of Solesmes style.

The English Hymnal (*1933 edition*)

By the time the second edition of *The English Hymnal* appeared in 1933 (EH2), the new style of singing and accompanying plainsong was well established. It is readily evident in *A Plainsong Hymn Book* (1932: PHB), a book published by the proprietors of *Hymns Ancient & Modern*, recovering some of the ground lost after the 1916 edition of *Hymns Ancient & Modern* had returned to its pre-1904 content, style and balance. Under the editorship of Sydney Nicholson (1875–1947) (and the watchful eye of Frere, no doubt), PHB included 165 items. About 20 musicians contributed to the accompaniments, including Martin and Geoffrey Shaw, J H Arnold, E T Cooke, W S Vale, Percy Buck, H C Colles, the young John Dykes Bower and Gerald Knight, and Nicholson himself.[49] The new culture of plainsong singing and accompaniment – inspired by Solesmes and made English in certain leading parish churches in London and other urban centres, and one or two cathedrals – was flourishing. J H Arnold's accompaniments in EH2 set a new standard, one that was widely adopted and has remained the principal model in Anglican plainsong accompaniment to the present day. The accompaniments and the advice in the preface indicate the changes in the style of singing the chant – more lightly, flexibly, and (implicitly) with choir rather than with congregation.

In preparing EH2, the texts remained unchanged. There were 125 changes in the music for those texts, all helpfully listed.[50] For the most part, the plain-song melodies were unchanged. In 14 hymns minor matters of pitch (e.g. EH2 123 and 214 are pitched in their normal modal range), grouping of neums (e.g. one instance in the third line of EH2 67), and accidentals (e.g. 'Christe, sanctorum decus angelorum', EH2 242) are corrected or annotated. More noticeable is the re-instatement of the normative melody for the Transfiguration hymn (EH2 233), and of the form of the melody of 'Ave maris stella' found in PHS (PHS 64, EH2 213 – the previous melody retained as an alternative). In all of these instances EH2 follows the readings of PHS instead of SHM.

An expanded edition of PHS had appeared in 1920. From this and other sources, Arnold selected new melodies for nine hymns, originally found in the *Antiphonale Romanum* (EH2 237), the mediaeval hymnals of Barking (EH2 229), Guisborough (EH2 56, 57), Hereford (EH2 180) and York (EH2 249), and one possibly of Sarum provenance (EH2 61, 62). A different Sarum melody was selected for 'Virginis proles' (EH191). Palmer's editions of the Reproaches, 'Crux fidelis' and 'In manus tuas' replaced those in EH (EH2 737, 740), and the elaborate chant of 'Haec dies' (properly used instead of an office hymn in Easter week) was omitted.

The introduction of new melodies increased the overall range in EH2. It also diluted the integrity of the original scheme, based on the mediaeval association of the texts and melodies of the Use of Sarum. By the 1930s, with aspirations for higher standards of singing in the wake of the report of the Archbishops' Commission on Music (1922) and the establishment of the School of English Church Music (1927; renamed The Royal School of Church Music in 1945), choirs in major churches became increasingly skilled. Plainsong was becoming something to be heard rather than shared. With the gradual decline of morning prayer and of a body of clergy and laity to sing the weekday offices, more of the book became redundant. Some of the central liturgical and pastoral princi-ples that underpinned the first edition of EH were under threat.

The New English Hymnal

The New English Hymnal (1986: NEH) is a practical and urbane product of its time. It was compiled at a time when morning prayer even on Sundays and in colleges and cathedrals had become a rarity, when both morning and evening prayer had been displaced by the parish Eucharist in most churches inclined to use EH and EH2, and when the Eucharist displaced the singing of evensong on holy days. The cycle of hymns for the office in EH and EH2 could claim no substantial place, liturgically or pastorally, in NEH.

On first acquaintance, NEH gives the impression of being a less 'liturgical' hymn book than its predecessor. The texts of the propers for Holy

Communion (EH657–753) are omitted. However, a comparison of items with music reveals that NEH is numerically more 'liturgical': of 665 items with music in EH, 362 (54%) have a liturgical placement; of 541 items with music in NEH, 346 (64%) have a liturgical placement (as shown in the table below).

The liturgical contents of each book can be grouped into six sections typical of mediaeval liturgy: temporal, diurnal, common of saints, proper of saints, dedication and processions. To these may be added hymns for Holy Communion and other liturgical items with music.

Comparisons of EH and NEH

Overall contents of each section of the two books

	EH		NEH		Variance
Temporal	146	40%	142	41%	−4
Diurnal	51	14%	36	10%	−15
Dedication	5	1%	9	3%	4
Common of Saints	31	9%	19	5%	−12
Proper of Saints	49	14%	51	15%	2
Communion	36	10%	48	14%	12
Processions	34	9%	0		−34
Other liturgical items	10	3%	41	12%	31
Total	**362**		**346**		**−16**

Plainsong items as a proportion of the overall contents of each section

	EH			NEH			Variance
	Total	Plainsong		Total	Plainsong		
Temporal	146	32	22%	142	18	12.7%	−14
Diurnal	51	21	41%	36	7	19.4%	−14
Dedication	5	3	60%	9	1	11.1%	−2
Common of Saints	31	11	35%	19	7	36.8%	−4
Proper of Saints	49	19	39%	51	12	23.5%	−7
Communion	36	3	8%	48	5	10.4%	2
Processions	34	7	21%	0			−7
Other liturgical items	10	9	90%	41	19	46.3%	10
Total	**362**	**105**	**29%**	**346**	**69**	**19.9%**	**−36**

The proportionate size of each section differs in the two books, as can be seen in the table. In NEH the notable differences are the omission of a processional section, and the expansion of the liturgical section. Some of the processional hymns are included in other sections of NEH. For instance, 'All glory, laud and honour' for Palm Sunday appears in the liturgical section of NEH, 'Hail thee, festival day' for Easter and Ascension appears (in a conflated form) in the Temporal section, and 'For all the saints' for All Saints is found in the proper of the saints.

Two factors account for the size of the liturgical section in NEH. First, it includes the selection of 13 responsorial psalms first published in *English Praise* (EP), and two settings of music for Holy Communion. Second, seven sequences included in the main body of EH are placed here in NEH. As in EH, NEH makes provision for other chants in this section. Five of those which appeared in EH are transferred. Additional provision is made for the Presentation of Christ in the Temple, Palm Sunday, Maundy Thursday, and the Easter Vigil. Furthermore, the Advent Antiphons, printed without music in EH, are set out with the chant in full and with the accompanying plainsong Magnificat.

Given the predominance of Holy Communion as the principal Sunday service in the Church of England in the last quarter of the twentieth century, it is not surprising to find that there is greater provision of hymns intended for the Eucharist in NEH. The temporal is also well provided for. More notable is the larger provision for the proper of the saints. NEH includes hymns for 34 saints' days, compared with 25 in EH. Three saints' days in Christmas week, traditionally included in the temporal, are placed in the Proper of the Saints in NEH.

Two categories of liturgical hymns are significantly smaller in NEH: the diurnal and the common of the saints. The change in the common of the saints is one of scale rather than comprehensiveness. The principal losses in the diurnal are the hymns for morning and evening prayer on weekdays, and the little day offices. These represent the core of the mediaeval hymnal; the hymns sung most frequently, day by day. Herein lies the real distinction between EH and NEH: EH provided hymnody for the daily sung office; NEH is a book for Sundays and greater feasts. In this respect NEH is, like the Latin *Liber Usualis*, 'a useful book', in comparison with the Latin Antiphonal and Gradual, which are 'books of liturgical Use'. Overall, NEH is far less liturgical than its predecessor.

There are further liturgical distinctions. In contrast with EH, there is generally no designation in the temporal, sanctoral or common hymns of NEH for specific use at morning or evening prayer, or on the eve rather than the feast day. There are also some new allocations of office hymns in the diurnal. 'O lux, beata Trinitas', traditionally sung at first evensong of Sunday in the period between Trinity and Advent (i.e. on Saturday evening), is now set for Sunday evening between Epiphany and Lent. 'Lucis creator optime', traditionally sung on Sunday evening between Epiphany and Lent and Trinity and Advent, is designated only for the period between Trinity and Advent. 'Deus, creator omnium', sung at first evensong on Sunday (i.e. Saturday evening) between Epiphany and Lent, is now the sole hymn provided for weekday evenings. (The hymn for Prime, 'Iam lucis orto sidere', is the only hymn provided for weekday mornings.) There is pragmatism in these allocations: accepting that only a small number of places sing morning or evening prayer except on Sunday, core texts are at least sustained in the repertory of NEH, though not always in their traditional position.

NEH is a conflation of two books, EH and EP, which together contain a total of 785 items with music. In reducing this total to 541 items, it is remarkable that so much of the ancient repertory of hymns is included in NEH. Even more surprising, in the climate of the 1980s, is the inclusion of plainsong settings for 69 texts (20% of the texts in the book). This compares with 105 items with plainsong in the first edition of EH (29% of the texts). Nevertheless, 38 office hymns and four processional items found in EH are omitted from NEH: that represents a loss of 40% of the plainsong; a significantly larger proportion than the 'slightly reduced' number of plainsong melodies claimed by the editors of NEH.

The selection of the plainsong melodies demonstrates a change in criteria as well as quantity. The editors state that the plainsong 'melodies of the office hymns … were taken from MS versions of the Sarum Antiphoner'. Of the 67 Sarum hymn melodies compiled in the first edition of *Plainsong Hymn-Melodies and Sequences*, 28 (42%) are included in NEH. This compares with 47 Sarum melodies (70%) in EH. One melody introduced into EH2 by J H Arnold (EH2 61, 62, origin uncertain, but thought to be Sarum) is also used. For 'Veni, creator Spiritus' (NEH138; EH2 154) and the two versions of 'Verbum supernum prodiens' (NEH2 269; EH2 330) the Sarum melodies are omitted, and the nineteenth-century form of the Roman chant (Mechlin edition, 1835) alone is retained. (The Sarum melody for 'Veni, creator' appears at NEH136.)

Seven plainsong hymn melodies are new to NEH. Roman melodies are introduced for 'Ut queant laxis' (NEH168, also NEH222) and 'Aeterna Christi munera' (NEH213). The latter is found in *A Plainsong Hymn Book* (1932, the companion volume to *Hymns Ancient & Modern*, edited by Nicholson, PHB87), as are the remaining four melodies newly introduced: 'Aurora lucis rutilat' (NEH100; PHB53ii), 'Jesu, nostra redemptio' (NEH153, 196; PHB62ii), 'Te laeta mundi' (NEH154; PHB33), 'Jesu, dulcedo carminum' (NEH214, 221, 292; PHB137). In the case of the last example, both melody and text of NEH292 ('Jesu, thou joy of loving hearts') are taken from PHB137.[51]

In ten of the office hymns transferred from EH the allocated plainsong melody is different in NEH. For the most part, melodies allocated to another hymn of the same season or feast in EH is used. Thus, the Pentecost hymn 'Beata nobis gaudia' (NEH136; EH151) is allocated the Pentecost melody for Terce (the well-known 'Veni, creator Spiritus', EH154); the Lenten hymn

'Audi, benigne conditor' (NEH60; EH66) has the melody of 'Ex more docti mystico' (EH65); and the Marian hymn 'Quem terra, pontus' (NEH181; EH214) is set to the more widely used melody of 'Veni, redemptor gentium' (NEH19; EH14), a melody used for five hymns in all in EH. In one case, the hymn 'O Maria, non flere' for St Mary Magdalen (NEH174, EH231), the editors of NEH follow the allocation of melody preferred by PHS. There are only two real surprises: the evening hymn 'Deus, creator omnium' (NEH152, EH49) is set to a melody strongly associated with weekday mornings (EH52–6, *passim*); and the melody for weekday evenings (EH58–62, *passim*) is used for the martyr's hymn 'Martyr dei, qui unicum' (NEH217; EH180). Evidently this offered the editors the only means of including these well-established tunes, notwithstanding the very different earlier associations of words and melodies.[52]

One melody ('O Pater sancte', NEH144; EH160) is applied to an office hymn new to NEH: the hymn for St Joseph's day 'Lord, hear the praises of thy faithful people' (NEH160). This is one of a number of texts compiled by the editors, and has echoes of the Latin hymn 'Caelitum, Joseph' (*Liber Hymnarius*, p.358). Like the Latin hymn, it is in Sapphic metre. Throughout NEH, the musical editors treat this metre as 11.11.11.5, and omit the customary caesura that divides the first three lines as 5+6 (though it is observed in the cadences of the accompaniments). This practice follows *A Plainsong Hymn Book*, rather than either EH or PHS or the Solesmes editions; indeed, the Solesmes editions include lengthenings that further emphasize the caesura. In 'Lord, hear the praises' the text carefully maintains the caesura; but this is not always the case in NEH. Of the other seven hymns in Sapphic metre, four have texts by the editors (NEH156, 168, 220, 222). All four have origins in the Latin, and none is so careful about the treatment of the caesura as earlier translations and adaptations. In two cases this causes problems. The adaptation of 'Quod chorus vatum', which replaces Lacey's translation (EH208), has a problematic third verse:

In God's high temple, | Simeon the righteous
Takes to his loving | arms with holy rapture
That one for whom his | longing eyes had waited
Jesus, Messiah.

The second line of 'As we remember, Lord, thy faithful handmaid' (NEH222, based on 'Virginis proles') is even more unfortunate:

As we remember, | Lord, thy faithful handmaid,
Who on this this day at-|tained the heavenly mansions,

These metrical infelicities highlight the tensions evidently felt by the editors in dealing with the old Latin hymns. On the one hand, there was evidently the wish to sustain the ideal of EH in maintaining the continuity of ancient hymnody; on the other hand, the original texts were often obscure and archaic in imagery and allusions, and the previous translations were some-times stiff. What may be acceptable in one context because it is Scriptural may be unacceptable in the writings of the early Church, particularly where they are versified both in Latin and in translation. The level of editorial revision in NEH varies from light touches (indicated by † as in EH) to wholesale re-writing. Benson's translation of 'Jesu, redemptor omnium' (NEH223; EH189) was, for instance, heavily revised: though little change was made in the dox-ology, only six of sixteen lines otherwise survive unaltered. In some cases, the Latin was used only as a reference point or abandoned. George Timms wrote a new hymn for All Saints, 'Father, in whom thy saints are one' (NEH196), which draws on 'Jesu, salvator saeculi' (see EH249) and 'Christe, redemptor omnium, conserva' (not included in EH). He also wrote the hymn for the Conversion of St Paul, 'A heavenly splendour from on high' (NEH154), which retains the formality of the office hymn tradition and makes free refer-ence to the Latin hymns for the feast, but is in other respects a strong new text.

NEH is a product of its time and denomination, seeking a balance between comprehensibility and liturgical continuity. With its frequent resonances of the past, including the use of the 'thou' form even in the new office hymns, the plainsong hymns and other chants, it comes closer to the Church of England's Rite B (traditional language) rather than to the utilitarian language of the *Alternative Service Book*'s Rite A (contemporary language) or the more radical idioms of the Roman Catholic vernacular liturgy. As a hymn book for the office it falls short of EH, which is more comprehensive, more authentic, and far more liturgically disciplined. The nearest replacement for EH as a hymn book for the office is *Hymns for Prayer and Praise* (1996), a collaboration between Anglican and Roman Catholic religious, whose texts are generally strong but whose music is sometimes compromised by the perceived need for accessibility. The need for an authentic but modern collection of hymns for the Anglican office is still outstanding, and more pressing with the reinvigorated predilection for the recitation of the new Daily Prayer of *Common Worship*.

Postscript: **The New Oxford Book of Carols**
If the second half of the nineteenth century was witness to the revived interest in plainsong in church, the second half of the twentieth century was witness to the revival of interest in early music in the concert hall, in broad-casts, and among amateur performers. Often the liturgical music revived has had little connection with the church or liturgy; worse still, some has been subjected to the nonsense of historical reconstructions of liturgical services without any actual liturgy.

Something of the vibrancy, mission and energy that brought performance and scholarship together in the revival of plainsong and in the re-connection with pre-Reformation patterns of worship in the later nineteenth century can be discerned in the early music movement. These characteristics are also found in *The New Oxford Book of Carols* (1992). Like EH and *The Oxford Book of Carols* (OBC), NOBC is in part a reaction to the taste of previous decades – here the choral carol industry that burgeoned in the 1960s and 1970s. In many ways NOBC is more radical than its predecessor (OBC) in its approach to authenticity, and more scholarly. Something of the same directness can be observed, not least in the plainsong melodies that are included. Interestingly they are placed in the category of 'composed carols' of part one, rather than the 'traditional carols' of part two.

A group of liturgical items is included in the first section, The Middle Ages. The anthology begins with four classic Advent and Christmas plainsong hymns, with Sarum chant and texts, and (mostly) Neale's translations: 'Verbum supernum prodiens', 'Veni, redemptor omnium', 'Christe, redemptor omnium', and 'A solis ortus cardine'; there is also the Christmas sequence 'Laetabundus' (NOBC1–5). All five items are found in EH. Here the plainsong neums on four-line staves are replaced by black blobs on five-line staves, and the melodies are transposed to a mezzo/baritone range. What is lost in flow and shape gained from the neums is at least compensated by the total absence of accompaniment. The melody stands alone – fresh and clear on the page.

Sixteen of the remaining 17 items in the section confirm the hazy borderline between plainsong and monophony, and between the liturgical and the sacred. Given the combination of great liturgical celebration and related feasting over the twelve days of Christmas, this blurring is not surprising. There is the plainsong office hymn 'Corde natus ex parentis' from the Use of York (NOBC20) set alongside the sixteenth-century Continental version from *Piae Cantiones*; and the processional of the nuns of Chester, 'Qui creavit caelum', here with the additional antiphons (NOBC17; cf. OBC67). 'Veni, Emmanuel' is edited from a fifteenth-century French processional: it is no invention of the eighteenth century, let alone of Helmore, and may be as early as the thirteenth century (NOBC16). There are two Latin songs associated with ceremonies (processions, and marking the time of the day with the Angelus), as well as a group of songs which may have been used to substitute for the Benedicamus Domino at the end of the office services at Christmastide.

The strength of good melody, boldly but straightforwardly treated when harmony is required, is a hallmark of NOBC. Musically it is a worthy contributor to the heritage of the *English Hymnal* tradition. In other respects it is a reminder of the growing gulf between the church and the ancient musical and liturgical endowment that Dearmer cherished and made alive.

Notes

1 Katherine Bergeron, *Decadent Enchantments: The revival of Gregorian chant at Solesmes,* Berkeley, Los Angeles and London, University of California Press, 1998.

2 John Harper, 'Gothic revivals: issues of influence, ethos and idiom in late nineteenth-century English monasteries', *Nineteenth-Century British Music Studies*, vol. 2 , Aldershot, Ashgate, 2002, 15–31.

3 Nicholas Temperley, *The Music of the English Parish Church*, 2 vols, Cambridge, 1979. Dale Adelmann, *The Contribution of Cambridge Eccelesiologists to the Revival of Anglican Choral Worship 1839–62*, Aldershot, Ashgate, 1997. Bennett Zon, *The English Plainchant Revival*, Oxford, OUP, 1999.

4 For a table summarizing the distribution of the office repertory in the Uses of Salisbury, York and Hereford, see John Harper, 'Music and Liturgy 1300–1600', in *Hereford Cathedral: a history*, ed. Gerald Aylmer and John Tiller, London, Hambledon Press, 2000, 397. This table is based on the comparative index compiled in W H Frere and L E G Brown, eds, *The Hereford Breviary*, 3 vols, London, Henry Bradshaw Society, 1903–15, vol. 3, 95–233.

5 It is difficult to be absolutely definitive since there are minor variants across the centuries and between sources. Furthermore, some texts that are treated as a single text in one source are divided into two hymns in another – particularly by the 19th-century editors (e.g. 'Aurora lucis rutilat' and its second part, 'Tristes erant apostoli', used as a hymn in its own right on certain days).

6 Donald Gray, 'The Birth and Background of *The English Hymnal*' above, and also *Percy Dearmer: A Parson's Pilgrimage*, Norwich, Canterbury Press, 2000, 68.

7 The early records of the society are scanty. On its formation, see *Grove's Dictionary of Music and Musicians*, 2nd edition, London, Macmillan, 1913, vol. iv; articles on the society also appear in all later editions of the dictionary. On its history and publications, see Anselm Hughes, *Septuagesima,* London, PMMS, 1959, and David Hiley, 'The Plainsong and Mediaeval Music Society, 1888–1998', in *Music in the Mediaeval English Liturgy*, ed. David Hiley and Susan Rankin, Oxford, OUP, 1993, 1–7.

8 One other publication, *The Order of Compline* (1928), should be mentioned. Edited by J H Arnold, and published amid great controversy because of the use of copyright words from the failed 1928 Prayer Book, it continues to be sold in significant numbers.

9 Currently in the archives held by the society.

10 The archives of St Barnabas Pimlico are either dispersed or unsorted, and it has not been possible to explore the precise involvement of Birkbeck or Riley with the church.

11 Mary Sackville Lawson, ed., *Collected Hymns, Sequences and Carols of John Mason Neale,* London, Hodder and Stoughton, 1914, viii. There is a conflict of ascription for two hymns: the translation of 'Telluris ingens Conditor' ('Earth's might maker, who's command') is regarded as anonymous in *Songs of Syon* and *The English Hymnal*, but is included in Neale's *Collected Hymns*, p.98; the translation of 'Magnae Deus potentiae' ('Almighty God, who from the flood') is ascribed to Neale in the same hymnals, but does not appear in the *Collected Hymns*.

12 The numbering of the 67 Sarum melodies is different in the two books, and there are some small melodic variants, but only one melody (SHM50, and PHS51) is unique to each collection. PHS also includes 5 Sarum processional chants, 5 hymn melodies from York, Hereford and Barking hymnals, and 15 sequences. SHM includes just 2 sequence melodies.

13 Sequences and processionals that appeared among the hymns in TH1891 are collected in two separate sections in TH1904.

14 Several Continental chants taken from late sources are not presented in plainsong notation, and are not counted as 'plainsong' either by the editors or here. The four versions of 'Salve, festa dies' in EH are treated as one item in this table, but not in the table below where all separately numbered items are counted. This means that, taking into account the liturgical chants at the end of the book, almost all the music in plainsong notation is taken from English sources.

15 EH, preface, v.
16 *Ibid.*, iv.
17 *Ibid.*, v.
18 Three further hymn texts from the Use of Sarum occur elsewhere in the book, but in other metres and with measured tunes.
19 These texts are in any case incorporated as the second part of the Easter hymns 'Aurora lucis rutliat' (EH123) and 'Sermone blando angelus' (EH124).
20 See EH Preface, vii.
21 Neale's translation of 'Creator lucis optime' (NEH150) is incorrectly ascribed to Dearmer (cf.EH 51).
22 For a recent appraisal of Birkbeck and Russia, see Michael Hughes, 'The English Slavophile: W J Birkbeck and Russia', *The Slavonic and East European Review*, 82 (2004), 680–706, also available on-line.
23 Athelstan Riley, *Concerning Hymn Tunes and Sequences*, London and Oxford, 1915. All the musical examples are taken from EH, including the typography.
24 [Rose Katharine Birkbeck], *Life and Letters of W J Birkbeck, M.A., F.S.A, by his wife*, London, Longmans, 1922, 18.
25 Initially at 221 Brompton Road, the organ appears to have been moved to two other London addresses, most likely Thurloe Square (1883–95) and 32 Sloane Gardens (1895–1916). Information compiled in 2001 by Nicholas Groves on the Paston School (North Walsham, Norfolk) alumni website (www.pastonschool.co.uk). The organ reached the school in 1938 (via Ely, Oxford and Booton), and was placed in the school hall. It was rebuilt in 1959 as a three-manual instrument, and further altered by Bower & Son in 1992.
26 *Life and Letters of W J Birkbeck*, 230–6.
27 *Ibid.*, 237.
28 *The Works of the Rt. Rev. Charles C Grafton*, ed. B Talbot Rogers, New York, 1914, vol. 7, 134–64. On-line extracts, http://justus.anglican.org/resources/pc/grafton/v7/134.html
29 EH, preface, xxiv.
30 EH2, preface, xvi. Palmer's editions of the Introits for Holy Communion were intended to be used with EH. Only their texts are included in EH (657–733), together with those of the other propers. While the Introit could be legitimately sung (since it was sung before the *Book of Common Prayer* service began), the other texts could have authorized status since they were included within the service.
31 PHS, preface, [v].
32 It is part of the preparation for the Eucharist in *Common Worship*.
33 EH2, preface, xvi.
34 Riley, *Concerning Hymn Tunes and Sequences*, 9.
35 The Mechlin melody of 'Stabat mater dolorosa' was introduced as the third tune in the second edition, EH2 115.
36 This may account for the inclusion of the one hymn from the Use of York in EH.
37 They are found in the appendix of *Liber Usualis*.
38 EH, preface, xix.
39 Riley, *Concerning Hymn Tunes and Sequences*, 28. Croft's collection passed to the Community of the Resurrection, Mirfield.
40 Cyril E Pocknee, *The French Diocesan Hymns and Their Melodies*, Alcuin Club Tracts 29, London, Faith Press, 1954, 11–12.
41 *Ibid.*, 21–2.
42 *Ibid.*, 38, 161–2. The table is supported by a short commentary on the sources of the musical examples.
43 Some, though not all, are emended in *The New English Hymnal* (1986).
44 EH165, 188, 191, 208, 223, 224, 242. In EH2, the 'Angers' melody (EH2 223) was replaced by the German chorale *Herr deinen Zornen*.

45 EH335, 435, 636.
46 The two editions of *Songs of Praise* (SP1 and SP2) have different numberings. However, a comparative table of the plainsong hymns in the two editions, and their respective numberings in EH, appears at the end of this section.
47 SP1, viii.
48 *The Processional of the Nuns of Chester*, ed. J W Legg, Henry Bradshaw Society, vol. 18, London, 1899.
49 The Shaws, Arnold and Cooke all served at St Mary, Primrose Hill, at one time or another, and Arnold, Cooke and Vale published text-books on the use and accompaniment of plainsong.
50 EH2, xxi.
51 In conversation, Michael Fleming confirmed to me his own close knowledge of PHB, gained during his time as a student of Gerald Knight at the Royal School of Church Music.
52 The other hymns with re-allocated plainsong melodies are NEH128, 166, 176, 190 (respectively EH141, 228, 234, 242). The NEH melodies for these hymns are found at EH125, 169, 150, 191; all but NEH176 (EH150) are used for at least one other text in NEH.

FOLK-SONGS IN *THE ENGLISH HYMNAL*[1]

Julian Onderdonk

The inclusion of folk-songs in *The English Hymnal* is one of its most striking and original features. Erik Routley observes that the hymnal broke 'new ground in introducing to hymnody a very large number of traditional English folk songs', and C S Phillips accounts the adaptation of folk-songs one of the book's main musical innovations, along with its inclusion of nineteenth-century Welsh Methodist tunes and sixteenth- and seventeenth-century French Diocesan melodies.[2] This policy of adapting traditional melodies for use as hymn tunes has also been a source of criticism. As early as 1921, Herbert Westerby praised *The English Hymnal* for its superior musicianship but asserted that the folk-songs were not a complete success because 'it is not easy to get away from the atmosphere of secularity'.[3] Fifty years later, Kenneth Long expressed similar views, arguing that 'many of these folk tunes have become widely popular – *Forest Green, Sussex, Shipston, Monks Gate, Kings Lynn, Kingsfold, Herongate,* and *Rodmell,* for example – but others still seem somewhat incongruous in the framework of Prayer Book services'.[4]

Ralph Vaughan Williams, the music editor, was keenly aware of the objection and met it head on in the essay he wrote for the booklet marking the fiftieth anniversary of *The English Hymnal*'s publication:

> I have been blamed for using adaptations of folk tunes for hymn purposes, but this is, surely, an age-old custom. Tierrsot has proved, to my mind conclusively, that certain church melodies of the Middle Ages were adapted from secular tunes, for example, the *Tonus Peregrinus*. In Germany also, is not *Innsbruck* adapted from a popular tune? And we know that the words of *Jesu Meine Freude* were originally a love song, 'Flora meine freude'. The well-known German tune which we sing as 'Glory, laud and honor' is certainly first cousin to 'Sellinger's Round'. The magnificently solemn tune for which Wesley wrote 'Lo, he comes', is an adaptation from a popular song of the day.[5]

Vaughan Williams knew whereof he spoke. Recent scholarship has substantiated the views he expressed here and shown that secular and traditional melodies have indeed long formed the basis of many hymn and psalm tunes, from the office hymns of the Old Roman Rite to the Lutheran hymns and Calvinist psalms of the Reformation and beyond.[6] What the composer did not mention in the quotation above was that the practice had fallen into disuse during the Victorian period. The increased demand for new hymns and hymn tunes in those years, coupled with the emergence of a Romantic

191

aesthetic stressing individual expression above all else, meant that 'originality' became the *sine qua non* of hymn-tune production while the kind of 'arranging' that characterized the older methods of adaptation fell into disrepute.[7] The result was a huge increase in the writing of wholly original hymns and hymn tunes that significantly altered the way congregational church music had traditionally been produced. Viewed in this context, Vaughan Williams' adaptation of folk-songs and other secular melodies for *The English Hymnal* did not so much constitute a 'breaking of new ground' as a renewal of past practices, one consistent with the other features of his editorial policy – the emphasis on early psalm tunes, Tudor and Restoration composers, and sixteenth- to eighteenth-century German church melodies – that expressed a revivalist agenda.

Nevertheless, there was one important difference between Vaughan Williams' editorial methods in *The English Hymnal* and the way folk and secular tunes had traditionally been converted into hymns. '[T]he motive in this case was new,' Nicholas Temperley writes: 'it was not so much to take advantage of familiar tunes by allying them to religious words, as to bring in unfamiliar tunes from a fresh and native stock.'[8] In other words, instead of choosing well-known melodies for their potential to attract newcomers to church worship (the principal motivation for such adaptations in the past), Vaughan Williams selected obscure and, in many cases, newly-collected folk-songs that he hoped would *become* popular. Indeed, over the course of his work with the major hymnals, he adapted 39 such traditional melodies, collected by himself and by Cecil Sharp, Lucy Broadwood, W E P Merrick and others active in the Folk Revival around the turn of the twentieth century. Thirty-one of these appeared in the 1906 *English Hymnal* while many of these were reprinted, along with yet other adaptations of recently-collected folk-songs, in the 1933 edition and in the two editions of *Songs of Praise*. Table 1 summarizes this information and provides the names of the original folk-songs and their collectors, where known, as well as the hymn numbers where these arrangements are found in each book. For convenience, a column giving the publications where these folk-songs first appeared in print – and where Vaughan Williams likely found those not collected by himself – is also included.[9] It is important to note in passing that these 39 tunes do not represent the sum total of the English folk-songs included in *The English Hymnal* and its sister publications. A further 24 traditional tunes drawn from older printed collections – Playford's *The English Dancing Master*, the *Fitzwilliam Virginal Book*, Sandys' *Christmas Carols* – also appeared there but are not included in Table 1 as they were not of recent collection. Nonetheless, the importance of these 'older' folk-songs to the composer's artistic conception will be clear, not least because they served to validate the 'new' tunes by rooting them in an age-old tradition.

The rationale usually given for Vaughan Williams' conversion of recently-collected folk-songs into hymn tunes has centred on his own nationalist

Table 1 Hymn tunes adapted from recently-collected English folk-songs and published in *The English Hymnal* and *Songs of Praise*

No.	Hymn-Tune Name	Folk-song Name	Collector	Hymn-Tune Arranger	Earliest Printed Source	EH	SP	SPE
1.	Bridgwater (see Stowey)	Sweet Europe	Cecil Sharp	RVW	Somerset(2), 42–3	656(1)	—	—
2.	Butler	The Holy Well	Cecil Sharp	Martin Shaw	JFSS 5, 4	—	—	378
3.	Capel (carol)	King Pharim	Lucy Broadwood	RVW	JFSS 4, 183–4	488	253	248
4.	Danby	A Brisk Young Farmer	RVW	RVW (2nd arr.)	unpublished	295	12	16
5.	Decree	The Black Decree	Cecil Sharp	Martin Shaw	JFSS 8, 31	—	—	484
6.	Dent Dale	Tarry Woo	RVW	RVW	JFSS 8, 215	23	248	88
7.	Devonshire	The Unquiet Grave	Lucy Broadwood	RVW	English Traditional, 54	294	211(1)	459(1)
8.	Dunstan	Psalm Tune	RVW	RVW	JFSS 10, 45	638 [1933]	—	393(2)
9.	Eardisley	Dives and Lazarus	Miss E Andrews	RVW	JFSS 7, 125	601	328	393(3)
10.	East Horndon	The Fisherman	RVW	RVW	unpublished	595	427	—
11.	Essex	Newport Street	RVW	RVW	JFSS 8, 157	—	352(2)	637(2)
12.	Exile	unknown	RVW?	Martin Shaw	unknown	572, 594	—	573(2)
13.	Farnham	The Bailiff's Daughter	RVW	RVW	unpublished	525(1)	156	285
14.	Forest Green	The Ploughboy's Dream	RVW	RVW	JFSS 8, 203	15	53	79(1)
15.	Gosterwood	The Brisk Young Lively Lad	RVW	RVW	unpublished	299	107(1)	21
16.	Hambridge	The Unquiet Grave	Cecil Sharp	RVW	JFSS 6, 6	355	11	15
17.	Hardwick	Virgin Unspotted	RVW	RVW or Shaw	unpublished	—	438	34
18.	Herongate	In Jessie's City	RVW	RVW	JFSS 8, 159	597	321	602
19.	Horsham	Stinson the Deserter	Lucy Broadwood	RVW	JFSS 4, 168–9	344, 609	139	258
20.	Ingrave	The Sheffield Apprentice	RVW	RVW	unpublished	607	—	—
21.	Kingsfold	Lazarus	A J Hipkins	RVW	English County, 102–3	574	267	529
22.	King's Langley (carol)	The Moon Shines Bright	Lucy Broadwood	RVW	English County, 108	221	5	229
23.	Kings Lynn	Van Dieman's Land or Young Henry the Poacher	RVW	RVW	JFSS 8, 166	562	177	308
24.	Langport	Lord Rendell	Cecil Sharp	RVW	Somerset(1), 46–7	656(2)	234	—
25.	Lew Trenchard	unknown	S Baring-Gould	RVW	unknown	591(2)	407(2)	493
26.	Lodsworth	The Unquiet Grave	W P Merrick	RVW	JFSS 3, 119	275	408	336
27.	Mariners	unknown	RVW?	RVW or Shaw	unknown	—	125	—
28.	Mendip	The Miller's Apprentice	Cecil Sharp	RVW	unpublished	498	201	201

Table 1 Hymn tunes adapted from recently-collected English folk-songs and published in *The English Hymnal* and *Songs of Praise* (continued)

No.	Hymn-Tune Name	Folk-song Name	Collector	Hymn-Tune Arranger	Earliest Printed Source	EH	SP	SPE
29.	Monks Gate	Our Captain Calls	RVW	RVW	JFSS 8, 202	402	255	515
30.	Newbury (carol)	Christmas Mummers' Carol	Godfrey Arkwright	RVW	JFSS 4, 178–9	16	54	395(3)
31.	Northumbria	Lullaby	RVW	Martin Shaw	unpublished	—	—	382
32.	Rodmell	The Bailiff's Daughter	RVW	RVW	unpublished	186 611	441	221
33.	Rusper	The Merchant's Daughter	Lucy Broadwood	RVW	JFSS 4, 160–1	379	—	—
34.	St. Hugh	Little Sir William	M H Mason	RVW	Nursery Rhymes	606	437	371
35.	Shepton-Beauchamp	Tarry Trowsers	Cecil Sharp	RVW	Somerset(2), 30–1	389	—	—
36.	Shipston	Bedlam City	J A Fuller Maitland	RVW	English County, 71	390 599	430	364
37.	Southill (carol)	May Day Carol	A Foxton Ferguson	RVW	JFSS 7, 132	638(2)	446(2)	395(2)
38.	Stalham	If There Be Danger	E J Moeran	RVW	JFSS 26, 14	638(3) [1933]	—	393(1)
39.	Stowey (see Bridgwater)	Sweet Europe	Cecil Sharp	RVW or Shaw	Somerset(2), 42–3	—	426	377
40.	Sussex	The Royal George	RVW	RVW	unpublished	239 385	190	321 —

musical agenda. Thus Michael Kennedy, in his full-length study of the composer, suggests that his work on *The English Hymnal* 'was, in fact, by coming as a tributary from, and corollary to, his folk-song collecting, another "liberating" influence', while the hymnologist Robin Leaver, in his overview of twentieth-century developments in British hymnody, relates the composer's adaptation of folk-songs to the 'revolution' occurring in British music in the years before and after World War One.[10] There is good reason for this as the composer was an outspoken proponent of the nationalist viewpoint that English composers needed to return to indigenous musical roots in order to throw off foreign musical domination. Subscribing to the rhetoric of 'national spirit' promoted by the nineteenth-century German philosophers Hegel and Herder, he asserted that folk-songs contained the 'spiritual life-blood of a people'[11] and he set about promoting them throughout society at large. His hope was that the dissemination of folk-song – via arrangements for school, home, or, as here, church use – would break English audiences of their centuries-old preference for continental music and help create a demand for the works of English composers who were themselves inspired by these melodies. It was in many ways the same strategy that underpinned his advocacy of early English music, both as composer of the *Fantasia on a Theme by Thomas Tallis* (1910) and as editor of two volumes of Henry Purcell's *Welcome Songs* (1905, 1910).[12] (It is no coincidence that *The English Hymnal* includes music by both of these composers as well as an unprecedented number of tunes by Orlando Gibbons and Henry Lawes.) But the promotion of folk-song was possibly more important for it gave proof that England, far from being 'Das Land ohne Musik', possessed a musical tradition all its own. The emphasis on *recently*-collected folk-songs was also important, not merely because they were well placed to demonstrate that folk-song was a living tradition in England, but also because the improved 'scientific' collecting methods of recent fieldworkers drew attention, in a way that older collections did not, to the unusual modal and gapped scales of English traditional music. Indeed, it was precisely these features that seemed to differentiate native folk-song from those of other parts of Europe, particularly Germany, whose folk-songs were more purely diatonic. Certainly, when it comes to the strictly Aeolian outlines of a hymn tune like *Kings Lynn* (Example 1 below), adapted from Mr Anderson's 1905 rendition of 'Van Dieman's Land', the resulting sound world is something that might convincingly be called 'English' (*Example 1*).

The respect Vaughan Williams felt for the folk tradition is palpable here. The Aeolian outlines of Mr Anderson's tune, which appears in the treble line, are faithfully matched in the accompaniment, which studiously avoids functional tonal harmony in its approach to the tonic d minor. Modal cadences occur in bars 4, 12 and 16 and when a dominant function does appear (as at bars 5, 10, 12 and 13) it is always the strictly modal form (v) that is used. The v chord (an A minor triad) is in fact the harmonic goal of the third phrase and

Example 1: Kings Lynn

it is approached via a series of shifting F and C chords whose mediant modal relationship to the A minor goal Vaughan Williams brilliantly exploits by placing the three chords in unpredictable non-functional combination. So thoroughgoing a use of modal harmony not only signalled a striking departure from typical hymn-tune accompaniments of the period but also represented an effective alternative to the nineteenth-century chromaticism that was, by 1906, leading German composers like Richard Strauss and Arnold Schönberg to the brink of atonality. Strict modal diatonicism of this kind was in fact to become a hallmark of Vaughan Williams' mature style, observable in minor works like the original hymn tune *King's Weston* (1925) as well as in portions of major masterpieces like the Fifth Symphony (1943). As such, his adaptation of folk-songs in *The English Hymnal* represented a first step in what would become perhaps his most important contribution to twentieth-century musical composition.

At the same time, it would be a mistake to claim too much originality for *Kings Lynn*. Its striking modal diatonicism is informed by a sturdy craftsmanship that has its roots firmly in the musical conventions of the Church. Fundamental here is the part-writing, which in every case results in predominantly conjunct lines that are eminently singable (even if a note above the tune – 'To be sung in unison' – indicates that these lines are to be played by the organ). More importantly, the harmony employs distinctly functional elements that point to a compromise with tradition. Vaughan Williams's frequent harmonization of Mr Anderson's pitch C, the flat seventh degree, with a C major triad (bars 2, 5, 6 and elsewhere) represents a bold modal gesture, but he then treats this chord as a secondary dominant of F, to which it consistently moves. F major is in fact the harmonic goal of the entire second phrase, and, as befits the relative major of the tonic d minor, is actually tonicized in bars 6–7 with one of the most common devices of functional harmony, a I-IV-V-I chord progression. The v chord (an A minor triad) is similarly tonicized in bars 12–13 in a manner that necessitates the introduction of non-diatonic B♮s in the accompaniment. Here, however, Vaughan Williams places the secondary dominant (an E triad) in the minor, thereby maintaining consistency not only with Mr Anderson's modal G♮, but also with the idea of avoiding dominant functions lying outside the Aeolian scale.

I point out these 'compromises' with common practice tonality not to minimize the originality of *Kings Lynn*, but rather to suggest that, when it came to *The English Hymnal* at least, Vaughan Williams did not ruthlessly pursue the 'nationalistic' musical implications of folk-song to the exclusion of all else. The hymn tune *Danby*, a reworking of the folk-song 'A Brisk Young Farmer', which Vaughan Williams collected from Mr Bowes in 1904, offers another case in point. Example 2 reprints the arrangement found in *The English Hymnal*, not the substitute one that appeared in *Songs of Praise* (*Example 2*).

Example 2: Danby

Mr Bowes' tune (in the treble) provides a good example of the kind of folk melody that attracted the composer: its use of both a tonal F# and a modal F♮ in the opening phrase, and its avoidance of either pitch in the 'gapped' second half of the tune, mark it as 'different' from most melodies and, as such, potentially useful in the work of creating a unique national style. Yet, note how Vaughan Williams' arrangement avoids the implications of these unusual features. The modal F♮ is treated as the seventh of a secondary dominant chord (V7 of C) that then resolves smoothly back to the tonic, while the gapped features of the second half of the tune are overlooked completely by an accompaniment that employs F#s in abundance. The result is a harmonization that essentially ignores the most 'characteristic' features of 'A Brisk Young Farmer' by presenting it in unambiguous G major throughout. Nor is this approach unique to *Danby*. Of the 20 modal and/or gapped folk-songs appearing in Table 1, only seven of them – *Kings Lynn, Kingsfold, Decree, Southill, Dunstan, Stalham* and the substitute arrangement of *Danby* appearing in *Songs of Praise* – were fitted with modal (or semi-modal) accompaniments that accentuate those features. The remaining 13, by contrast, were given wholly *tonal* accompaniments that essentially bypassed them – either by 'filling in' the absent scale degrees to create a wholly diatonic (major/minor) harmonization or by outright ignoring the modal inflections of the tune by incorporating them into firmly tonal harmony.

The reasons for this 'mainstreaming' of the modal and gapped elements of folk-songs in *The English Hymnal* and its sister publications will be readily apparent. Vaughan Williams' four-year stint as organist and choirmaster of St Barnabas South Lambeth from 1895 to 1899 gave him first-hand experience of the musical limitations of church congregations and he knew just how important it was to provide harmonizations that simplified the tunes and made them easier to sing. In the case of *Danby*, for example, it is likely that he suspected the abrupt juxtaposition of a truly modal F♮ with the preceding F# leading tone would confuse unskilled singers and so found a way to incorporate the F♮ into a tonal harmonization. Similarly, his continued use of F#s in the harmony during the gapped second half of the tune surely stemmed from the need to maintain continuity with the already-established tonal context. Such a concern for the 'singability' of the entire arrangement is consistent with other features of his editorial work, notably the pitching of tunes as low as possible and the introduction of slower tempi, that reflect his democratic concern for congregational abilities. In some cases, congregational considerations actually prompted him to *alter* the tune as sung. Example 3 reprints *Rusper* from *The English Hymnal* as well as the folk-song on which it was based, 'The Merchant's Daughter', as sung by Henry Burstow and collected by Lucy Broadwood (*Example 3a and 3b*).

Example 3a: The Merchant's Daughter

RUSPER (76 76 D)

Moderately slow ♩ = 80   From an English Traditional Melody

Example 3b: Rusper

In its rhythmic variety and freedom, Mr Burstow's tune constitutes a good example of the rhythmic peculiarities of certain English folk-songs – qualities that, once again, were attractive to Vaughan Williams in his pursuit of a distinctive national style. But as a tune for congregational singing, 'The Merchant's Daughter' was far too complex and required significant alteration and simplification. The syncopation in the first and fourth phrases, as well as the triplet figure in the second, in particular, represented potential stumbling blocks, and Vaughan Williams simplified them not merely by smoothing out the rhythmic figure in each case but by seeing to it that all three phrases used the *same* rhythmic figure (♩♪♩♪). Rhythmic repetition and predictability of this sort could only help unskilled singers to learn, and possibly even retain, a tune. Other changes are less drastic and serve to standardize the crotchet upbeat found at the beginning of all four phrases, although the melodic alteration before bar 1 – a change that actually runs contrary to this standardization – may be due to the composer's concern to ease singers into the beginning of the tune. (As Vaughan Williams well knew, congregations are most apt to falter at the start of a hymn tune.)

Taken together, the changes to 'The Merchant's Daughter' are considerable enough to result in a significantly altered tune, a fact that Vaughan Williams acknowledged by printing the words *'from* an English Traditional Melody' above the music (my emphasis).[15] For the most part, however, the editorial alterations that he introduced for congregational purposes are slight, and include, among other things, the insertion of an occasional passing tone (*Kings Lynn, Stowey*), the diminution of rhythm (*Hambridge, Gosterwood*), the mixing and matching of variant passages from different verses (*Rodmell, Sussex)*, and even the transposition of individual pitches (*Dunstan*). (This list of alterations and of tunes exemplifying each is far from complete.) Nonetheless, it is a testament to Vaughan Williams' concern for congregational involvement that, of the 37 hymn tunes for which I have so far found the folk-song originals, fully 19 of them introduce changes that serve to simplify the tune or otherwise make it easier to sing.

Also impacting the editorial process were considerations of text. In order for a folk-song to be converted into a hymn tune it had to be matched with a hymn that was compatible with it. Compatibility in this case meant considerations of general mood – it clearly would not do to set a transcendently radiant hymn to a sombre Aeolian tune – but especially issues of verbal metre. In the absence of correspondence or committee minutes it is often difficult to know whether Vaughan Williams searched for folk-songs that fitted pre-chosen texts or whether those texts were selected to match folk-songs he had already chosen (although we do know of a few instances where texts were specially written by Percy Dearmer and others for specific tunes[16]). Whatever the precise negotiations, the committee clearly did their best to find matching metres, for 32 of the 37 hymn tunes for which we have the folk-song originals are in metres either exactly matching or closely approximating those of the melodies to which they were set. In these instances, Vaughan Williams' editorial alterations to the tune are minimal, involving the occasional dropping of an anacrusis (*Dent Dale, Shepton-Beauchamp*), the substitution of one crotchet for two quavers or vice versa (*King's Langley, Farnham, Forest Green*), even the omission or repetition of an entire phrase of the melody (*Kingsfold, Lodsworth*). In some cases, prosody and not metre *per se* prompted change, as in the conversion of the folk-song 'Little Sir William' into the hymn tune *St Hugh*, where the substitution of the words 'Sing to the Lord the children's hymn' for the original folk text 'Easter day was a holiday' necessitated a switch from the original rhythm ♩♩♩♫♩.♪♩ to the ♩♫♩♩♩.♪♩ of the hymn-tune version. (The prosody given here is retained in the subsequent verses of both texts.) But it is the traditional melodies whose metres significantly diverged from those of the hymns with which they were coupled that naturally produced the greatest editorial challenge. A case in point is the hymn tune *Langport*, set to the words 'See him in raiment rent' and derived from Mrs Perry's version of 'Lord Rendal' as collected by Cecil Sharp in Somerset (*Example 4a and 4b*).

The metrical incompatibility of the original folk text – itself compiled from various printed sources, according to Sharp[19] – with the hymn text is obvious. The latter juxtaposes poetic lines of 10 and 9 syllables, grouped into a

Example 4a: Lord Rendal

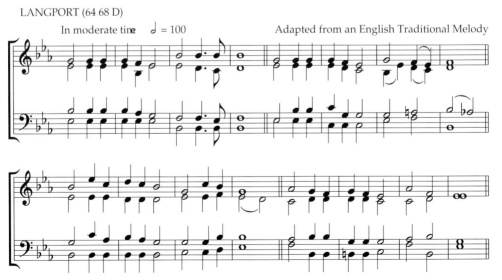

Example 4b: Langport

repeating 6 4. 6 3. metrical pattern, while the former reflects the notorious rhythmic and verbal flexibility of traditional song by running anywhere from 6 to 12 syllables per line, often in unpredictable sequence. (This is especially true of the first two lines of each stanza – only the first is printed here – which fluctuate randomly between 10 and 12 lines per stanza.) This unpredictability is matched by the tune which, in bar 9, undergoes a rhythmic slowdown and change of mood as the son tries to prepare his nervously chattering mother for his impending death. Vaughan Williams' solution to this metrical challenge, after changing the overall metre to 2/2, was to place the first two phrases firmly in the new verbal metre by replacing the opening quavers with a crotchet and then, in the third and fourth phrases, to craft an essentially *new* melody based loosely on the original. Here, the repeated phrase 'I've been to my sweet-heart, mother' is heard only once, its jaunty rhythms and some of its melodic leaps severely curtailed. The melodic outlines of this 'new' phrase then form the point of departure for the remainder of the third phrase (bars 11–12) as well as for the entire fourth phrase, which ignores the corresponding phrase of the original entirely (including the switch to 6/4) except for its use of the falling fa-re-do (4–2–1) figure at the cadence. The result is an eminently singable and well-crafted tune, shorn of its original melodic and rhythmic eccentricities, that admirably suits the verbal metre of the hymn.[20]

The editorial alterations and choices outlined above will come as no surprise, of course. Compilers of hymn books and psalm-tune collections have throughout the ages grappled with the need to adapt melodies to the straightjacket of the text's metre, to smooth out awkward rhythms and intervals, and to provide a consistent and familiar harmonic framework. In adapting folk-songs in this manner, Vaughan Williams unequivocally situated himself at the centre of a long and distinguished tradition. The irony is that the practical requirements of conversion actively prompted him to *blunt* the very features of English traditional music that were presumed to be most unique. How could it be otherwise? Modal and gapped scales, awkward and unexpected intervals, rhythmic irregularities and eccentricities – all such departures from conventional musical syntax may have been characteristic of individual folk-song performance but they were quite unsuitable for congregational singing, where the musical abilities of the participants vary widely. The few 'deviations' that do find a place in *The English Hymnal* – the modality of *Kings Lynn*, the shifting metre of *Hambridge*, the three-bar phrases of *Horsham* – may very well reflect the direction his most striking creative work was to take, but they are decidedly the exception not the rule. Indeed, it is no exaggeration to say that, from an editorial standpoint, Vaughan Williams' folk-song adaptations differ very little from the arrangements he made of hymn tunes, like *Christe Sanctorum* or *Was Lebet Was Schwebet*, that have no basis in the folk tradition.

This is not to say that Vaughan Williams' transformation of English folk-songs into hymn tunes had no connections to a nationalist musical agenda. The very inclusion of these melodies in *The English Hymnal* and related publications sent a strong nationalist message, whether the arrangements communicated uniquely English musical characteristics or not. Indeed, when we consider that folk-songs were included in the hymnal as a means to help *reform* the music of the Anglican Church, the suppression of 'characteristic' scales and rhythms and the improved 'singability' of the arrangements emerge as distinct advantages. Other contributors to the present volume of essays have written about this push for reform, which grew out of the dissatisfaction of Percy Dearmer and his High Church colleagues with the treacly sentimentalism and emotional excesses of *Hymns Ancient & Modern*. Principally, their objections were directed to the words of Victorian hymns. The triumph of Evangelical Christianity in the nineteenth century had resulted in hymn texts that emphasized subjective emotion in their focus on the soul's personal relationship with God. It was precisely such texts that Dearmer had in mind when, in his preface to *The English Hymnal*, he countered that the 'best hymns of Christendom are as free as the Bible from the self-centred sentimentalism, the weakness and unreality which mark inferior productions', and offered the new hymnal as an attempt to redress these 'defects'.[21] But the committee's objections were also focused on the musical settings of these hymns. In his preface on 'The Music', Vaughan Williams wrote of the 'languishing and sentimental hymn tunes which so often disfigure our services', and boldly declared that the aim of the new book was to keep 'enervating tunes ... to a minimum'.[22] His 1902 Bournemouth lectures on folk-song, given two years before his appointment as music editor, went even further and attacked the 'maudlin sentiment' of contemporary hymn tunes, flatly stating that 'hard-working men and women should be given bracing and stimulating music, not the unhealthy outcome of theatrical and hysterical sentiment'.[23] What he objected to was Victorian composers' reliance on the 'sickly harmonies of Spohr' (i.e. excessive chromaticism) and on the 'operatic sensationalism of Gounod', by which he probably meant the use of dramatic organ swells and pedals as well as the Victorian practice of providing vividly contrasting dynamic markings for different lines of text. Along with such techniques as phrase elision and over-elaborate part-writing, these were the standard devices by which late-Victorian composers brought the 'grand effects' of contemporary instrumental music to bear on the humble hymn tune.[24]

Against such harmonic and textural elaborations, Vaughan Williams posed the unadorned folk-song – simple, diatonic and completely devoid of sensational effect. Avoiding chromaticism, employing a relatively narrow range and containing easily memorized phrase repetitions, folk-songs were easy to sing and, as he said of the old psalm tunes that he no less pointedly revived for *The English Hymnal*, were 'absolutely suitable for congregational singing'.[25] Perhaps more importantly, folk-songs were also *impersonal* in tone and expression. The theory of folk-song's communal origin, which maintained that folk-songs had been passed down from generation to generation, meant that any given tune reflected not the tastes of the individual but rather those of the community.[26] This, he believed, explained the 'tightly shut eyes' and the 'impersonal detachment' of the 'true traditional ... singer', who understood that 'a fine ballad tune only begins to show its quality when it has been repeated several times' in strophic performance.[27] Such detachment provided a powerful antidote to the extroverted emotionalism of Victorian hymnody, as Vaughan Williams made clear in his 1926 essay 'How to Sing a Folk-Song' where he contrasted the 'cumulative effect' of 'impersonal' folk-singing with:

> the terrible results of the 'personal' element applied to congregational singing – such vandalisms as the following rendering of a well-known hymn as recommended, I believe, in a popular hymnal;
> (*ff*) In life, (*pp*) in death. (*p*) O Lord (*cresc*) abide with me.[28]

Viewed in this context, the editorial simplifications that Vaughan Williams introduced in *Rusper* and *Langport* had strong connections to the reform movement. Folk-songs already possessed a simpler melodic outline than most Victorian hymn tunes, and by smoothing out the edges of the more 'awkward' ones he made them even more so. Even the 'compromises' with functional harmony in the modal *Kings Lynn* and the partially-modal *Danby* (Examples 1 and 2 above) can be seen as contributing to reform in that those harmonies met congregational expectations and improved the singability of each tune. (The modal elements of *Kings Lynn*, which otherwise relate to his compositional agenda, as we have seen, can also be viewed as contributing to reform insofar as they are rigorously diatonic and so avoid chromaticism.) The link with his efforts to revive psalm tunes – another great achievement of *The English Hymnal* – is significant here, for psalm tunes also possessed qualities of directness and simplicity that Vaughan Williams attributed to the fact that many of them ultimately derived from folk-songs.[29]

Some writers have claimed that the eradication of Victorian excesses was tantamount to the purging of recent continental influences from English hymnody, and by extension from English music.[30] There is much truth to the assertion, as Vaughan Williams' own dig at Spohr and Gounod, above, indicates; and certainly, when we consider the significance he attributed to indigenous folk-song as a means to deflect continental influences and so pave the way for a truly national style, the suggestion is placed beyond debate. Nonetheless, it should be noted that Vaughan Williams' attitude towards Victorian hymnody was not uniformly dismissive. By my count, he included 118 tunes and arrangements by 64 known Victorian composers – including 33 by the likes of J B Dykes, W H Monk, H J Gauntlett, Arthur Sullivan and

Joseph Barnby – in the 1906 *English Hymnal*. His preface to that book even expressed regret that he could not for copyright reasons 'include such beautiful tunes as Dykes' *Dominus Regit Me* or Stainer's *In Memoriam*'.[31] Admittedly, a number of these tunes were printed by dictate of the committee – nine were relegated to the Appendix, or as he called it, the 'Chamber of Horrors'[32] – but he still included 70 tunes and arrangements by 43 Victorian composers in *Songs of Praise Enlarged*, where he was under no such obligation. His fondness for certain specimens of Victorian hymnody, meanwhile, is suggested by later compositional activity. When preparing *Songs of Praise* for publication in 1925, for example, he thought enough of Monk's *Eventide* to fit it out with a descant, when as music editor he could easily have passed on the assignment to someone else. Even more significant, his ethereal 1936 composition *Two Hymn-Tune Preludes* for small orchestra, premiered at the Three Choirs Festival, constitutes a loving meditation on *Eventide* and Dykes' *Dominus Regit Me* – hardly the choice of a man who was indifferent to Victorian hymnody. Still other compositions are founded on hymn tunes by nineteenth-century Welsh composers like Joseph Parry and R H Prichard.[33]

No doubt Vaughan Williams was selective in his approach to Victorian hymnody: the hymn tunes mentioned here, including those selected for *Songs of Praise Enlarged*, are notable for their avoidance of the features he found most offensive (excessive chromaticism, wide dynamic contrasts, over-elaborate part-writing, etc.); moreover, the Welsh tunes all have a distinctly folk-song feel. The point, however, is that this allowance for qualification and exception indicates that the composer was not rigidly dogmatic on the subject of Victorian hymnody. Indeed, the striking thing is just how open-minded he was about specific hymn tunes, even despite the strong stance he took on them generally. This has important implications for our understanding of *The English Hymnal*. It is often forgotten, perhaps because of its very title, just how eclectic this book was and is. It may have privileged early English composers and melodies, but it did so while casting its net widely into Italian, Spanish, Dutch and American repertories.[34] It also drew extensively on *German* tunes of the fifteenth to nineteenth centuries – far more, in fact, than *Hymns Ancient & Modern*. The 1889 edition of that book, dissatisfaction with which prompted the initial conversations that would lead to the formation of Dearmer's committee, printed 67 tunes and arrangements from 50 German composers and/or sources, whereas the 1906 *English Hymnal* printed 152 tunes and arrangements from 94 German composers and/or sources, including 27 by J S Bach alone.[35] This is remarkable by any standard, but especially in view of the supposedly anti-Germanic basis of Vaughan Williams' compositional agenda. (Expressing perhaps the common view, especially of the interwar years, Herbert Westerby declared that 'the great number of German tunes [*The English Hymnal*] contains is against the book'.[36]) Even nineteenth-century German music is better represented in *The English Hymnal* than in *Hymns Ancient & Modern* (18 tunes from 11 composers/sources as opposed to 11 tunes from 7 composers/sources), and this despite the fact that Vaughan Williams' dislike of the earlier hymnal supposedly stemmed from its over-dependence on contemporaneous German musical styles. Such dislike evidently did not prevent him from including a tune from *Die Meistersinger von Nürnberg* (*Da zu dir der Heiland kam*) by his beloved Wagner, nor from arranging a second one, *Parsifal*, from the opera of the same name for the 1933 edition. Nor did it prevent him from printing in *Songs of Praise* an arrange-ment of a German folk-song (*Ich Fahr Dahin*) by Johannes Brahms, the nineteenth-century German composer he later called 'one of the greatest [men] in my lifetime'.[37]

Mention of German folk-song raises yet another point about the broad-mindedness and eclecticism of *The English Hymnal* – its inclusion of folk-songs from nations other than England. Table 2 lists the hymn tunes derived from *non*-English folk-songs that Vaughan Williams published in *The English Hymnal* and both versions of *Songs of Praise*.[38] One is immediately struck by their sheer number: 44 tunes drawn from eleven different nations. This is more than two thirds of the 63 English folk-songs included in the three publications (i.e. the 39 'new' folk-songs listed in Table 1 plus the 24 'older' ones mentioned in passing above) – again, a remarkably high percentage in view of Vaughan Williams' rigidly nationalist associations. Admittedly, with the exception of *Marylebone* and *The Birds*[39] none of these are of recent collec-tion, as is the case with so many of the English folk-songs appearing in the hymnal. It is further true that 23 of these 44, being of Welsh, Irish and Scottish origin, hail from the British Isles. Nonetheless, this leaves 11 tunes from France, Switzerland, the Low Countries, Norway and the Czech lands, as well as a further 10 tunes from Germany alone. Such inclusiveness was no mere nod to prevailing editorial practice, as Victorian hymn books ignored this repertory just as they had English folk-song; rather, it reflected nothing less than a fascination with folk-songs of every kind. Vaughan Williams, we must remember, arranged a number of non-English folk-songs over the course of his career, not merely in his hymn-tune editing but also in his work as free-lance composer. Between 1902 and 1904, just as his own collecting work was starting up, he arranged six German and seven French folk-songs for voice(s) and piano, and he returned to this repertory (as well as to Scottish, Irish and Manx folk-songs) intermittently throughout his career.[40] He also knew a great deal about the folk-songs of other nations. His essays and lectures frequently make reference to continental folk-songs and show an intimate familiarity with the work of nineteenth-century French and German folk-song scholars like Julien Tiersot and Franz Böhme, both of whom he quotes liberally. It seems likely, in fact, that their researches into the secular origins of many Lutheran and Calvinist church melodies, which Vaughan Williams closely documents in his essay 'The Influence of Folk-song on the Music of the Church', informed his own opinions and directly influenced his decision to include recently-collected folk-songs in *The English Hymnal*. Their

Table 2 Hymn tunes adapted from non-English traditional melodies and published in *The English Hymnal* and *Songs of Praise*

No.	Hymn-Tune Name	Place of Origin	Folk-song Name or Published Source from which tune probably taken	Arranger	EH	SP	SPE
1.	A Little Child	Flanders	'Er is een kindeken geboren op d'aard' from *Oxford Book of Carols* (OBC)	Julius Röntgen	—	—	352
2.	Ar hyd y nos	Wales	known in England as 'All through the night'	RVW	268	31	46
3.	Cormac	Ireland	*Feis Coíl Collection of Irish Music*	Martin Shaw	—	—	495
4.	Daniel	Ireland	*Songs of Praise for Boys and Girls* (1929)	Martin Shaw	246 [1933]	—	376
5.	Das Leiden des Herrn	Germany	Erk and Böhme's *Deutsche Liederhort* (1894)	E W Goldsmith RVW? (2nd arr.)	387 111 [1906] App. 11 [1933]	82(1)	— 119
6.	De Boodschap (carol)	Holland	'De Boodschap van Maria' from *Nederlandsch Volksliederenboek* (1896)	Martin Shaw	—	—	226
7.	Deirdre	Ireland	Bunting's *Ancient Music of Ireland* (1840)	RVW?	212(2) [1906]	—	—
8.	Dun Aluinn	Ireland	adapted by 'The Irish Guild of the Church'	Martin Shaw	356 [1933]	—	115(2)
9.	Es ist ein Ros' entsprungen	Germany	Praetorius' *Musae Sioniae* (1609)	Michael Praetorius	19	46	70
10.	Faithful	Scotland	'Faithful Johnny' from *Daily Express Community Song Book* (1927)	Martin Shaw	—	—	282
11.	Fanad Head	Ireland	*Petrie Collection of Ancient Irish Music*	C H Kitson	—	164	294
12.	Flanders	Flanders	'De Dryvoudige Geboorte' from OBC	Martin Shaw	—	—	448
13.	Grafton	France	*Chants Ordinaires de l'Office Divin* (1881)	Sydney Nicholson	33 [1933]	405(1)	129(2)
14.	Herzlich thut mich erfreuen	Germany	Walther's *Ein schooner Geistlicher und Christlicher newer Berckreyen* (1552)	RVW?	284	132(1)	249(1)
15.	Ich fahr dahin	Germany	'Ich fahr dahin' from Brahms' *Deutsche Volkslieder* (1864)	Johannes Brahms	—	376	667
16.	In Babilone	Holland	from unspecified collection of Dutch folk-songs by Julius Röntgen	Julius Röntgen	145	99(1)	173(1)
17.	Innsbruck	Germany	'Innsbruck Ich muss lassen,' possibly composed by Heinrich Isaac; this arr. from Bach *St. Matthew Passion*	J S Bach	86 278	40	57
18.	Jesu meine Freunde	Germany	arr. from Bach Cantata 'Jesu Meine Freude'	J S Bach	—	276	544
19.	Layriz (Ins Feld geh)	Germany	*Kern des Deutschen Kirchengesänge* (1853)	RVW?	440 [1933]	—	—
20.	Londonderry	Ireland	'Londonderry Air'	Henry G Ley	—	330	230 611
21.	Magdalena	Germany	unspecified	RVW	285 [1906] 392	314	591
22.	Martyrdom	Scotland	poss. derived from 'Helen of Kirkconnel'	R A Smith	367	205	449

Table 2 Hymn tunes adapted from non-English traditional melodies and published in *The English Hymnal* and *Songs of Praise* (continued)

No.	Hymn-Tune Name	Place of Origin	Folk-song Name or Published Source from which tune probably taken	Arranger	EH	SP	SPE
23.	Marylebone	Ireland	'My Bogeling Down' (collected by Cecil Sharp in London, 1908)	RVW?	—	184(1)	315(1)
24.	Morley	Ireland	unspecified	C Burke	626(1)	266(2)	528(2)
25.	O Filii et Filiae	France	unspecified	E W Goldsmith	626(2)	97	—
				S Webbe (2nd arr.)			—
				RVW? (3rd arr.)			143(1)
26.	Oslo	Norway	unspecified	RVW	—	—	232
27.	Petrie	Ireland	*Petrie Collection of Ancient Irish Music*	Martin Shaw	—	—	102
28.	Picardy (carol)	France	'Romancero' in Tiersot's *Mélodies* (1887)	RVW	318	147	273
29.	Pilgrims of the Night	Switzerland	unspecified	RVW?	399	—	—
30.	Remember the Poor	Ireland	*Petrie Collection of Irish Airs*	Irish Hymnal 1919	—	179	310
31.	Rhuddlan	Wales	'Dowch I'r Frwydr' from Edward Jones' *Musical Relicks of the Welsh Bards* (1800)	RVW?	423	284	552
32.	St. Patrick	Ireland	*Petrie's Collection of Ancient Irish Music*	RVW?	212(1)	266(1)	528(1)
33.	St. Sechnall	Ireland	from unspecified collection of Irish folk-songs by W H Grattan Flood	L L Dix	—	—	268
34.	Selma	Arran Islands	unspecified; poss. composed by Smith	R A Smith	290	208	10
35.	Slane	Ireland	'With My Love on the Road' from Joyce's *Old Irish Folk Music and Songs* (1909)	Martin Shaw	—	—	565
36.	Solothurn	Switzerland	'Dursli und Babeli' from *Sammlung von Schweitzer Kuhreihen und Volkslieder* (1826)	RVW	243	108	239
37.	Suo-Gan	Wales	'Lullaby Song' from Edward Jones' *Musical Relicks of the Welsh Bards* (1794)	Martin Shaw	—	—	380
38.	The Birds (carol)	Czech lands	'Zezulka z lesa vylítla, kuku' from OBC (collected by Miss Jacubickova in 1921)	Martin Shaw	—	—	381
39.	Thule	Germany	unspecified	G R Woodward	371 [1933]	—	—
40.	Trefaenan	Wales	unspecified	Martin Shaw	—	—	158
				Martin Shaw (2nd arr.)			462
41.	Valor	Ireland	unspecified	RVW	91 [1933]	163(2)	293(2)
42.	Wachterlied	Germany	'Wolauf, wolauf mit lauter stimm' from C Egenolf's *Reutterliedlein* (1535)	RVW	—	273	562
43.	Wicklow	Ireland	Joyce's *Old Irish Folk Music and Songs* (1909)	RVW	157 [1933]	—	182
44.	Ymdaith Mwngc or Monk's March	Wales	'Ymdaith y Mwnge' from Playford's *Dancing Master* (1665)	RVW?	203	127	209

discussion of the fluid origins and uncertain authorship of many hymn tunes, so close in spirit to his own evolutionary theories of folk-song, may even account for the large number of settings of this repertory by Bach and his contemporaries that the book contains.

Clearly, then, our understanding of the folk-song element in *The English Hymnal* is in need of substantial revision. Far from reflecting a narrowly English compositional agenda or chauvinistic world view, the inclusion of folk-songs originated in a spirit of broadminded inclusiveness that sought to expose congregations to the best music irrespective of nationality. By this reasoning, the incorporation of folk-songs was a logical extension of Vaughan Williams' stated desire that the book be 'a compendium of all the tunes of worth which were already in use' and 'a thesaurus of all the finest hymn tunes in the world'.[41] It is true that he viewed indigenous folk-song as an effective tool in the reform of Victorian hymnody, but then again he recruited Calvinist psalm tunes, Lutheran melodies of the sixteenth and seventeenth centuries, and even *continental* folk-songs for the same purpose. Indeed, the wide range of sources he drew on to effect this reform is wholly in keeping with the current revaluation of the composer as a more cosmopolitan and international figure than has previously been supposed.[42]

If we really wish to understand the 'nationalism' informing Vaughan Williams' transformation of folk-songs into hymn tunes, we must place his actions in the context of the times. After all, the interest in folk-song was not just a localized musical or aesthetic concern but rather part of a much larger vogue for things rural in the late-Victorian and Edwardian periods. The years 1880 to 1914 witnessed an explosion of enthusiasm for the countryside, manifested by the Arts and Crafts movement, the founding of the Commons Preservation Society and the National Footpaths Preservation Society, the establishment of agrarian communes and farming cooperatives, the rise of the wild 'English' garden, 'alternative' rural schools and even planned 'Garden City' suburbs, among much else.[43] Like the Folk Revival, these movements emerged in response to the perceived threat of the expansion of modern urban life and culture into the 'timeless' traditions of the countryside. But they also reflected a deeper uneasiness about perceived problems in the national life, particularly the growth of military and economic rivalry with Germany and the United States, the apparently insatiable needs of an expanding empire, and the re-emergence of class antagonism at home after a period of domestic peace. Indeed, the cry of 'Back to the Land' signalled nothing less than the abandonment of the Victorian 'compromise' and symbolized a seismic shift in the national self-image from one that embraced the Victorian industrial experience to one that looked principally to the nation's pre-industrial past.[44]

Cultural historians have argued that the emergence of this 'ruralist nationalism' helped sustain the status quo precisely by giving the ruling elite the *appearance* of assimilating aspects of rural working-class culture.[45] The truth is more complicated, however, since the embrace of the rural resulted not in the evasion of promised or implied social reforms but rather in their active and efficient implementation. The non-competitive and anti-commercial nature of folk-song and comparable artifacts of rural life was in fact a powerful inspiration for those who sought to redress the abuses of industrial capitalism through direct government action.[46] Certainly, it is no coincidence that Vaughan Williams and Dearmer, and indeed the majority of the *English Hymnal* committee, were political progressives who were dedicated to the extension of democratic reforms into every aspect of British economic and social life. Dearmer was a Christian socialist who famously preached against unfair labour conditions, supported the suffragettes and the idea of a female clergy, and attracted a Left-leaning congregation to St Mary's Primrose Hill where he emphasized social mission and outreach.[47] Vaughan Williams was a socialist in early life, read the Fabian tracts while an undergraduate, voted Radical or Labour throughout his career, and held strong views about the role of centralized administration in the equitable distribution of resources and services.[48] It was the support of figures such as these, inspired in part by a musical expression of rural working-class life, folk-song, that helped ease the transition from an outmoded Victorian Liberalism to new forms of political and economic centralization that would eventually result in the establishment of the Welfare State after 1945.

Vaughan Williams' and Dearmer's concern was not, however, focused exclusively on the poorest members of society. The social and cultural dislocations resulting from the political and economic transformations of the period were profound and affected Englishmen and women of all social classes. The appeal of the idea of 'rural England' lay precisely in the reassurance it gave to society in general about the rootedness of English life in a period of change. Its idealized projection of communal stability and individual equality, in particular, offered a prescription for social cohesion and cooperation at a time when forces from without and within were threatening to break society apart. Here is the true source of the nationalism informing Vaughan Williams' adaptation of native folk-songs for hymn tunes. Much more than an attempt self-consciously to create a 'national' compositional style, his adaptations reflected an ambition to bring his compatriots into a more profound relation with their English heritage and in so doing to forge connections between social classes. The 'purest' remnants of folk-song may have been found among a few scattered and rapidly-dwindling representatives of the rural poor, but this did not mean that folk-song was the exclusive possession of the working classes. Rather, it was the possession of *all* social classes, the 'spiritual life-blood of a race', and it was in the attempt to reintroduce English citizens to this cultural heritage – to remind them, as it were, of their relationship to the rest of society – that he set about arranging folk-songs for inclusion in church worship. '[If] the folk song has nothing to say to us *as we are now* – without a sham return to an imaginary (probably quite illusory)

211

arcadia of several centuries ago,' Vaughan Williams wrote to Cecil Sharp around 1907, 'then I would burn all the collections I could lay my hands on and their singers with them.'[49] Or as he put it in 1956 with specific reference to *The English Hymnal*: '[By 1906] Cecil Sharp had just made his epoch-making discovery of the beautiful melody hidden in the countryside: why should we not enter into our inheritance in the church as well as the concert room?'[50]

The notion of nationalism as a kind of code for 'social cohesion' was of course the guiding idea behind *The English Hymnal*, which was conceived as a uniting force within the Church. Unhappy with the sectarian rivalries and infighting threatening the Anglican communion from every side, Dearmer offered the book 'to all broad-minded men' in the belief that 'the hymns of Christendom show more clearly than anything else that there is even now such a thing as the unity of the Spirit'.[51] But 'unity' in this case went beyond the confines of the Church to encompass society itself. Hence the title of the book, and hence *Songs of Praise* (1925), which expanded the scope of the earlier hymnal by eliminating the strictly liturgical material and expanding the general content to include hymns on broadly humanistic themes, some of them only tangentially connected to Christian tradition. The result was a truly 'national' collection of song, adopted by schools and by the BBC 'Daily Service' broadcasts, that was at the forefront of the ecumenical movement of the mid-twentieth century.[52] The importance of native folk-song to these developments will be obvious. Their very inclusion in *The English Hymnal* and related publications served to validate the 'national' aspirations of these collections and to authenticate the compilers' genuinely populist and democratic aims. As such, they underscore the fundamentally social and cultural – *not* the compositional – thrust of the *English Hymnal* project, and possibly even of Vaughan Williams' own nationalist agenda. Writing in 1934, he asked:

> Is not folk-song the bond of union where all our musical tastes can meet? We are too apt to divide our music into popular and classical, the highbrow and the lowbrow. One day perhaps we shall find an ideal music which will be neither popular nor classical, highbrow or lowbrow, but an art in which all can take part.[53]

Notes

1 My thanks to Drs Mark Rimple, Ray M Beccam and the Revd Canon Alan Luff for much help and advice in the preparation of this essay. Thanks also to Dr Paul Emmons for the loan of valuable books and hymnals and to John Bawden for sharing his important work on Vaughan Williams and hymnody with me.

2 Erik Routley, *The Music of Christian Hymnody,* London, Independent Press, 1957, 139; C S Phillips, *Hymnody Past and Present*, London, SPCK, 1937, 238–9.

3 Herbert Westerby, quoted in the panel discussion following the delivery of Charles W Pearce's paper, 'English Sacred Folk Song of the West Gallery Period (c. 1695–1820)', *Proceedings of the Music Association,* 48 (1921–2), 26.

4 Kenneth R Long, *The Music of the English Church* (London, Hodder & Stoughton, 1972), 423.

5 R Vaughan Williams, 'Some Reminiscences of the English Hymnal', in *The First Fifty Years: A brief account of The English Hymnal from 1906 to 1956* (London, OUP, 1956), 4–5.

6 Nicholas Temperley, *The Hymn Tune Index: A Census of English-Language Hymn Tunes in Printed Sources from 1535 to 1820*, Oxford, 1998, Vol. 1, 30–58. See also the present author's 'Folk Music in Hymnody', in *A New Dictionary of Hymnology*, ed. J R Watson, London, Canterbury Press, forthcoming.

7 In the course of a longer 1934 essay, Vaughan Williams made these very points, attributing the decline of secular influence on hymn tunes in the Victorian period to 'clerical disapproval' and to the 'modern craze for personality'. See R Vaughan Williams, 'The Influence of Folk-Song on the Music of the Church', in *National Music and Other Essays*, Oxford, OUP, 1987, 74–82 (quotations at pp.78 and 82). Incidentally, it is not strictly true that the adaptation of traditional and secular tunes was wholly abandoned by Victorian church composers. Certainly, traditional carol melodies were frequently arranged by them, and while most of these were printed in carol collections, some actually appeared in mainstream hymnals. A famous example is Arthur Sullivan's *Noel*. See Maurice Frost, ed., *Historical Companion to Hymns Ancient and Modern* (London, William Clowes, 1962), 168. Nicholas Temperley's provocative suggestion that *Hymns Ancient & Modern* contained 'many traditional English tunes [that were] subtly altered to conform with the times' is unfortunately not discussed in detail. (*The Music of the English Parish Church*, Cambridge, CUP, 1979, Vol. 1, 302.)

8 *Ibid.*, Vol. 1, 323.

9 Table 1 is organized by hymn-tune name, with other columns provided for the names of the original folk-song, collector and arranger, where known. (Where a tune has been arranged more than once, the words '2nd arr.', '3rd arr.', etc., are used.) The column headed 'Earliest Printed Source' lists in abbreviated form the location of the earliest version of the folk-song used for a hymn tune, where known. (Here, 'Somerset' indicates Cecil Sharp's *Folk Songs from Somerset* (5 series, 1904–9); 'JFSS', *Journal of the Folk Song Society* (thirty-five issues, 1899–1931); 'English Traditional', Lucy Broadwood, *English Traditional Songs and Carols* (1908); 'English County', Lucy Broadwood and J A Fuller-Maitland, *English County Songs* (1893); and 'Nursery Rhymes', M H Mason, *Nursery Rhymes and Country Songs* (1877). Note that pagination of these sources is included.) The three columns for the principal hymn books – *The English Hymnal*, *Songs of Praise* and *Songs of Praise Enlarged* – indicate the hymn number as well as the tune number (in parentheses) in cases of multiple tunes for a hymn text. '1906' or '1933' after a hymn number indicates that the tune in question appears only in the 1906 or 1933 editions of *The English Hymnal*; where no date is given, it may be assumed that the tune appears in both. Note, finally, that while the hymn tunes adapted from folk-songs are 40 in number, *Bridgwater* and *Stowey* are both derived from the same folk-song collected by Cecil Sharp, 'Sweet Europe', creating a total of 39 folk-songs used.

10 M Kennedy, *The Works of Ralph Vaughan Williams*, rev. ed., London, OUP, 1980, 74; R Leaver, 'British Hymnody, 1900–1950', in *The Hymnal 1982 Companion*, ed. Raymond Glover, New York, The Church Hymnal Corporation, 1990, Vol. 1, 491–2.

11 Vaughan Williams, *National Music*, 23.

12 Unless otherwise noted, dates of works and editions given in this essay are for the year of completion as found in Michael Kennedy, *A Catalogue of the Work of Ralph Vaughan Williams*, 2nd ed., London, OUP, 1996.

13 This and all subsequent hymn-tune transcriptions reprint the tunes as they appear in *The English Hymnal* (for convenience, the 1933 edition is used), although space limitations necessitate that only the first verse of each text appear.

14 My transcription of 'The Merchant's Daughter' reproduces all musical notation just as it appears in the printed original. Space limitations again prevent the reproduction of more than the first verse of verbal text – which in the original appears directly underneath the

music, as here. My thanks to the English Folk Dance and Song Society for permission to print this folk-song from the *Journal*.

15 The more common heading, used for tunes that received little if no editorial alteration, was simply 'English Traditional Melody'. However, heavily-altered tunes were given the heading 'adapted from an English Traditional Melody', suggesting that the changes to 'The Merchant's Daughter' were middle-of-the-road.

16 Dearmer wrote 'The winter's sleep was long and deep' for *King's Langley*, and of course famously adapted Bunyan's 'He who would valiant be' for *Monks Gate*. See Percy Dearmer and Archibald Jacobs, *Songs of Praise Discussed*, London, OUP, 1933, 139. Some other examples possibly include Athelstan Riley's 'Saints of God' (for *Sussex)* and the text written for *Bridgwater* and *Langport* by Edward Monro and 'M.D.' (Mabel Dearmer?). *Langport* is discussed below.

17 My transcription of 'Lord Rendal' exactly reproduces the melody line of Mrs Perry's tune, not the newly-composed piano harmonies with which Sharp set the tune. (The texture and harmonies of Vaughan Williams' setting appear to owe very little to Sharp's version, incidentally.) The only exception to this is that I have transposed the tune from its original D major to E♭ major in order to facilitate comparison with the hymn tune version. I also provide only the first verse of text from the original; again, this appears directly underneath the music, as here.

18 Hymn No.656 employs two folk-song-derived hymn tunes in alternation. *Bridgwater* (Parts 1, 2 and 3) is set to verses 1–8 and 21–4, while *Langport* (Parts 3 and 4) is set to verses 9–20.

19 *Folk Songs From Somerset*, Vol. 1, London, Simpkin, Marshall, 1905, 68.

20 Vaughan Williams' adaptation of Mr Punt's 'The Fisherman' for the hymn tune *East Horndon* offers another example of radical editing resulting from metrical incompatibility. For a musical analysis, see the present author's 'Hymn Tunes from Folk-Songs: Vaughan Williams and English Hymnody', in *Vaughan Williams Essays*, ed. Byron Adams and Robin Wells, Aldershot, Ashgate, 2003, 114–16.

21 'Preface' to *The English Hymnal with Tunes*, rev. ed., London, OUP, 1933, v.

22 'The Music' in *ibid.*, ix. It is also worth suggesting that Vaughan Williams, who often spoke of the beauty of the King James version of the Bible, probably shared Dearmer's views on the poor state of the words of Victorian hymns. See R Vaughan Williams, *National Music*, 173–4.

23 This and the next two quotations from Kennedy, *Works*, 33–4. Percy Dearmer held similar views on the music of Victorian hymns. See *The Parson's Handbook*, 8th ed., London, Humphrey Milford, 1913, 217.

24 Temperley, *Parish Church*, 303–10, offers a detailed discussion of the musical characteristics of the Victorian hymn tune.

25 Quoted in Kennedy, *Works*, 33.

26 See Vaughan Williams, *National Music*, 28–39, for his views on this matter.

27 Quotations from R Vaughan Williams, 'The Justification of Folk Song', *English Dance and Song* 5/6 (July–August 1941), 66; and R Vaughan Williams, 'How to Sing a Folk-Song', *The Midland Musician* 1/4 (April 1926), 127.

28 'How to Sing a Folk-Song', 127.

29 Vaughan Williams, *National Music*, 79–81

30 Leaver, 'British Hymnody', 490–2; and John Bawden, 'Vaughan Williams and the Hymnals: A New Perspective', *Journal of the Ralph Vaughan Williams Society,* 29 (February 2004), 4–11.

31 Vaughan Williams, 'Preface', ix.

32 'While trying to include all the good tunes, I did my best to eliminate the bad ones. This was difficult because I was not entirely my own master. My committee insisted that certain very popular tunes should be retained.' Vaughan Williams, 'Some Reminiscences', 3.

33 *Household Music* (1941), for string quartet or alternative instruments, includes a movement founded on Joseph Parry's *Aberystwyth*. *Three Preludes founded on Welsh Hymn Tunes* (1920), for organ, are based on William Owen's *Bryn Calfaria*, John Edward's *Rhosymedre*, and R H

Prichard's *Hyfrydol*. *Prelude on Three Welsh Hymn Tunes* (1955), for brass band, also employs *Bryn Calfaria* and *Hyfrydol*.

34 See, for example, David W Music, 'Americans in *The English Hymnal* of 1906', in *With Ever Joyful Hearts: Essays on Liturgy and Music Honoring Marion J Hatchett*, ed. J Neil Alexander, New York, Church Publishing, 1999, 272–95, for an account of the extensive American texts and tunes that the hymnal drew on; also in this volume the chapter by Alan Luff.

35 Since the 1889 edition of *Hymns Ancient & Modern* lacks any composer or source information, I have compiled my data with the help of the 1916 Standard Edition. I include under 'sources' any instance where composer authorship is unclear or ambiguous but the published or manuscript source is given. Thus the 1889 edition includes 39 tunes and arrangements by 30 known German composers and 22 tunes and arrangements from 20 German sources. (A further 6 tunes, identified as 'German' in origin, have no attribution of any kind.) The 1906 *English Hymnal* includes 88 tunes and arrangements by 54 German composers as well 55 tunes from 40 German sources, along with a final 2 'German' tunes with no attribution. It was of course their disappointment with the revised 1904 edition of *Hymns Ancient & Modern* that finally galvanized Dearmer and the committee into action. It seems likely that the greater representation of German music in that edition had some bearing on the *English Hymnal*'s policies, although its figures (103 tunes and arrangements from 73 composers and/or sources) still fall well short of its 1906 rival's.

36 Herbert Westerby, quoted in *Proceedings of the Music Association*, 48 (1921–2), 26. For Westerby, see note 3 above.

37 Quoted in Kennedy, *Works*, 388.

38 The general approach used in Table 1 is retained in Table 2 – organization by hymn-tune name, columns listing the arranger(s), hymn-book locations, and folk-song name and/or source location. The information for this last column, which I must stress is very preliminary, comes mostly from Dearmer, *Songs of Praise Discussed*; K L Parry and Erik Routley, *Companion to Congregational Praise*, London, Independent Press, 1953; and *The Hymnal 1940 Companion*, New York, The Church Pension Fund, 1940. There is also a column listing the regional locations of the folk-songs used. Table 2 includes all non-English tunes that are listed as 'traditional' or 'ancient' either at the head of the tune or in the 'Composers, Arrangers, and Sources of Melodies' index of the various hymnals. I adopt this approach since, in a very few instances, such designations appear in one location but not the other – for example, *Pilgrims of the Night*, described as 'probably adapted from a Swiss Melody' at *English Hymnal* No.399, appears as 'Swiss Traditional Melody' in the index. Similarly, I include here any tunes that are designated as 'traditional' in one publication but not in another – for example *Grafton*, which is listed as a 'French traditional melody' in *Songs of Praise* but as a 'French Church Melody' in the 1933 *English Hymnal* and *Songs of Praise Enlarged*. The important point, in my view, is to identify the tunes that Vaughan Williams and Dearmer *believed* were traditional at the time of publication, even if subsequent research resulted in the revision of earlier opinions. Such vacillations are common in the scholarly examination of the fluid borderline between folk-song and hymnody. But again, instances of inconsistent attribution such as these are very few in number in Table 2.

39 Cecil Sharp collected *Marylebone* from an Irish immigrant living in a central London workhouse. *The Birds* was collected in 1921 in the Czech lands. See Dearmer, *Songs of Praise Discussed*, 206.

40 Kennedy, *Catalogue*, 16, 18, 19, 21, 27, 65, 85, 91, 178, 214 and 219. The total number of Vaughan Williams' non-English folk-song arrangements, outside of those he made for hymn books, is 22.

41 Vaughan Williams, 'Some Reminiscences', 2.

42 Alain Frogley, 'Constructing Englishness in Music: National Character and the Reception of Ralph Vaughan Williams', in *Vaughan Williams Studies*, ed. Frogley, Cambridge, CUP, 1996, 1–22.

43 Jan Marsh, *Back to the Land: The Pastoral Impulse in England, from 1880 to 1914*, London, Quartet Books, 1982.

44 Martin J Weiner, *English Culture and the Decline of the Industrial Spirit, 1850–1980*, Cambridge, CUP, 1981.

45 Alun Howkins, 'The Discovery of Rural England', in *Englishness: Politics and Culture 1880–1920*, ed. Robert Colls and Philip Dodd, London, Croom Helm, 1986, 62–88; and Brian Doyle, 'The Invention of English,' in *ibid.*, 89–115. For an interpretation of the Folk Revival's role in this class manoeuvre, see Dave Harker, *Fakesong: The Manufacture of British 'Folksong' 1700 to the Present Day*, Milton Keynes, Open University Press, 1985, esp. Chapter 9; and Georgina Boyes, *The Imagined Village: Culture, Ideology and the English Folk Revival*, Manchester, Manchester University Press, 1993, esp. Chapter 3.

46 See Marsh, *Back to the Land*, 1–23; also Peter C Gould, *Early Green Politics: Back to Nature, Back to the Land, and Socialism in Britain 1880–1900*, Brighton, Harvester Press, 1988.

47 Donald Gray, *Percy Dearmer: A Parson's Pilgrimage*, Norwich, Canterbury Press, 2000, *passim*. For the political and social views of the other committee members, see *ibid.*, 62–3.

48 See Paul Harrington, 'Holst and Vaughan Williams: Radical Pastoral', in Christopher Norris, ed., *Music and the Politics of Culture*, London, Lawrence and Wishart, 1987, 106–27; and the present author's *Ralph Vaughan Williams's Folk-song Collecting: English Nationalism and the Rise of Professional Society*, Ph.D. diss., New York University, 1998, especially Chapter Two. Donald Gray further points out that the two men who separately advised Dearmer to hire Vaughan Williams as music editor, Canon Scott Holland and Cecil Sharp, were both socialists. (*Percy Dearmer*, 63–4.) He is incorrect, however, in linking Holland to Vaughan Williams through St Barnabas Pimlico, where Holland occasionally worshipped and where A F A Hanbury-Tracy, another member of the *English Hymnal* committee, was vicar. Vaughan Williams was organist and choirmaster at St Barnabas South Lambeth.

49 Undated letter concerning the proofs of Sharp's *English Folk Songs: Some Conclusions*. Cecil Sharp MS Collection: Correspondence T-Z [box 3], Vaughan Williams Memorial Library, English Folk Dance and Song Society, London. My thanks to librarian Malcolm Taylor for drawing my attention to this source and to the EFDSS for permission to quote the letter here.

50 Gustav Holst and R Vaughan Williams, *Heirs and Rebels: Letters Written to Each Other and Occasional Writings on Music by Ralph Vaughan Williams and Gustav Holst*, ed. Ursula Vaughan Williams and Imogen Holst, London, OUP, 1959, 38.

51 Dearmer, 'Preface', iii.

52 Leaver, 'British Hymnody', 493–9.

53 R Vaughan Williams, *National Music*, 39.

GERMAN CHORALE MELODIES IN *THE ENGLISH HYMNAL*

Bernard S. Massey

In the 1520s a key aim of Martin Luther, as prime mover of the Reformation in Germany, was to provide opportunity for the laity to take an integral part in liturgical worship. To this end he introduced the vernacular hymns now generally referred to as chorales.

They were not the first German hymns. But earlier hymns had been the preserve of monastic choirs or restricted to non-liturgical occasions. Luther's innovation was to use hymns as a vehicle for congregational contribution at the centre of the liturgy. Many of the early chorales were adapted from a variety of older sources, especially Gregorian hymns and sequences. Luther himself, however, wrote several chorale texts and, as a canny and capable musician, he also composed or adapted suitable melodies. He encouraged others to follow his example and thus, over the next 200 years or so, a size-able body of vernacular hymnody was built up.

The writers of the chorale texts gave free rein to their poetic imaginations and their enterprise resulted in a great variety of metre and form. Notwithstanding this diversity the associated melodies acquired certain familial characteristics arising from the need for confident congregational participation. In normal use (that is not in oratorios or cantatas) the melodies would be sung entirely in unison, whether or not organ accompaniment was provided. The classic chorale setting would be mostly one note per syllable, although congregations, then as now, would no doubt insert extra (passing) notes to smooth over melodic intervals. In any case, intervals that would be difficult for untrained singers relying on memory were avoided. In the longer melodies the last phrase (or pair of phrases) often repeated an earlier part of the melody (e.g. *Ave Virgo Virginum* (131)): this is of course a potent aid to the memory.

These German developments were in sharp contrast to the contemporaneous situation in Britain for example. Here the stimulus for the Reformation came more from Switzerland than Germany. For British Protestants congregational praise consisted almost solely of metrical psalms with a very restricted range of metres. A congregation's musical needs could thus be met by just a handful of tunes. Early hymn-writers, such as Isaac Watts, mostly used the metres of the metrical psalms, so ensuring a supply of ready-made tunes. Only later did writers spread their wings into other metres and so require a much larger tune repertoire.

Victorian Britain saw massive changes. Increasing industrialization led to large movements of population and thus the building of churches of all denominations at an unprecedented rate. Literacy improved. Anglican (and to a lesser extent other) churches came to regard a four-part choir as a status symbol and the choir rather than the congregation at large was the focus of musical attention. Much church music was composed in, or cast into, a part-song style. Whatever beauties or benefits this might have had in its own terms its intricacy, refinement of expression and particularly the high pitch of melodic lines were discouragements to congregational participation. Choirs, moreover, were apt to resent the intrusion of uncouth congregational voices into their own choice contribution.

Hymn books proliferated and wealthier churches produced their own. This gave rise to a large demand for hymn tunes which many an amateur composer, talented or not, hastened to meet. Dilution of quality was inevitable.

Vaughan Williams in editing *The English Hymnal* did not disguise his disdain for much of the hymn music in circulation as the twentieth century dawned. Furthermore, as he made clear in the Musical Editor's preface, a particular concern of the book was to restore hymn singing to the whole congregation. What better for that purpose than the sturdy, easily singable melodies of German chorales that had stood the test of time?

The English Hymnal was not the first book to draw on chorale melodies. By the mid-nineteenth century a handful had become known, at least to musical cognoscenti, through the works of Bach and more particularly Mendelssohn. Of these melodies the most celebrated is doubtless *Nun Danket* (533). Then in 1847, the year of Mendelssohn's death, the Revd W H Havergal published his *Old Church Psalmody* in which, with perhaps more enthusiasm than discernment, he included what Vaughan Williams termed 'distorted and mutilated' versions of various originals. In Havergal's defence it may be said that he sought to bring something of the richness of other traditions to the restricted repertoire used in Britain at that time. One of the best-known examples of Havergal's cut-and-paste approach is the serviceable, if unexciting, short-metre tune *Franconia* (370), the result of piecing together snippets of an original in 67.67.66 metre.

Another enthusiast for bringing chorale melodies to Britain was Baron von Bunsen (1791–1860), the Prussian ambassador to Britain, 1841–54. As he could not countenance the adaptation of German melodies to fit English metres he persuaded Catherine Winkworth to produce translations of German texts in the metres of the originals. This was a tall order because of the different natural rhythms and word order of German and English and the need to match the metres of original and translation. But Miss Winkworth rose to the challenge and the result was *The Chorale Book for England*, 1863, a volume of 200 hymns set to 121 different tunes harmonized by William Sterndale Bennett and Otto Goldschmidt. The book did not make the impact in English churches that had been hoped for and not many of its contents entered the standard British repertoire. A shining exception, however, is the metrical *tour de force* 'Praise to the Lord, the Almighty' (536) in 14.14.4.7.8.

Other translators of chorale texts, and indeed Catherine Winkworth herself in some of her earlier work, were little concerned to preserve the German metres. Thus the importation of chorale melodies was largely on an individual basis, and too often they were squashed into rather lifeless foursquare versions similar to native hymn tunes. (Compare, for example, *Nun Danket All*, 421, with No.459 in the old Standard edition of *Hymns Ancient & Modern*.)

Vaughan Williams was, he said, concerned not only to utilize chorale melodies but 'as far as possible' to restore them to their 'original' forms. But what were the original forms? Many of the melodies had in fact undergone change over the years, even in Germany. The most notable reviser was J S Bach who, when incorporating chorale melodies into his cantatas, passions and oratorios, was not averse to producing versions of his own. In particular he would usually 'square up' the rhythm into regular common or triple time. Bach was VW's great hero; thus he would normally prefer a Bach version of a melody over any other. In the EH preface (p. xv) VW says 'the object has been to print the finest version of every tune, not necessarily the earliest'. In fact, for VW the golden age of the chorale was evidently the early eighteenth century, and 'the finest version' was one in a modern major or minor mode with regularly placed bar-lines.

The new broom swept energetically. Of the 555 different (non-plainsong) tunes in EH's first edition, approximately 121 (22%) were, or were derived from, chorale melodies, and 22 of them were printed twice. (The numbers are approximate because the category inevitably has slightly blurred boundaries.) A similar count for the new (1904) edition of *Hymns Ancient & Modern*, expected at the time to be EH's chief rival, shows chorale melodies accounting for about 10% of the total, with only five doing double duty.

Among the books likely to have been at VW's elbow when he began his task of selecting tunes would of course have been *Hymns A&M*. About 25 of EH's chorale melodies came direct from the old or new editions of A&M with little or no alteration. Surprisingly perhaps, there seems to have been no direct input from *The Chorale Book for England*, although some items such as *Nun Danket* (533) and *Hast Du Denn, Jesu* (536) had travelled indirectly via A&M.

VW also availed himself of 27 of the less complex of Bach's chorale settings. When a choice was on offer, for example with *Passion Chorale* (102), he normally opted for the most straightforward and therefore most congregational setting. In one instance, *Herzliebster Jesu* (70), he produced a conflation of two harmonizations (*St Matthew Passion* No.3 and *St John Passion* No.7) which has since become the standard version in British hymn books. However, he also included the more elaborate harmonization from *St Matthew Passion* No.55 with the stern injunction that it was for use only in verses where the choir sings alone. For *Passion Chorale* he added as alternative the version from *St Matthew Passion* No.72 with the even sterner instruction that it must be sung by the choir alone. Each of these alternative settings, he warned, should be attempted only by good choirs.

EH is notable not only for the care but also for the astonishing speed with which it was produced. As musical editor VW simply did not have the time (and probably not the inclination) to research the origins of chorale melodies in countless German tune books. So he must have rejoiced in being able to use Johannes Zahn's monumental metrical index[1] of nearly 9000 chorale melodies and their variants. This massive work not only printed the melodies but documented in detail the principal changes they had undergone over the years. For most tunes only the melody line was given: consequently VW, or one of his associates (honoured on p. xix of the preface) had to supply the accompanying harmonies.

In several instances the style of these harmonizations is clearly modelled on Bach, with baroque detailing involving many short-length notes. Hymns in general, maintained VW, were sung too fast: EH abounds with the warning *Slow* or even *Very Slow*. Impressive as the elaborate settings may sound in a large building, the harmonic speed humps slow down singers in more intimate surroundings. In any case, much faster tempi are now in vogue and the impatient twenty-first century is apt to find the harmonic curlicues less acceptable.

There is no doubt of EH's indebtedness to Zahn. A telling piece of evidence is a small slip which had eluded Zahn's usual attention to detail. In J G Schicht's tune *Zu Meinem Herrn* (119) Zahn miscopied or misprinted the first note of the final phrase a tone too high. This error was duly reproduced in EH. There would be no point now in trying to 'correct' the error: the 'wrong' melody is perfectly satisfactory even though it does not fit the original harmony (in Schicht's *Allgemeines Choral-Buch,* Leipzig, 1819).

Zahn was no doubt again called on in the selection of tunes for *Songs of Praise* 1925 and 1931 which had VW as joint musical editor with Martin Shaw. It drew on a very wide range of literary sources, many of which had not previously been considered hymn material. Thus the book presented a remarkable variety of metres for which Zahn would have proved an invaluable resource.

The second edition of EH in 1933 included no new hymn texts (apart from Blake's 'Jerusalem' which has its own inseparable tune); strictly therefore no new tunes were called for. However, VW took the opportunity to add more than 100 tunes, the majority of them from *Songs of Praise*. Among the newcomers were 14 chorale tunes, all but three from *Songs of Praise*.

But there in 1933 the story of EH and the chorales effectively ends. The team's next publication was *Hymnal for Scotland*, 1950, for the Scottish Episcopal Church. This incorporated the whole of the 1933 EH plus a supplement of 15 items especially for Scottish use. The sole chorale tune in the supplement, *O Jesu*, was repeated from the parent book. Neither *The English Hymnal Service Book*, 1962, nor the supplement *English Praise*, 1975, added further to the chorale stock.

The New English Hymnal, 1986, smaller in content than EH (though much greater in bulk), dropped 12 chorale tunes: two in favour of less austere, more popular, alternatives; the others because the corresponding hymn texts had been discarded.

It seems, then, that the introduction of German chorale melodies to Anglican congregations, and indeed to the British in general, has run its course. And, given the huge changes in musical taste and styles of worship over the past hundred years, there is little likelihood of this import trade being resumed. Not all the chorale melodies in EH proved to be sure-fire winners. Yet a measure of VW's success is the very small number of them that were not subsequently adopted in books beyond the EH family.

Note

1   Johannes Zahn, *Die Melodien der Deutschen evangelischen Kirchenlieder, aus den Quellen geschöpft und mitgeteilt*, six volumes, Gütersloh, 1889–93.

WELSH TUNES IN *THE ENGLISH HYMNAL*

Rhidian Griffiths

One of the achievements of *The English Hymnal* was the introduction to a wider audience of a number of Welsh tunes, some of which have become mainstays of the repertoire of English hymnody. Tentative steps had been taken in this direction by, for instance, *The Methodist Hymn Book* (1904), but the selection of Welsh tunes provided by Vaughan Williams in 1906 was unique in its depth and range.

It is hard to say what prompted Vaughan Williams to seek out Welsh tunes. He may have been aware that Welsh hymnody had developed markedly during the late nineteenth century and that Welsh hymnals contained a number of stirring tunes unknown outside Wales. Welsh hymn singing had been praised by English musicians, who had admired its fiery quality and harmonic richness. As a collector of folk-songs, and one who was involved with the English Folk-Song Society, Vaughan Williams may have come into contact with the nascent folk-song movement in Wales. Or he may simply have come across tunes like R H Prichard's *Hyfrydol* and Joseph Parry's *Aberystwyth*, and been sufficiently impressed to find out more about the tradition from which they had sprung.

He had two principal sources of Welsh tunes. On p. xix of the Preface to the 1906 edition he acknowledges the help of:

> the Rev. Hugh Davies, L.T.S.C. (Pencerdd Maelor), editor of 'Caniadau y Cyssegr a'r Teulu', and the Rev. W L Richards, editor of 'Emyniadur yr Eglwys yng Nghymru', for much valuable information concerning Welsh hymn melodies ...

Hugh Davies (1844–1907), originally from Garth, near Rhiwabon in north-east Wales, was from 1895 until his death a Calvinistic Methodist minister at Plasmarl, Swansea. In 1889 he edited a revised edition of a non-denominational collection of hymn tunes entitled *Caniadau y Cyssegr a'r Teulu* (Songs of the Sanctuary and the Family), originally published in 1878 by Gee and Son of Denbigh. The collection comprises Welsh traditional tunes and more recent compositions, and a single stanza of text (Welsh and English) is given with each tune as an example of words to which it may be sung. The revised edition, containing 825 tunes, was to prove a valuable source-book for *The English Hymnal*.

It is possible that Vaughan Williams was introduced to Davies by his other Welsh associate, the Anglican W L Richards. William Lewis Richards (1861–1921), son of the rector of Cemaes in Montgomeryshire, served as a curate at Merthyr Tydfil, Oswestry and Llandudno, where he showed his musical gifts by editing choral versions of the Prayer Book and Psalter in Welsh. He was then appointed to the living of Penstrowed in Montgomeryshire, where he concentrated on editing the musical portion of *Emyniadur yr Eglwys yng Nghymru* (The Hymnal of the Church in Wales). This was one of several Welsh hymnals produced for the Anglican Church in Wales during the late nineteenth century. The initiative for it seems to have come from Lewis Lloyd, Bishop of Bangor, and his name appears as one of the editors, alongside Chancellor D Silvan Evans and W L Richards. Acknowledgement is also made of the contribution of Roland Rogers (1847–1927), organist of Bangor Cathedral from 1871 to 1891 and again from 1902 to 1927, who harmonized many of the tunes in the book. The *Emyniadur* appeared in a words only edition in 1895, and the music edition followed in 1898. It contains a mixture of Welsh traditional tunes, tunes by Welsh composers, and tunes imported from England.

The 1906 *English Hymnal* contains 23 tunes of Welsh origin or attribution. Of these, twelve are attributed to specific composers or sources; three are described as 'Welsh traditional melody', and the remaining eight as 'Welsh hymn melody'. Two belong to the seventeenth-century psalter tradition. *St Mary* (84) first appeared in Edmwnd Prys's metrical *Llyfr y Psalmau* (Book of Psalms) in 1621, and may be of Welsh origin. Prys has it as a Dorian melody, but *The English Hymnal*, like all other hymnals which have included it, follows Playford's *The Whole Book of Psalms* (1677) in reproducing it in the minor key. *St David* (166) is one of a group of tunes found in Ravenscroft's *The Whole Book of Psalms* (1621), said to be Welsh in origin and named after the Welsh cathedrals. Both these tunes, however, appear to have reached *The English Hymnal* via English sources, not directly from Wales.

Of the remainder, most belong to the category of Welsh tunes composed, collected and published during the first three quarters of the nineteenth century. No Welsh tune books are known to have been published before 1800, even though many of the tunes recorded in the 1830s and 1840s may have been in circulation for some time. Several of them appear in one or more of the seminal collections *Peroriaeth Hyfryd* (Sweet Music) by John Parry (1837), *Caniadau y Cyssegr* (Songs of the Sanctuary) by John Roberts (1839) and *Caniadau Seion* (Songs of Zion) by Richard Mills (1840), all of which record tunes as sung by contemporary congregations and preserved in a largely oral tradition. The best Welsh tunes in these collections are strong and simple, often working within a limited melodic compass, and having powerful rhythmic drive, with 'an insistence on the notes of the common chord'.[1] Six of the best of the *English Hymnal* tunes may be found in one or more of these volumes.

From *Peroriaeth Hyfryd* come *Llanfair, Caersalem* and *Moriah. Llanfair* (143) first appeared here, unattributed and under the name *Bethel*: it was the music journal *Y Cerddor* (The Musician) which in 1896 definitively attributed it to the blind Robert Williams (1782–1818) of Llanfechell, Anglesey. *Caersalem* (397) is the only Welsh tune in *The English Hymnal* set to words of Welsh origin, William Williams' 'Guide me, O thou great Jehovah'. Its composer, Robert Edwards, was a precentor of Welsh congregations in Liverpool. *Moriah* (437) is an interesting example of a Welsh tune made popular in eighteenth-century English sources. It appeared in Madan's *Collection of Psalm and Hymn Tunes* in 1769 as *Love Divine* and is called *Welsh* in Aaron Williams' *Universal Psalmodist* of 1770. *Peroriaeth Hyfryd* also gives it the name *Welsh*. It follows a classic AABA pattern common in Welsh tunes.

Caniadau y Cyssegr is the source of the two tunes *Ffigysbren* and *St Denio*. *Ffigysbren* (324) is usually known as *Clod*[2] (Praise) in Welsh hymnals, and appears in numerous variant forms. It is called *Bethesda* in *Caniadau y Cyssegr* and *Clod* in *Caniadau Seion*, and although most sources describe it as a Welsh tune, it may be of English origin. It bears similarities to 'The fashionable lady' in *The Cobblers' Opera* (1729) and is apparently the same as 'Death and the lady' in Chappell's *Old English Popular Music* (1893). Its use as a hymn tune appears, however, to originate in Wales. *St Denio* (407), one of the most celebrated of the *English Hymnal* 'discoveries', is in origin a Welsh ballad tune, 'Can mlynedd i nawr' (A hundred years from now). Its first appearance as a hymn tune is in an English source, namely Edward Miller's collection of *Sacred Music*, published around 1800, where it is called *Rowlands* and described as 'An old original Welsh melody, never before printed'. It seems certain, however, that its publication in John Roberts' *Caniadau y Cyssegr* in 1839 is derived not from Miller but from contemporary Welsh usage. Roberts calls the tune *Palestina*. Only William Lloyd's *Meirionydd* (473) appears exclusively in *Caniadau Seion*, but this collection also contains *St Denio*, under the name *Joanna*, by which it is commonly known to Welsh congregations, and *Ffigysbren* under the name *Clod*.

These six tunes represent the cream of Welsh traditional hymn tunes from the late eighteenth and early nineteenth centuries. But Vaughan Williams also ventured to include three tunes defined as 'Welsh traditional melodies' and not typically in use as hymn tunes before 1906. All three may be derived from Brinley Richards' immensely popular collection, *Songs of Wales*, published by Boosey in 1873. *Ymdaith Mwngc* (203), an unconvincing setting of words by Christina Rossetti, is now thought to be of English origin: it appeared as *Restoration Tune* in the 1665 edition of Playford's *Dancing Master*, where it is described in the index as *The Lord Monk's March*. Edward Jones adopted an arrangement published in 1719 and made a spurious connection with the march of the monks of Bangor Is-y-Coed to the battle of Chester in 613, before claiming the tune as Welsh in his *Musical and Poetical Relicks of the Welsh Bards* in 1784.

The much more familiar *Ar hyd y nos* (All through the night) likewise appeared in Jones' *Relicks* in 1784, and became a popular tune in the London of the early nineteenth century. Vaughan Williams may have known that this was the melody which Heber had in mind for his 'God that madest earth and heaven', but he may equally have taken it from *Caniadau y Cyssegr a'r Teulu*. Welsh congregations have been much slower to adopt it as a hymn tune, partly no doubt because of its strong associations with secular words in the Welsh mind. *Rhuddlan* (423) first appeared as *Dewch i'r frwydr* (Come to the battle) in the revised 1794 edition of Jones' *Relicks*, though the rhythm adopted in *The English Hymnal* appears to have been derived from *Songs of Wales*. In 1870 Morris Davies conjectured that William Williams had written his 87.87.67 metre hymns to this melody, but in Welsh hymnic usage the tune was transmuted into the minor key and was known as *Iorddonen* or *Jordan*. Its absence from Welsh hymnals tends to reinforce the view that Vaughan Williams took the tune from *Songs of Wales*, though it is a puzzle why he chose to give the fourth note of the melody as the tonic rather than the super-tonic, which it invariably is in Welsh sources. Nor is it clear why he adopted the name *Rhuddlan* for the tune. It was not apparently until 1951 that it was brought back to Wales in this form, in the Anglican *Emynau'r Eglwys* (Church Hymns).

The remaining tunes were composed from the 1830s onward, but most of them may be said to be traditionally Welsh in character. *Lovely* (303) appears in later books under the name *Rhosymedre*, the name of the parish in Denbighshire where its composer, J D Edwards (1805–85), was the incumbent for many years. It was first printed in the periodical *Y Drysorfa* (The Treasury) in May 1838, and subsequently in the composer's collection of *Original Sacred Music* (1839). *Hyfrydol* (301) by Rowland Hugh Pritchard, a weaver from Bala in Merionethshire, first appeared in the composer's *Cyfaill y Cantorion* (Singers' Friend) in 1844. It was published in the *Methodist Hymn Book* of 1904, and this was perhaps Vaughan Williams' immediate source. The dotted rhythm in the melody of the second bar, firmly established in English practice, appears to be derived from the form of the melody in *Hymnau yr Eglwys* (Hymns of the Church) (1897), whereas most Welsh sources have equal notes at that point (the original had no movement between the first and third beats of the bar). William Owen's *Bryn Calfaria* (319) appeared in 1853 in the com-poser's *Y Perl Cerddorol* (The Musical Pearl), and subsequently in many Welsh collections. *The English Hymnal* and other English collections retain the orig-inal barring, which has the tune opening on the first beat of the bar: most Welsh collections – to Owen's annoyance – amended this to give an anacrusis. *Caniadau y Cyssegr a'r Teulu* does, however, retain the original barring, and this was no doubt the source Vaughan Williams used, though he edited out the antiphony between the melody and lower parts which characterizes the last three lines of the original, and reharmonized the whole. It was on three of these tunes that Vaughan Williams chose to compose his *Three Preludes on Welsh Hymn Tunes*: *Bryn Calfaria*, *Lovely* and *Hyfrydol*.

Prysgol (575), again by William Owen, is an interesting example of a tune unknown to Welsh congregations but accorded a place of honour in *The*

English Hymnal. Derived from *Caniadau y Cyssegr a'r Teulu* where it is called *Pren Afalau* (Apple Tree), it was written for words by the poet John Thomas (1742–1818) of Pentrefoelas, Denbighshire, which liken Christ to an apple tree under which the believer may take shelter. Prysgol is the name of Owen's home near Caernarfon. This undistinguished tune is not included in other Welsh collections, and it is hard to see why Vaughan Williams wished to use it. One of the great triumphs of *The English Hymnal* on the other hand was the inspired setting of *Gwalchmai* (424) to George Herbert's 'King of glory, King of peace', a marriage that now seems indissoluble. The tune first appeared in *Llyfr Tonau ac Emynau* (Book of Tunes and Hymns), edited by the composer J D Jones (1827–70) and Edward Stephen, and published in 1868. *Hope* (551) by Robert Davies also first appeared in *Llyfr Tonau ac Emynau* in 1868, under the name *Gobaith*, but in subsequent collections this name was translated to its English equivalent, *Hope*. Joseph Parry's *Aberystwyth* (87) was introduced to accompany Richard Grant's 'Saviour, when in dust to thee'. The tune, first published in 1879 in Edward Stephen (Tanymarian)'s *Ail Lyfr Tonau ac Emynau* (Second Book of Tunes and Hymns), had appeared in *The Methodist Hymn Book* in 1904. It is interesting, however, that in the 1889 *Caniadau y Cyssegr a'r Teulu*, *Aberystwyth* is linked to the same English text by Richard Grant.

The remaining eight Welsh tunes are described as 'Welsh hymn melodies' and include some which have become well established in English usage. Of these, *Ebenezer* (108) is one of the best known. This is perhaps the only trace of the influence on *The English Hymnal* of the Welsh religious revival of 1904–5, during which the tune was widely sung. It is odd that it should be labelled a 'Welsh hymn melody' even in the 1933 edition, when its known composer, T J Williams (1869–1944), was still alive. The tune had been printed in the periodical *Yr Athraw* (The Teacher) in 1897, and subsequently the composer used it as part of an anthem. The tune *Arfon* (116) is derived from *Caniadau y Cyssegr a'r Teulu*, apparently the only Welsh book in which the tune is to be found in a six-line form: to Welsh congregations it is now well known in an eight-line version. Though described as a Welsh melody, it is thought to be a carol tune of French origin, found in Charpentier's *Messe de Minuit* (c1690). Given the strong links between Wales and Brittany, it may have been brought to Wales and have gained popularity in oral tradition, so being assumed to be Welsh. *Llangloffan* (207) on the other hand has every claim to be thought a Welsh tune, though some have tried to associate it with 'The miller of Dee'. It was collected by David Lewis of Llanrhystud, Ceredigion and first published in the Baptist collection *Llwybrau Moliant* (Paths of Praise), edited by Lewis Jones (1872). It subsequently appeared in the 1875 supplement to *Hymnau a Thonau er gwasanaeth yr Eglwys yn Nghymru* (Hymns and Tunes for the Service of the Church in Wales).

The *Emyniadur* is the source of the tune *Dolgelly* (349), printed in Griffith Harris's *Halelwiah Drachefn* (Hallelujah Again) (1855) where it is called

Canaan's Banks (which may suggest an origin outside Wales). It is in a more extended form there, with the fifth and sixth lines repeated. The present form, with some variations of rhythm, has appeared in several Welsh books. *The English Hymnal*, however, repeats one curiosity found only in the *Emyniadur*, and which may be a simple misprint: the first note of the melody in the fifth line is the third of the chord, whereas elsewhere it is invariably the fifth. *Llansannan* (514) is again derived from the *Emyniadur*, and is an arrangement of a secular song, 'Y gwelltyn glas' (The green blade), which first appeared as a hymn tune in *Aberth Moliant* (Sacrifice of Praise) (1873), arranged by W J Hughes, though possibly in congregational use before then. *The English Hymnal* reproduces a feature of the *Emyniadur* version which is unlike other printings by giving the first note of the melody in the seventh line as the sub-mediant rather than the tonic – again possibly a misprint in the *Emyniadur*. The 1933 edition reverted to the established form, describing it as a 'more correct' version.

Vaughan Williams relied on his two principal sources for most of the tunes he used. From *Emyniadur yr Eglwys yng Nghymru* he appears to have derived *Llanfair, Caersalem, Meirionydd, Ffigysbren, St Denio* (though the name is taken from Thomas Jones' *Welsh Church Tune and Chant Book*; the *Emyniadur* calls it *Joanna*), *Moriah, Lovely, Llangloffan, Dolgelly* and *Llansannan*. From *Caniadau y Cyssegr a'r Teulu* he took *Arfon, Prysgol, Hope* and *Gwalchmai*, and perhaps *Ar Hyd y Nos*.

He harmonized or reharmonized virtually all these tunes, to a greater or lesser extent. *Moriah*, for instance, appears exactly as it is in the *Emyniadur*, complete with the grace notes characteristic of the Welsh style of the early nineteenth century, but very few others go unamended. In academic terms Vaughan Williams' harmonies and arrangements are superior to those found in the Welsh collections from which he took the tunes, but they do not always accord with Welsh practice. *Ffigysbren* is extended from its usual four lines to six by repeating the first couplet, a device which sounds strange to a Welsh ear, as does the more exotic harmony of the final line. *Lovely* on the other hand is treated in a simple and sympathetic way which enhances the melody. *St Denio* appears in a dignified, unadorned harmonization which follows the *Emyniadur* and ultimately the *Welsh Church Tune and Chant Book* in eliminating the passing notes in the melody line which are a characteristic of the tune as sung in Wales. The most obvious example of reharmonization is *Ebenezer*. Presumably in the belief that the melody was traditional, Vaughan Williams reharmonized the whole. The cadence at the end of the sixth line is quite different from T J Williams' original harmony, retained in Welsh hymnals, which has a characteristically Welsh major chord at that point.

Was Vaughan Williams' experiment successful? Certainly, in terms of some tunes: *Aberystwyth, Ar hyd y nos, Ebenezer, Gwalchmai, Hyfrydol, Llanfair, Rhuddlan* and *St Denio* have achieved lasting fame, and most are still regularly associated with the words to which they were set in *The English Hymnal*.

WELSH TUNES IN *THE ENGLISH HYMNAL*

Others – *Bryn Calfaria, Llangloffan, Lovely (Rhosymedre), Meirionydd* and *St Mary* – still find a place in English hymnals, though they are less well known than the tunes of the premier league. Some were not well served by the words to which they were set, or have had to face competition from tunes that are better known. *Ffigysbren*, for instance, does not compete successfully with Gibbons' *Song 1* as a tune for 'O Thou who at thy Eucharist didst pray'; and it is fair to say that *Ffigysbren* (or *Clod*) is by now rarely sung by Welsh congregations. The solemn and prayerful *Dolgelly* is not well matched with a rather weak hymn for the sick. *Moriah* has been supplanted by *Blaenwern* for 'Love divine, all loves excelling', while *Llansannan*, though it seems suited to Walsham How's 'Who is this so weak and helpless', has an intensity of emotion that perhaps does not appeal to English-speaking congregations. That several tunes are still in use one hundred years on suggests nevertheless that Vaughan Williams' experiment was well worth the risk.

The 1933 edition added thirteen Welsh tunes to the complement of 1906 (*Aberystwyth* was also printed a second time as an alternative to *Hollingside* for 'Jesu, lover of my soul').

The years between 1906 and 1933 were a period of considerable musical development in Wales. New collections were published which, through the agency of editors like Walford Davies and David Evans, brought to the fore good Welsh tunes both traditional and new: several appeared in *Songs of Praise* in 1925 and its revision in 1931. Some of these tunes, such as *Rhyddid* (EH1933, 222) are in the canonical tradition established in 1906; others are new compositions, such as Morfydd Owen's angular *Richard* (EH1933, 56) and David Evans' *Ton-mân* (EH1933, 270) and *Yn y Glyn* (EH1933, 563). Few have enjoyed much success among English congregations, certainly none on the scale of *Gwalchmai, Aberystwyth* or *St Denio*. It is significant that of the sixteen Welsh tunes included in *The New English Hymnal* in 1986, thirteen are to be found in the 1906 *English Hymnal*. Only one, John Ambrose Lloyd's *Cromer* (an unexpected choice), is an addition from 1933. The other two Welsh tunes in *The New English Hymnal* are the now ubiquitous and inevitable *Blaenwern* and *Cwm Rhondda*, which for so many, outside Wales and within, have come to epitomize the Welsh hymn tune. Comparison of these two with the original *English Hymnal* list of 1906 may suggest that the true riches of the Welsh tradition were those uncovered by Vaughan Williams a century ago.

Notes

1   Erik Routley, 'Welsh hymnody' in *The Music of Christian Hymnody*, London, Independent Press, 1957, 160–4, at p. 163.
2   Pronounced 'Cload' (the 'o' is long).

VAUGHAN WILLIAMS' 'CHAMBER OF HORRORS' – CHANGING ATTITUDES TOWARDS VICTORIAN HYMNS

Ian Bradley

One of the best known and most intriguing features of *The English Hymnal* is the appendix of 'additional tunes which do not enter into the general scheme of the book'. Famously referred to by Vaughan Williams as 'the Chamber of Horrors', it represents a significant assault on Victorian hymn tunes.

Ralph Vaughan Williams was not, of course, the first musician to express his distaste for the emotionalism, sentimentality and shallowness of many of the hymn tunes composed in the latter half of the nineteenth century. Several Victorian critics had railed against their contemporaries for suspending their usual critical musical faculties and standards when it came to writing tunes for hymns. W H Hadow, editor of *The Oxford History of Music*, could not forgive John Stainer for defending the work of J B Dykes. In a savage review of Stainer's own collected hymn tunes, Hadow praised plainsong melodies, German chorales and French and Swiss psalm tunes and tore into modern British hymn tunes for their cloying sentimentality and second-rate musicality: 'They seek the honeyed cadence and the perfumed phrase ... they can touch the surface of emotion, but can never sound its depths.'[1] Robert Bridges felt much the same way, noting that his daughter's confirmation service in Exeter had been 'ruined by the introduction of some of the most maudlin and washy hymns with their tunes out of *Hymns Ancient & Modern*'.[2]

Bridges' *Yattendon Hymnal*, which appeared in four parts between 1895 and 1899, was a reaction against nearly all that Victorian hymn-writers and hymn tune composers stood for. It emphasized musical and literary purity rather than singability, emotional power and didactic impact. The editors of *The English Hymnal* took a very similar approach to that adopted by Bridges, as did G R Woodward in his *Songs of Syon* which appeared in 1910. Whereas both the *Yattendon Hymnal* and *Songs of Syon* had small circulations and only limited impact, however, *The English Hymnal* was a mainstream publication widely taken up in the Church of England. As such, it gave considerable impetus to the movement against Victorian hymnody.

It is worth examining the contents of the infamous appendix as they give a significant pointer to what Vaughan Williams did not like. Altogether there are 16 items in his 'Chamber of Horrors'. Two are higher settings of tunes found in the main body of the book – Dykes' *Nicaea* set in E rather than D and *Easter Hymn* set in D rather than C. It is not clear why Vaughan Williams felt the need to include these two settings. His preference for unison over part-singing and for lowering the pitch of hymns explains why in the body of the book he took them down a tone. In their higher form, both contain a sustained high E which is certainly not comfortable for those singing the melody line in unison. Perhaps his inclusion of the higher settings in the Chamber of Horrors signalled a quiet protest against the too high pitching of hymns in his own time. He wanted to show just how uncomfortable Victorian hymn book editors made life for congregations who were not into or up to part-singing.

The other 14 items are all mid- or late-nineteenth-century tunes. Most of the leading Victorian hymn tune composers find their way into the Chamber of Horrors – W H Monk tops the list with three entries (*St Philip*, *Wirtemburg* and *Nutfield*), Barnby appears twice (with *For All the Saints* and *St Chrysostom*) and Thrupp (*Epiphany*), Dykes (*St Cross*), Scholefield (*St Clement*), Sullivan (*Golden Sheaves*), Bullinger (*Bullinger*), Schulthes (*Requiem*), W B Gilbert (*Maidstone*), Sankey (*Beneath the Cross*) and Northrop (*Northrop*) all make one appearance.

Relegation to the appendix is not the only indicator of Vaughan Williams' disapproval of modern hymn tunes. Perhaps even more indicative is the very poor showing of Victorian composers in the main body of the book. Sullivan is almost completely excluded, with *St Gertrude*, the only tune of his to be included, being pointedly given as the alternative tune for 'Onward, Christian soldiers' and a second best to *Haydn*. 'Alleluia! Alleluia! Hearts to heaven and voices raise', which cries out for Sullivan's gloriously affirmative *Lux Eoi*, is set in *The English Hymnal* to Smart's *Everton* (which was itself relegated to a further appendix in the 1933 edition with *Wurzburg* being substituted as the preferred tune for this hymn). Barnby is treated in a similar fashion, being given only one tune in the body of the book, *Cantate Domino* for 'The Lord is come!' Among the tunes consciously rejected by Vaughan Williams was his *Cloisters* for 'Lord of our life'. W H Monk has just five tunes in *The English Hymnal*. Dykes appears on the face of it to be rather better treated, with ten tunes in the body of the book although this represents a significant drop from his showing in earlier Anglican hymnals – the 1875 edition of *Hymns Ancient & Modern*, for example, contained 56 Dykes tunes. Stainer does not make a single appearance in the book.

This poor showing by recent and contemporary composers was partly a result of copyright restrictions. Vaughan Williams himself noted in his preface the regret of the editorial committee 'that they are not able for a few years to include such beautiful tunes as Dykes' *Dominus Regit Me* or Stainer's *In Memoriam*'. He went on, however, in the next sentence to add that 'nothing but gain can result from the exclusion of certain other tunes, which are worthy neither of the congregation who sing them, the occasions on which they are sung, nor the composers who wrote them'. Overall, his preface constitutes a sustained attack on the genre of the late Victorian hymn tune. He noted that 'many of the tunes of the present day which have become familiar and, probably from association, popular with congregations are quite unsuitable for their purpose. More often than not they are positively harmful to those who sing and hear them.' He left his readers in no doubt that this was 'a moral rather than a musical issue' and singled out two particular bones of contention – the congregational 'old favourites' which 'in fact are of very recent growth, dating at the earliest from the year 1861' and the tune composed specially to fit a particular hymn. In *The English Hymnal*, he promised, 'the "specially composed tune"– that bane of many a hymnal – has been avoided as far as possible'.[3]

What did Vaughan Williams have against recently written tunes and especially against those composed to fit a specific hymn? It is difficult to resist the temptation that, like many church musicians of all ages, he had deeply conservative instincts and a dislike of the new and modern. It is significant that after castigating 'the specially composed tune' he goes on to remark that 'there are already many hundreds of fine tunes in existence, so many indeed that it is impossible to include more than a small part of them in any one collection'. Here surely he speaks very much with the voice of the musician rather than the liturgist. He wants to fill his hymn book with fine melodies, of which he feels there are plenty in the great and long-standing traditions of English folk-song, German chorales and Geneva psalmody. He sees no need to craft new tunes specifically to fit the words of a particular hymn (although of course he himself does this superbly with *Sine Nomine* for 'For all the Saints' and *Down Ampney* for 'Come down, O love divine'). This was the art, or the craft, in which the Victorian composers that he so despised excelled. It was a relatively recent craft. The great innovation of *Hymns Ancient & Modern* had been the dedicated hymn tune, often specially written for a particular set of words. Vaughan Williams, one feels, would have been happier with the previous practice of having a separate tune book to which hymns could be matched up depending on metre. Ironically, he himself commissioned dedicated new tunes from contemporary composers like Harold Darke and Martin Shaw for *Songs of Praise*. Presumably because they were not Victorian composers, with the particular vices to which that species was prone, this was quite acceptable – although it must be said that the results of his commissions were very varying in terms of durability. Some of the new dedicated tunes, like Shaw's *Marching* for 'Through the night of doubt and sorrow' worked wonderfully and have established themselves as classics but others did not.

To understand what Vaughan Williams did not like about the specially composed Victorian hymn tune we need to look at a specific example. One that will do well is Dykes' *Vox Dilecti* for 'I heard the voice of Jesus say'. It is a classic expression of the Victorian hymn composer's art of enhancing the meaning and emotional charge of a particular hymn through a tune carefully crafted to fits its mood and message. The key change in the middle of each verse perfectly complements the switch in the text from Jesus' words of invitation to the response of the weary pilgrim and the beneficial effect that he experiences. The tune greatly enhances the dramatic power and emotional effect of the hymn. *Kingsfold*, the lyrical, all-purpose folk tune which Vaughan Williams substituted as the companion for Bonar's words could equally well be sung to any hymn of this metre in a way that *Vox Dilecti* emphatically could not. It is easy on the ear, highly singable and memorable but it does not really bring out the feelings and the faith behind Bonar's words.

Vaughan Williams doubtless dismissed *Vox Dilecti* as trite, maudlin and sentimental. He did not like emotionalism and subjectivity in his hymn tunes, even when those qualities were very clearly there in the texts to which they were set. As the reviewer of *The English Hymnal* for *The Standard* noted, the choice of him as musical editor 'ensures purity of musical taste, perhaps even leaning to the side of severity'.[4] This quality of severity perhaps comes out most clearly in his relegation of *St Clement* to the 'Chamber of Horrors' and substitution of the Genevan psalm tune *Les Commandements de Dieu* as the preferred tune for 'The day thou gavest, Lord, is ended'. The simple foursquare psalm melody certainly gives a gentler and more reverential feel to Ellerton's evening hymn than Scholefield's lilting waltz tune (in which I and others have argued Sullivan almost certainly had a major hand). But one wonders whether if Vaughan Williams' rather austere coupling had been adopted by other hymnal editors 'The day thou gavest' would ever have come anywhere near occupying the favourite place among British hymns that it held for much of the twentieth century.

Victorian hymn tunes are often sentimental, emotional and subjective because they were written for very sentimental, emotional and subjective words. What, one wonders, did Vaughan Williams make of Albert Peace's ultra-chromatic *St Margaret* for Matheson's 'O love that will not let me go' or Sullivan's supremely sensitive and wistful *Lux in Tenebris* for Newman's 'Lead, kindly light'? Doubtless they would have come into the category of the 'enervating tunes' which he proudly proclaimed were reduced to a minimum in *The English Hymnal*. In his preface, he reflected just how easy it is 'to dwell in the miasma of the languishing and sentimental hymn tunes which so easily disfigure our services'. Yet if the words are sentimental and sad, or, indeed, as in the case of both Matheson's and Newman's texts, highly nuanced and ambiguous expressions of doubt-tinged faith and spiritual soul-searching, do they not deserve something more than a pleasant sounding folk melody or a rigidly objective and passionless Genevan psalm tune?

It is perhaps most obviously those great Victorian expressions of doubt-filled faith (or faith-filled doubt) that cry out for the 'specially composed tune' that Vaughan Williams so much disliked. His provision of the stately and measured *Song 5* for Tennyson's 'Strong Son of God, immortal love' rather softens and weakens the power of the poet's extraordinarily honest wrestling with the ambivalence of faith and doubt. One senses that for all his agnosticism, Vaughan Williams did not like struggle and ambiguity. One of the Victorian tunes he rejected for *The English Hymnal* was William Boyd's

Pentecost for Monsell's 'Fight the good fight'. Originally written for 'Veni Creator', it had first been set to Monsell's text by Sullivan in the 1874 *Church Hymns*, an inspired coupling because, as Iain Mackenzie has observed, it 'burned and crunched with a sense of the profound inner struggle, not a macho display of prowess'.[5] *Shepton Beauchamp*, the traditional English melody which Vaughan Williams substituted, and which has not stood the test of time as well as some of his other importations, is altogether too bland and smooth without possessing the singability and memorability of the later substitute, *Duke Street*, which is also really rather too catchy and bouncy for these particular words. At least 'Fight the good fight' is a hymn which can take a clean, masculine, unison melody. Others need something rather more tentative and feminine.

Vaughan Williams' assault on Victorian hymn tunes and their composers was echoed and continued by many musicians and hymn book editors in the decades following the publication of *The English Hymnal*. George Gardner's *Worship and Music* (1918) deplored the 'vulgar lusciousness' of Dykes' melodies and the 'thin and rowdy sentimentalism' of Barnby's work.[6] In 1925 Percy Dearmer's son Geoffrey wrote a paper on 'The Fall and Rise of the Hymn Tune' which identified *Hymns Ancient & Modern* as representing the low-point and 'plunging religious music into an abyss'.[7] The introduction to the music in the 1927 handbook to *The Revised Church Hymnary*, written by G Wauchope Stewart, a leading musical authority in the Church of Scotland, expressed the view that Victorian tunes 'are too often of a weak and sentimental character, depending for their appeal not on bold and clearly outlined curves of melody or on strong and forceful rhythms, but on chromatic harmonies which are apt to cloy and become loathsome in their own deliciousness'.[8] In 1932 the Archbishop of Canterbury, Cosmo Gordon Lang, forcefully condemned Scholefield's *St Clement*, sparking off a long correspondence in *The Times* in which many sided with him in wishing to see a 'feeble waltz' dismissed from service.

Most of those writing about church music in the middle decades of the twentieth century shared Vaughan Williams' animus against Victorian hymn tunes and praised him for initiating the reaction against them. C H Phillips, writing in the early 1940s, echoes his criticisms, dealing especially harshly with Dykes whose style he castigates as 'self-satisfied and unctuous optimism' and whose output he describes as 'the type *par excellence* of the Victorian hymn-tune'. He singled out *Lux Benigna* as 'rhythmically unadventurous', over-emotional and making too much use of the dominant seventh – 'a chord of fatal fascination to the Victorian'.[9] In his important and scholarly study, *Church Music in the Nineteenth Century* (1967), Arthur Hutchings describes Victorian hymnody as 'semi-sophisticated popular music in which we may meet phrases and bits of tune or harmony unconsciously borrowed from famous poets and musicians'. For him it is Sullivan rather than Dykes who is the chief villain:

It is not in the deeply religious Dykes that one finds revolting sanctimosity but in the charmingly worldly Sullivan ... if he had not felt the need to be a different Sullivan on Sundays, he might have contributed something enduring to church music ... Sullivan's church music is best forgotten; from it we can but illustrate only the nadir of sanctimonious vulgarity.[10]

One of the strongest condemnations of Victorian hymnody is to be found in Kenneth Long's 1971 study, *The Music of the English Church*. Dykes, Gauntlett, Sullivan, Stainer and Barnby are here bracketed together under the heading 'Victoriana' with the dismissive comment that 'most of their music has long since been discounted by sensitive musicians'. After complaining of 'the comforting warm glow of spurious religiosity induced by trivial and sentimental ear-ticklers', Long enumerates the specific faults of these composers' hymn tunes as 'a static bass, enfeebled chromatic harmony, stilted rhythms, rigid four-bar phrases, meretricious tunes, and a complete disregard for the rhythms, inflections, meaning and mood of the words'. More fundamentally, he finds 'a basic insincerity ... the deliberate attempt to write down to popular taste ... the music is not only highly emotional but the emotions are patently stage emotions, the tears are crocodile tears, and the humility and self-abasement are never allowed to obscure the fact that the sun never sets on the British Empire'. Alluding to Gauntlett's estimated 10,000 tunes, he comments tartly that 'not surprisingly, Homer not only nods but sleeps pretty soundly for some 9,990 of them'. Dykes is castigated for 'weaknesses that make musicians blush...slipping and sliding over treacherous chromatics' while Barnby's church music is dismissed as 'simply mawkish'. Sullivan receives a less severe ticking-off, being guilty only of 'the far more healthy fault of sheer vulgarity'.[11]

In this atmosphere, it is hardly surprising that several writers felt that Vaughan Williams had not gone far enough in his purge of Victorian hymn tunes from the pages of *The English Hymnal*. His biographer, A E F Dickinson, writing in 1963, complained that despite the rejections made 'as a matter of religious obligation, moral decision and sheer artistic distaste', there were still 'some appalling things' remaining including *Mendelssohn* for 'Hark! The herald angels sing', *Redhead 47 & 76*, *St Oswald*, *Hursley* and *Leominster*. He went on:

After these, it hardly seems consistent to rail off, in an appendix, what the editor used to call his Chamber of Horrors. By this device, he curiously retains a number of tunes under magisterial disapproval as 'not entering into the general scheme of the book', but with a tolerant assent to deviations for the weaker-minded organist or other musical executive; languishing things like Barnby's *St Chrysostom* and *For All the Saints*, and the singularly named hospital hymn *Requiem* along with *St Cross*, *Northrop* and various higher settings of approved tunes.[12]

VAUGHAN WILLIAMS' 'CHAMBER OF HORRORS'

The figure generally regarded as the greatest hymnologist of the twentieth century, Erik Routley, also felt that, if anything, Vaughan Williams had been rather too kind on the Victorians. He noted that 'the *English Hymnal*, for all its editor's critical attitude towards the Victorians, contains 69 tunes by 30 English Victorians'.[13] In general terms, however, Routley was an enthusiastic supporter of what Vaughan Williams had done for hymnody. In his *Twentieth Century Church Music* (1964), he lauded him as 'the pioneer of the first major English musical dissent of the twentieth century' and praised his move away from 'the whole harmonic and contrapuntal orthodoxy of the eighteenth and nineteenth centuries' and his questioning of 'the near axiomatic requisite of four-part harmony'.[14] Vaughan Williams, Routley enthused, wrote music that 'did true honour to the real English tradition' and popularized a 'revised standard of good taste … educating churchgoers towards a wider vocabulary in which the religious emotion of stiff solemnity might be lessened in favour of a new eagerness and vitality'.[15] He was the great hero who rescued the Church of England from 'the debased coinage of Victorian hymnody':

> Vaughan Williams said in effect 'Radical revolution is required, and we shall substitute for the narrow canons of Victorian church music that freedom which will be gained from reverently studying and using the music of the whole treasury of three hundred years; and especially, we shall substitute for the secular idiom of the nineteenth century, the secular idiom of the sixteenth century; away with "Daisy, Daisy" and let the floor be given to "Greensleeves".'[16]

Routley's own animus against Victorian hymn tune composers is as strong as anyone's in the twentieth century. 'Take a hundred assorted hymn tunes from the period 1861–1900', he notes dismissively, 'and there will be a good case against ninety-seven of them.'[17] He spells out his objections in his remarks about Dykes:

> His defects can be summarized under a single head – the flight from reason, and from the tensions and controversies to which reason leads, which is the mark of Victorian England at its worst … Whenever Dykes is weak, it is always here, in his reasonable principle. When he is vulgar it is always because he renounces the discipline of modesty which is the secret of good hymn-tune writing. When he is 'unctuous' or 'sentimental' it is because his superficial effects are achieved not in consequence of but as a refuge from the tension of his musical argument.[18]

More specifically and technically, Routley criticizes Dykes and other Victorian hymn tune composers for the 'too dramatic and pictorial device of rhythmically repeated notes' and for their general degeneration into the 'cushioned ease of the salon'.[19] Sullivan is treated with even more contempt than Dykes, his hymn tunes attacked for 'vacillating between appalling vulgarity and glum monotony' and representing 'the disastrous rubbish which a musician of outstanding gifts thought appropriate for church use ... Sullivan wrote hardly a tune that is not virtually intolerable for modern singing.'[20] Barnby is damned with the faint praise that 'he could write a good drawing room ballad' while S S Wesley's *Aurelia* is dismissed for its 'depressing and threadbare quality'.[21]

Erik Routley felt that much of the blame for the poor quality of Victorian hymn tunes could be attributed to the complacent atmosphere of the Victorian church.

> It was not so much Dykes who was at fault, as Lady Lufton at Framley and Archdeacon Grantley at Plumstead Episcopi, who took such pleasure in these musical evidences of security and ease, in hearing the choirboys enunciate these mellifluous melodies, in thus being reassured that their duties as clergy and people were confined to preserving the present state of things rather than to prophesying and preaching to dying men.[22]

This seems a rather debatable thesis on a number of grounds. As we have already noted, there is, in fact, considerably more 'security and ease' in the folk melodies Vaughan Williams introduced than in the Victorian hymn tunes which they replaced. This is manifestly true of *Kingsfold* as against *Vox Dilecti*, for example, or of *Shepton Beauchamp* as against *Pentecost*. There is certainly more doubt in many Victorian hymn tunes, as in their words, than in those which replaced them. It is also strange to castigate the Victorians for not prophesying and preaching. Their hymn tunes often have a preachy quality – rather too preachy for their critics who dislike the way that they emphasize and enhance the emotional power and message of the words. The device which Routley so disliked of repeated notes is often used precisely in this preachy way. Arguably, it is the timeless folk tunes which Vaughan Williams introduced which give several Victorian hymns a more conservative and less contemporary feel than they originally had. It is also somewhat ironic and misleading that Routley, good Congregationalist that he was, should see the dreaded Victorian hymn tune as a distinctly Anglican malady. The composers may predominantly have been Anglican but their greatest fans were non-Anglicans. It was the Presbyterians who took up Stainer as musical editor of the 1898 *Church Hymnary*. Sullivan, Stainer, Barnby and Gauntlett were, on the whole, much better represented in Nonconformist than in Anglican hymnals throughout the twentieth century.

Did *The English Hymnal* initiate a rejection of Victorian hymn tunes from twentieth-century hymnals? The table below shows the number of tunes by five leading Victorian composers, J B Dykes, W H Monk, Arthur Sullivan, John Stainer and Joseph Barnby, which have appeared in successive editions of four major denominational hymnals in the twentieth century. The books surveyed are the 1906 *English Hymnal*, the 1927 *Revised Church Hymnary* (Presbyterian), the 1933 *Methodist Hymnbook*, the 1950 *Hymns Ancient & Modern Revised*, the 1973 (third) edition of *The Church Hymnary*, the 1983 *Hymns and Psalms* (Methodist), the 1986 *New English Hymnal* and the 2000 *Common Praise* (from the *Hymns Ancient & Modern* stable). The figures represent the number of original tunes by each composer appearing in the book – tunes that are used more than once are only counted once and adaptations and arrangements are not included. The figures in brackets represent appearances in the 1906 'Chamber of Horrors' Appendix.

Victorian hymn tunes in twentieth-century hymn books

	EH 1906	RCH 1927	MHB 1933	AMR 1950	CH3 1973	HP 1983	NEH 1986	CP 2000
Dykes	10 (+1)	26	26	31	9	21	10	20
Monk	5 (+3)	14	11	15	2	8	6	9
Sullivan	1 (+1)	12	12	3	5	3	3	3
Stainer	0	14	12	15	2	8	7	7
Barnby	1 (+2)	11	16	4	0	4	1	2
Total	17 (+7)	77	77	68	18	44	27	41

Several interesting facts emerge from this table. Of all the books surveyed the 1906 *English Hymnal* has the fewest tunes by the five leading Victorian composers. The other hymnal in which they have a very poor showing, the 1973 edition of *The Church Hymnary*, was compiled and published during the period when the reaction against Victorian hymn tunes was perhaps at its strongest and most widespread. Overall, the table shows a fairly clear picture of declining fortunes for Victorian hymn tunes through the twentieth century with the number of tunes by the five composers dropping from 77 to 44 in the main Methodist hymnal and from 68 to 41 in *Hymns Ancient & Modern* and its replacement over the space of fifty years. However, the picture is not entirely one of decline. The 1986 *New English Hymnal* had a much better showing of Victorian hymn tunes than the 1906 edition. Indeed, overall it restored 25 tunes from the Victorian period which were not included in the original edition. The fourth edition of *The Church Hymnary* (2005) has also restored several Victorian tunes knocked out of the 1973 third edition, including Sullivan's *Lux Eoi*, Stainer's *All for Jesus*, *Cross of Jesus* and *Charity*, Hopkins' *Culford* (for 'Take my life and let it be'), *Leominster* (for Matheson's 'Make me a captive, Lord'), S S Wesley's *Winscott* (for 'God, speak to me, that I may speak') Smart's *Misericordia* (for 'Just as I am') and Dykes' *St Agnes, Durham* (for 'Jesus, the very thought of thee').

Are Victorian hymn tunes now coming back into favour and if so, why? Certainly those writing about church music in recent decades have not been as snooty about them as those quoted above from the 1960s and 1970s. I suspect that an important harbinger of the changing mood was Nicholas Temperley's *The Music of the English Parish Church* (1979) which staunchly defended Victorian hymn tunes against their many detractors. The Hymn Society of Great Britain and Ireland has taken a noticeably more charitable view of Victorian hymns, publishing several important articles in their defence in its Bulletin, notably Donald Webster's 'Victoriana Revisited' in 1987. General surveys like Andrew Wilson Dickson's *The Story of Christian Music* (1992) have avoided the kind of gratuitous attacks on Victorian hymn tunes that one would have expected as a matter of course in books published thirty or forty years earlier. Some recent writers have been positively kind about them. Bertram Barnby's *In Concert Sing – Concerning Hymns and their Usage* (1996) is generally complimentary of the genre, as one might expect from a direct descendant of the much-maligned Joseph Barnby. Lionel Dakers' *Beauty Beyond Words: Enriching Worship Through Music* (2000) has the usual gripe against 'the over-loading of sentimentality' in Victorian tunes but he does single this out as their 'one failing' and has much good to say about them, although Dykes' *St Oswald*, *Gerontius* and *Lux Benigna* do come in for criticism. Dakers even takes Vaughan Williams to task for diminishing the effect of one particular hymn through his substitution of a folk tune in preference to an eighteenth-century melody. The words of 'Firmly I believe and truly', he notes, 'are enhanced in no uncertain way when married to William Boyce's tune *Halton Holgate* ... By marked contrast, the tune *Shipston*, which has always been used in *The English Hymnal*, though nice enough, is a jaunty folk tune and comes off second best.'[23]

The principal reason why musicians have stopped attacking Victorian hymn tunes with such fervour is almost certainly that they have found newer and even more tempting targets. Dykes' harmonies seem models of sober objectivity compared to much of the music associated with modern worship songs. Lionel Dakers noted in his *Parish Music* (1991) that the work of certain late-twentieth-century church musicians 'reveals a degree of mediocrity and poverty of musical invention which would be hard to equal anywhere, even in the worst excesses of many Victorian hymns'.[24] This may be damning with faint praise but at least it is more positive than the remarks made by a previous generation of church musicians. What Vaughan Williams wrote about Victorian hymn tunes is now being written about contemporary worship songs. Congregations enjoy singing both, when they are allowed to.

The attitude towards Victorian tunes displayed by their relegation to the 'Chamber of Horrors' in the 1906 *English Hymnal* ultimately raises questions that are beyond the scope of this article. Should hymn tunes and worship songs be judged by different standards than are applied to other musical compositions? Is the all-purpose folk melody, psalm tune or chorale with its timeless and unspecific feel to be preferred to the dedicated tune written for particular words? Is appealing to the emotions and the sentiments always wrong in a hymn tune? Surely the truth is that there is room for many different styles of music – for *Sine Nomine* and *Down Ampney* just as much as for *Lux Eoi* and *Cross of Jesus*, all in their different ways great hymn tunes which serve to bring the singer nearer to God and illumine the meaning and spirit of the words to which they are set.

Notes

1 *The Guardian*, 31 October 1900, 1532.
2 C Phillips, *Robert Bridges. A Biography*, OUP, 1992, 198.
3 *The English Hymnal*, 1906, OUP, x–xi
4 Quoted in U Vaughan Williams, *R V W: A Biography of Ralph Vaughan Williams*, Oxford, Clarendon Press, 1992.
5 I Mackenzie, *Tunes of Glory*, Edinburgh, Handsel Press, 1993, 170.
6 Quoted in L Benson, *The Hymnody of the Christian Church*, Richmond, Virginia, John Knox Press, 1927, 253.
7 *Ibid.*
8 J Moffatt and M Patrick, eds., *Handbook to the Church Hymnary*, Revised Edition, OUP, 1927, xxv–xxvi.
9 C H Phillips, *The Singing Church*, Revised Edition, London, Mowbrays, 1979, 171–2.
10 A Hutchings, *Church Music in the Nineteenth Century*, London, Herbert Jenkins, 1967, 109.
11 K Long, *The Music of the English Church*, London, Hodder, 1971, 359, 360, 361, 366.
12 A E F Dickinson, *Vaughan Williams*, London, Faber & Faber, 1963, 130.
13 E Routley, *The Music of Christian Hymnody*, London, Independent Press, 1957, 140.
14 E Routley, *Twentieth Century Church Music*, London, Herbert Jenkins, 1964, 23–4.
15 *Ibid.*, 97–8.
16 E Routley, *The Music of Christian Hymnody*, 134.
17 E Routley, *The Musical Wesleys*, London, Herbert Jenkins, 1968, 198.
18 E Routley, *The Music of Christian Hymnody*, 122–3.
19 *Ibid.*, 123.
20 *Ibid.*, 124.
21 *Ibid.*, 128.
22 *Ibid.*, 124.
23 L Dakers, *Beauty Beyond Words: Enriching Worship Through Music*, Norwich, Canterbury Press, 2000, 16–17.
24 L Dakers, *Parish Music*, Norwich, Canterbury Press, 1991, 63.

A HUNDRED YEARS ON: THE VIEW FROM PRIMROSE HILL

Robert Atwell

It always comes as a surprise to realize that when *The English Hymnal* – now such an established and conventional part of Anglican parochial and cathedral worship – was first published on Ascension Day 1906, it did not meet with universal enthusiasm. Musicians may have been warm in their approval of the achievement of its Musical Editor, Ralph Vaughan Williams, but the ecclesiastical Establishment gave the new hymnal a decidedly frosty reception. A phalanx of bishops let their hostility be known in the press, and foremost among them was the Archbishop of Canterbury, Randall Davidson, who went so far as to express the strong wish that the hymnal should not be adopted in any parish in his diocese.

The focus of their disapproval was the high profile *The English Hymnal* gave to the commemoration of the saints, and specifically to their invocation in prayer. The bone of contention was Canon Stuckey Coles' Marian hymn, 'Ye who own the faith of Jesus', with its outrageous couplet, 'For the faithful gone before us, may the holy Virgin pray'. As Percy Dearmer, its Literary Editor, protested, 'Does the Bishop [of Bristol] think we should sing, "May the holy Virgin *not* pray"?' At St Mary's Primrose Hill where Dearmer was Vicar and where a number of the editorial meetings were held, congregations have sung the hymn in procession on their Patronal Festival for a hundred years now without noticeable ill effects or loss of faith; and it is difficult at this distance to conceive how hymnody could have raised the theological temperature of the Church of England if not exactly to white heat, then certainly way beyond its comfort-zone. But then again, as T S Eliot lamented as long ago as 1934 in *Choruses from 'The Rock'*:

> Our age is an age of moderate virtue
> And of moderate vice
> When men will not lay down the Cross
> Because they will never assume it.

If critical attention in 1906 focused on the hymns for the commemoration of saints, other more radical (or at any rate unconventional) theological emphases seem to have passed most people by. Beneath its handsome but unconventional green covers, the book was uncompromising in its liturgical structure and presentation. It presumed a sacramental view of the world and promoted the Catholic ideal of objectivity in worship as the normative

243

expression of all Anglican public worship, giving centre stage to the celebration of the Eucharist. This was in sharp contradistinction to the emphasis in Evangelical circles upon the centrality of the sermon, which many High Churchmen perceived as being vulnerable to an unhealthy dependence on the personality of the preacher.

The strong liturgical nature of the book seems unremarkable today, but at the time it was innovative. Besides the excellence of its music, what makes the hymn book noteworthy, and to a degree controversial from the perspective of historical theology, is what the editors chose to include and exclude. Positively, they gathered an extraordinarily wide range of material from the whole gamut of the Christian tradition, making amongst other things the riches of ancient and mediaeval hymnody available to a wider public. But they also included great hymns from English literature, some of them, like John Bunyan's 'He who would valiant be' (though shorn of its 'hobgoblins and foul fiends'), making their first appearance in a church hymnal. Negatively, the editors were determined to exclude the worst excesses of Victorian sentimentality, what Martin Shaw called 'slushiness'.[1] They were concerned to challenge the Evangelical preoccupation with personal salvation to the exclusion of all else.

In combination with fine new tunes, such as Vaughan Williams' wonderful melody *Sine Nomine* for 'For all the Saints', now universally adopted, this policy succeeded in raising the whole standard of English hymnody. The book represented a conscious attempt not merely to reflect the spirit of the new century in the worship of the Church, a sort of theological-musical *aggiornamento*, but to set forth a broader vision of Christian life and society. In the preface to the hymnal, Dearmer claimed that they were not interested in producing a 'party-book, expressing this or that phase of negation or excess'. Their appeal (they claimed) was to 'all broad-minded men'. But they were being disingenuous. Instinctively, they knew what has to be discovered afresh in each generation, that there is no renewal in the Church which is not spiritual. In the production of *The English Hymnal* they were consciously trying to disturb the complacency of the Edwardian Church, and to push it into a more profound engagement with the world. In short, they were trying to set the agenda for the Church of England in their generation.

This seems a lot to claim for a hymn book. But in a pre-television age, as Donald Gray points out in his introductory essay, 'hymns and hymn singing was a significant ingredient in the musical repertoire of most people'. In Edwardian England it formed a key part of what we would now call 'popular culture'. Historians of the early Church regularly coin the Latin tag *lex orandi, lex credendi* (the rule of prayer and the rule of belief) to highlight the significance of the interface of prayer and belief in the life of the Christian Church. If you want to understand what Christians believe, look how they pray and worship. By the same token, how Christians worship and pray will be informed by what they believe about God. There is a pattern of religious osmosis to be observed. To this two-fold cord, one might add a third strand, *lex cantandi*: what Christians sing also exercises a formative influence. The combination of word and melody is a powerful tool in shaping the spirituality not only of individuals but of an entire community. It fosters a corporate sense of belonging to the pilgrim people of God. The editors of *The English Hymnal* grasped this intuitively.

But to return to the origins of the project and the theological motives of the hymnal's editors: what was it that they were rebelling against? What was it they were so concerned to exclude?

From the outset it is clear that Dearmer and his fellow editors were decisive in wanting to outlaw the banal, the sentimental, and all narrowly focused evangelical piety. Dearmer had long been dismissive of *Hymns Ancient & Modern* in its original edition (1861), and was happy to adopt the new edition at St Mary's as soon as it was published in 1904. But apart from its maroon covers of which he approved (in contrast to the 'lamp-black' or 'London fog' colour usual for Bibles and hymnals)[2] the new edition proved to be a big disappointment to him. In the opinion of Martin Shaw (later to be appointed by Dearmer organist and choirmaster at St Mary's) it was a 'dull compromise, and as such compromises will, it fell flat. It was certainly not the new hymnbook that the new century needed.'[3] Compromise was not a word in Percy Dearmer's vocabulary. He had high standards and applied them equally to music, to religious texts, and to the performance of the liturgy itself. To quote Martin Shaw again:

> Our musical policy, never put into words but mutually understood and agreed upon, was that the music should be chosen on its own merits. The obvious thing to do, it might be thought; yet I really believe that St Mary's, Primrose Hill, was the only church in London where, for instance, the popular weak Victorian hymn tune was never heard. The usual argument is – you must give people what they like. Percy said – 'You must give people what is good and they will come to like it'.[4]

Here we glimpse the driving force and the vision behind the project for a new hymnal, at least as it was being expressed in Primrose Hill. In the new dispensation, sentimental lines like:

> Weary of earth, and laden with my sin,
> I look at heaven and long to enter in.

or

> O Paradise, O Paradise, who doth not crave for thee?

were out. The editors did not see the world as negatively or as unredeemable as their *Ancient & Modern* counterparts; nor was their image of God, in the words of Shaw, 'a kind of angry policeman waiting to catch us out'.[5] In general, their choice of hymns reflected a belief that the earth is good, that God has put us on it to enjoy it, and to say the least, it is ungrateful to declare that we are weary of it. No attempt was made to pretend before God or to adopt a devotional pose.

In pursuit of these principles, the hymns selected ('the best hymns in the English language' or so they claimed) reflected a more generous vision of the Christian life, and a less stern and judgemental image of God. In general the hymns they chose tended to be theologically transcendent. When focusing upon the Incarnation, their language tended to be more 'Christ-centred' than 'Jesus-centred' as was customary in Evangelical circles. Following Tractarian custom, when the focus was specifically upon the person of Jesus it tended to be in a Eucharistic context. That said, there are notable exceptions such as Horatio Bonar's hymn, 'I heard the voice of Jesus say' (sung to that wonderful folk tune, *Kingsfold*); or Charles Wesley's hymn, 'Jesu, Lover of my soul', or indeed, Percy Dearmer's own hymn, 'Jesus, good above all other'. But in each case, the theology is rich and strong. There is passion in *The English Hymnal*, but it is without syrup.

So much for what was excluded. But what was included?

The declared intention of the editors that their new hymnal should not be a 'party-book' is certainly reflected in its wide array of texts. It was truly catholic, in the sense of being broadly based and international in flavour. They selected material which was (dare one say) both ancient and modern. Their wish to be 'inclusive', and in the preface they specifically use this term, enabled them to embrace office hymns ascribed to St Ambrose, the riches of the American Quaker tradition, seen for example in the inclusion of John Greenleaf Whittier's hymns, 'Dear Lord and Father of mankind' and 'Immortal love for ever full', the poetry of Herbert, Donne and Milton, and, from the Orthodox Church, the Russian *Kontakion for the Dead*.

Were there limits to their inclusivity? The answer lies in a series of preparatory meetings which took place in 1903 in London to discuss the parlous state of English hymnody. Besides Dearmer, the group consisted of A Hanbury-Tracy, D C Lathbury, G R Woodward and Athelstan Riley. The majority of these would become the core of the editorial board of the new hymnal, but this was some way off. Early in their discussions, Woodward, a pioneer in the revival of plainsong in the Church of England and a prominent member of the group, resigned on the grounds that he could not tolerate the inclusion of William Blake's poem, 'To Mercy, Pity, Peace, and Love' on the grounds that Blake was not a committed Christian.[6] The disagreement brought to the surface underlying ideological tensions. In contrast to Woodward, Dearmer stood for the generous embrace of those whose theological credentials may not have been entirely orthodox, but whose contribution was still valuable in their pursuit of excellence. Ecclesiastical affiliation (or lack of it) was unimportant. In the end, the only valid criterion for assessing the worth of a melody or of a text was merit.

A HUNDRED YEARS ON: THE VIEW FROM PRIMROSE HILL

It should come as no surprise, therefore, that when *The English Hymnal* eventually rolled off the printing presses three years later, contrary to Woodward's wishes, it included Blake's hymn with its powerful, though alas, no longer politically correct, final verse:

And all must love the human form,
In heathen, Turk, or Jew;
Where Mercy, Love, and Pity dwell,
There God is dwelling too.

Dearmer was a Christian Socialist, and for him God was to be encountered in all men and women, in the 'heathen, Turk and Jew', and closer to home, in the poor and disadvantaged. In parallel with his instinctive desire to celebrate beauty went a passion to eradicate all forms of ugliness in society. Beauty in worship had to go hand-in-hand with 'mercy, love and pity' and a commitment to address the causes of poverty. According to his second wife, Nan, Dearmer's subsequent impatience with ritual was due to the fact that for him it had little value if it was divorced from Christian social teaching.[7] This passion is behind his inclusion of Henry Scott Holland's hymn, 'Judge Eternal, throned in splendour', and G K Chesterton's hymn, 'O God of earth and altar'. The latter was a late inclusion, having only been published early in 1906 in *Commonwealth*, a Christian Socialist magazine for which Dearmer also wrote. At the time Chesterton was still a lapsed Nonconformist, sixteen years away from his conversion to Roman Catholicism.[8]

The hand of Dearmer is also evident in the editing of Mrs C F Alexander's hymn, 'All things bright and beautiful', made even more popular by its subsequent setting to 'Royal Oak', an arrangement by Martin Shaw of an English traditional melody. The original version of the hymn, however, contained the infamous verse:

The rich man in his castle,
The poor man at his gate:
God made them high and lowly,
And ordered their estate.

This was precisely what Dearmer did *not* believe. As he pointed out acerbically in his *Songs of Praise Discussed*, Mrs Alexander 'must have forgotten Dives, and how Lazarus lay "at his gate"; but then she had been brought up in the atmosphere of a land-agent on an Irish estate'.[9] It was the passivity and inertia at the heart of the British Establishment in the face of huge inequalities in Edwardian society that Dearmer felt called to challenge.

One hundred years on from its publication, *The English Hymnal* in its successive editions continues to enrich the worship of St Mary's Primrose Hill. It is still the faithful 'companion' of our liturgy, to use a phrase from the preface, albeit these days liturgy drawn from *Common Worship* rather than from *The Book of Common Prayer,* which we only retain for Choral Evensong. The parish continues to stand four-square in the Catholic tradition of the Church of England, though not in a partisan way. Its style of worship is unmistakably Anglican, with unfussy ceremonial, good music and sensitive preaching. It has an openness and robustness and a commitment to social engagement which we like to think Percy would have approved of.

The strong liturgical structure of the hymnal continues to invite and encourage a disciplined adherence to the rhythm of the Christian Year as it moves inexorably from creation to judgement, from the birth of Christ to his passion and resurrection. And if one is obedient to this discipline, the hymnal creates a rich and effective musical counterpoint to the Church's lectionary and reinforces the theological themes being celebrated, enabling a congregation to engage more profoundly with the great religious themes of the Christian story.

To give an example, at St Mary's we still mark the beginning of Lent with the singing of the Litany in procession, and throughout the season there are neither jolly hymns nor organ voluntaries. Musical fasting contrasts starkly with the musical feasting of Easter. As part of this self-imposed discipline, some hymns are sung only once or twice a year in spite of their popularity. 'My song is love unknown', for example, is sung only on Palm Sunday and Good Friday. The restricted use of such hymns makes them all the more powerful through their lack of exposure. In the context of the liturgy of the day they become very evocative.

Like many parish churches, and indeed as the original editors of the hymnal anticipated, we make no attempt to use all the hymns or liturgical material contained in its successor volume, *The New English Hymnal.* England has changed hugely and rapidly over the last twenty-five years, and as a result there is already much that feels dated. Some things just no longer work. We use all the responsorial psalms in tandem with singing the Gradual Psalm to plainchant (maintaining our long-standing commitment to plainsong in English) but we find that the introits, sequences and stations of the liturgical section no longer sit easily with a modern Parish Eucharist.

Happily, the Advent Prose has found a new home in the Advent Carol Service, and the Lent Prose serves as the recessional at the Ash Wednesday Eucharist. Liturgical *aficionados* will be glad to know that certain ceremonies, doubtless unique to St Mary's and of Dearmer's creation, but which are reflected in the hymnal, survive unchanged. We still use the original Lenten array designed by Percy Dearmer, complete with his great Lenten veil suspended before the Rood. The Palm Sunday procession, having begun at the summit of Primrose Hill with the blessing of palms, much to the puzzlement of sundry Japanese tourists, Tai-chi enthusiasts and dog-walkers, eventually enters St Mary's and stands before the chancel arch. At this point the great Lenten veil is lowered and the so-called 'Prophetic Anthem' included in the liturgical section of the hymnal is sung, revealing the *Christus Rex* figure. It is a good example of how ancient music and ceremonial, words, drama and prayer can still coalesce into an incredibly powerful liturgical moment.

Conrad Noel, sometime assistant priest at St Mary's, records Dearmer's like of congregational singing and their frustration at the rigidity of the then organist, Dr Goldsmith. 'When I said to Goldsmith one day: "I think, at last, the people are beginning to join in that hymn," he answered: "Oh! Then I'll change it".'[10] Dearmer had pioneered regular congregational practices on Friday evenings as a means to greater lay participation in the liturgy. And it was in the context of such practices that new hymns and tunes were tried out before their inclusion in the hymnal. In the parish records for December 1905, for example, we have a note of the debut of Christina Rossetti's poem 'In the bleak mid-winter' as a Christmas carol. The editors had specially commissioned Gustav Holst to write a tune for it, which he named 'Cranham', the village outside Cheltenham where he was born. It is strange to think how this Christmas carol, now an established part of the English repertoire, along with many other famous hymns began their life on a Friday evening congregational practice in north London.

Such midweek practices are not feasible today. Nevertheless, we maintain a broad, if selective, palette of hymns, mindful of the importance of allowing them (contrary to the wishes of Dr Goldsmith) to become familiar to a congregation which is not only constantly changing, but which is nowadays very international and diverse. Learning by rote has gone out of fashion. But there is value as well as virtue in instilling spiritual truths through the gentle but steady drip of the familiar, so that they enter more deeply into minds and memories. Familiarity doesn't necessarily breed contempt: it can bring comfort and reassurance. In old age when memories are fragmenting, or in times of crisis or stress, remembrance of a hymn tune can become a moment of grace, conjuring up an association of words and feelings that refreshes us and enables us to pray.

One hundred years ago *The English Hymnal* related to a culture that was English, that was Christian, and, although not necessarily Anglican, was still familiar with and valued hymns. This is no longer the case, and it presents a fresh series of challenges to clergy and musicians alike. At St Mary's, for example, if we are unmistakably Anglican, we are no longer unmistakably English.

Recently at Pentecost we celebrated our own version of the Acts of the Apostles narrative, inviting members of the congregation for whom English was not their first language simultaneously to say the Lord's Prayer in their mother tongue. Twenty-two different languages emerged, including Icelandic, the African languages Twi and Fante, Greek, Russian and Lithuanian. Such a range of languages and cultures is absent in rural England, but is no longer unusual in our major cities. It is both exhilarating and challenging to minister in such contexts. The editors of *The English*

Hymnal intended their book to be inclusive. The question is how to make that vision a reality for this generation, given the complexity and fragmented nature of British society, and the sheer diversity of the Church in England. It may be an impossible task. Time will tell.

As always, high ideals need to be matched by pastoral realism. What is possible musically in a parish is invariably determined by the quality of its leadership, and the willingness of clergy and musicians to work together. Without patronizing anyone, both have to be more modest than Percy Dearmer in their expectations about what is possible for the average congregation to sustain comfortably. Not least because increasingly (whether one likes it or not) being a regular and committed Anglican often means attending church every other week – certainly not twice on a Sunday plus a hymn and plainsong practice on a Friday night. Being realistic, however, does not mean opting for lowest-common-denominator worship. Nothing is solved by bad music, and the worth of some hymns only emerges the third time round. One can make too much of the need for accessibility. The trouble is, sometimes you only get one chance. It's a case of getting the balance right. In this, as in all things, we are talking about the art of the possible.

In 1906 the editors of *The English Hymnal* said that it would 'stand or fall on its merits'. One hundred years on, as this volume of essays has revealed, the reason why it had such an impact on the worship of the Church of England (and beyond) was precisely because of its merits. We need to be loyal to our musical inheritance, but not in a narrow antiquarian way. Dearmer, Vaughan Williams and their fellow editors faced the challenge of their new century with enthusiasm, and we need to find the same energy and vision to do the same for ours. The Church is not a support-group or a club, but the Body of Christ, a *worshipping* community witnessing to Christ and to the power of God to change lives. In every generation the Church needs good hymns and good music. 'Prefer nothing to the love of Christ,' wrote St Benedict; and it is the worship of God that must always claim the Church's first priority. Only worship that is real permits others to be real. Only worship that looks outward to the needs of the world and consciously brings them before God in prayer can have space to welcome fellow pilgrims who may call upon God by another name. Only worship that goes deep can sustain us in our journey to the gates of heaven. In the words of St Augustine:

How happy will be our shout of 'Alleluia' as we enter heaven. How carefree we will be, secure at last from being attacked, where no enemy lurks and where our friends do not die. In heaven praise is offered to God, but here on earth too. Here it is offered by anxious people, there by those who have been freed from anxiety. Here it is offered in hope, in heaven by those who enjoy the reality; here by pilgrims in transit, there by those who have reached their homeland. So my dear friends let us sing 'Alleluia' even though we are not yet in enjoyment of our heavenly rest. In so doing we will sweeten our toil in this life. Let us sing as travellers do on a journey to keep up their spirits and help them keep on walking. Press on from good to better in this life. Sing up, my friends, and above all, keep on walking.[11]

Notes

1 Martin Shaw, *Up to Now*, London, 1929, 100.
2 Percy Dearmer, reviewing the new edition of *Hymns Ancient & Modern* for *Commonwealth* in 1904.
3 Shaw, *Up to Now*, 101.
4 Quoted by Nan Dearmer, *The Life of Percy Dearmer,* London, The Book Club, 1941, 164. No source given.
5 Shaw, *Up to Now*, 100.
6 Nan Dearmer, *Life,* 178.
7 *Ibid.,* 115.
8 See Ian Bradley, ed., *The Penguin Book of Hymns,* London, Penguin, 1990, 301.
9 Percy Dearmer, *Songs of Praise Discussed: A Handbook to the best-known hymns and to others recently introduced,* Oxford, 1933, 239.
10 *Conrad Noel: An Autobiography*, edited with foreword by Sidney Dark, London, 1945, 80.
11 Augustine, *Sermon* 256, 1, 3.

SELECT BIBLIOGRAPHY

Benson, L, *The Hymnody of the Christian Church*, Richmond, USA, John Knox, 1927.

—— *The English Hymn: Its Development and Use in Worship*, USA, George Doran, 1915, reprinted Richmond, Virginia, John Knox, 1962.

Bergeron, K, *Decadent Enchantments: The Revival of Gregorian Chant at Solesmes*, Berkeley, Los Angeles and London, University of California Press, 1998.

Bradley, I, *Abide With Me: The World of Victorian Hymns*, London, SCM Press, 1997.

Clarke, W, *A Hundred Years of Hymns Ancient and Modern*, London, William Clowes, 1960.

Davies, H, *Worship and Theology in England*, USA, Princeton University Press, 1970.

Dakers, L, *Parish Music*, Norwich, Canterbury Press, 1991.

Dearmer, N, *The Life of Percy Dearmer*, London, The Book Club, 1941.

Dearmer, P, Preface to *The English Hymnal*, London, OUP, 1906.

—— Preface to *The Oxford Book of Carols*, London, OUP, 1928.

Dearmer, P and Jacob, A, *Songs of Praise Discussed*, London, OUP, 1933.

Dickinson, A E F, *Vaughan Williams*, London, Faber, 1963.

—— 'Some Thoughts About *The English Hymnal*', in *The Musical Times*, May 1956.

Ellinwood, L and Lockwood, E, *Dictionary of North American Hymnology*, eds P Powell and M Vandyke, USA, The Hymn Society in the United States and Canada, 2003, CD-ROM.

Frost, M, *English and Scottish Psalm and Hymn Tunes c.1543–1677*, London, SPCK and OUP, 1953.

—— ed., *Historical Companion to Hymns Ancient and Modern*, London, William Clowes, 1962.

Gray, D, *Percy Dearmer: A Parson's Pilgrimage*, Norwich, Canterbury Press, 2000.

Higginson, J, *History of American Catholic Hymnals*, USA, The Hymn Society of America, 1982.

Hiley, D and Rankin, S, *Music in the Medieval English Liturgy*, Oxford, OUP, 1993.

Hughes, A, *The Rivers of the Flood*, London, Faith Press, 1961.

Hutchings, A, *Church Music in the Nineteenth Century*, London, Herbert Jenkins, 1967.

Jefferson, H, *Hymns in Christian Worship*, London, Rockliff, 1950.

Julian, J, ed., *A Dictionary of Hymnology*, London, John Murray, 1892, reprinted New York, Dover, 1957.

Kennedy, M, *The Works of Ralph Vaughan Williams*, Oxford, Clarendon, 1964/1980/1992.

Long, K, *The Music of the English Church*, London, Hodder and Stoughton, 1972.

Luff, A, *Welsh Hymns and Their Tunes*, USA, Hope Publishing, 1990.

Manning, B, *The Hymns of Wesley and Watts*, London, Epworth Press, 1942.

Millar, P, *Four Centuries of Scottish Psalmody*, London, OUP, 1949.

Onderdonk, J, 'Hymn Tunes From Folk-Songs: Vaughan Williams and English Hymnody', in *Vaughan Williams Essays*, eds B Adams and R Wells, Aldershot, Ashgate, 2002.

—— 'Folk Music in Hymnody', in *A New Dictionary of Hymnology*, ed. J R Watson, London, Canterbury Press, 2007.

Phillips, C S, *Hymnody Past and Present*, London, SPCK, 1937.

Phillips, C Henry, *The Singing Church*, London, Faber, 1945.

Pocknee, C, *The French Diocesan Hymns and their Melodies*, London, Faith Press, 1954.

Routley, E, *Hymns and Human Life*, London, 1952.

—— *The Music of Christian Hymnody*, London, Independent Press, 1957.

—— *Twentieth Century Church Music*, London, Herbert Jenkins, 1964.

—— 'Percy Dearmer, Hymnologist', in *Hymn Society Bulletin No.111*, Winter 1967.

—— *The Musical Wesleys*, London, Herbert Jenkins, 1968.

—— *An English Speaking Hymnal Guide* (first published 1979), revised and expanded by P W Cutts, Chicago, GIA Publications, 2005.

—— *A Panorama of Christian Hymnody* (first published 1979), revised and expanded by P Richardson, Chicago, GIA Publications, 2005.

Stephen, F, *St Mary's, Primrose Hill*, London, St Mary's, 1972.

Temperley, N, *The Music of the English Parish Church*, Cambridge, CUP, 1979.

Vaughan Williams, R, 'The Music', in the Preface to *The English Hymnal*, London, OUP, 1906.

—— *The First Fifty Years: A Brief Account of The English Hymnal From 1906 to 1956*, London, OUP, 1956.

—— 'A Musical Autobiography', in *National Music and Other Essays*, London, OUP, 1963.

—— *National Music and Other Essays*, Oxford, OUP, 1987.

—— *RVW: A Biography of Ralph Vaughan Williams*, London, OUP, 1964.

Watson, J R, *The English Hymn*, Oxford, Clarendon Press, 1997.

Watson, R and Trickett, K, eds, *Companion to Hymns and Psalms*, Peterborough, Methodist Publishing House, 1988.

INDICES

Abbreviations used for hymn books

A&M	Hymns Ancient and Modern
EH	English Hymnal
EP	English Praise
HN	The Hymnal Noted
NEH	New English Hymnal
NOBC	New Oxford Book of Carols
OBC	Oxford Book of Carols
PHB	A Plainsong Hymn Book
PHS	Plainsong Hymn-melodies and Sequences
SHM	Sarum Hymn Melodies
SP	Songs of Praise
SPE	Songs of Praise Enlarged
SS	Songs of Syon
TH	The Hymner

INDEX OF GENERAL SUBJECTS

INDEX OF GENERAL SUBJECTS

INDEX OF TITLES OF HYMN TUNES

INDEX OF TITLES OF HYMN TUNES

INDEX OF TITLES OF HYMN TUNES

INDEX OF COMPOSERS AND ARRANGERS OF HYMN TUNES

INDEX OF COMPOSERS AND ARRANGERS OF HYMN TUNES

INDEX OF AUTHORS AND POETS
OF HYMNS

INDEX OF FIRST LINES OF HYMNS

INDEX OF FIRST LINES OF HYMNS

277